SPATIAL POLITICS IN ISTANBUL

SPATIAL POLITICS IN ISTANBUL

Turning Points in Contemporary Turkey

**Courtney Dorroll and
Philip Dorroll**

EDINBURGH
University Press

Edinburgh University Press is one of the leading university presses in the UK. We publish academic books and journals in our selected subject areas across the humanities and social sciences, combining cutting-edge scholarship with high editorial and production values to produce academic works of lasting importance. For more information visit our website: edinburghuniversitypress.com

Edinburgh University Press Ltd
13 Infirmary Street,
Edinburgh, EH1 1LT

First published in hardback by Edinburgh University Press 2023

Typeset in 11/15 EB Garamond by
IDSUK (DataConnection) Ltd

A CIP record for this book is available from the British Library

ISBN 978 1 3995 0337 2 (hardback)
ISBN 978 1 3995 0338 9 (paperback)
ISBN 978 1 3995 0339 6 (webready PDF)
ISBN 978 1 3995 0340 2 (epub)

CONTENTS

List of Figures   vi
Acknowledgements   vii
Abbreviations and Selected Technical Terms   x

Introduction   1
1   Turning Points: Theory, Background and Methods of Analysis   14
2   Istanbul as European Capital of Culture, 2010: The AKP's
    Final Turn towards Europe   55
3   Gezi Park, 2013: Protesting and Resisting the AKP   99
4   The Station of the Martyrs, 2017: Memorialisation and
    Consolidation of the AKP   138
5   The Reconversion of Hagia Sophia, 2020: Final Conquest and
    Victory of the AKP   169
Conclusion   216

Bibliography   227
Index   256

FIGURES

3.1   Gezi Park, July 2013   100
3.2   Holy Trinity Greek Orthodox Church, Taksim Square, July 2013   125
5.1   Hagia Sophia, January 2022   170
5.2   Hagia Sophia interior, January 2022   174
5.3   Hagia Sophia interior, January 2022   175
5.4   Hagia Sophia dome and upper galleries, January 2022   176
5.5   Hagia Sophia *mihrab* (with view of covered mosaic icons),
       January 2022   177
5.6   Hagia Sophia panel donated by President Erdoğan, January 2022   200
5.7   Hagia Sophia *mihrab* (with panel donated by President Erdoğan),
       January 2022   201
C.1   Şehitlik Mosque, Berlin, June 2022   221
C.2   Şehitlik Mosque interior, Berlin, June 2022   222
C.3   Şehitlik Mosque dome, Berlin, June 2022   222

ACKNOWLEDGEMENTS

The start to this book occurred during Courtney Dorroll's dissertation research, fieldwork and writing. Portions of it appeared in Courtney Dorroll's 2015 dissertation titled 'The Spatial Politics of Turkey's Justice and Development Party (AK Party): On Erdoğanian Neo-Ottomanism', which is available through the University of Arizona's library records. The project has since been expanded to include events that occurred after her dissertation, and Philip Dorroll focused on the expansion chapters as well as timely updates to the sections that Courtney originally wrote for her dissertation. The final product is a collaborative effort from both Courtney and Phil, and they are fortunate to have had the opportunity to work together in their respective field of Turkish Studies.

Courtney Dorroll would like to thank her dissertation committee: co-advisers Drs Leila Hudson and Amy Newhall, and committee members Drs Linda Darling and Aomar Boum. Courtney Dorroll's PhD was generously funded by the Jacob K. Javits Fellowship (stewarded by Dean Dorian Vorhees), the Critical Language Scholarship, the Department of Education's Title VI Foreign Language and Area Studies Fellowship, and the Confluence Center for Critical Inquiry at the University of Arizona. Ideas from the dissertation that are now incorporated into this book have been better honed because of presentations and feedback from the American Academy of Religion, American Anthropological Association, the Middle East

Studies Association, the Southeast Regional Middle East and Islamic Studies Society, University of Tubingen's Center for Islamic Theology and its Department of Oriental and Islamic Studies, the Heritage, Aesthetics and Belonging: Gender in Turkish neo-Ottomanism workshop organised by the Many Roads in Modernity Research Centre, University of Copenhagen, held at the Swedish Institute in Istanbul by Drs Catharina Raudvere and Petek Onur (an edited volume from those talks, *Neo-Ottoman Imaginaries in Contemporary Turkey. Gendered Discourses, Agencies, and Visions* is forthcoming), and the 2021 Teaching the South Caucasus Workshop at the University of Illinois. Being part of the University of Arizona's Center for Turkish Studies has allowed Courtney Dorroll to continue to stay engaged with innovative and interdisciplinary approaches to researching and teaching about contemporary Turkey.

Philip Dorroll would like to thank his first mentors in the field of Islamic and Religious Studies, including Vincent and Rkia Cornell, Stacy Holden, Zaineb Istrabadi, Kevin Jaques, Scott Kugle, Jacqueline Mariña, Kevin Martin, Richard Martin, Gordon Newby, Thomas Ryba and Devin Stewart. Several friends and colleagues who have done important work on the intersection of religion, human rights and national identity have also deeply impacted Philip Dorroll's recent thinking on topics related to this book, including Mustafa Akyol, Sarah Eltantawi and M. Hakan Yavuz. He would also like to thank friends and colleagues in Orthodox Christian Studies whose work over the past several years has alerted him to the need to consider the experiences of Orthodox Christian minorities when thinking about issues of global human rights, including George Demacopoulos, Katherine Kelaidis, Candace Lukasik, Aristotle Papanikolaou and Sarah Riccardi-Swartz. Philip Dorroll would also like to thank the many friends and colleagues whose insights have laid the foundation for his current work in this field, and whose names are too numerous to indicate, but who prominently include Brandon Gallaher, Inga Leonova, Ashley Purpura, Andrew Sharp and Angeliki Ziaka.

At Wofford College, both authors would like to thank the Faculty Development Committee, the Office of the Provost and the Board of Trustees for extending funding for summer work devoted to writing and research and research sabbaticals (Philip Dorroll spring 2020 and Courtney Dorroll spring 2021) to give time to work on this book. They would also like to thank their inspiring colleagues in the Middle Eastern and North African Studies Program that make them excited to discuss issues in the region and learn more from each person's disciplinary focus and theoretical perspective. They are also grateful for their Religion Department colleagues who promote the growth mindset and autonomy within one's classroom and research trajectory. Both authors are forever grateful for the meaningful conversations they have been able to have with their thoughtful and committed Wofford students. Wofford's President Nayef Samhat is a wonderful leader who has been a supporter of the MENA Program, expanded the college to incorporate Arabic and created more space for scholar-teachers which has directly allowed both authors to thrive at Wofford College.

Finally, as parents, both authors would like to thank their phenomenal childcare family: the Church of the Advent preschool and the Trinity United Methodist Church both in Spartanburg, South Carolina. Specific gratitude goes to to Ms Jennifer, Ms Mya and Ms Tracie. The love and care you provide each work day allowed this book to happen.

ABBREVIATIONS AND SELECTED TECHNICAL TERMS

Political Parties

AKP	Adalet ve Kalkınma Partisi (Justice and Development Party)
CHP	Cumhuriyet Halk Partisi (Republican People's Party)
FP	Fazilet Partisi (Virtue Party)
GP	Gelecek Partisi (Future Party)
HDP	Halkların Demokratik Partisi (Democratic People's Party)
İYİ	İyi Parti (Good Party)
MHP	Milliyetçi Hareket Partisi (Nationalist Action Party)
MNP	Milli Nizam Partisi (National Order Party)
MSP	Milli Selamet Partisi (National Salvation Party)
RP	Refah Partisi (Welfare Party)
SP	Saadet Partisi (Felicity Party)

Selected Terms

Diyanet	The Turkish Directorate of Religious Affairs (Diyanet İşleri Başkanlığı).
Kemalism	The revolutionary secularist ideology associated with the political programme of the founder of the Republic of Turkey, Mustafa Kemal Atatürk.

Rum/Ρωμιοί/ Romioi   The indigenous Greek Orthodox Christian community of Istanbul, the modern descendants of the Byzantines. These names are all derivations of 'Roman', the term that 'Byzantine' Greeks used for themselves, because their medieval empire was the continuation of the Roman Empire in its eastern territories (the term 'Byzantine' was invented by modern Western historians; the empire was always known to itself and others as simply the Roman Empire). Beginning in the fouth century, the Byzantines ruled territories in Anatolia, the Balkans, the Middle East and the eastern Mediterranean from their ancient capital city of Constantinople. This city was conquered by the Ottomans in 1453, who converted it into their imperial capital. It later became known as Istanbul.

INTRODUCTION

This book explores the momentous shifts in power during a crucial decade in Turkish history, 2010 to 2020, by analysing how these events have produced shifts in the physical landscape of Istanbul. The book's analysis focuses on the role of the Turkish state in the restoration of conservative Islamic and neo-Ottoman imagery and iconography in public space through the intentional transformation of architecture and the built environment. The specific case studies were selected to act as various nodes in the overarching constellation of the Adalet ve Kalkınma Partisi's (AKP; Justice and Development Party) conceptions of the built environment. As the book demonstrates, a specific ideological framework undergirded the AKP's conception of the built environment, the plans it implemented to transform it, and the forms of resistance that these plans generated. This specific ideological framework is Erdoğanian neo-Ottomanism. This term was introduced by C. Dorroll (2015; 2016) and is used in this book to illustrate the ideological driving forces that have driven the transformation of Turkish politics over the past decade as they are reflected in public space and the built environment. Put simply, 'Erdoğanian Neo-Ottomanism' means the AKP's use of the power of the state to shape the urban landscape in their social and ideological image. This phenomenon is the subject of this book's analysis.

The AKP under Erdoğan's leadership remembers the Ottoman past in homogeneous Sunni Turkish Muslim terms, and it is the specific form of cultural memory that constitutes the new cultural capital that is shifting the political and urban landscape of Turkey. Erdoğan's AKP is not concerned with ethnic, religious, or political plurality or heterogeneity in Turkish society and public life. Instead, it actively discourages the growth of a pluralistic social life and public sphere by cracking down on counter movements that dissent to, or are simply different from, the AKP's conception of conservative Sunni Turkish cultural capital. This book will argue in particular that one of the key and unique features of this ideology is that it seeks to establish and perpetuate its homogenising vision specifically through manipulation of the urban land-scape. In other words, Erdoğan's AKP seeks to transform Turkey's political landscape through transforming Turkey's architectural landscape, especially in Istanbul.

The four specific case studies in the book will illuminate the key dynamics and transformations of the last decade of Turkish politics by analysing discrete instances where Erdoğan's AKP has attempted to inscribe its vision in the pub-lic sphere through public architectural sites. The first case study will analyse how Istanbul's designation as 'European Capital of Culture' in 2010 became a way to reshape the urban landscape by displacing ethnic minorities from the city centre. The second case study will analyse the 2013 Gezi Park protests as a pluralist site of protest to the AKP's homogenising social vision, while noting the historical ironies of the protests' enactment in the area of the displacement and marginalisation of indigenous Greek Orthodox in the twentieth century. The third case study will analyse the Monument to the Martyrs of 15 July and associated memorial practices related to the 2016 coup attempt in order to uncover how experiences of trauma and acts of memorialisation intersect with the dynamics of the AKP's spatial politics. The fourth case study will analyse how the change in Hagia Sophia's status from museum to mosque in 2020 epitomises the political and ideological dynamics of Erdoğan's AKP as a political project of conservative Turkish Islamic national identity. This project will be contrasted to histories and prominent responses from the indigenous Greek Orthodox community that illuminate the significance of the AKP's spa-tial politics in Istanbul with particular clarity.

In all of our case studies a common question lurks under the surface: who has the right to this space? We argue that the AKP is dictating public space, its use and its aesthetics, as part of its methods of political rule. This is not surprising, as political parties in power do have more rights over the physical space that they control. The elite, political powers have top-down ability to dictate Turkey's public space in ways that accord with that party's ideals. As will be discussed more fully in Chapter 1, political manipulation of public space in modern Turkey did not begin with the AKP. The founder of the Turkish Republic, Mustafa Kemal Atatürk, did this when he physically moved the cultural capital of the capital city away from Istanbul (and its Byzantine and Ottoman cultural legacies and remains) and transformed the small village of Angora into the Turkish Republic's capital of Ankara. Mustafa Kemal Atatürk used his power position to create a landscape that aligned with his aspiration to shape Turkey through the eyes of the West and secularism.

This book will therefore read architecture, monuments, public ceremony and similar phenomena as text. It will unpack its ideologies and meanings and also analyse people's response to these phenomena. It is not just those in power that control the material culture and landscape of their time; it is also members of the public that engage, repurpose and protest the spaces in their city, neighbourhoods and parks. This conversation and dialectic between the official dictates of public space and the response by the public will also be explored. Most significant to this project is the documenting and analysing of the specific ways the AKP is using and manipulating space, particularly public space, because this process directly affects the use of this space by the public and the possibilities for its use as a public sphere.

The concept of 'cultural capital' is particularly important to this book's analysis (as will be discussed in more detail in Chapter 1). In *Outline of a Theory of Practice*, Pierre Bourdieu defines cultural capital as things that are deemed cultural assets, not financial capital, but have value and can be 'used' to gain access and power in society.[1] This book argues that it is through the urban landscape, the arts and architecture that the AKP is inscribing their political ideology onto the urban landscape of Istanbul and thereby creating a shift in cultural capital of the urban landscape. This book provides tangible examples of the effects of this shift on the Istanbul built environment. The built environment can therefore be read as a 'text' to show the lasting power and reappropriation of power through the Turkish landscape. It is not simply the AKP's implementation of neoliberal economic policies, but also their implementation of cultural capital that allows them to change the architectural landscape of contemporary Istanbul. This is what is meant here when referring to the 'spatial politics' of the AKP.

Analysing Istanbul: Disciplinary Context and Scope of the Argument

There are an endless variety of ways to analyse a city, particularly when attempting to capture the intricacies of a city such as Istanbul, whose historical roots are some two millennia old and whose current population is almost 15 million people. Istanbul in particular has been the subject of globally renowned artistic accounts that focus on the particular affective power of the city's unique urban landscape, such as Orhan Pamuk's *Istanbul: Memories of a City,*[2] a personal and nostalgic journey through the city as an object of memory and melancholy, and Nuri Bilge Ceylan's anlaysis of alienation and distance in *Uzak* (2002). Specialised studies have utilised the city from more meta-perspectives[3] and historical analyses[4] engaged with Istanbul in a wide variety of illuminating micro-level analyses. These have included: how Istanbul is depicted in television[5] or how the AKP's ideology is infused in Islamic media out of Istanbul networks;[6] female poverty in the city;[7] research on how one uses an archive in Istanbul;[8] neighbourhood- or location-specific studies;[9] museum and art specific studies;[10] daily traffic ways and how these illustrate class hierarchies;[11] analyses of Pamuk;[12] the activism and violence embedded in Istanbul's contemporary conversation and past;[13] animals in the city;[14] nationalism and football in the city;[15] and Istanbul's identity through its culinary scene[16] (to name only a few examples). There have also been numerous thought-provoking works on the recent AKP's distinct style of politics,[17] neo-Ottomanism as a cultural and political phenomenon[18] and neo-Ottomanism as a form of Turkish foreign policy and global relations.[19] Beyond situating this book with other works on Istanbul, Turkey and Turkey's influence globally, we also situate the book in broader conversations on nationalism,[20] the built environment[21] and urban studies.[22]

This book's contribution is a consideration of architecture and public space that sheds new light on our understanding of the political changes caused by the last decade of AKP administration in Turkey. Within the discipline of Turkish Studies in particular, this book engages questions and builds on scholarly approaches that concern what we have referred to above as the spatial politics of the city of Istanbul. Our understanding of space concurs with Kathrin Wildner and Frank Eckardt, who aptly point out in their edited volume, *Public Istanbul: Spaces and Spheres of the Urban*:

> Urban space is analyzed as a social process that is based on spatial structures and space constructing activities. Urban spaces are continuously (re)constructed in planning processes, as well as in everyday practices. In this sense, the existence of public space – where spatial structures are materialized and social interactions take place – is a central characteristic of 'urbanity'. It is temporarily used for different utilizations and has differing attributions of meaning. It is thus a heterogeneous space of negotiation, materially and discursively disputed . . .[23]

Public space and the urban built environment are inherently politicised because they are areas for 'negotiation, materially and discursively disputed' by and for a variety of ideological perspectives and worldviews. Reading urban space this way therefore becomes a way to read Turkish politics and social dynamics in general, and changes in the urban space reflect and contribute to changes in society and politics. As the title of the book suggests, the urban space is so dynamic that we can observe turning points in Turkish history in general by examining shifts, turns and changes within the landscape of the city that stands at the centre of Turkish history, Istanbul.

Moreover, in Turkey the role of the state in these changes is particularly decisive. Changes in the urban landscape are often deliberately caused by the state in pursuit of political objectives. Amy Mills' work in particular has inspired and motivated the methods employed in this book because it calls attention to precisely this dynamic, or in her words: 'how the process of nation-imagining occurs through a transformation of the city'.[24] Istanbul is particularly important in this respect: 'Since the foundation of the Turkish Republic in 1923, Istanbul has had unique importance as a site through and against which the Turkish state asserts and represents national identity.'[25] Mills' analyses of secular Turkish nationalism in the early republican period focuses on how ways of seeing and interacting with the urban landscape of Istanbul were not merely *products* of a new vision of national identity, but were in fact *producers* of this new identity. We argue that the same is true for the AKP in contemporary Istanbul.

In order to somehow force the highly multi-ethnic and cosmopolitan reality of Istanbul into the restrictive vision of Turkish nationalism, the Turkish state and its supporters had to deliberately and radically reimagine the city itself. As Mills' work powerfully demonstrates, at the very beginning of the history of the republic, 'Ethno-nationalist Turkish belonging in Istanbul was a form of urbanism, composed of place-based norms for behavior and a commonly understood cultural geography of the city.'[26] Our work extends this insight by delving into how the AKP has manipulated the urban and public space of Istanbul in the service of its own form of nationalist identity, which importantly is formed in conscious opposition to the secular Turkish nationalism analysed in Mills' work. In this book we argue that Erdoğan's particular form of neo-Ottomanism is the key to understanding how and why the AKP has gone to such great lengths to instantiate its social and political vision via its manipulation of Istanbul's urban space. Our analysis of the spatial politics in Istanbul is therefore an analysis of how the AKP under Erdoğan has changed Istanbul in order to change Turkish identity itself. The case studies below show how the AKP endeavoured to shape and contour Istanbul's landscape so that when they viewed it, and showed it to others, they saw themselves in reflection.

The methods employed in this book's analysis enable close analysis of concrete changes in one place over time and enables consideration of the interconnectedness of the specific sites under analysis, as they all exist in the same urban context of Istanbul. This method focuses on a city that is particularly important to AKP interpretations of Turkish history because of its status as a kind of symbolic battleground for modern debates over the nature of Turkish identity more generally, as described above; and as we will see, this is particularly true of the contemporary AKP due to the importance of neo-Ottomanism in its social and political worldview. This method is therefore not meant to represent or homogenise the complex political experiences of rural or other urban areas in Turkey, but rather to reveal the particular role the cityscape of Istanbul has played in recent Turkish politics. Our focus on Istanbul is not meant to make arguments that apply to all of Turkey, but rather to reveal dynamics particular to the way in which the AKP has interacted with Istanbul specifically.

Finally, it is important to note the positionalities of the authors of this book. Both Courtney and Philip trained in Turkish Studies, but they specialised in different approaches within this field. This is reflected in the multidisciplinary approach of this book's analysis, an approach we felt was uniquely well-suited to addressing the complex and multidimensional nature of the book's topic. Courtney's research has focused on ethnographic approaches, while Philip's has focused on textual approaches. These two methods and their specific contributions are woven together throughout the book, with some chapters relying more heavily on one approach over another, depending on the nature of the specific subject matter in question. Neither author is Turkish, but both have studied and trained extensively in Turkey. Philip is a practicing Orthodox Christian who is also a member of the Greek Orthodox Archdiocese of America.

Chapter Summaries

Chapter 1 outlines the key theoretical and methodological components of the book's larger argument that the AKP has utilised a specific type of spatial politics to alter cultural capital in Turkey by creating a neo-Ottoman architectural public sphere. It describes the methods of research used in the book, including ethnographic research, textual analysis and the analysis of architectural sites as texts. This chapter also lays the theoretical groundwork for the case studies in the rest of the book by discussing how the Ottoman Empire has been remembered, forgotten or reimagined in modern Turkey. The authors will conceptualise and define the various modes of Turkish nationalism. It discusses the cultural movement of neo-Ottomanism and its roots in the new social class of the Turkish Islamic bourgeoisie, exploring how this movement is the latest in a series of attempts by hegemonic elites to shape the public sphere in modern Turkey, and specifically introduces the concept of Erdoğanian neo-Ottomanism.

Chapter 2 discusses how the AKP utilised Istanbul's 2010 designation as the European Capital of Culture (ECoC) and the attendant arts and culture programming to reinvigorate and rebrand the importance of Turkey's Ottoman past. This moment represented a possible turn towards Europe and the possibility of multicultural Turkish identity. At the same time, the ECoC designation acted as the catalyst for the Sulukule Gentrification Project which 'cleaned' the area of Roma residents that had been residing there since the eleventh century and replaced them with representatives of the Islamic bourgeoisie that much more closely conform to the interests of AKP spatial politics. The utilisation of pluralistic neo-Ottoman rhetoric stood in stark contrast to the actual effects of the Sulukule Gentrification Project. Through specific examples of arts programming, the Ottoman past was romanticised as being inclusive and multi-ethnic, while in the actual architectural public sphere of Sulukule the historic ethnic identity of the Roma was displaced to make room for apartments built by the Mass Housing Authority (Toplu Konut İdaresi; TOKİ) in the peripheral Taşoluk neighbourhood. This chapter explores documents and public events associated with the ECoC in order to show the AKP utilised this designation as an opportunity to inscribe its hegemonic vision through the political utilisation of arts and culture projects in public space. This chapter focuses in particular on the tensions and ambiguities present in this early stage of the development of Erdoğanian neo-Ottomanism as it still looked towards the West while beginning to manifest the authoritarian nationalism that would come to characterise it over the course of the decade.

Chapter 3 analyses how Gezi Park developed into the main site of protest against the AKP's attempts to manipulate the urban landscape to reflect its own political and social vision. This chapter utilises on-site research conducted in summer 2013, specifically participant observation in Gezi Park and survey research of respondents at Boğaziçi University in Istanbul associated with or opposed to the protests. This chapter analyses how the Gezi Park protests, which were sparked by AKP plans to demolish this important public green space in Istanbul, marked the beginning of significant public opposition to the restructuring of public space by Erdoğan's AKP. This chapter will also analyse the tensions and historical ironies in the protestor's multicultural rhetoric, as they are analysed in the context of the twentieth-century removal and marginalisation of the Greek Orthodox populations that once thrived in and dominated the parts of the city where the Gezi movement arose and flourished, and also by considering the reaction of contemporary Greek residents to the Gezi movement. While the previous chapter analyses a moment of ambiguity in the AKP's relationship with Istanbul's urban landscape, this chapter shows how the Gezi movement marked the decisive turning point the AKP's approach to the city of Istanbul where it forever turned away from the possibilities of cosmopolitan identity, and towards conservative Turkish nationalism.

Chapter 4 analyses the events of the attempted coup of July 2016 as traumatic experiences that were understood and processed through sites of memorialisation in public space and public architecture. Focusing in particular on the significance of the renaming of the Bosphorus Bridge as the 15 July Martyrs' Bridge, the imagery and AKP-related public discourse and ritual associated with the memory and mourning of the victims of the coup attempt, this chapter will discuss how the traumatic aftermath of these events led the AKP to attempt to silence all public resistance to its agenda. This analysis will therefore open up an analytical space to discuss how the dramatic turning points of the past decade in Turkish politics are connected not only with ideological agendas, but also with traumatic social memory and practices of memorialisation and remembrance. At the same time, this chapter considers how such practices serve to construct and reinforce the power and dominance of the AKP's conservative Islamic nationalism and its construal of the ideal Turkish citizen.

Chapter 5 analyses the shift from Hagia Sophia's status as a museum to a mosque in summer 2020 as the paradigmatic example of the public dominance and triumphalism of the AKP's conservative Turkish Muslim political vision. This chapter will argue that the architectural site of Hagia Sophia is one of the most central and contentious sites in all of Istanbul, and that the shift in its status marks the high-point of the AKP's use of architecture and public space to exclude multicultural or pluralistic narratives of Turkish national identity. This chapter will analyse the spatial politics of the building of Hagia Sophia, and will consider the importance of this public monument to the identity of the city of Istanbul throughout its history in terms of both its Greek Orthodox and Turkish Sunni identities in the past and the present. This chapter's analysis will focus on the political and social discourse, public ceremony and physical changes related to the reconversion of the museum of Hagia Sophia by the AKP in order to reveal this moment as the climax of the dynamics charted throughout the course of this book. It will also consider the reactions of prominent representatives of the indigenous Greek Orthodox community of Istanbul to the reconversion of Hagia Sophia, as these reactions shed dramatic light on the specific nature of Erdoğanian neo-Ottomanism as a homogenising form of conservative Turkish Muslim nationalism that specifically denies cosmopolitan identities and histories.

Notes

1. Pierre Bourdieu, *Outline of a Theory of Practice*, trans. Richard Nice (Cambridge: Cambridge University Press, 1977), 8.

2. Orhan Pamuk, *Istanbul: Memories and the City*, trans. Maureen Freely (New York: Vintage, 2006).

3. Ipek Türeli, *Istanbul, Open City: Exhibiting Anxieties of Urban Modernity* (London: Routledge 2018); Nora Fisher-Onar, Susan C. Pearce, and E. Fuat Keyman (eds), *Istanbul: Living with Difference in a Global City* (New Brunswick, NJ: Rutgers University Press, 2018).

4. Murat Gül, *The Emergence of Modern Istanbul: Transformation and Modernisation of a City* (London: I. B. Tauris, 2009); Çağlar Keyder, 'A Brief History of Modern Istanbul', in Reşat Kasaba (ed.), *The Cambridge History of Turkey*, vol. 4 (Cambridge: Cambridge University Press, 2008), 504–23.

5. Ipek A. Celik Rappas and Sezen Kayhan, 'TV Series Production and the Urban Restructuring of Istanbul', *Television & New Media* 19:1 (2018): 3–23.

6. Hikmet Kocamaner, 'Strengthening the Family through Television: Islamic Broadcasting, Secularism, and the Politics of Responsibility in Turkey', *Anthropological Quarterly* 90:3 (2017): 675–714.

7. Ilkim Markoc, 'Poverty and Difficulties in Participation of Urban Social Life: Young Women in Istanbul', *Journal of International Women's Studies* 22:9 (2021): 49–67.

8. Timur Hammond, 'Papering, Arranging, and Depositing: Learning from Working with an Istanbul Archive', *Area (London 1969)* 52:1 (2020): 204–12.

9. Kristen Sarah Biehl, 'A Dwelling Lens: Migration, Diversity and Boundary-Making in an Istanbul Neighbourhood', *Ethnic and Racial Studies* 43:12 (2020): 2236–54; Deniz Neriman Duru, 'From Mosaic to Ebru: Conviviality in Multi-Ethnic, Multi-Faith Burgazadası, Istanbul', *South European Society & Politics* 20:2 (2015): 243–63; Serife Genis, 'Producing Elite Localities: The Rise of Gated Communities in Istanbul', *Urban Studies* 44:4 (2007): 771–98; Amy Mills, *Streets of Memory: Landscape, Tolerance, and National Identity in Istanbul* (Athens, GA: University of Georgia Press, 2010); Danielle van Dobben Schoon, '"Sulukule is the Gun and We are its Bullets": Urban Renewal and Romani Identity in Istanbul', *CITY* 18:6 (2014): 720–31; Emine Yetiskul and Sule Demirel, 'Assembling Gentrification in Istanbul: The Cihangir Neighbourhood of Beyoğlu', *Urban Studies* 55:15 (2018): 3336–52.

10. Gönül Bozoğlu, 'A Great Bliss to Keep the Sensation of Conquest Alive!: The Emotional Politics of the Panorama 1453 Museum in Istanbul', in Chiara de Cesari and Ayhan Kaya (eds), *European Memory in Populism* (London: Routledge, 2020), 91–111; Koray Değirmenci, 'Homegrown Sounds of Istanbul: World Music, Place, and Authenticity', *Turkish Studies* 11:2 (2010): 251–68; A. G. Papadopoulos and Aslı Duru (eds), *Landscapes of Music in Istanbul: A Cultural*

Politics of Place and Exclusion (Bielefeld, Germany: Transcript, 2017); Jean-Francois Polo, 'The Istanbul Modern Art Museum: An Urban Regeneration Project?' *European Planning Studies* 23:8 (2015): 1511–28; Lorenzo Posocco, 'Museum Politics in Turkey under the Islamic Justice and Development Party (AKP): The Case of the Istanbul Museum of the History of Science and Technology in Islam', *International Journal of Politics, Culture, and Society* 32:1 (2018): 83–103; İpek Türeli, 'Modeling Citizenship in Turkey's Miniature Park', *Traditional Dwellings and Settlements Review* 17:2 (2006): 55–69; Daniel Xerri, 'The Poetry of Cities: On Discovering Poems in Istanbul, Sarajevo, and Bratislava', *Journeys (New York, N.Y.)* 15:1 (2014): 90–108.

11. Berna Yazıcı, 'Towards an Anthropology of Traffic: A Ride Through Class Hierarchies on Istanbul's Roadways', *Ethnos* 78:4 (2013): 515–42.

12. Sibel Erol, 'The Chronotope of Istanbul in Orhan Pamuk's Memoir *Istanbul*', *International Journal of Middle East Studies* 43:4 (2011): 655–76; Erdag Goknar, 'Orhan Pamuk and the "Ottoman" Theme', *World Literature Today* 80:6 (2006): 34–8.

13. Asli Duru, '"A Walk down the Shore": A Visual Geography of Ordinary Violence in Istanbul', *Environment and Planning* 37:6 (2019): 1064–80; Christopher Houston, *Istanbul, City of the Fearless: Urban Activism, Coup d'État, and Memory in Turkey* (Oakland, CA: University of California Press, 2020); Defne Kadıoğlu Polat, 'No One Is Larger than the State: Consent, Dissent, and Vigilant Violence during Turkey's Neoliberal Urban Transition', *Journal of Southeast European and Black Sea Studies* 21:2 (2021): 189–211; Danielle V. Schoon and Funda Oral, 'The Role of Communities of Practice in Urban Rights Activism in Istanbul, Turkey', in Carl A. Maida and Sam Beck (eds), *Global Sustainability and Communities of Practice* (New York: Berghahn, 2018), 94–108.

14. Kimberly Hart, 'Istanbul's Intangible Cultural Heritage as Embodied by Street Animals', *History and Anthropology* 30:4 (2019): 448–59.

15. John Konuk Blasing, 'Hegemonic Discourses Clash in the Stadium: Sport, Nationalism, and Globalization in Turkey', *International Journal of Middle East Studies* 51:3 (2019): 475–8.

16. Bendegul Okumus and Gurel Cetin, 'Marketing Istanbul as a Culinary Destination', *Journal of Destination Marketing & Management* 9 (2018): 340–6.

17. Senem Aslan, 'Public Tears: Populism and the Politics of Emotion in AKP's Turkey', *International Journal of Middle East Studies* 53:1 (2021): 1–17; Rasim Özgür Dönmez, 'Nationalism in Turkey under Justice and Development

Party Rule: The Logic of Masculinist Protection', *Turkish Studies* 16:4 (2015): 554–71; Simon A. Waldman and Emre Caliskan, *The New Turkey and Its Discontents* (Oxford: Oxford University Press, 2017).

18. Yılmaz Çolak, 'Ottomanism vs. Kemalism: Collective Memory and Cultural Pluralism in 1990s Turkey', *Middle Eastern Studies* 42:4 (2006): 587–602; Chien Yang Erdem, 'Ottomentality: Neoliberal Governance of Culture and neo-Ottoman Management of Diversity', *Turkish Studies* 18:4 (2017): 710–28; Husik Gulyan, 'The Spatialization of Islamist, Populist, and neo-Ottoman Discourses in the Turkish Capital under AKP Rule', *New Perspectives on Turkey* 61 (2019): 125–53; Murat Ergin and Yağmur Karakaya, 'Between neo-Ottomanism and Ottomania: Navigating State-Led and Popular Cultural Representations of the Past', *New Perspectives on Turkey* 56 (2017): 33–59; Nora Fisher-Onar, 'Echoes of a Universalism Lost: Rival Representations of the Ottomans in Today's Turkey', *Middle Eastern Studies* 45:2 (2009): 229–41; Jeremy Walton, 'Practices of neo-Ottomanism: Making Space and Place Virtkuious in Istanbul', in Deniz Göktürk, Levent Soysal and İpek Türeli (eds), *Orienting Istanbul: Cultural Captial of Europe?* (London: Routledge 2010), 88–103; M. Hakan Yavuz, *Nostalgia for the Empire: The Politics of Neo-Ottomanism* (Oxford: Oxford University Press, 2020).

19. Sunnie Rucker-Chang, 'The Turkish Connection: Neo-Ottoman Influence in post-Dayton Bosnia', *Journal of Muslim Minority Affairs* 34:2 (2014): 152–64; Mark Langan, 'Virtuous Power Turkey in Sub-Saharan Africa: The "neo-Ottoman" Challenge to the European Union'," *Third World Quarterly* 38:6 (2017): 1399–414; Ipek Z. Ruacan, 'Bringing the Empire Back In: The Gradual Discovery of the Ottoman Empire in Turkish Foreign Policy', *Welt Des Islams* 56:3/4 (2016): 466–88; Göktürk Tüysüzoğlu, 'Strategic Depth: A neo-Ottomanist Interpretation of Turkish Eurasianism', *Mediterranean Quarterly* 25:2 (2014): 85–104.

20. Benedict Anderson, *Imagined Communities: Reflections on the Origin and Spread of Nationalism* (New York: Verso, 2006); Ernest Gellner, *Nations and Nationalism* (Ithaca, NY: Cornell University Press, 1983); Michael Hechter, *Containing Nationalism* (Oxford: Oxford University Press, 2000).

21. Nezar AlSayyad, *Traditions: The 'Real', the Hyper, and the Virtual in the Built Environment* (London: Routledge, 2014).

22. Henri Lefebvre, *The Production of Space*, trans. Donald Nicholson-Smith (Malden, MA: Blackwell, 2016); Gülçin Erdi-Lelandais (ed.), *Understanding the City: Henri Lefebvre and Urban Studies* (Newcastle upon Tyne: Cambridge Scholars, 2014);

Thomas Bender and Alev Cinar, *Urban Imaginaries: Locating the Modern City* (Minneapolis: University of Minnesota Press, 2007).

23. Kathrin Wildner and Frank Eckhardt, 'Preface', *Public Istanbul: Spaces and Spheres of the Urban* (Bielefeld: Transcript Verlag, 2015), 7–8.

24. Mills, *Streets of Memory*, 10.

25. Mills, *Streets of Memory*, 7.

26. Amy Mills, 'The Cultural Politics of Ethnic Nationalism: Turkish Urbanism in Occupied Istanbul (1918–1923)', *Annals of the American Association of Geographers* 107:5 (2017), 1179.

1

TURNING POINTS:
THEORY, BACKGROUND AND
METHODS OF ANALYSIS

This chapter[1] lays the groundwork for the rest of the book by outlining the key theoretical concepts used in its analysis, discussing the Turkish historical and political background necessary to contextualise the specific case studies analysed and clarifying the specific methods of analysis used in these case studies. The key theoretical concepts include cultural capital, cultural memory and public spheres. The necessary historical background focuses on how the historical legacy of the Ottoman Empire has been remembered, forgotten or reimagined in modern Turkey. The key analytical methods that will be applied to the case studies occurring between 2010 and 2020 include ethnographic research, textual analysis and the analysis of architectural sites as texts. This book's broad assertion is that studying key moments of change in the urban landscape and built environment of Istanbul over this ten-year period reveals key social and political dynamics that took place during this period.

The specific argument of this book is that the AKP under the leadership of Recep Tayyip Erdoğan has utilised a specific type of spatial politics to alter cultural capital in Turkey by creating a neo-Ottoman architectural public sphere. Put another way, the AKP administration of the past ten years under Erdoğan's leadership has altered public and architectural spaces in the city of Istanbul in order to establish and enforce the dominance of its social vision. The book describes a series of decisive turning points, where the AKP was presented with the possibility of supporting a pluralistic or heterogenous vision of Turkish politics and national identity, but decisively turned away from this possibility and chose to embrace a politics of homogeneous and conservative Turkish Islamic national identity. At each turning point the AKP, by appealing to Ottoman history and identity, consolidated this shift by altering the public sphere in the city that is the heart of Turkish cultural identity. This analysis focuses on the cultural movement of neo-Ottomanism and its roots in the new social class of the Turkish Islamic bourgeoisie, exploring how this movement is the latest in a series of attempts by hegemonic elites to shape the public sphere in modern Turkey. It specifically introduces C. Dorroll's concept of Erdoğanian neo-Ottomanism, and explains how this type of neo-Ottomanism was used to create an architectural public sphere and reshapes cultural capital in contemporary Istanbul.

Moreover, such dynamics are not unique to contemporary Turkey, but point to a universal trend that spans time and space: people in power inscribe meaning on things. As David Harvey famously argued, 'Place, in whatever guise, is like space and time, a social construct.'[2] We see those in power inscribe, dictate, erect and immortalise their legacies. As time goes by and power dynamics shift, new people come to power and re-inscribe, tear down and change the meaning on the landscape of their rule. In some cases, we can also see those at the margins fight back and try to regain, re-claim or somehow hold onto their claim to space; yet, in most cases, the decisive factor is what regime is in power and how that regime rewrites, transcribes and creates the hegemonic voice. In the time period under consideration in this book, prime minister and then president Recep Tayyip Erdoğan constitutes the primary source of the hegemonic political voice in Turkey. Therefore, this book analyses how Erdoğan and his party have told the story of Istanbul during a specific decade (2010–20).

Yet in between the lines of powerful rhetoric and official narrative come the voices of those moved out, pushed to the side and written out of the context. In the case studies analysed below, these include the Roma, Greek Orthodox Christians, Gülenists, secularists, protesters and others. The telling of this story is unique to its time and place, and reveals how architecture has the power to display, reorient and contest systems of power. Here we will show that representations are multilayered and ever-changing. The power of the ruler and the ruling elite is both demonstrated and contested through these public visual forms. Reading architecture and public space, including the discourses and practices associated with architecture and public space, therefore reveals important insights about the AKP's consolidation of power, and the resistance to it, over this critical ten-year period in modern Turkish history.

The narrative of this analysis is structured around specific 'turning points', which we define here as key moments in time where the AKP under Erdoğan's leadership decisively turned Turkish politics in the direction of conservative Turkish Islamic national identity. In each case, this turn was accomplished by the utilisation of Erdoğan's specific form of neo-Ottomanism, which is distinguished by the manipulation of architecture and public space as a way to consolidate and display political and social power. Each case study therefore examines the use of neo-Ottomanism at a specific site and how this usage stands as a turning point for broader Turkish political shifts.

The 2010 European Capital of Culture (ECoC) designation for the whole city of Istanbul marked the moment and climax of Turkey's aspirations to join the European Union. This climax of the long turn towards Europe in modern Turkish history proved to be deeply ambiguous, however, as it also contained an early example of the AKP's manipulation of public space to fit a specific Turkish national identity. In preparation for that year's festivities that would focus on the celebration of Istanbul's multicultural identity, Roma residents were forcibly displaced in order to make room for the Islamic bourgeoise that underpinned the AKP administration. The 2010 ECoC designation reveals the tensions, gaps and ambiguities at the early stages in the development of Erdoğanian neo-Ottomanism, most notably the way the AKP administration utilised multiculturalist and pluralist rhetoric to celebrate the Ottoman past of Istanbul while at the same time erasing the actual multiculturalism of the city's present. In addition, the AKP's presentation of Ottoman Istanbul ironically reinscribed the Orientalising tropes that had underpinned Western Europe's rejection of Turkey as a member of Europe.

The protests at Gezi Park and Taksim Square in 2013 reveal the moment when Erdoğan's specifically authoritarian vision of AKP rule began to emerge and to consciously turn away from Europe and the West, effectively reversing the historical trend that had led to the 2010 ECoC designation. The protesters at Gezi Park were viewed as anti-AKP, secular, Westerners that were quite literally standing in the way of Erdoğan and the AKP's broader plan for that space – a commercial centre that was to be built in the style of the Ottoman barracks that had once stood there. The plural, multicultural and heterogeneous possibilities for Turkish identity represented both at Gezi and in Taksim's history were forcibly repressed in favour of a hegemonic and homogeneous vision of Turkish national identity that privileged Turkish ethnicity and Muslim faith, a dynamic that would be dramatically accelerated over the decade. This dynamic also had roots in the previous urban history of this very neighbourhood, as it was the exact location where cosmopolitan identity had been attacked decades before by secular Turkish nationalists through violence against the indigenous Greek Orthodox of Istanbul, whose cultural and religious life was centred in this part of the city.

The violent coup attempt against the AKP government that followed only three years later in 2016 was yet another decisive turning point in Turkish history under Erdoğan's AKP. This event was a moment of national trauma that profoundly altered Turkish society and politics. In response, Erdoğan and the AKP mobilised deeply neo-Ottoman Sunni Islamic spiritual motifs in the public memorial and mourning ceremonies associated with the Istanbul bridge at the centre of popular resistance to the coup plotters – especially the Monument to the Martyrs of 15 July (15 Temmuz Şehitler Makamı). This use of neo-Ottomanism had the dual effect of addressing the real trauma experienced by Turkish society, while also reinforcing the homogenising conservative Turkish Sunni nationalism favoured by Erdoğan. This was also accompanied by massive political repression of the perceived enemies of and potential traitors to Erdoğan's AKP, who were now reckoned not only to be found in the secular opposition such as the Gezi movement, but potentially in any devout religious opposition movements as well, such as any follower of Fethullah Gülen.

The apex of the AKP's neo-Ottomanism under Erdoğan came in 2020 when the Hagia Sophia museum was reconverted into a mosque. This move was the climax of the central dynamic of Erdoğanian neo-Ottomanism: the inscription of a conservative and homogeneous Turkish Muslim nationalism on the public space of Istanbul that deliberately displaces pluralistic or heterogeneous conceptions of identity. The most famous building in all of Istanbul's history, and an architectural monument and achievement of staggering proportions and significance, the Hagia Sophia is also the most powerful representation of the pluralist possibilities and heterogeneous nature of Istanbul's historical identity. It possesses unparalleled spiritual significance for Eastern Orthodox Christians, the spiritual descendants of Byzantine Christianity that was once centred at Constantinople before it was conquered by the Ottomans in 1453 and made the Ottoman capital of Istanbul. The Hagia Sophia also embodies the experiences of the besieged and diminishing indigenous Greek Orthodox community of Istanbul, whose claim to the city has long been seen as deeply threatening to Turkish nationalism. The AKP's reconquest of the architectural centre of Istanbul represented the final victory of its political identity in Tukey itself.

Theories, Concepts, and Methods: Interdisciplinary Analysis of Cultural Capital, Cultural Memory, Public Spheres and the Politics of Architecture

Pierre Bourdieu's concepts of symbolic and cultural capital demonstrate how the manipulation of architecture and public space can both effect and reflect political changes and power. Bourdieu's concepts of symbolic and cultural capital expand the understanding of social worth and value beyond that which is economic. Bourdieu argues that within society there are values and capital that are accessed, traded and learned on the symbolic level and the cultural level. In his work *Distinctions*, Bourdieu outlines in further detail these expanded terms of value. Culture is divided among groups and maintains differing values in order to retain groups and classes. This is accomplished through privilege in the case of who is able to access certain types of culture. According to Bourdieu, 'There is no way out of the game of culture; and one's only chance of objectifying the true nature of the game is to objectify as fully as possible the very operations which one is obliged to use in order to achieve that objectification.'[3]

Institutions that reproduce concepts of cultural and symbolic value are cultural and artistic organisations, which are used in order to establish and maintain levels of culture. Social, cultural and economic class also become key with respect to who is able to pursue art and culture in a given society. The legitimation process that includes cultural competence must be decoded, and it is those with the privilege to access the knowledge of said code that can hold the title of cultural noble, elite or bourgeois in a society.[4] This is the process of creating hierarchical levels of 'taste'. Bourdieu explains that it is not only the institutions themselves, but it is the normative view by society that these institutions are important and legitimate that allows the prolonged and continued reproduction of hierarchies of taste and the evaluation of cultural value. The very phenomenon of one believing in the naturalness of cultural inheritance instead of unpacking the power relations that are inherently involved in creating cultural legitimacy is what Bourdieu calls symbolic violence. Symbolic violence creates the cultivated person and reproduces the institution of power that is cultural heritage.[5]

Bourdieu's discussion of cultural capital as an analytical category that goes beyond the pure economics of a society to evaluate structures of power and that accounts for social mobility is central to this book's analysis. It is through the specifically artistic mediums of architecture and attendant forms of landscape and urban design that we argue the AKP is impressing their ideological, neo-Ottoman traces onto the built environment of Turkey and thereby enacting a shift in cultural capital. In addition to the neoliberal economic dimension of the AKP's power and governance, our analysis focuses on the non-economic values that are amassed through the manipulation and utilisation of architecture and public space in Turkey in accordance with the AKP's social and political ideals. It is not simply the AKP's use of the economy, but also its implementation of cultural capital that allows it to change the spatial aspects of contemporary Turkey that thereby consolidate and reinforce their power. We also use the phrase 'spatial politics' to describe these processes. At the heart of this argument is the theoretical argument Bourdieu has provided through the concept of cultural capital: that art and culture have value and hierarchical systems, which mean that at different times different types of art and culture are more powerful for one segment of society than others, and that this power differential can be used to construct and maintain social and political hierarchy.

A key component of cultural capital in the present is how the past is currently being interpreted and constructed in the form of cultural memory. Marita Sturken describes memory as constantly trying to compete for a spot in history. Sturken argues that different individual's memories of the past are in constant competition for the status of official history.[6] Specific readings of history are the necessary building blocks of cultural memory and therefore of cultural capital. Because cultural memory is by necessity a highly selective construction of the vast complexity of past events and societies, processes of forgetting are in fact important components of cultural remembering, and therefore of cultural capital itself and the identities built on these constructions. This book will explore the most recent shifts in cultural capital and cultural memory in Turkey and how these shifts have both reflected and effected key political and social changes. These shifts were accomplished by the AKP's utilisation of Erdoğanian neo-Ottomanism, a politicised way of remembering a specific type of Ottoman past (in this case, one that is focused on portraying an orthodox Sunni, Turkish version of the Ottoman past that elides or represses religious and ethnic diversity). Our case studies stand as examples of the types of cultural capital that have held significant value during the AKP rule of Turkey and how they are rooted in specific forms of cultural memory.

Finally, our analysis argues that cultural memory and cultural capital are rendered visible by being inscribed in the public sphere through architecture and the built environment. In *The Structural Transformation of the Public Sphere*, Jürgen Habermas famously provides an account of the development of civil society in the post-French Revolution cultural environment in England, France and Germany. Habermas argues that the formation of the public press and literary criticism sparked the emergence of the public sphere comprising the private, property-owning, educated man. According to Habermas, rational-critical discourse spread throughout the bourgeois public sphere through the literary criticism movement and communicative action. Key to Habermas' analysis is the understanding of publics formed by the reading of shared written texts.[7]

This book's understanding of the public sphere moves beyond the idea of the Habermasian public sphere by arguing that non-written materials can also serve as 'texts' in the Habermasian sense. As Leila Hudson argues, 'The modern environment is symbolically rich, creates a visual grammar of power, is inscribed on the land, involves the investment of finite resources, and the circumscription of people of new structures.'[8] Similar to Hudson's exploration of structures of governmentality in late Ottoman Damascus, this book will analyse how the architectural built environment constructed by the AKP in Turkey creates a visual and spatial 'grammar of power' in the contemporary Turkish public sphere. Using Hudson's terminology, the contemporary AKP's architectural projects that visually reconstruct and re-imagine the Ottoman past may be described as constituting a 'centrally orchestrated campaign of public tradition'.[9]

In other words, though Habermas focused his analysis on the reading public and literature, our study extends the idea of the 'text' to include architecture and what is written architecturally on the urban landscape, because these inscriptions tell us a great deal about the political dynamics in a given society when these architectural changes were made. As described above, the reason why such architectural changes can be used to analyse political dynamics is because cultural capital and cultural memory are key to political projects – and cultural memory and cultural capital are rendered visible in architecture and the built environment. Architectural sites and places of public culture will exhibit the changing cultural capital in Turkey depending on time period, class and dominant ideological stance. We see that the building's message is ever-changing as power regimes shift and new contexts and beliefs are transcribed onto the building's physical surface. This means that one can read a building or a public site as 'text' in much the same vein as reading a literary text in context: architecture and the built environment can be read as forms of political discourse.

It is also important to note that the spatial politics and politics of architecture described above constitute a key feature of modern nation-building and the development of national identities globally, and are not restricted to the Turkish context. Throughout the nineteenth and twentieth centuries, new nation-states arose after empires or larger ruling powers dissolved. These territories became sites of contestation in the context of an identity flux and shift, as new national governments that were no longer under a larger umbrella organisation or power now needed to create their own identity, write new legal codes, and decide who now constitutes an insider and who constitutes an outsider. In the case of many nation-states in the early twentieth century, this meant drastic restructuring of societies at every level, even leading to mass violence where ethnic cleansing and war were used to create an idealised 'citizen', including the genocide and ethnic cleansing of minority populations in Turkey (such as indigenous Armenians and Greeks). Multicultural and cosmopolitan urban spaces were radically and violently restructured to fit a new national identity. As Lawrence Vale notes regarding monumental governmental architecture, 'The manipulation of civic space thus tends both to sanction the leadership's exercise of power and to promote the continued quiescence of those who are excluded'.[10]

This phenomenon of homogenising and eliminating certain populations was written into architectural plans, and occurred at all levels of society. At the broadest, national level, this included the production of a specific 'national style' that homogenised previously cosmopolitan traditions of architecture. At the individual level of ownership, the homes of those that were forced to leave were taken over by those allowed to stay, resulting in massive changes in demographics and property ownership throughout the urban landscape. The nationalist drive to uphold one culture, one ethnic group and one particular religious tradition also resulted in the destruction of significant cultural and religious buildings that were used by the now eliminated minority. Resurgent nationalist architecture replaced pluralistic landscapes and represented the new nation-state identity that glorified one culture, one ethnic identity and one religion. Since the nineteenth century, therefore, modern architecture has served as a canvas that those in power are able to manipulate in order to construct and uphold their vision of identity.[11]

Global examples of these dynamics are nearly endless, but a few notable cases can be highlighted here. One of the most notorious and consequential examples of mass violence against cosmopolitan urban public space was Germany's Kristallnacht in 1938, which resulted in the mass and nation-wide destruction of synagogues, public businesses and other property, in a violent attempt to force the urban landscape to fit a homogeneous and racialised vision of identity.[12] Public buildings could also signify radical shifts in identity. In 1931, after the atheist Soviets had taken over the territories of the former Russian Empire, the massive Cathedral of Christ the Saviour in Moscow was entirely demolished; but was then rebuilt in the 1990s after the fall of the Soviet Union when Russian national identity reconnected itself with Orthodox Christianity.[13] The architectural space of entire cities was designed or redesigned to reflect a new national identity, including building new capitals where none had existed before, as in the famous case of modern Athens.[14]

Importantly, on the subject of nationalist architectural style and spatial politics, modern Turkey is in fact one of the most well-known and illustrative examples, recalling how the case studies in this book echo patterns in previous histories of the politics of architecture in modern Turkey. Sibel Bozdoğan's important study *Modernism and Nation Building: Turkish Architectural Culture in the Early Republic*, demonstrates that in the early Turkish Republic

'Modern architecture was imported as both a visible symbol and an effective instrument of [Kemalism's] radical program to create a thoroughly Westernized, modern, and secular new nation dissociated from the country's own Ottoman and Islamic past.'[15] As this book will discuss in detail, architecture and public space under Erdoğan's AKP have been equally important, but used to precisely the opposite effect. Zeynep Kezer's essential study of the same early republican period, *Building Modern Turkey: State, Space, and Ideology in the Early Republic*, details important ways in which the Kemalist project manipulated and constructed public space in accordance with its radically new social vision, including how 'the country's dwindling non-Muslim citizens were marginalized in the public sphere, their properties appropriated, and the vestiges of their existence deliberately eradicated'.[16]

This book's analysis will analyse a public space in contemporary Turkey that is top-down and inscribed by power by the ruling AKP and that can be understood as an 'architectural public sphere'. By this term, we refer to the ways in which architecture and the public built environment can be structured to reflect and inculcate certain political and social values, thus allowing them to be 'read' and experienced by the public as, to use Hudson's phrase above, 'visual grammars of power'.[17] The case studies below focus on the role of the Turkish state in the restoration of conservative Islamic and neo-Ottoman imagery and iconography in public space through the intentional transformation of architecture and the built environment. The specific case studies were selected to act as various nodes in the overarching constellation of the AKP's conceptions of the built environment. As the book demonstrates, a specific ideological framework undergirded the AKP's conception of the built environment, the plans it implemented to transform it, and the forms of resistance that these plans generated. This specific ideological framework is Erdoğanian neo-Ottomanism. This term was introduced by C. Dorroll (2015; 2016) and is used in this book to illustrate the ideological forces that have driven the transformation of Turkish politics over the past decade as they are reflected in public space and the built environment.

The case studies below will demonstrate that the AKP under Erdoğan's leadership remembers the Ottoman past in homogeneous Sunni Turkish Muslim terms, and it is the specific form of cultural memory that constitutes the new cultural capital that is shifting the political and urban landscape of

Turkey. Erdoğan's AKP is not concerned with ascribing cultural and therefore political value to ethnic, religious or political plurality or heterogeneity in Turkish society and public life. Instead, Erdoğan's AKP actively discourages the growth of a pluralistic social life and public sphere by cracking down on counter movements that dissent to, or are simply different from, the AKP's conception of conservative Sunni Turkish cultural capital. This book will argue in particular that one of the key and unique features of this ideology is that it seeks to establish and perpetuate its homogenising vision specifically through manipulation of the urban landscape. In other words, Erdoğan's AKP seeks to transform Turkey's political landscape through transforming Turkey's architectural landscape, especially in Istanbul.

The case studies below make use of a wide range of interdisciplinary methodologies in order to read and interpret architecture and public space in contemporary Turkey. Architecture and public space are highly complex phenomena when regarded as 'texts', because they refer to and are composed of textual discourse, artistic form, public ceremony, media discourse, political speeches and statements, public activism, to name only a few essential elements. Therefore, the case studies below will combine a variety of specific methodologies in order to bring out the dimensions of architecture and public space that are important for analysis, including ethnography, analysis of discourse and text, historical analysis, and analysis of the artistic style and history of specific buildings and sites. A multidisciplinary and interdisciplinary approach has therefore been chosen for this book due to the inherently multidimensional nature of subjects under analysis: actual structures, ceremonies and activities in public space, which are also intimately connected with political discourse, religious discourse, historical context, and the irreducibly complex experiences of the people that live in and interact with public and urban space.

Cultural Capital, Cultural Memory and Public Spheres in Modern Turkish History

The Ottoman Public Sphere, Cultural Memory and Cultural Capital

The interplay between the public sphere, cultural memory and cultural capital that come together to form the architectural public sphere is the theoretical heart of this book's analysis. These theoretical dynamics have been chosen to underpin our analysis because they have been crucial to political and social developments throughout modern Turkish history. It is therefore necessary to provide a discussion of how these dynamics played out in this history leading up to and including the development of the AKP. In other words, the dynamics of the AKP's neo-Ottomanism under Erdoğan are not new to Turkey, but are instead contemporary versions of trends that are central to modern Turkish history from its beginnings in the late Ottoman Empire up to the present day.

During the late nineteenth century under the rule of Sultan Abdül Hamid II, Islamic symbol and ritual received a new level of emphasis in an attempt to combat the surging ethnic nationalisms that were rending the territorial fabric of the Ottoman Empire.[18] This period is especially important because it immediately precedes the takeover by the Young Turk junta and the eventual secularisation and nationalisation of the Turkish polity under Mustafa Kemal Atatürk, the founder of the present-day Republic of Turkey in 1923 after the disintegration of the Ottoman Empire. The Islamic component of Ottoman cultural memory in this period is in sharp contrast to what followed it, and had a dialectical influence on the rise of secular nationalism that became the foundation for cultural memory under Atatürk. In addition, it must be pointed out that though the level of explicit emphasis on Islam in Ottoman cultural consciousness during this period was distinctly revivalist, its basic contours and symbolism were similar to Ottoman history as a whole.

The ideological constructs of the Ottoman ruling elite are important because they formed the frame of reference for much of Ottoman high culture in general, and therefore played a significant role in the elaboration of the contours of Ottoman cultural memory. In the late nineteenth century, the Ottoman sultan made numerous significant gestures that pointed to the broadly religious frame of Ottoman cultural memory. The few times that the sultan appeared in public often occurred on religious occasions, thereby highlighting the link between state and faith and therefore the ubiquity of Islam in Ottoman cultural life. These appearances included elaborate and highly publicised visits to the sacred shrine of Eyüp during Ramadan, said to be the burial place of the standard bearer of the army of Muhammad.[19] The sultan also conducted elaborate and highly ritualised visits to the Holy Relics of the Prophet Muhammad in Topkapı Palace. These expeditions included not only the sultan himself, but an entourage of 300 carriages, his entire harem and the whole of his royal entourage.[20] That Topkapı Palace housed such valuable holy relics as the sword and mantle of the Prophet simultaneously emphasised the Islamic and military framework of Ottoman cultural memory and the importance of both to imperial legitimacy.

During this period the sultan also made a concerted effort to acquire more supposed relics of the Prophet to add to his distinguished collection, including the reputed sandals of the Prophet in 1872 and a letter said to be written in the Prophet's handwriting in 1875.[21] One of the most striking manifestations for this society-wide admiration for, and cultural deference to, religious tradition was the fact that the sultan himself showed honour to members of the class of Islamic religious learning, the ulema. During the annual holiday of the holy month of Ramadan, the sultan would receive a host of distinguished visitors, and rose in the presence of none of them, save the ulema.[22]

The lineage of the sultanate itself also loomed large in Ottoman cultural memory. Alternately construed as the product of the nomadic Turkic past and a classical Islamic 'civilised' culture, the origins of the sultanate itself combined a host of powerful myths in the ideological constellation of Ottoman cultural memory. The nomadic and Turkic past of the sultanate was the subject of royal honour in both the medieval and early modern stages of Ottoman history. Mehmed I, for instance, during his reign in the early fifteenth century went to great lengths to ensure that a mosque was built in Söğüd, the mythical homeland of the Ottoman house.[23] Here again, Islam emerges as a potent ideological force: Mehmed I's way of honouring this site in western Anatolia was the construction of a Muslim place of worship.

Abdül Hamid II made similar gestures almost four centuries later, only on a much grander scale. Abdül Hamid II constructed a whole new commemorative complex on the site and endowed it with a special air of ideological grace: 'The complex became the site for annual celebrations when the "original Ottoman tribe" the Karakeçili, would ride into Söğüd dressed as Central Asian nomadic horsemen and stage a parade where they would sing a "national march" with the refrain: "We are soldiers of the Ertuğrul Regiment . . . we are ready to die for our Sultan Abdül Hamid".'[24] This special regiment was itself named for the mythical father of the founder of the Ottoman dynasty, Osman I.

Early fifteenth-century Ottoman literature, in an attempt to separate itself from Timur, created a new ideology that elaborated the genealogy of

Turkish ancestry and mapped Ottomans as descendants of the Central Asian Kayı tribe. This attempt created a type of royal lineage that then predates Chengiz Khan and therefore gives the Ottomans the right to sovereignty from the Timurids.[25] During the Kemalist period discussed below, secular Turkish nationalists co-opted these fifteenth-century ideologies in their pursuit of Turkish origin literature that tied Turks to Central Asia. Ironically, this was done in a way to separate the new republic from the Ottoman past.[26] The Turkic nomadic origins of the Ottoman state were also conceptually intertwined with its Islamic origins.

The Ottoman sultan was not only the descendent of the steppe tribes, but also of Noah and therefore the primordial human being, Adam himself; interestingly, this mode of direct lineage was debunked as early as the sixteenth century, but found favor again in the late nineteenth century.[27] Similar to the ways in which Abdül Hamid II appealed to Islamic and Ottoman dynastic tradition to legitimate his rule, this book will explore how the AKP's urban renewal projects attempted to create an ideological basis of legitimacy derived from an idealised remembering of the Ottoman past. As the chapters below will show, Erdoğanian neo-Ottomanism's construction of Ottoman cultural memory in order to underpin its post-Kemalist form of Turkish cultural capital echoed the constructed idealisation of Ottoman tradition practiced by the late Ottoman state itself towards the end of its existence.

The Kemalist Public Sphere, Cultural Memory and Cultural Capital

Turkish cultural memory and cultural capital have undergone profound shifts in content and emphasis in the past century. When the Ottoman Empire collapsed following the First World War, a series of nationalist republics emerged out of its old territories, with the Republic of Turkey comprising the environs of its old imperial capital in Istanbul and the territory of Anatolia. The change of government from a multi-ethnic, multireligious Muslim-ruled imperial dynasty to a nationalistic, ethnocentric, monolingual secular republic engendered new forms of cultural memory and cultural capital. Out of this dramatic social and cultural experience emerged a new narrative of Turkish selfhood promoted by Kemalism. In the early Turkish republican period from the 1920s to the 1950s, Kemalist nationalism silenced the Ottoman past by locating Turkish national origins in Central Asia, believed to be the archaic home of the Turkish ethnicity. The neo-Ottomanism discussed in this book would emerge at the end of the twentieth century in order to challenge this Kemalist notion of Turkish identity, in particular by resurrecting the Ottoman identity that the Kemalist repressed.

The shift away from dynastic, religious and multi-ethnic politics in the Ottoman Empire to a nationalised state epitomises the dynamic that Mustafa Kemal Atatürk established in his revolution and brought to actualisation in the founding the Republic of Turkey in 1923. Nora Fisher-Onar describes this identity shift as the disappearance of the universalisms of the Ottoman Empire due to the onslaught of the new identity politics where the definition of political belonging is based on ethnic 'Turkishness' in the Turkish nation-state. Onar explains that 'this led to an emphasis – officially – on a volunta-ristic form of national belonging in which all citizens regardless of ethnic or religious background were first-class members of the nation'.[28] Atatürk and the Turkish nationalist movement believed that this shift was necessary for the modernisation and progress of Turkish society, and therefore described his social programme this way: 'The aim of the reforms we have already carried out and are continuing to carry out is to form Turkish society into a modern society in every aspect.'[29] Atatürk's engagement with shaping Turkish cul-ture was conducted along these ideological lines: a commitment to populist politics, republican and democratic government, nationalist ideology, a secular basis of social legitimacy, and rapid and revolutionary progress in economics and social values.[30]

Massive shifts in cultural capital that were accompanied by the collective forgetting of the Ottoman Empire were necessary to construct the new nation-alist narrative of the Turkish Republic. Like the Ottomans before him, and the AKP in the present day, Mustafa Kemal Atatürk and the Turkish nationalist movement that he led manipulated cultural capital and cultural memory in order to consolidate and solidify their political power and their conception of national identity. The project of building a new ethnic nation from the ruins of the multiethnic Ottoman Empire would not have been possible without the prescriptive forgetting measures enacted through the new Kemalist regime. In fact, one of the most crucial spatial modifications at the heart of the Kemalist national project was the rejection of the city of Istanbul itself, the capital of the dynastic Ottoman past. Istanbul was abandoned as a governmental centre and the capital for the Turkish Republic was quite literally built from scratch in central Anatolia in a city named Ankara.

Kemalism's manipulation and modification of cultural capital and cultural memory extended to nearly every realm of Turkish culture. The Arabic and Persian linguistic and cultural influence was extracted from the hybrid Ottoman courtly language during the Turkish-language reform that created a new national language using the Latin alphabet, and Ottoman Islamic traditions were deliberately forgotten in the public sphere as Turkey set out to construct a secular governmental system.[31] The language reform also diluted the power once held by Ottoman elites that was connected to knowledge of the cultural capital of Arabic, a linguistic expertise that was the basis for Islamic religious authority. Likewise, Persian cultural capital undergirded authority in art.[32] The new linguistic cultural capital, however, was geared to the vernacular and the construction of the national language of Öztürkçe (pure Turkish).[33] These strategic silences allowed for a constructed memory that aligned with nation-state, Kemalist ideals.

These reforms outlawed the Ottoman Arabic script and effectively destroyed the Ottoman language, replacing it with a national Turkish tongue based on Turkish vernacular and written in the Latin alphabet. This reform reflected the spirit of a wedding of Western civilisation and Turkish national culture. As Feroz Ahmad observes, 'this reform, more than virtually any other, loosened Turkey's ties with the Islamic world to its east and irrevocably forced the country to face West'.[34] In accordance with the populist mode of governance of the new republic, Atatürk used the language of reform as an opportunity to drastically increase public literacy.[35]

Language reform therefore allowed the new republican elites to mould a new public sphere that was not associated with the voice of Islam as spoken through Arabic and Persian languages. The Turkish language was promoted by the Society for the Study of Turkish Language through the creation of new textbooks standardised with modern Turkish and the establishing of new cultural institutions across Turkey, such as the famous People's Houses.[36] These 'People's Houses" were educational institutes operated and funded by the government to promote the indoctrination of Kemalism and the new national language of the Republic of Turkey.[37] Atatürk also dramatically increased the role of women in the public sphere and public life, although he sought to do so largely by example rather than through direct legislative action. For example, one of his adopted daughters became a professor of history at Ankara University, while another became a famous fighter pilot.[38] Atatürk's wife also did not wear the traditional head covering donned by Muslim women of the Ottoman Empire.

Atatürk's construction of the new Turkish public sphere centred on nationalist, secular Turks as the basis of the state. This dynamic created a climate of exclusion for ethnic minorities (e.g., Armenians, Greeks, Jews and Kurds) and conservative Turkish Muslims. Talal Asad usefully points to the limitations of this kind of Kemalist mentality, pointing out 'that "the secular" should not be thought of as the space in which *real* human life gradually emancipates itself from the controlling power of "religion" and thus achieves the latter's relocation'.[39] In other words, the public sphere of Kemalism was not the purely emancipatory project that it claimed to be, and it did not eliminate the exclusionary and constricting implications of the Ottoman Islamic public sphere. Instead, it simply created new hegemonies and exclusions. Throughout the secularisation and Westernisation process, the construction of secular and ethnic 'Turkishness' played an overarching role in the emergence of a comprehensive identity which based itself on assimilating the multiplicity of the Ottoman Empire to one concise, homogenised group bound together by the new nation-state.[40] The Kemalist stance intended ultimately to eradicate religion from the public sphere and contain it within the confines of the private sphere.[41] In pursuit of this goal, during Atatürk's rule religious institutions in society were pushed out of political power and marginalised.[42]

This modernisation programme ironically developed as the radical offshoot of the efforts of liberal Ottoman thinkers towards the end of the empire. Atatürk sought to continue and complete the radical social changes that late Ottoman reformers such as the Committee of Union and Progress inaugurated and also built his programme on a shared theoretical foundation.[43] An important instance of this shared foundation that decisively shaped the republican attitude towards the Ottoman past was Atatürk's adoption of the Turkish nationalist thinker Ziya Gökalp's distinction between culture and civilisation, seeing the former as the exclusive property of a particular national community and the latter as the common property of all mankind and best exemplified in Atatürk's lifetime in Western European culture.[44]

Thus, in Atatürk's view, a Turk could maintain a sense of national and religious particularity while at the same time adopting all facets of Western civilisation wholesale, for the Turk would be Turkish in national culture and Western in civilised progress. This mindset informed the Kemalist reforms that aimed to demolish the Ottoman social order as relics of an uncivilised past and wed Turkish nationalism with Western civilisation. Towards this end, Atatürk outlawed and closed all Sufi lodges; banned the wearing of the fez, the traditional symbol of Ottoman dress; adopted the Western Gregorian calendar and Sunday as the weekly day of rest; and initiated the establishment of a secular civil code of laws.[45]

The era of Atatürk and the first few decades of the Turkish Republic was therefore the era that saw the construction of cultural memory, cultural capital and a new public sphere all designed to support the new secular Turkish nation-state. Atatürk sought to remake Ottoman society into a Turkish national society, based not on loyalty to a multi-ethnic and multireligious empire ruled by an imperial dynasty, but based on a national space constructed by Turks for Turks. Above all, this meant targeting not only cultural memory but the physical and public elements of Ottoman Islamic culture that would later be so crucial to neo-Ottomanism. As Asad notes, religious structures cannot be separated from power structures in society, so in this case the hegemonic ideals of Kemalism directly impacted Islam in Turkey, as rituals, symbols and meanings of a religion are 'disciplinary practices' based on history and power.[46] Atatürk closed the tombs (*türbes*) of saints and holy people that were so central to popular Ottoman Islamic devotion and by 1933 religion classes in Turkish state-operated schools were eliminated, further de-legitimising Islam in the nascent Turkish Republic.[47] Another way of understanding this radical shift in cultural capital and cultural memory is provided by Robert Heffner, who applies the term 'internalized orientalism' to describe this phenomenon, pointing out that Turkish nationalism interpreted Islamic practice and tradition as 'backwards' in much the same way that Western European colonists did in other contexts.[48]

The Shift from Kemalism to an Islamic Bourgeoisie

The complete and encompassing control of Turkey by Kemalists eventually waned. By the 1980s economic markets and media markets began to open, allowing devout, conservative Turks and others pushed to the margins under

Kemalism to gain power and public visibility in Turkish politics and culture. This phenomenon allowed for the revival of Islamic identities in Turkey. As Janine Clark points out, the rise of conservative Muslim and Islamist groups in the history of republican Turkey has occurred directly in response to the secularisation practices of the Kemalist nation-state.[49] Under the leadership of Turgut Özal, prime minister from 1983 to 1989 and president from 1989 to 1993, a tendency towards harmonising Islamist and nationalist discourses emerged. The end of the 1980s and the beginning of the 1990s saw movements that argued that possible coexistence outweighed old binaries between secularists and Islamists in Turkey. The political and cultural reset that came about as a result of the 1980 military coup undermined Kemalist hegemony by allowing for the flourishing of innovative political voices.[50]

Beginning in the 1980s, conservative Islamic thinkers entered the mainstream with their own politics and intellectual power.[51] This period saw the beginning of a decisive shift in cultural capital in Turkey, which the AKP built itself on and continues to develop via its deployment of neo-Ottomanism, as this book will discuss in detail. Consequently, Kemalist ideology began to lose its hegemonic status in the same period.[52] The revival of Islamic identities in the 1980s are an example of how the previously restrictive secularist measures in Kemalist Turkey recast and inadvertently revitalised religious and cultural idioms and identities.[53] Devout Muslims in Turkey began to use Islam to create their own version of modernity which revitalised Ottoman–Islamic cultural capital as a symbol of identity in the public sphere. One particularly widespread example of deliberate and popular return of Ottoman Islamic cultural capital to the public sphere has been the proliferation of headscarves that utilise Ottoman design motifs, including even Ottoman sultans' calligraphic signatures, or tughra, as key artistic design elements. Anna Secor's research has described the bourgeoisie, upper-class fashion industry of devout Turkish women and how this industry incorporates Ottoman elements and elements that combine fashion and practices of piety.[54]

These Muslims in essence redefined the Kemalist consensus on modernity by melding nationalism, secularism, democracy, human rights, the liberal market and personal autonomy into a synthesis based on Islamic terms: Hakan Yavuz terms this phenomenon the vernacularisation of modernity.[55] Market liberalisation under Özal in the 1980s and 1990s allowed this alternative vision of modernity to spread and consolidate among certain sectors of Turkish society. As will be described in detail below, Turkey's Islamic movements during the same time period peacefully made their way to the centre of power in Turkey through a variety of political and social means. As Yavuz points out, such movements sought to reclaim the Muslim self within the Turkish nation-state.[56] As Sena Karasipahi demonstrates, Islamic discourse strengthened when the secular Kemalist state failed to deliver its promised utopia.[57] Like Yavuz, Karasipahi points to the failures of Kemalist ideology as authoritarian, statist and fundamentally oppressive.[58] In the end, the Kemalist modernisation project did not yield a purely secular state: instead, a homogeneous secularism existed with hybrid forms of life.[59]

Yavuz shows that the new Muslim bourgeoisie in Turkey produced a new 'network of shared meaning' through their control of key forms of economic power such as large business ventures supported by neoliberalism.[60] Prime Minister Turgut Özal's privatisation programme created space separate from state control that focused on free-market policies, thereby empowering the Muslim bourgeoisie to support a new Islamic lifestyle based on new avenues of consumption.[61] We can therefore observe the dual formation of the new pious Muslim bourgeoisie and the Islamisation of leisure and fashion, especially as they manifested themselves in the public sphere.[62] Middle-class Islamist women in Turkey, for instance, exhibited particular dress that emphasises their class distinction while allowing them to remain a part of the Islamist movement. Anna Secor shows that the form of veiling known as *tesettür* connoted an alternative and previously outlawed Islamist political orientation that is often known as a 'turban' style of veiling.[63] The Islamist elite and middle class thereby emerged and valued material styles and lifestyles, particularly those that reflected their political orientation.[64] This elite veiling also symbolically tied Islamism to the Muslim culture of the Ottoman court instead of the diverse Ottoman masses.[65]

In other words, in Turkey the process of economic privatisation and the formation of the new Islamic bourgeoisie and their attendant lifestyle went hand in hand. Increased access to new spaces created the possibility for the entrance and enhancement of new voices; economic liberalisation created separation from state control over religion and allowed the Muslim identity to penetrate the Turkish public sphere.[66] Yavuz convincingly describes the rise of political Islamism in Turkey (and of the originally moderate religious conservatism of the AKP that grew from it, as will be seen below) as a process supported by the opening of new 'opportunity spaces' that integrated previously marginalised Islamic conservative voices into Turkish electoral politics.[67]

The first of these spaces was an opening for the participation of devout Muslim businesspeople based in rural Anatolia in the Turkish economy. This was accomplished through the neoliberal economics of Turgut Özal who reversed the Kemalist import-substitution policies that had previously been marginalising local Anatolian economies and enriching the urban secularist business elite.[68] The new neoliberal economy produced what Yavuz calls the new 'Anatolian Muslim bourgeoisie' who brought with their success markers of cultural and political identity different from the previously dominant Kemalist elite. As Jenny White has noted, this period allowed the Islamic political and cultural movement in Turkey to form a viable economic basis supported by devout, politically engaged businesspeople and industrialists.[69] This was the cultural and economic basis that would lay the groundwork for the electoral success of the AKP in the future.

Newly empowered by increasing wealth, the Muslim bourgeoisie helped to fund cultural and religious institutions to promote the social and cultural values of the Anatolian heartland, including a religiously conservative and public Islamic lifestyle. The new Muslim bourgeoisie helped to fund and establish a second type of opportunity space: new media outlets that promoted a conservative Turkish Islamic viewpoint. As Yavuz notes, these media outlets helped to create a devout and conservative Muslim reading public that evolved counter narratives to Kemalist hegemony but at the same time fostered the Muslim bourgeoisie's 'commitment to democratic values through supporting various cultural and political activities'.[70] The publishing and business activities of the new Muslim bourgeoisie produced a third opportunity space, a political opportunity space, as these classes became politically organised. Turkey's electoral landscape now featured 'competitive political spaces' that allowed for a conservative Islamic voice, which could no longer be ignored due to the economic, and consequently social and political, power it had accrued due to Turkish neoliberal economics.[71]

The Rise of the AKP

Since its first electoral victory in 2002, the AKP has built its political power on the basis of the economic and cultural shifts described above that produced the new Islamic bourgeoisie. The AKP is the latest iteration of a series of Islamically inspired political parties that formed in response to Kemalist hegemony. It has its roots in Islamist movements dating from the early 1970s, but is the offshoot of a moderate wing of these movements that in its original platform significantly modified the rhetoric and policies of the earlier parties. The original AKP platform was notable for its strong stance in favour of neoliberal capitalist economic policies and its promotion of conservative social ethics, alongside an appeal to universalist human rights discourses and pro-European Union politics. The central arc that this book will analyse are the moments over the course of the pivotal decade of 2010–20 where the AKP's politics shifted towards an authoritarian nationalism that stands in stark contrast to the possibilities offered by its original vision.[72]

The AKP is the result of a long and gradual shift in the views of the political Islamist movement in Turkey. Its roots can be traced as far back as the National Outlook Movement (Milli Görüş Hareketi). The National Outlook Movement was founded in the late 1960s and early 1970s with the support of the Nakşibendi sheikh Mehmet Zahid Kotku (1897–1980), a conservative Sufi leader who mobilised his order in support of political Islamist movements and who had close connections with pious Muslim politicians of the past few decades, including the family of Turgut Özal and members of the AKP.[73] With the help and support of Kotku and his followers, Necmettin Erbakan, who would go on to lead every major political Islamist party in Turkey until moderate dissenters of his movement founded the AKP, was elected to the Turkish parliament from Konya in 1969.[74]

The National Outlook Movement was the first movement in modern Turkish history to outline a specifically Islamic political identity.[75] Its ideological underpinnings are very well described by a conversation between Lütfi Doğan, head of the Presidency of Religious Affairs from 1968 to 1971 and Kotku himself. Doğan reports that Kotku said to him: 'The core identity and character of this wounded nation is Islam. Your main heritage is Islam and as Muslims you can heal this wound by listening to what our Turkish people want. What they want is an Islamic sense of justice and the restoration of their

Ottoman-Islamic identity.'[76] This exchange is very important in a number of respects. It reveals how this movement created the beginnings of a specifically Islamic political discourse in Turkey that was not based on a rejection of Turkish national identity but on a reorientation of it away from the Kemalist vision of Turkish national identity. The National Outlook Movement sowed the seeds of contemporary political neo-Ottomanism by turning away from Kemalist laicism as the epicentre of Turkish national heritage and instead turning Turkish nationalist memory to face the Ottoman Empire. Thus, a strain of Islamist political activism was born that recreated Turkish national identity in Ottoman terms and combined this with conservative social politics.

The National Outlook Movement was transformed by Kotku and Erbakan into a series of Islamist political parties beginning with the National Order Party (Milli Nizam Partisi; MNP) on 26 January 1970.[77] The MNP lasted until 11 October 1972 when the National Salvation Party (Milli Selamet Partisi; MSP) was founded. The MSP continued the politics of the National Outlook Movement as a 'direct protest against the radical Kemalist project'.[78] The party embraced political and economic modernisation, as evidenced in its four ideological pillars: culture, industrialisation, social justice and education.[79] However, it introduced into Turkish politics a dichotomy between modernisation and Westernisation, an alliance that had been assumed since the days of Atatürk and the early Turkish Republic, as described above. The MSP, like its successor parties and the National Outlook platform, argued for economic advancement, social justice, and political reform on Islamic and Turkish cultural bases, instead of appealing to discourses that were pro-West or held up Western Europe as the ideal of universal human rights. Instead, the MSP argued for a politics of cultural authenticity, pitting Turkish Islamic heritage against the Westernising foreignness of the Kemalist elite.

The MSP was closed down by the Turkish military following the 1980 coup and was replaced by the Welfare Party (Refah Partisi; RP) that remained in operation from 1983 to 1998. While the previous incarnations of Erbakan's movement had seen little mass success at the ballot box, the RP performed surprisingly well in the municipal elections of 1994 and the national elections of 1995, when it captured the largest amount of votes at 21.4 per cent. Although these results did not produce a RP majority, it did allow the RP to form a coalition government, arousing the suspicions of the staunchly Kemalist armed forces and the secularist wing of Turkish public opinion, who for the first time in Turkish history were dramatically confronted with the power of political Islamism in Turkey. This suspicion would lead to the eventual demise of the party. On 4 February 1997, the RP mayor of Sincan (a suburb of Ankara) held a rally with the Iranian ambassador featuring attendees waving Hamas and Hizbullah flags. Alarmed at this, the military sent tanks to Sincan and forced the local government to arrest the mayor for anti-secular activities.[80] On 28 February the military issued an ultimatum to the RP, and the government was disbanded. The party was shut down in 1998, and was succeeded by the short-lived Virtue Party (Fazilet Partisi; FP). In 2001, the FP closed and its supporters split into two factions, one moderate conservative and one openly Islamist. The former group (composed of such figures as Recep Tayyip Erdoğan and Abdullah Gül) founded the AKP in August 2001, while the latter group founded the Felicity Party (Saadet Partisi; SP) in July 2001.

The foundation of the RP's success was its ability to leverage disaffection with the ineffective Turkish state and economy into support for political Islamism.[81] Though the party's previous incarnations had attempted to do the same, the RP was the first political party in Turkish history to successfully craft a social, political and cultural identity expressed in explicitly Islamic terms that attracted significant support.[82] According to the RP, 'national outlook' meant a rejection of 'imitating the West' and a reassertion of what is most distinctive about Turkish national identity: adherence to Islam.[83] The RP also vocally condemned Western imperialism and Zionism, seeing both as natural allies in a global effort to suppress Muslim societies, including Turkey. The RP also accomplished the integration of a large section of the Turkish population, rural and poor pious Muslims, into the political process; this achievement revolutionised Turkish politics by turning a pious conservative Muslim identity into a recognisable political platform against social injustice and economic advancement.[84]

As noted above, the RP distinguished between modernisation and Westernisation, and rejected the latter in favour of an Islamically inspired version of the former. However, the RP also made subtle shifts in its political rhetoric in the 1980s that decisively broadened its base of support and laid the groundwork for the future successes of the AKP. During this period, the RP 'successfully framed the global agenda in Turkey in terms of a quest for more democratization, freedom, and human rights in order to appeal to a broader sector of the citizenry'.[85] Thanks to the RP, political Islamism in Turkey now spoke the language of universal human rights, a discourse that would have a much better chance of appealing to the majority of Turkish voters than an appeal to strict conservative Islam. This discursive shift would prove to be decisive for the AKP as well, and became a key part of its political discourse and the political identity that it presented to the public before its authoritarian transformation under Erdoğan.

After it was created in 2002, the AKP managed to capture the votes of not only conservative Muslims but also a large cross-section of Turkish society. The AKP consolidated the appeal of a conservative Muslim identity, but at the same time rejected the polarising anti-Western and anti-secular discourses of the RP and earlier Turkish Islamist parties. The AKP's political discourse instead appealed to universal human rights discourse and the party pursued a policy of European Union membership as a way to further democratisatise its own goals for political reform.[86] The AKP has also adopted a discourse of personal freedom and personal choice as a way to promote the rights of pious Muslims to assert their identity in the Turkish public sphere. The early political discourse of the AKP represents 'the liberalization of Muslim conceptions of practices and politics, whereby conservative Muslims attenuate their demand for normative hegemony ... and subsume adherence to such norms to the sphere of personal choice'.[87] Thus, the AKP depicted itself as the true heir to the tradition of secular democracy in the Turkish Republic, in contrast to the Kemalist opposition, which it described as undemocratic and oppressive. During this period, the AKP often presented its model of secular democracy as an 'American' model, in which the state does not interfere in the religious affairs of private citizens.[88]

The party platform document 'The Political Vision of the AKP', released on 30 September 2012, represents the clearest example of the discourses the party used to describe itself and its ideals at the beginning of the decade under consideration in this book (2010–20). This document describes the AKP's oft-touted 'conservative democrat political identity'.[89] It argues that the AKP has done more than any other political party in Turkish history to advance democracy, and also claims that the party's values are based on the defence of universal human rights, 'civility', 'tolerance' and 'intellectual and behavioural pluralism'. Even more strikingly, the platform describes the whole reason for the existence of the AKP as the defence of fairness, justice and the promotion of universal human rights: 'The essence of an administration and understanding of politics focused on the human individual is the advancement of fundamental rights and freedoms at every level and in universal measure.'

However, as this book will discuss through its consideration of Istanbul's urban landscape and built environment, the AKP decisively turned away from its initial commitment to pluralism and secular human rights and turned towards a conservative nationalist authoritarianism over the decade 2010–20. Beginning with the 2010 constitutional referendum, this period also saw Erdoğan's emergence as the undisputed leader of the AKP, and therefore the most powerful politician in the country. As Yavuz explains: 'Erdoğan's domineering role in the AKP is a norm for Turkish politics. Party leaders preside over a rigorous centralized decision making process in which they determine the list of candidates and establish their respective policy platforms. Due to his deeply internalized authoritarian tendencies and intolerance toward diverse lifestyles, it would be prudent and proper to call him a dictator.'[90] Susannah Verney, Anna Bosco and Senem Aydın describe this process as the development of an authoritarian presidentialism: over the course of this decade, Erdoğan consolidated and expanded the powers of the presidency over all elements of the Turkish federal government, including the judiciary – effectively eliminating any separation of powers or checks on Erdoğan's individual authority.[91]

As Jenny White has pointed out, the AKP features 'contradictory discourses supporting universalist principles of human rights while at the same time curtailing freedom of speech and openly opposing lifestyles that do not conform to a conservative worldview'.[92] When the success of the AKP following the 2002 elections did not go unchallenged by the secular establishment, the AKP responded in kind. Throughout the mid- to late 2000s, the party used the trial against an alleged secularist conspiracy to overthrow the government (the 'Ergenekon' organisation) to imprison dissident journalists, politicians and other public figures that have openly opposed the neoliberal and socially conservative policies of the AKP.[93] As will be discussed in detail throughout this book, the AKP enacted policies that assumed the right of the ruling party to determine social mores, dictate social norms and recreate the Turkish public sphere. The party's attempt to reshape the built environment of Istanbul in pursuit of these goals is what our analysis terms 'Erdoğanian neo-Ottomanism'.

The Politics of Cultural Memory: Neo-Ottomanism in Turkey

One of the key tasks of this book is therefore elaborating the concept of Erdoğanian neo-Ottomanism as a way to understand the authoritarian shifts in Turkish politics over the crucial decade 2010–20. Key to this elaboration is understanding and clarifying how Erdoğan's use of neo-Ottomanism is distinct from other forms of this major cultural movement in modern Turkey, which has gained particular strength and salience over the past few decades. As described above, the nascent Turkish Republic was characterised by a hegemonic Kemalist ideology that deliberately forgot the Ottoman past in order to recreate and rewrite the historical memory to focus on a Turkish origin-story that began in Central Asia and Anatolia, and followed the outline of Western civilisation and created the rhetoric of the 'civilised Turk'. This actively silenced Ottoman historiography and vilified the sultanate and described Ottoman rule as the 'dark age' of the Turks.[94] 'Turkishness' was formulated in opposition to the nineteenth-century Ottoman view of Ottomanism as an identity marker that allowed differing ethnic–religious groups a unifying form of identity. Turkish nationalist identity homogenised the Ottoman Muslim populations under one general identity marker: Turk. This national identity marker was mobilised under the newly created secular state and society in Turkey.

Yılmaz Çolak's work underscores that official, nascent Turkish narratives may have forgotten the Ottoman past but it remained salient within Turkish popular culture.[95] As Yavuz has demonstrated, Ottoman cultural memory also remained alive in artistic and religious spaces in the Turkish Republic, such as in literature and in Sufi religious culture.[96] The active silencing of the Ottoman past over time produced a counter-reaction in the form of neo-Ottomanism. As Yavuz explains, 'Turkey's march toward Westernization and economic development engendered the formation of a counter-elite, who defined themselves contrary to the Republic by highlighting Ottoman and Islamic traditions.'[97] 'Neo-Ottomanism' therefore refers to the broad cultural movement in modern Turkey that revives awareness of and appreciation for Ottoman culture and history in order to re-imagine what it means to be a citizen of the Republic of Turkey. As Çağaptay notes, neo-Ottomanism refers to a very wide array of actors and cultural products, but it 'distills, ultimately, to a single assumption: that Turkey's "genuine" identity resides somewhere in the recesses of its Ottoman past'.[98] Yavuz's treatment of this topic focuses on the nostalgia at the heart of neo-Ottomanism: 'The discourse of Neo-Otto-manism is largely nostalgic, critical of the present, and romantic about the past before the decline of the Ottoman world'.[99]

Yavuz also importantly calls attention to the role that historic and genera-tional trauma plays in the development of neo-Ottomanism, most notably the trauma experienced by Muslims who were the victims of genocidal ethnic cleans-ing in the Balkans and the Caucasus in the nineteenth and twentieth centuries, whose descendants would become Turkish citizens of the new republic. Genera-tional memories of these trials and threats, combined with memories of the more recent trauma experienced by devout Turks under the militant secularism of the early republic, have caused many conservative Muslim Turks to recentre Otto-man Muslim identity as something to be revived, cultivated and protected.[100] Chapter 4 in this book will also address the role of trauma in the production of neo-Ottomanism in the context of the aftermath of the 2016 coup attempt.

As Yavuz also notes, Christian victims of genocide and ethnic cleansing during the same period were also displaced from memory in the early Turkish Republic, during which time 'There was no acknowledgment of ethno-religious persecution neither of the Balkan Muslims nor of the Christians.'[101] We will also engage the memories and discourses of Greek Orthodox Christians in Turkey, whose identity and experiences are key to understanding the dynamics of cul-tural capital and cultural memory in the modern Turkish Republic, as will be discussed in detail throughout this book. As this book will also show, the experi-ences of Greek Orthodox in Turkey in particular are key to understanding both the ideology of Erdoğanian neo-Ottomanism itself and the responses to it.

Neo-Ottomanism began to have significant political impact beginning in the closing decades of the twentieth century. As Çolak and Yavuz also demon-strate, it was Prime Minister Turgut Özal who re-introduced Ottoman mem-ory into the political arena in 1980s and 1990s Turkey. By actively 'defining the Republic of Turkey as the heir to the Ottoman Empire, he attempted to make Ottomanism part of the Turkish identity'.[102] In this project he utilised the rhet-oric of the melting pot and cultural pluralism. Özalian neo-Ottomanism was publicised as an 'imperial vision' of an Ottoman pluralist system.[103] He argued that Ottoman Islam was flexible and tolerant, which he described as giving Turkish society 'a different outlook from that of other Islamic societies: "as a result of its cosmopolitan foundations, moreover, the Ottoman State was open to other cultural influences"'.[104] As Umut Uzer argues, Özal's neo-Ottomanism was meant to correct the ideological and political deficiencies of secular Turkish nationalism by 'fostering a more comprehensive national identity'.[105]

This early variety of neo-Ottomanism argued that the existence of the so-called 'millet system' in the classical Ottoman period, in which various ethnic and religious groups were supposed to have been granted their own internal autonomy based on their status as individual 'millets', proves that the Ottoman Empire represented a kind of pluralist society.[106] As Yavuz notes, 'Özal's Neo-Ottomanism was inclusive and tolerant of diversity.'[107] It was distinctly 'cosmopolitan' and 'saw ethnic and religious diversity through the lens of pluralism and regarded it as a source of strength and cultural richness rather than a security threat to the state'.[108] As Fisher-Onar shows, Özal's vision of Ottoman cultural memory represented an example of the revival of the universalism of Ottoman imperial identity as a corrective to the nationalist strictures of Kemalism. Her analysis also importantly points out that during this period (and therefore in stark contrast to the period under consideration in this book) conservative Islamist political thinkers and activists in Turkey followed Özal's lead and argued that Ottoman cultural revival could produce a kind of pluralism, tolerance and cosmopolitanism that was superior to Western, secular versions.[109]

Therefore, under the Özal government a new way of remembering the Ottoman past as an integral component of Turkish national identity was formulated; this was the beginning of neo-Ottomansim in general in Turkey, and what might be called Özalian neo-Ottomanism (in contrast to the later Erdoğanian neo-Ottomanism). Çolak focuses on Özalian neo-Ottomanism as a form of remembering the Ottoman Empire to elicit a notion of pluralism, which in the mid-1990s also became Islamised. He argues that Özal fostered government projects and policies that subsumed former Ottoman territories, especially in the Balkans, under an appeal to Ottoman cultural memory as a way to perpetuate the idea, or myth, of a pluralist Ottoman past. Çolak notes that in the nineteenth century (and as described in the historical summary above) 'the idea of a common homeland and common traits based on modern patriotic citizenship and universal law, was developed to provide Ottoman unity in the context of each ethnic–religious groups efforts to develop its own nationalism'.[110]

Çolak points out that Özalian neo-Ottomanism was developed with the same goal in mind as Ottomanist patriotism, its nineteenth-century imperial ideological precursor. This goal was the unification of a diverse populace under a single cultural identity. While noting that Özalian neo-Ottomanism and nineteenth-century Ottomanism were not the same in every respect, Çolak demonstrates that they both were 'technique[s] of cultural pluralism'.[111] Özalian neo-Ottomanism's understanding of pluralism was also inclusive of a wider array of Muslim ethnic identities than simply Kemalist Turkishness due its universalising and cosmopolitan orientation, demonstrating its potential transnationalism. As Çolak notes, 'Serbian nationalists' attempt at ethnic cleansing of the Bosnians and later the Albanian minority in Kosovo (by equating the terms Muslim/Turk/Ottoman) . . . were tragic events that reminded both the Balkan Muslim population and Turkish citizens of their common Ottoman ancestors', leading to a strong sense of solidarity among the Turkish public with persecuted Muslims in the Balkans.[112]

It is also important to note here, however, that Özal's pluralist construction of neo-Ottomanism involved its own selective remembering and construction of the Ottoman past. Leslie Peirce contests the 'natural' and common assumption that the Ottoman Empire was pluralistic in the modern sense of the term. Instead, Pierce demonstrates that Ottoman society is better understood as an example of polyglotism, in that the empire capitalised on the skills and functions of its diverse population (e.g., specialisation, artisanal talents, fiscal expertise, etc).[113] A pluralistic outlook originated from the intimacy of contact and experience.[114] Yet one cannot apply the overly positivist contemporary terms of multiculturalism to the Ottoman Empire, for in this case Peirce shows that this utilisation of diversity was a tactic of governing, not a device for inclusion with utopian undertones as exhibited in much Özalian neo-Ottoman rhetoric.

Benjamin Braude's work also disproves the idea that the Ottoman government in its classical period during the fifteenth and sixteenth centuries featured a well-defined 'millet system', thereby rendering visible the mythological content of a key feature of pluralist neo-Ottoman reconstructions of the Ottoman past. Instead of reflecting a classical Ottoman social reality or policy, the notion of a pluralistic millet system has been projected back in time. According to Braude, '*millet* means a religiously-defined people'.[115] It does not usually refer to non-Muslims when in use in pre-Tanzimat sources. Braude found that '*millet* in the empire's heyday did not denote an autonomous protected community of non-Muslim Ottoman subjects'.[116] Ottoman officials in fact used the term millet to refer to themselves, Christian sovereigns or rare Jewish favourites, but not the mass of non-Muslim subjects because the term had a meaning of sovereignty attached to it in the pre-Tanzimat period.[117] Though it was not used for non-Muslim communities prior to the nineteenth century, today the term is commonly projected backwards in time by neo-Ottoman rhetoric to denote a form of pluralistic social organisation, as mentioned above. Braude illustrates that by the 1820s and onward millet was understood to mean a non-Muslim protected community, but in previous decades it could have meant the opposite.[118] Lately the term has become, according to Braude, a 'historiographical fetish'. His research 'strongly suggests that there was no overall administrative system, structure, or set of institutions for dealing with non-Muslims . . . the absence of an explicit technical term is highly significant in such a term-conscious bureaucracy . . . [and] suggests the absence of an institutionalized policy.'[119] The term has experienced significant changes over time and place and this must be considered when attempting to describe Ottoman society.[120]

Describing and Theorising Erdoğanian Ottomanism

Though Özal's construction of neo-Ottomanism featured the same processes of selective constructions of cultural memory and cultural capital, it did so in order to advance a social vision and public sphere where diversity, pluralism and heterogeneous identities were considered natural and non-threatening in the Turkish Republic. The analysis in the following chapters will show how Erdoğanian neo-Ottomanism took the precisely opposite approach to Turkish identity, and that it did so via the manipulation of the architectural and urban public landscape of the city of Istanbul. As outlined above, we refer to the type of neo-Ottomanism that depicts the Ottoman Empire as a pluralistic, tolerant and multicultural space as 'Özalian neo-Ottomanism'. As Çolak and Yavuz demonstrate, Özalian neo-Ottomanism employed the memory of the Ottoman Empire to differentiate itself from the Kemalist ideals of the early Turkish nation-state, and at the same time promote a vision of pluralism based on a mythological and romantic reading of the Ottoman past. We will extend this analysis and outline what we will refer to as *Erdoğanian* neo-Ottomanism, a concept that unpacks how Ottoman memory has been politicised and employed in recent years by the AKP under the control of Recep Tayyip Erdoğan. This version of neo-Ottomanism maintains a mythic vision of the Ottoman past yet rejects the pluralistic policy orientation of Özalian neo-Ottomanism.

C. Dorroll's term 'Erdoğanian neo-Ottomanism' refers to the way in which the AKP under the leadership of Erdoğan frames the Ottoman past.[121] Put simply, 'Erdoğanian neo-Ottomanism' means the AKP used the power of the state to shape the urban landscape in their social and ideological image. Specifically, this term refers to how the AKP under Erdoğan's leadership actively manipulates and transforms public space through architecture, urban renewal, public ceremony and similar cultural phenomena to create a neo-Ottomanism top-down architectural public sphere that reflects the homogenising social vision of the AKP and its neoliberal economic policies. Our use of this concept is meant to highlight how important this specific technique is to AKP governance under Erdoğan. Manipulations and transformations of public space – especially in the highly symbolic city of Istanbul, the centre of Ottoman cultural memory – are not merely by-products of Erdoğan and the AKP's policies and social vision. On the contrary, they are some of the primary means of enacting them.

What therefore is the specific ideology that is being (quite literally) instantiated in Istanbul by Erdoğanian neo-Ottomanism? We refer to this ideology as 'conservative Turkish Islamic nationalism'. This ideology can also be termed conservative Turkish Sunni nationalism, because its understanding of Islam refers predominately (if not entirely exclusively) to Sunnism. In our usage, Erdoğan's conservative Turkish Islamic nationalism is composed of: the promotion or enforcement of religiously conservative social values in the public sphere; the assertion that a conservative Muslim identity anchored in Ottoman tradition is the most authentic form of Turkishness; and the assertion that this reading of conservative Turkish Islam is entitled to social and political dominance. As this book argues, Erdoğanian neo-Ottomanism is distinctive for its manipulation of cultural memory and cultural capital via its manipulation of the urban landscape and built environment in order to promote and accomplish these policies and assertions.

Our analysis of Erdoğan's conservative Turkish Islamic nationalism is also meant to build on, and contribute to, broader discussions of Turkish nationalism as it has developed throughout the history of the Turkish Republic. Umut Uzer identifies three distinct forms of nationalist ideology that contribute to the development of Turkish nationalism: (1) Kemalist nationalism, which is 'a territorial and civic form of nationalism with strong ethnic tones'; (2) ethnic nationalism, which 'defined the nation according to race or ethnicity'; (3) conservative nationalism, which developed as a criticism of Kemalism following the 1950s when the social values of Turks from Anatolia began to influence politics in large urban areas such as Istanbul and Ankara, as people from poorer urban areas migrated there in search of economic opportunity and social mobility.[122] Our analysis considers Erdoğan's conservative Turkish Islamic nationalism to have developed from the third ideological current that Uzer identifies, and that its strength is rooted in the social and political rise of conservative Anatolian Muslim culture (as described in previous sections above).

The relationship between Erdoğan's conservative Turkish Islamic nationalism and Turkishness is also important to consider here. We classify Erdoğanian neo-Ottomanism as a type of Turkish nationalism because this ideology understands and reconstructs the Ottoman past specifically through the lens of Turkish Muslim identity and experiences. This is why Turkishness cannot be divorced from Erdoğan's Islamic nationalism. As Yavuz has noted, the combination of Muslim and Turkish identities has long been central to Erdoğan's conception of Turkish nationhood, and Erdoğan can therefore also be described as an 'Islamo-Turkish nationalist' whose political and social goal is 'Islamo-Turkish restoration'.[123] The crucial importance of Turkishness in Erdoğanian neo-Ottomanism is also why we do not refer to Erdoğan as simply or exclusively an 'Islamist' in this book. As Yavuz explains, 'puritanical Islamism' is not a part of his ideological platform, which is better understood as a kind of populism.[124]

As Yavuz notes, Erdoğan's ideology can also be described as 'his own hybrid mix of Islamism and nationalism infused into a majoritarian democratic system'.[125] He insightfully summarises his ideology by noting that 'Erdoğan's imagined Ottomanism is authoritarian, inward looking, and aggressive, offering no space for diversity.'[126] Lisel Hintz also draws attention to this conservative political hybrid in her analysis of contemporary Turkish 'Ottoman Islamism' as an 'identity proposal' that 'contains constitutive norms of pious

Sunni Muslim membership and reverence for the Ottoman Empire's glory and wide-reaching authority, the social purposes of spreading Sunni Islam in the domestic sphere and strengthening ties with Muslim and former Ottoman populations, a relational meaning of Europe (and "the West") in general as the salient out-group, and a cognitive worldview of Turkey as the legitimate inheritor of Ottoman legacies and leader of the Islamic world.'[127]

Turkishness, in a specifically nationalist sense, is also central to understanding Erdoğan's ideology as a religious Islamic nationalism precisely because Turkishness throughout the history of the modern republic has been defined by its connection with Islam. As Çağaptay has demonstrated, 'After Kemalist secularization, nominal Islamic identity as well as the cultural heritage of the former Muslim millet became important in defining Turkishness.'[128] If the Kemalist conception of Turkishness assumed a nominal, privatised or progressive Muslim identity, Erdoğan's conception of Turkishness assumes an active, devout and conservative Muslim identity. Turkish nationalism remains central to both, for as Uzer notes, 'In modern Turkey the general answer to the question "Who is a Turk?" was Turkish-speaking Muslims living in Turkey.'[129] Importantly, this has meant that the identity of non-Muslims who are indigenous to Turkey (such as Greek Orthodox Christian identity as discussed throughout this book) has long been seen as alien and even threatening to Turkish national identity because it is fundamentally 'inassimilable into Turkishness', as Çağaptay helpfully puts it.[130] Non-ethnic Turks who are Muslim (such as Circassians) have been seen as assimilable into Turkishness, while ethnic identities associated with Christianity, such as Armenian or Greek, have been seen as by definition threatening to Turkishness because they cannot be accepted as 'Turkish'.[131] As will also be discussed in the following chapters, this makes these and other minority identities threatening to Erdoğanian neo-Ottomanism in particular because of its homogenising and exclusive view of Turkish national identity.

Finally, Erdoğan's conservative Turkish Islamic nationalism exhibits other shared characteristics with the broader dynamics of Turkish nationalist ideologies as described in the important work of Behlül Özkan and Hale Yılmaz. As Özkan notes, 'the ideology of nationalism . . . insists on an isomorphism between place and ethnicity and considers the linkage between citizens of states and their territories as natural'.[132] Özkan therefore explicates the concept of *vatan* – homeland – as crucial for understanding Turkish nationalism in particular. Identifying

Turkishness with the territorial homeland of the republic will emerge in our analysis as central to Erdoğan's conservative Turkish Islamic nationalism, especially in Chapter 4's analysis of the neo-Ottoman response to the 2016 coup attempt. Yılmaz identifies cultural and public practices as key 'sites of the state's attempt to produce a new Turk and modern Turkish nation' in the early years of the Kemalist republic.[133] Our analysis will show how Erdoğanian Neo-Ottomanism functions in a parallel fashion as it endeavors to shape architecture, urban public space, and the urban built environment in order to promote and instantiate its conservative and religious vision of idel Turkishness.

Notes

1. Parts of this chapter are from Courtney Dorroll, 'The Spatial Politics of Turkey's Justice and Development Party (AK Party): On Erdoğanian Neo-Ottomanism', PhD dissertation, University of Arizona, 2015.

2. David Harvey, *Justice, Nature, and the Geography of Difference* (Oxford: Blackwell, 1996), 293–5.

3. Pierre Bourdieu, *Distinction: A Social Critique of the Judgment of Taste*, trans. Richard Nice (Cambridge, MA: Harvard University Press, 1984), 12.

4. Bourdieu, *Distinction*, 2.

5. Pierre Bourdieu, *The Field of Cultural Production: Essays on Art and Literature*, Randal Johnson (ed.) (New York: Columbia University Press, 1993), 121.

6. Marita Sturken, *Tangled Memories: The Vietnam War, the AIDS Epidemic, and the Politics of Remembering* (Berkeley: University of California Press, 1997), 4.

7. Jürgen Habermas, *The Structural Transformation of the Public Sphere: An Inquiry into a Category of Bourgeoisie Society*, trans. Thomas Burger and Frederick Lawrence (Boston, MA: MIT Press, 1991).

8. Leila Hudson, 'Late Ottoman Damascus: Investments in Public Space and the Emergence of Popular Sovereignty', *Critique: Critical Middle Eastern Studies* 15:2 (2006): 152.

9. Hudson, 'Late Ottoman Damascus', 155.

10. Lawrence J. Vale, *Architecture, Power, and National Identity* (New Haven, CT: Yale University Press, 1992), 8.

11. On this general point, see Paul Jones, *The Sociology of Architecture* (Liverpool: Liverpool University Press, 2011), 49–66.

12. On the scale of destruction, see 'Map: Synagogues Destroyed during Kristallnacht', *United States Holocaust Memorial Museum*, available at: https://www.ushmm.org/information/exhibitions/online-exhibitions/special-focus/kristallnacht/synagogues/

how-was-kristallnacht-carried-out/map-synagogues-destroyed-during-kristallnacht, last accessed 6 July 2022.

13. Konstantin Akinsha, Grigorij Kozlov and Sylvia Hochfield, *The Holy Place: Architecture, Ideology, and History in Russia* (New Haven, CT: Yale University Press, 2007).

14. Eleni Bastéa, *The Creation of Modern Athens: Planning the Myth* (Cambridge: Cambridge University Press, 1999).

15. Sibel Bozdoğan, *Modernism and Nation Building: Turkish Architectural Culture in the Early Republic* (Seattle, WA: University of Washington Press, 2001), 6.

16. Zeynep Kezer, *Building Modern Turkey: State, Space, and Ideology in the Early Republic* (Pittsburgh, PA: University of Pittsburgh Press, 2015), 12.

17. Our use of the term 'architectural public sphere' therefore refers to architecture and public space as politicised, and as being read as such in its urban built environment. This usage is distinct, therefore, from uses of this term that refer to curated, indoor exhibitions of architecture, as in Léa-Catherine Szacka, 'The Architectural Public Sphere', *Multi* 2:1 (2008): 19–34.

18. Selim Deringil, *The Well-Protected Domains: Ideology and the Legitimation of Power in the Ottoman Empire, 1876–1909* (London: I. B. Tauris, 1999), 18–19.

19. Deringil, *The Well-Protected Domains*, 24.

20. Deringil, *The Well-Protected Domains*, 24.

21. Deringil, *The Well-Protected Domains*, 37–8.

22. Deringil, *The Well-Protected Domains*, 25.

23. Deringil, *The Well-Protected Domains*, 33.

24. Deringil, *The Well-Protected Domains*, 32.

25. Stanford Shaw, *The History of the Ottoman Empire and Modern Turkey, vol. 1: Empire of the Gazis: The Rise and Decline of the Ottoman Empire, 1280–1808* (New York: Cambridge University Press, [1976] 1997), 13.

26. Geoffrey Lewis, *The Turkish Language Reform: A Catastrophic Success* (Oxford: Oxford University Press, [1999] 2002), 45.

27. Deringil, *The Well-Protected Domains*, 27.

28. Onar, 'Echoes of a Universalism Lost', 232.

29. Enver Ziya Karal, 'The Principles of Kemalism', in Ali Kazangıcil and Ergun Özbudun (eds), *Atatürk: The Founder of a Modern State* (London: Hurst, 1994), 15.

30. Karal, 'he Principles of Kemalism', 16.

31. Lewis, *The Turkish Language Reform*, 2.

32. Lewis, *The Turkish Language Reform*, 45.

33. Lewis, *The Turkish Language Reform*, 68.

34. Feroz Ahmad, *The Making of Modern Turkey* (New York: Routledge, 2002), 82.

35. Ahmad, *The Making of Modern Turkey*, 81.

36. Feyzi Baban, 'The Public Sphere and the Question of Identity in Turkey', in E. Fuat Keyman (ed.), *Remaking Turkey: Globalization, Alternative Modernities and Democracy* (Lanham, MD: Lexington Books, 2007), 87.

37. Erik Zürcher, *Turkey: A Modern History* (London: I. B. Tauris, [2004] 2005), 180.

38. Ahmad, *The Making of Modern Turkey*, 87.

39. Talal Asad, *Formations of the Secular: Christianity, Islam, Modernity* (Palo Alto, CA: Stanford University Press, 2005), 191.

40. Baban, 'The Public Sphere and the Question of Identity in Turkey', 87.

41. Hakkı Taş and Meral Ugur, 'Roads "Drawn" to Modernity: Religion and Secularism in Contemporary Turkey', *PS: Political Science and Politics* 40:2 (2007), 311.

42. Taş and Ugur, 'Roads "Drawn" to Modernity', 311.

43. Karal, 'The Principles of Kemalism', 13.

44. Karal, 'The Principles of Kemalism', 27.

45. Ahmad, *The Making of Modern Turkey*, 79.

46. Talal Asad, *Genealogies of Religion: Discipline and Reasons of Power in Christianity and Islam* (Baltimore, MD: Johns Hopkins University Press, 1993), 79.

47. Niyazi Berkes, *The Development of Secularism in Turkey* (Montreal: McGill University Press, 1964), 466, 477.

48. Robert Hefner, 'Shari'a Politics: Law and Society in the Modern Muslim World', in Robert Hefner (ed.), *Shari'a Politics: Islamic Law and Society in the Modern World* (Bloomington: Indiana University Press, 2011), 33.

49. Janine Clark, *Islam, Charity and Activism: Middle Class Networks and Social Welfare in Egypt, Jordan and Yemen* (Bloomington: Indiana University Press, 2004), 5.

50. Filiz Şahin and Tahir Uluç, 'Contemporary Turkish Thought', in Ibrahim M. Abu-Rabi (ed.), *The Blackwell Companion to Contemporary Islamic Thought* (Oxford: Blackwell, 2006), 35.

51. Carter Vaughn Findley, *Turkey, Islam, Nationalism, and Modernity: A History, 1789–2007* (New Haven, CT: Yale University Press, 2010), 21.

52. Sena Karasipahi, *Muslims in Modern Turkey: Islamism, Modernism and the Revolt of the Islamic Intellectuals* (New York: I. B. Tauris, 2009), 30.

53. Hakan Yavuz, *Islamic Political Identity in Turkey* (New York: Oxford University Press, 2003), 4.

54. Anna Secor, 'Islamism, Democracy, and the Political Production of the Headscarf Issue in Turkey', in Ghazi-Walid Falah and Caroline Nagel (eds), *Geographies of*

Muslim Women: Gender, Religion and Space (New York: Guilford Press, 2005), 203–25.

55. Yavuz, *Islamic Political Identity in Turkey*, 5.
56. Yavuz, *Islamic Political Identity in Turkey*, 7.
57. Karasipahi, *Muslims in Modern Turkey*, 11.
58. Karasipahi, *Muslims in Modern Turkey*, 12.
59. Hakan Yavuz, *Secularism and Muslim Democracy in Turkey* (New York: Cambridge University Press, 2009), 43.
60. Hakan Yavuz, 'Opportunity Spaces, Identity, and Islamic Meaning in Turkey', in Quintan Wiktorowicz (ed.), *Islamic Activism: A Social Movement Theory Approach* (Bloomington: Indiana University Press, 2004), 271.
61. Yavuz, 'Opportunity Spaces, Identity, and Islamic Meaning in Turkey', 277.
62. Yavuz, 'Opportunity Spaces, Identity, and Islamic Meaning in Turkey', 279–80.
63. Secor, 'Islamism, Democracy, and the Political Production of the Headscarf Issue in Turkey', 208.
64. Jenny White, *Muslim Nationalism and the New Turks* (Princeton, NJ: Princeton University Press, 2013), 23.
65. White, *Muslim Nationalism and the New Turks*, 23.
66. Yavuz, 'Opportunity Spaces, Identity, and Islamic Meaning in Turkey', 285.
67. Yavuz, 'Opportunity Spaces, Identity, and Islamic Meaning in Turkey', 270–1.
68. Yavuz, *Secularism and Muslim Democracy in Turkey*, 53.
69. White, *Muslim Nationalism and the New Turks*, 115.
70. Yavuz, *Secularism and Muslim Democracy in Turkey*, 47.
71. Yavuz, *Secularism and Muslim Democracy in Turkey*, 47.
72. For thorough discussions of the details of this authoritarian transition in AKP governance, see Bahar Başer and Ahmet Erdi Öztürk (eds), *Authoritarian Politics in Turkey: Elections, Resistance, and the AKP* (London: I. B. Tauris, 2017); Necati Polat, *Regime Change in Contemporary Turkey: Politics, Rights, Mimesis* (Edinburgh: Edinburgh University Press, 2016).
73. Şerif Mardin, 'The Nakşibendi Order in Turkish History', in Richard Tapper (ed.), *Islam in Modern Turkey: Religion, Politics and Literature in a Secular State* (New York: I. B. Tauris, 1994), 134; Brian Silverstein, *Islam and Modernity in Turkey* (New York: Palgrave Macmillan, 2011), 98.
74. Banu Eligür, *The Mobilization of Political Islam in Turkey* (Cambridge: Cambridge University Press, 2010), 57; Yavuz, *Islamic Political Identity in Turkey*, 207.
75. Yavuz, *Islamic Political Identity in Turkey*, 208.
76. Quoted in Yavuz, *Islamic Political Identity in Turkey*, 207.

77. Eligür, *The Mobilization of Political Islam in Turkey*, 57; Yavuz, *Islamic Political Identity in Turkey*, 209.

78. Yavuz, *Islamic Political Identity in Turkey*, 212.

79. Yavuz, *Islamic Political Identity in Turkey*, 212.

80. Yavuz, *Islamic Political Identity in Turkey*, 243.

81. Eligür, *The Mobilization of Political Islam in Turkey*, 144.

82. Jenny White, *Islamist Mobilization in Turkey: A Study in Vernacular Politics* (Seattle, WA: University of Washington Press, 2002), 6; Yavuz, *Islamic Political Identity in Turkey*, 215.

83. Eligür, *The Mobilization of Political Islam in Turkey*, 145.

84. Yavuz, *Islamic Political Identity in Turkey*, 217.

85. Eligür, *The Mobilization of Political Islam in Turkey*, 147.

86. Eligür, *The Mobilization of Political Islam in Turkey*, 248.

87. Silverstein, *Islam and Modernity in Turkey*, 182.

88. White, *Muslim Nationalism and the New Turks*, 46.

89. The current version is available at: https://www.akparti.org.tr/parti/2023-siyasi-vizyon, last accessed 23 June 2022.

90. M. Hakan Yavuz, *Erdoğan: The Making of An Autocrat* (Edinburgh: Edinburgh University Press, 2021), 17, 176.

91. Susannah Verney, Anna Bosco and Senem Aydın-Düzgit, 'The AKP on the Road to Presidentialism', in Susannah Verney, Anna Bosco and Senem Aydın-Düzgit (eds), *The AKP since Gezi Park: Moving to Regime Change in Turkey* (New York: Routledge, 2020), 2.

92. White, *Muslim Nationalism and the New Turks*, 17.

93. Eligür, *The Mobilization of Political Islam in Turkey*, 263.

94. Çolak, 'Ottomanism vs. Kemalism', 590.

95. Çolak, 'Ottomanism vs. Kemalism', 591.

96. Yavuz, *Nostalgia for the Empire*, 68–106, 238.

97. Yavuz, *Nostalgia for the Empire*, 4.

98. Soner Çağaptay, *Erdoğan's Empire: Turkey and the Politics of the Middle East* (London: I. B. Tauris, 2018), 285.

99. Yavuz, *Nostalgia for the Empire*, 5.

100. Yavuz, *Nostalgia for the Empire*, 46.

101. Yavuz, *Nostalgia for the Empire*, 5.

102. Çolak, 'Ottomanism vs. Kemalism', 592.

103. Çolak, 'Ottomanism vs. Kemalism', 592.

104. Turgut Özal, *Turkey in Europe and Europe in Turkey* (Northern Cyprus: K. Rustem, 1991), 290; Çolak, 'Ottomanism vs. Kemalism', 593.

105. Umut Uzer, 'Conservative Narrative: Contemporary neo-Ottomanist Approaches in Turkish Politics', *Middle East Critique* 29:3 (2020), 279.

106. Fisher-Onar, 'Echoes of a Universalism Lost', 236.

107. Yavuz, *Nostalgia for the Empire*, 111.

108. Yavuz, *Nostalgia for the Empire*, 110.

109. Fisher-Onar, 'Echoes of a Universalism Lost', 233–6; Çolak, 'Ottomanism vs. Kemalism', 595–8.

110. Çolak, 'Ottomanism vs. Kemalism', 589.

111. Çolak, 'Ottomanism vs. Kemalism', 593.

112. Çolak, 'Ottomanism vs. Kemalism', 594.

113. Leslie Peirce, 'Polyglottism in the Ottoman Empire: A Reconsideration', in Gabriel Piterberg, Teofilo F. Ruiz and Geoffrey Symcox (eds), *Braudel Revisited: The Mediterranean World, 1600–1800* (Toronto: University of Toronto Press, 2010), 77.

114. Peirce, 'Polyglottism', 79.

115. Benjamin Braude, 'Foundation Myths of the Millet System', in Benjamin Braude and Bernard Lewis (eds), *Christians and Jews in the Ottoman Empire: The Functioning of a Plural Society* (New York: Holmes & Meier, 1982), 69.

116. Braude, 'Foundation Myths of the Millet System', 70.

117. Braude, 'Foundation Myths of the Millet System', 71.

118. Braude, 'Foundation Myths of the Millet System', 73.

119. Braude, 'Foundation Myths of the Millet System', 74.

120. Braude, 'Foundation Myths of the Millet System', 74.

121. Although this book details specific forms of Erdoğanian neo-Ottomanism in Istanbul, C. Dorroll has published on this phenomenon in Ankara in her article Courtney Dorroll, 'Hamamönü: Reconfiguring an Ankara Neighborhood', *Journal of Ethnography and Folklore* 1/2 (2016), 55–86, and Courtney Dorroll, 'Between Memory and Forgetting and Purity and Danger: The Case of the Ulucanlar Prison Museum', in Catharina Raudvere and Petek Onur (eds), *Neo-Ottoman Imaginaries in Contemporary Turkey: Gendered Discourses, Agencies, and Visions* (London: Palgrave Macmillan, forthcoming). Both of these examples are located in Ankara, Turkey.

122. Umut Uzer, *An Intellectual History of Turkish Nationalism: Between Turkish Ethnicity and Islamic Identity* (Salt Lake City: University of Utah Press, 2016), 3–4.

123. Yavuz, *Erdoğan*, 299.

124. Yavuz, *Erdoğan*, 80.

125. Yavuz, *Erdoğan*, 78.

126. Yavuz, *Nostalgia for the Empire*, 243.

127. Lisel Hintz, *Identity Politics Inside Out: National Identity Contestation and Foreign Policy in Turkey* (Oxford: Oxford University Press, 2018), 57.

128. Soner Çağaptay, *Islam, Secularism, and Nationalism in Modern Turkey: Who is a Turk?* (London: Routledge, 2006), 156.

129. Uzer, *An Intellectual History of Turkish Nationalism*, 8.

130. Çağaptay, *Islam, Secularism, and Nationalism in Modern Turkey*, 158.

131. Samim Akgönül, *The Minority Concept in the Turkish Context: Practices and Perceptions in Turkey, Greece, and France* (Leiden: Brill, 2013), 75–7; Samim Akgönül, *Türkiye Rumları: Ulus-Devlet Çağından Küreselleşme Çağına Bir Azınlığın Yok Oluç Süreci* (Istanbul: İletişim Yayınları, 2007), 19; Yavuz, *Erdoğan*, 87.

132. Behlül Özkan, *From the Abode of Islam to the Turkish Vatan: The Making of a National Homeland* (New Haven, CT: Yale University Press, 2012), 103.

133. Hale Yılmaz, *Becoming Turkish: Nationalist Reforms and Cultural Negotiations in Early Republican Turkey, 1923–1945* (Syracuse, NY: Syracuse University Press, 2013), 2.

2

ISTANBUL AS EUROPEAN CAPITAL OF CULTURE, 2010: THE AKP'S FINAL TURN TOWARDS EUROPE

Summary Background and Context: Turkey and Western Europe[1]

Since the establishment of the Republic of Turkey in 1923, successive Turkish administrations have pursued legal and social policies designed to strengthen the connection between Turkey and Western Europe. The most dramatic of these policies was the unprecedented and revolutionary Westernisation project undertaken in the 1920s and 1930s by Turkey's first president, Mustafa Kemal Atatürk, that laid the social and legal foundations of the Turkish Republic. This comprehensive reform programme was driven by the abolition of the Ottoman Empire itself and its major social and governmental structures, such as the sultanate, the caliphate and Islamic elements of Ottoman legislation; and their replacement by a modern parliamentary republic with a legal system copied directly from secular Western European examples. As described above, the social dimension of this reform programme famously included the creation and standardisation of the modern Turkish language (written in Latin, unlike the Arabic script of its Ottoman Turkish predecessor), the closing and outlawing of popular Ottoman Islamic religious institutions such as Sufi (Muslim mystic) shrines and lodges and Sunni Islamic seminaries (*medreses*), and even the legal enforcement of Western European customs of dress in public (such as the famous 1925 law that declared fezes and turbans illegal).[2]

Though the radical Westernisation of the early Kemalist state was tempered relatively quickly, beginning in 1950 when the first democratic elections in modern Turkish history unseated Atatürk's party, the broader commitment of the Turkish government to a European cultural identity and foreign policy orientation remained strong throughout the twentieth century. In 1949, Turkey joined the Council of Europe; in 1952, Turkey joined NATO; and in 1975, Turkey joined the Organization for Security and Cooperation in Europe.[3] After the European Economic Community (EEC) was founded by six member states with the signing of the Treaty of Rome in 1957, Turkey applied for associate membership of the EEC (the precursor to the European Union (EU)) in 1959. After lengthy negotiations, a formal association agreement was signed by the EEC and Turkey in 1963.[4] In 1987, Turkey applied for full membership of the EEC, and in 1999 it was accepted as a candidate for membership in the EU (which had replaced the EEC with the Treaty of Maastricht in 1993).[5]

When the AKP was first voted into power in 2002, support within Turkey for EU accession was particularly high. EU accession was touted by the AKP as its key foreign policy objective in Turkey's longstanding relationship with Western Europe, and EU accession was seen as critical to Turkey's economic and democratic development. As with other candidates for membership, the criteria for Turkey's membership were primarily political, and consisted of the necessity of reforms that would meet EU criteria for the protection of human rights, democratisation and the rule of law. At the beginning of the AKP's administration in 2002, constituencies as diverse as religious conservatives, secular liberals, and the Turkish military supported EU membership and the reforms required to enhance protections for individual human rights and democratisation.[6] In addition, in 2002 there was wide popular support for EU accession: 64 per cent of Turks supported accession, including a majority of all but one of the existing political parties across the ideological spectrum.[7]

In the following years, successive administrations undertook significant structural reforms in order to conform to the Copenhagen Criteria (outlined at the 1993 European Council in Copenhagen), the political and economic criteria required for EU accession. These included constitutional amendments in 2001 and 2004, and a series of eight harmonisation packages adopted between 2002 and 2004.[8] During this period the EU also went through two periods of massive enlargement: in 2004, Cyprus, the Czech Republic, Estonia, Hungary, Latvia, Lithuania, Malta, Poland, Slovakia and Slovenia all became EU members; Bulgaria and Romania acceded to the EU in 2007. These enlargements, however, called into question the extent to which the EU was willing to seriously consider Turkey's candidacy, as Bulgaria and Romania in particular seemed to exhibit structural political and economic deficiencies similar to, or worse than, Turkey's that did not prevent them from becoming members. Due to their Christian heritage, these nations were seen as inherently includable in the definition of what it means to be European, whatever the technical specifics of the Copenhagen on issues such as democratisation, economic reform or political reform.

At the same time, as Çiğdem Nas explains, 'Turkey's candidacy and accession to the EU is not justified but contested on the grounds of Europeanness.'[9] While majority-Christian countries in Eastern Europe were able to make the case that they were sufficiently 'European', by 2006 it had become increasingly clear that many EU leaders, most notably the French president, considered it impossible for Turkey to ever be fully 'European' due to its nature as a Muslim-majority nation, regardless of whether or not it met the technical criteria for membership.[10] It was during this period, when the AKP administration in Turkey was at the height of its ambitions in the pursuit of EU accession, and while EU leaders were openly questioning whether or not Turkey could ever be European at all, that Turkey in 2006 submitted the city of Istanbul as a candidate for the ECoC. It was awarded the designation in 2007, in preparation for when it would officially hold the title in 2010. Ayse Banu Bıçakçı explains the relationship between Turkey's EU aspirations and the ECoC: 'the event is benefited as a catalyst for receding from the Middle Eastern identity and converging to its European one. The city brand based on "European common roots" narrative is a result of Turkish political standing, endeavoring to be an EU member.'[11]

Encountering Istanbul in 2010

Walking the streets of Istanbul in 2010 felt as though I was in a gigantic ad for Istanbul. The trendy blue jeans store, Mavi, designed a line of t-shirts for men and women that centered around Istanbul. Signs all around advertised Istanbul as the latest city to be designated the Cultural Capital of Europe. Tulips were everywhere and signs described the importance of the tulip to Turkey and how it was during the Ottoman Empire that Turkey exported the tulips to Western Europe. Istanbul in 2010 was different from other years because this was the year Istanbul became an open-air museum for European consumers of culture. The 2010 designation was the result of concentrated effort on the part of the AKP-led Istanbul city government to attract Western European tourists to the mega-city and not just to the seaside, all-inclusive resort towns. This was the year the AKP was able to rebrand Istanbul as the city that projected their Neo-Ottoman ideals. At the time, as a tourist this was not obvious to me; instead it seemed that Istanbul had simply become a fashion object. Only upon reflection have I realized what this designation meant and the power of framing the AKP had in their hands during the year they programed Istanbul to be the European Capital of Culture.[12]

The European Capital of Culture (ECoC) Programme

Turkey submitted Istanbul as a contender city for the ECoC in 2006 and was awarded the designation in 2007 to prepare for the title in 2010. This designation gave the AKP the opportunity to rebrand Istanbul in accordance with a neo-Ottoman vision designed to appeal to a European and international audience. Throughout this process, the urban and public space of Istanbul was transformed into a kind of open-air museum, and the programming of the ECoC events revealed the elements of Istanbul's cultural heritage (i.e., its cultural capital) that were officially approved by the AKP. This official relocation of Turkish cultural heritage to Istanbul is highly significant, given the attempt in the early republican period to shift the focus of cultural memory from the cosmopolitan Ottoman capital to the Anatolian heartland, represented by the dedication of Ankara as the new capital of the Turkish Republic. Yet since the early 1990s, Istanbul as the centre of Ottoman heritage had begun to play a key role in neo-Ottoman ideology, particularly in the spatial and cultural politics of the AKP.

This chapter focuses on how the AKP utilised Istanbul's designation as the ECoC and the attendant arts and culture programming to reinvigorate and rebrand the importance of Turkey's Ottoman past. At the same time, the AKP utilised the ECoC as a pretext to gentrify centrally located neighbourhoods that did not fit the AKP's narrative of the Ottoman past. Thus, as a consequence of the AKP's utilisation of the ECoC status, ethnic minority groups that once had significant presence in the Ottoman Empire (and even as far back as the Byzantine Empire), such as the Roma community, were silenced and moved to the periphery of Istanbul. This chapter argues that the turn towards Europe envisioned in the ECoC designation was deeply ironic and ambiguous, because this attempt by the AKP to market a pluralist form of neo-Ottoman Istanbul for an international audience also involved the destruction and removal of cultural heritage and cultural memory that did not fit the AKP's political and social narrative.

The ECoC designation acted as the catalyst for the Sulukule Gentrification Project, which 'cleaned' the area of Roma residents that had been residing in the area since the eleventh century and replaced it with representatives of the Islamic bourgeoisie that much more closely conform to the interests of AKP spatial politics. The architectural public sphere that was created was criticised by many as wiping away the historical roots of the Roma people in the historical peninsula known as Sulukule. At the same time, the ECoC itself utilised neo-Ottoman symbols in its programming that emphasised cultural diversity and pluralism. As will be discussed in detail below, the utilisation of pluralistic neo-Ottoman rhetoric stood in stark contrast to the actual effects of the Sulukule Gentrification Project. Through specific examples of arts programming, the Ottoman past was romanticised as being inclusive and multi-ethnic, while in the actual architectural public sphere of Sulukule the historic ethnic identity of the Roma was displaced to apartments built by TOKİ in the peripheral Taşoluk neighbourhood.

This chapter explores the rhetoric of the application submitted for ECoC status and the implementation of the Sulukule Gentrification Project in order to shed light on the rebranding of Istanbul in accordance with the AKP's neo-Ottomanism. We argue that Istanbul's designation as the ECoC provided the political rationale for gentrificaiton projects that empowered members of the Islamic bourgeoisie at the expense of minority communities. We demonstrate that these efforts on the part of the AKP were designed to implement a shift in Istanbul's cultural capital that inscribed the AKP's hegemonic vision through the political utilisation of architecture and public space. This chapter therefore discusses a key dynamic that would go on to define the AKP's governance throughout the 2010s, as the following chapters will each reveal in turn.

In 1985, the EU began the initiative of selecting cities to represent Europe under the title of 'European City of Culture' (today the 'European Capital of Culture' or ECoC). A city must complete an extensive dossier application in order to be considered. According to the EU, the stated purpose of the ECoC is to:

- Highlight the richness and diversity of European cultures
- Celebrate the cultural ties that link Europeans together
- Bring people from different European countries into contact with each other's culture and promote mutual understanding and foster a feeling of European citizenship and regenerate cities
- Raise their international profile and enhance their image in the eyes of their own inhabitants
- Give new vitality to their cultural life
- Raise their international profile, boost tourism and enhance their image in the eyes of their own inhabitants[13]

The goal of the programme was to encourage unity among European countries. Initially it focused largely on high culture and high art. In 2004, the Palmer/Rae Report was published in which data and outcomes from the ECoCs of 1995 to 2004 were analysed. The report showed that cities were trying to replicate the success of previous ECoCs and thereby losing local distinctiveness, a dynamic that will be reflected in our analysis of the urban renewal projects undertaken in preparation for Istanbul's designation. In May 1999, the European Parliament and Council passed decision 1419/1999.EC, which permitted the European Capital of Culture organisation to allow non-member countries to participate in the ECoC between 2005 and 2019. The project was headed by Robert Palmer of Palmer/Rae Associates in Brussels. Istanbul was the first non-EU member city to be designated the ECoC.

The capacity of the ECoC to widen the definition of Europe and participation in the European integration project was what first attracted the AKP to this initiative. Kiran Klaus Patel's important edited volume devoted to the study of the ECoC programme, *The Cultural Politics of Europe: European Capitals of Culture and European Union since the 1980s*, shows that the ECOC programme has expanded the view of 'Europe' beyond a stereotypical focus on Western Europe with Brussels as its capital, and urges researchers to see European cultural policy as relational and operating through various stakeholders (in this case, such various stakeholders might include the specific interests of the AKP and their political constituencies, most notable the new Islamic bourgeoisie). He importantly points out that the ECoC programme has directly impacted the expansion conversation of what it means to be 'European', as it forms part of 'the wider framework of EU cultural policy and European integration during this period'.[14] Banu Karaca highlights the way in which these conversations have particular importance for countries perceived to be on the margins of Europeanness, such as Turkey, because for these countries incorporation into Europeanness has particularly significant impact for both domestic development and international advancement.[15]

In an equally significant volume that narrows in on the ECoC in Istanbul, *Orienting Istanbul: Cultural Capital of Europe?* the editors summarise the dynamics underlying the AKP's participation in this programme:

> The 2010 European Captial of Culture programme causes excitement and dissent among policy-makers, intellectuals, and producers of culture. It seeks to forge new connections and to strengthen existing ones towards a new European identity. Istanbul's version presents itself primarily as a marketing strategy, highlighting new urban regeneration projects while supposedly celebrating cultural diversity. The EU programme evidently employs culture to remap or raise the status of its key cities with forward-looking economies which are not themselves key players in the global city network. Policy and resources are geared towards culture-led development rather than structural economic change, which could potentially benefit a broader demographic in cities participating in the programme. This is where the EU programme and popularized vision of the global city coalesce.[16]

Turkish commentators at the time of Istanbul's designation as the ECoC took note of exactly these dynamics, including the neo-Ottomanist discourses surrounding the events. The *Hürriyet Daily News* reported on the debate that Turkish intellectuals were conducting over Facebook regarding how the AKP was marketing Istanbul for the ECoC. One of the leaders of the debate, Hasan Anamur, a founding member and executive board chairman of the Turkish section of the International Association of Theatre Critics, was quoted stating 'I would paint a ballerina, who is flying over Istanbul in her tutu skirt, but it would be against the AKP government's conception of the world.'[17]

The debate centred on the contention that the AKP was using oriental-ist figures to promote Istanbul to the West. Specifically, a poster that read 'Meet the Roots of Fun – In Istanbul 2010' was heavily criticised for cari-caturising the Ottoman past with figures of a flute player, janissary, harem women, sultan and oil wrestlers. Historian Hüseyin Irmak was quoted saying 'This poster will trigger the oriental view on Turkey in the Western world. As it is assumed, Istanbul was not an oriental city in the Ottoman period, too. It was just asked to be perceived like this, that's all . . . In a period in which the AKP is the ruling party, we could not expect a different poster. Unfortunately, the subconscious of the AKP members collides with the modern world.'[18]

The *Hürriyet* article also sheds light on one of the more significant domestic arguments relating to Istanbul's preparation for being the ECoC in 2010: the AKP government's plan to restore the Atatürk Culture Centre (Atatürk Kültür Merkezi; AKM), a symbol of modernisation and Western European cultural capital and identity in Taksim Square in Istanbul. In the end the AKM was not restored, and was in fact eventually demolished and replaced with a similarly modernist structure in 2021. One widely read daily newspaper at the time, *Today's Zaman*, wrote: 'the stalled restoration of the Atatürk Cultural Centre (AKM), [is] one of the biggest flops of İstanbul 2010'.[19]

The restoration of the AKM was scheduled to be part of the city's prepa-ration for the designation, but was stalled because there was a lack of trust that the AKP-led restoration would respect the integrity of a public build-ing and space that was seen as one of the city's most important emblems of secular, Western-oriented cultural capital and heritage.[20] The Ernst & Young final assessment report of the ECoC in Istanbul also drew attention to this particular issue: 'One flagship project which faced particular difficulty was the renovation of Atatürk Cultural Centre . . . one of the most prominent performance venues in Istanbul. Whilst it was planned to reopen the Cen-tre during 2010, a number of legal difficulties prevented the completion of the building works and the building remains unused at the present time.'[21] Though a seemingly minor dispute, like the rest of the ECoC preparation process in Istanbul, it foreshadowed dynamics that would only intensify in the coming years.

Preparation for the ECoC: Shaping Public Space in Istanbul

One official report regarding the purposes of the ECoC designation shows how close the connection was between the intentional transformation of the public sphere through urban renewal, and the preparations for the ECoC in Istanbul:

> Cities which are ECoCs exhibit their local authenticity, display cultural and artistic activities with various activities one year long, and find the opportunity to revise their cities by producing new city plans and architectural plans . . . Today, it has the priority to come to a mutual understanding in urban planning and cultural heritage conservation issues and produce projects for and with public. It should be better understood that the European Capital of Culture project is neither a marketing project nor public relations campaign. It is mainly a cultural planning project in which the culture should really work for the public. Thus the vision of the project should be perceived by the authorities clearly and explained to the public, so they can get involved in the project both in the preparation process and during the year 2010. By achieving the public participation in a wide scale, the base for a democratic platform will be established. Thereby, the EcoC project will become a catalyst as it generates a new approach in planning and in conservation of the cultural heritage, if only the 4 year period can be evaluated efficiently.[22]

In other words, the reshaping of urban and the architectural public sphere in Istanbul was seen as key to the success of the ECoC designation in the city, thereby providing the AKP administration with an opportunity to begin to reshape Istanbul in their social and political image.

Commodification of cultural heritage and memory, along with the commodification of public space, also emerged as key dynamics in Istanbul as a result of the ECoC designation. In a report commissioned by the European Network on Housing Research (ENHR) and executed by Turgay Koramaz and Elif Kisar-Koramaz, culture was described as becoming in this process 'a "business" of cities, [where] the "property-based" perspective has developed policies based on centralization of the cultural infrastructure and facilities serving for the privileged groups'.[23] The report analysed Istanbul as a 'commodity'-based system of culture and analysed the cultural policies of the ECoC in Istanbul that became 'a catalyst for development, promotion and tourism' by showing that the majority of all the events with the ECoC occurred in one central location; there was a distinct lack of events in peripheral districts, meaning that the programme catered only to elite Istanbulites and tourists.[24] Istanbul took the approach of economic development as their key component in their application to the ECoC, but the ENHR report states that few cultural landmarks were created for the year, and the researchers called particular attention to the fact that the AKM was not restored or used: 'since the hall has strong meaning in [the] city's cultural and political landscape, it has not been renovated because of political conflicts'.[25] In other words, the cultural memory associated with particular public sites and buildings becomes a key site for contestation over broader political conflicts and conceptions of identity.

Given the tensions generated by the dynamics described above, Zeynep Gunay's important analysis warns that Istanbul as the ECoC could serve to further create problematic tensions between conservation and regeneration:

In Turkey, the role of conservation has changed significantly over the past two decades, and it has become an alternative contributor to urban regeneration. It has become a common phenomenon in recent years to put cultural heritage at the heart of urban regeneration projects that are not just performing a cultural or educational role, but are also boosting local and regional economies. However, the compatibility of conservation and regeneration has brought up ongoing tensions that stem from political and economic interpretations of cultural heritage. The perceived economic benefits from the re-usage of cultural heritage cause the transformation of historic sites into large-scale development projects. The community prefers illegal construction or destruction because of the restrictive measures and the long decision-making process taken by conservation plans and implementing authorities. With regard to this, Istanbul has become a major concern for a case study as it is the major industrial, economic and cultural centre of Turkey, and is now fighting to be the centre of the global world, as well as a European Capital.[26]

Gunay's critique is particularly significant as a warning against using the pretext of urban development to undermine or even destroy the historic integrity and complexity of a city's architecture and landscape:

The ECoC 2010 event should not only be evaluated as an opportunity for image creation or as a promotion tool but also as a potential for long-lasting integrated cultural policies through sustainable management in order to respect the appropriate standards that are necessary for the protection of the historic environment. This is the balance between historic appreciation and development pressures.[27]

One specific development project in particular epitomised the destruction of historic spaces and even communities: the forcible relocation of the Roma of Sulukule. *Time* journalist Pelin Turgut covered the contested urban renewal projects that would be implemented to prepare for the ECoC year. Specifically, she visited the Roma neighbourhood of Sulukule. Turgut's reporting revealed that the low-economic neighbourhood would soon be entirely demolished and replaced by luxury neo-Ottoman-style townhomes. Turgut detailed how Istanbul would be 'cleaned' of Gypsies in preparation for the 2010 ECoC events.

This is, in fact, exactly what took place. The Roma of Sulukule were relocated to TOKİ houses[28] in the periphery of Istanbul; as Turgut explained, 'They can sell their property at a rate far below market prices (or face having it expropriated), or they can move to public housing in Tasoluk, some 25 miles outside the city, for which they will have to pay a mortgage over a 15-year period that very few can afford.'[29] As Turgut's article hypothesised, the Roma neighbourhood has been destroyed and with it the area's communal life, which has been replaced with an AKP-led development project that rebrands the cultural history of the area to conform to the narrow hegemonic parameters of the AKP's neo-Ottomanism. The urban renewal project itself was run by Mustafa Demir, mayor of the conservative Fatih municipality in Istanbul.

During 2004 and 2005 relevant laws were altered to allow more power for urban policies, and as a consequence decentralised planning fell into the hands of municipalities.[30] This led to cooperation between municipalities and the private sector for urban regeneration projects in Turkey. Specifically, in June 2005, Law 5366 for Renovation, Protection, Cherishing and Use of Worn Historical and Cultural Immovable Properties (Yıpranan Tarihi ve Kültürel Taşınmaz Varlıkların Yenilenerek Korunması ve Yaşatılarak Kullanılması Hakkında Kanun) was passed by the Turkish parliament, which allowed municipalities the power to oversee large-scale urban regeneration projects with the right to expropriation in areas deemed to be deteriorated. Later in 2010, the Law of Municipalities, Article 73, was amended in order to give added authority to municipalities that would allow them to build public housing, industrial parks, technology parks and recreation areas in order to protect urban areas and preserve historical areas.[31]

In January 2006, the Istanbul Metropolitan Municipality Council approved the Sulukule Urban Regeneration Project; this project would be conducted primarily by the Fatih municipality, but also received aid from the Istanbul Metropolitan Municipality and TOKİ. This also came at the time when Istanbul was seeking to apply for the status of European Capital of Culture. It has been demonstrated that the ECoC spurred the Sulukule Regeneration Project in an attempt to 'clean-up' Istanbul for the year on display. In both regeneration projects the historical fabric of the neighbourhood was replaced with modern, 'Ottoman style' homes. Four hundred and eighty homes were built in Sulukule; families were displaced through expropriation. In Sulukule during October 2006 an 'urgent expropriation' was issued for residents that were resisting evacuation in Sulukule.[32]

In a 2008 report for UNESCO on Sulukule, the organisation stated that Sulukule was the world's most significant location for Roma music, a 'cultural mosaic of the Historical Peninsula' (old Istanbul, between the Golden Horn and the Sea of Marmara), and that the area's close proximity to the prime entertainment centres of Istanbul was a major economic factor for Roma people living in the area (before they were relocated).[33] The gentrification project has actually put central Istanbul at risk of being removed from UNESCO's World Heritage List due to a lack in conservation projects. Deniz İncedayı from the Istanbul Chamber of Architects stated that: 'Gentrification projects in Istanbul lack socio-cultural research in their planning. When you look at successful examples in the West, locals are equally included in planning processes via acknowledging their views through special legal statutes. But, the converse happens here as these people are excluded on the grounds of maintaining funding.'[34] İncedayı explained that even if Roma were relocated to TOKİ apartments their culture would be damaged and Sulukule would lose its historical context.

The gap between the AKP's initial commitment to minority rights and its practices while in government also emerged with particular clarity in the treatment

of the Roma of Sulukule. Funda Gençoğlu-Onbaşı has analysed the AKP rhetoric with respect to minority rights and these communities' relationship with the
Turkish government. Specifically, she problematises the so-called 'Romani Opening' that the AKP has claimed to have effected, along with the 'Kurdish Opening',
'Alevi Opening' and 'Armenian Opening'.[35] These so-called 'openings' describe
official political events that have been coordinated by the AKP that are perceived
to be opening dialogue regarding the Turkish state minority groups in Turkey.
In one particularly notable example of this kind of dialogue, on 11 November
2013 Erdoğan met with Massoud Barzani, president of the autonomous Kurdish
region in northern Iraq in Diyarbakir and it was reported that Erdoğan utilised
the term Kurdistan.[36] Yet the gap between rhetoric and reality in minority policies
proved to be vast (and, as will be discussed in later chapters, even the rhetoric of a
multicultural Istanbul would be abandoned and forcefully rejected).

Gençoğlu-Onbaşı demonstrates that these projects that aimed to fight
against ethno-religious discrimination actually turned out to be discriminatory in their implementation. She also ties these efforts to the AKP's attempts
to join the EU and their attempt to align Turkey with the Copenhagen Criteria
that puts a premium on minority rights.[37] She focuses on the Romani Opening and how the discussion during the politicised 'Roma Meeting' in March
2010 in Istanbul with Prime Minister Recep Tayyip Erdoğan, organised by the
AKP, actually occurred simultaneously with the eviction of Roma from their
Sulukule homes.[38] Gençoğlu-Onbaşı outlined three major problems with the
'Romani Opening' in particular:

> First, the government's approach to the issue, telling the Roma who they are,
> how they are supposed to live, what they need and what they want in a rather
> patronizing manner, has been disappointing. Second, the opposition parties in
> the parliament (although they remained silent in large part) have problematized
> the scheduling of the Romani Opening among some other 'more significant
> and urgent' problems of the country, by inference stating that the Roma and
> their problems do not have a significant place in their agenda. Third, the main-
> stream media supported the opening in a way that served the reproduction of
> the stereotypes about the Roma.[39]

The first of Gençoğlu-Onbaşı's critiques was particularly prescient with respect
to the development of a specifically authoritarian form of conservative Turkish

Sunni nationalism under Erdoğan's leadership of the AKP over the course of the decade between 2010 and 2020. The AKP 'telling the Roma who they are, how they are supposed to live', that is, its attempt to control their lifestyle and assimilate them to the AKP's social and political ideal, foreshadows the methods and goals of Erdoğanian neo-Ottomanism that would accelerate dramatically over the course of this decade. Moreover, these urban renewal projects also sought to tell the Romani people *where* they should be living. This project closed the Sulukule neighbourhood to the Romani people and relocated them to TOKİ houses in the city's periphery at the command of the AKP government, not the desire of the Romani themselves.

During the March 2010 Roma Meeting, Erdoğan stated:

> You are my Romani sisters and brothers. I am greeting, cherishing and embracing each of you with love . . . [w]e have faith in each other. We trust each other. We have opened our hearts to each other and we [speak] the language of sincerity, the language of our hearts and feelings. Our country, our soil, our civilization takes its inspiration from love and tolerance.[40]

In this same speech Erdoğan showed pictures of the TOKİ housing projects that had been specifically built to relocate the Romani of Sulukule to the state's social housing complex in Taşoluk.[41] He continued by saying: 'I do not want anymore to see my Roma citizens living in tents or in shacks; I do want you to live *humanely*.'[42] The original, Romani residents were not able to pay the difference between what their property was valued and the price of the newly constructed townhomes. In the end most Romani residents sold their properties and relocated to the TOKİ homes in Taşoluk.[43]

The relocation and gentrification project forcibly constructed a new identity on the Sulukule historic peninsula. Rolien Hoyng's important work provides a multivalent analysis of the varieties of urban activism in Istanbul that emerged opposed to the destruction of the Sulukule neighbourhood, which was planned as part of the AKP's 'creative city' rebranding of Istanbul for the ECoC. Hoyng also makes the point that although these forms of activism did not prevent the destruction of the neighbourhood, they pointed the way towards different conceptions of what the city might be, and left 'continuing traces . . . on the city's pratico-material order'.[44] The Roma's historical and cultural heritage was ultimately erased and replaced by a homogenised version of an Ottoman past outlined by the AKP. Sulukule points to the politicised nature of gentrification projects. One must ask which type of cultural heritage is being preserved and which types are being erased.

Finally, the Sulukule project also foreshadowed the direct and personal role that Erdoğan would come to play in the reshaping of Istanbul's built environment. This aspect of the Sulukule project would emerge as the project that came under scrutiny in anti-corruption investigations targeting the AKP administration in Istanbul. Between 17 December and 19 December 2013 Turkey was rocked by the news that Istanbul police had detained the sons of three AKP minsters and over fifty other suspects in connection with massive anti-corruption investigations that had been underway for months without the knowledge of the AKP government.[45] Erdoğan immediately characterised the operations as being politically motivated, and retaliated by firing dozens of police chiefs across the country who had been instrumental in the massive probe.[46] The investigations accused suspects of 'rigging state tenders, accepting and facilitating bribes for major urbanization projects, obtaining construction permits for protected land areas in exchange for money, helping foreigners to obtain Turkish citizenship through falsified documents, involvement in export fraud, forgery of documents and gold smuggling'.[47] The mayor of Fatih municipality in Istanbul, the municipality responsible for the Sulukule gentrification project, was also detained by police; the municipality was accused of taking bribes from major developers in construction projects.[48]

The case against Fatih municipality, the location of the Sulukule gentrification project, began with the evidence gathered by whistleblower Azat Yalçın, who was fired from the municipality for uncovering evidence of corruption and who subsequently took his revelations to the Istanbul police at the beginning of 2013.[49] The son of Erdoğan Bayraktar, the AKP Minister of Environment and Urban Planning who was also in charge of TOKİ, was among those detained by police; Istanbul police alleged that Bayraktar's son and other officials at TOKİ took bribes from major construction companies and engaged in illegal building activities.[50] These cases and the many other investigations associated with anti-corruption dominated Turkish news and public debate when they were revealed; however, the most shocking comments on the scandal to date have come from Minister Bayraktar himself, who after being forced by Erdoğan to resign called for Erdoğan's resignation as well, claiming that he had approved and had knowledge of many of the projects now under legal investigation.[51] The former minister of culture, Ertuğrul Günay, also publicly claimed that Erdoğan was in close contact with the Istanbul city government throughout these projects and that 'every high rise was built with his approval'.[52]

Istanbul as the ECoC: The AKP's Neo-Ottoman City

A close analysis of the AKP's ECoC application for Istanbul and the public programming during the city's designation reveals the contours of the AKP's neo-Ottoman vision for the city. This vision, on the one hand, emphasised a multicultural, pluralist and tolerant reading of Ottoman history (along the lines of Turgut Özal's construction of neo-Ottomanism described in the previous chapter) that nevertheless clashed with the AKP's practices of governance, such as the treatment of the Roma of Sulukule. This analysis shows that this moment represented the high point of Turkey's turn towards Western Europe under the AKP: even as it was emphasising its connectedness with Europe, it was laying the groundwork for the exclusionary policies that would dominate its use of public space in the years following (especially after Gezi Park, as described in the next chapter).

Erdoğan himself went to great lengths to connect Istanbul with European identity, highlighting the oft-repeated metaphor of Istanbul as a 'bridge' between 'East and West' in the ECoC application. This common metaphor (which did appear in the Review of Selection of Istanbul for the ECoC) of the 'bridge' acts as a way to define spaces in accordance with hegemonic and homogenising versions of reality. This places a binary between 'East' and 'West' and uses the physical place of Turkey to fit the confines of the terms produced by the European cultural elite. As Aslı Iğsız has shown, Turkey under Erdoğan's leadership has often sought to position itself as a 'bridge' between 'East' and 'West' in the context of post-9/11 security anxieties, thus reinforcing such 'civilisational' binaries for the sake of its own power in the geopolitical arena.[53] What does this designation mean when Turkey is then incorporated as 'Europe': is it allowing Turkey a place in the dominant cultural position yet without allowing it in the political space of the European Union? Does it then mean that Turkey is a symbolic space that is utilised to access and allow Western thought and 'civilisation' to reach the place of the East? One must ask, in what direction is 'culture' flowing on this so-called bridge, who are the legitimisers and why would Turkey strive to be put in this liminal position?

In Erdoğan's endorsement letter in the ECoC application he clearly illustrates the flow of culture on this so-called 'bridge': 'Istanbul will develop a more visible European dimension and project European culture not only in Turkey, but in the Middle-East, the Caucasus and Central Asia as well, with European civil society at the centre.'[54] A stated point of the ECoC is its efforts to 'highlight the richness of cultural diversity in Europe', which begs the question, what is Europe and how is it defined?[55] There is also a sense of connecting and aligning Turkey with Europe and further othering the Middle East: 'Istanbul's strategic location means that it lies at the intersection of some of the most troublesome regions in the world. These regions stretch from the Caucasus to the Middle East and the instability also threatens Europe. The aim is for Istanbul as an ECoC to host an organization that will serve world peace.'[56] One event that clearly exhibited such motifs was titled 'Crossing the Bridge: A multitude of activities on the Bosphorus', which plays on the 'significance of Istanbul connecting Europe and Asia'.[57] Also exhibited in the application is the event titled 'Danube Bridge'.[58]

The bridge metaphor was also cited in the final report by the ECoC commission:

Although the city has a rich cultural heritage, the motivation for the ECoC centred on establishing Istanbul as a centre for modern and contemporary culture reflecting the diversity of cultures and ethnic groups in Istanbul as well as its young, dynamic population. More specifically, the objectives of the ECoC were to:

• Generate transformative energy and build capacity
• Restore cultural and industrial heritage
• Address the urban and cultural dimensions of citizenship
• Function as a bridge connecting Europe to its East[59]

The stated goal of the 'European Capital of Culture' project is to bring European citizens together to:

- Highlight the richness and diversity of cultures in Europe
- Celebrate the cultural features Europeans share
- Increase European citizens' sense of belonging to a common cultural area
- Foster the contribution of culture to the development of cities

In addition to this, experience has shown that the event is an excellent opportunity for:

- Regenerating cities
- Raising the international profile of cities;
- Enhancing the image of cities in the eyes of their own inhabitants
- Breathing new life into a city's culture
- Boosting tourism[60]

Who decided what is a common aspect of European culture? It is not just the gatekeepers on the Artistic and Application Committees, but the education and social institutions within a society that produce a hierarchy of cultural production. In other words, in its application to the ECoC the AKP was producing new cultural capital to orient Istanbul as the capital of culture over Ankara, the official nation-state capital.

A close analysis of the specific ECoC cultural events reveals the specifically neo-Ottoman contours of this programming's vision of Istanbul's cultural heritage and cultural capital. According to the official application document submitted by the Turkish government, the year's events were to be divided into four phases: Earth, Air, Wind and Fire. The first phase of events, Earth (1 January–20 March), is especially important for our analysis because this phase was titled 'Tradition and Transformation'; it was clearly intended to establish a normative vision of Istanbul's cultural heritage. This vision was decidedly neo-Ottoman.

The application document describes this phase this way: '"Earth" means the history, tradition and cultural heritage of the land. Under this heading comes the values of the past which have been preserved down to the present day and will be passed on to future generations – ancient values that take root and send forth fresh leaves like the seeds of new plants.'[61] The programming was designed to focus heavily on the Ottoman past, with far fewer references to Istanbul's classical and Byzantine heritage. Of the eleven events scheduled for this period (not including the general ECoC opening ceremony), eight were to be dominated by Ottoman or Ottoman-era themes:

(1)   The *Imperial Passions* exhibition at the Sakıp Sabancı Museum was to showcase art created or commissioned by the Ottoman sultans them-selves, including poems, calligraphy and illustrations by Mehmet II, Sül-eyman the Magnificent, Murad III, Abdül Hamid and Abdül Mecid.

When the exhibit opened it was named 'Legendary Istanbul: From Byzantion to Istanbul: 8000 Years of a Capital'. It ran from 5 June to 26 September 2010 and it was curated specifically for the European Cultural Capital year and pro-gramme of events. Sakıp Sabancı Museum Executive Director, Dr Nazan Ölçer aimed for the exhibit to be one of the most inclusive exhibits in the museum's history and focused on the legacy of Istanbul to frame it within the context of the European Cultural Capital. Five hundred pieces were displayed from forty different institutions, both Turkish and international. Objects as varied as massive stone walls, frescos and naval weaponry were put on display.[62]

As the Sakıp Sabancı Museum online literature puts it: 'Byzantion, Neo Roma, Constantinople, and Istanbul – the series of cities which have occupied the same site by turn – and their histories constitute a treasury of symbolic phenomena. Inarguably continuous with its past, Istanbul is a universal space that reflects historical encounters.[63] Earlier on the page, one can see the focused approach to the Ottoman era: 'Then in 1453, it was conquered by the young Ottoman ruler Sultan Mehmed II, who brought the Byzantine Empire to an end. Having had [sic] become one of the most splendid capital cities of the modern age, Istanbul reflected the ethnic and religious diversity of the Otto-man Empire through its rich demographic mosaic of the city, where Muslim, Christian, and Jewish communities lived together.'[64]

The online resource from the museum describes the exhibit as a whole in this way:

With a selection of objects that had opened with prehistoric findings, the exhibition covered the Roman, Byzantine, and Ottoman periods of the city through a lens focusing on these civilizations' influences upon each other. Accordingly, it aimed attention at the multicultural qualities of the colorful population that has characterized Istanbul throughout its history, the energy emanated from this dynamic crowd, its ability to adapt to innovations, and the spirit of youth it had continued to reflect despite its long past.[65]

The museum executive director hosted two Zoom events and posted on YouTube to discuss the exhibit,[66] the museum published a book[67] based on the exhibit and also maintains a web presence based on the exhibit.[68]

(2)   The *Istanbul Inspirations* programme was to include the performance of European operas that were set in the Ottoman Empire, such as Rossini's *Maometto II* and Krauss' *Soliman*. It was suggested in the application that the former be held at the Rumeli fortress and the latter be held inside Topkapı Palace.

(3)   The programme titled *Turkish Makam Music: Between the Past and the Future* was to include the performance of traditional Ottoman Turkish classical music 'in a series of concerts for local and foreign audiences at the venues where this form of music was born, such as the imperial palace, dervish lodges, and similar historical social structures'.[69]

(4)   An exhibition was to include a display of historical costumes from the Byzantine to the end of the Ottoman period, though the event was to be held at a distinctly Ottoman building: the Ottoman Feshane (fez factory).

During the actual year's events, the Istanbul Museum of Modern Art exhibited twenty-six designers to showcase modern fashion that represented the history and architecture of Istanbul.[70]

(5)   The *Topkapı Palace Cyber Museum* project was also proposed. This project would create a virtual platform for exploration of the entirety of the palace. The fact that this particular structure (a distinctly classical Ottoman palace) was chosen, instead of Byzantine-era structures or 'Westernised' examples of Ottoman imperial architecture (such as the Dolmabahçe Palace) speaks to the decision to highlight the classical Ottoman heritage of Istanbul, locating the essence of its architectural heritage in the heart of the most powerful era of Sunni Ottoman imperial dominance.

(6) The *Only in Istanbul Music Festival* was proposed as a way to showcase the flavour of Istanbul's musical heritage, 'a music festival project which will bring together the musical traditions of the Middle East, Caucasus, Balkans, and Eastern Mediterranean'.[71] In other words, the musical heritage of Istanbul is here being equated with the musical heritages of the former Ottoman Empire.

(7) The *International Istanbul Ülker Puppet Festival* was also suggested as a featured event, intended to highlight the heritage of puppetry arts from around the world. However, the focus on a puppetry motif clearly alludes to the importance of the Karagöz puppetry tradition, a Turkish folk art that was extremely popular in the Ottoman period and a practice widely associated with Ottoman cultural heritage.

During the year's events, the international Istanbul puppet festival was extended and combined with similar events: 'As part of the 13th International Istanbul Puppet Festival, World Puppet Day will be celebrated March 21 and the World Puppet Exhibition will open simultaneously. This year the International Istanbul Puppet Festival will be expanded to three months with the support of the Istanbul 2010 European Capital of Culture agency.'[72] The importance of the Ottoman-era Karagöz tradition in particular was reinforced: 'during the opening of the festival, Karagöz masters Tacettin Diker, Orhan Kurt and Metin Özlen, who have been regarded as "providers of cultural richness" since Karagöz is accepted as an oral heritage, will be presented a special [plaque]'.[73] This foregrounding of Ottoman heritage preceded a schedule of events that was highly international and included 'selected groups from France, Russian Federation, Hungary, Spain, Brazil, Japan, Czech Republic, Germany, Greece, Iran, Italy and Turkey' and the staging of the World Puppet Exhibition at the Taksim metro station.[74]

(8) The programming for the opening section of the ECoC year was also to close with a very distinctly Ottoman public festival, a meticulous re-enactment of the 1720 circumcision celebration parade held by Sultan Ahment III in honour of his son. The parade was to be recreated based on a description given by the poet Seyyid Vehbi and the famous book of miniatures that depicted the event by Levni, the *Şenlikname*.

It is also interesting to note here that the only major event specifically dedicated to the Christian and Jewish heritage of Istanbul actually frames these cultural heritages as 'European' and thus fundamentally other than the essence of Istanbul itself or of the Ottoman past. This event, titled '7000 Years at 7000 Meters', was a proposed series of guided tours of major Christian and Jewish architectural monuments. The specific goals of this project are stated as: 'the promotion of the "multi-cultural" identity of Istanbul in regard to its relationship with Europe'.[75] It is significant that the description of these ancient monuments characterises them in connection with Europe (a claim that is not made with regard to Islamic architecture), thereby othering these monuments and alluding to the presumption of a distinctly Turkish Muslim essence to Istanbul's cultural heritage.

The ECoC application makes extensive use of the neo-Ottoman rhetoric of pluralism when describing Istanbul and its cultural heritage. The application refers to Istanbul as a 'beautiful harmony' of 'countless societies and cultures'.[76] The city is also described as a place 'that has nurtured different cultures, religions and languages and molded them into an enduring synthesis'.[77] The application also describes Istanbul as 'a melting pot where many languages are spoken, a multitude of traditions followed and various ethnicities expressed: from Anatolia, the Balkans, the Crimea, the Black Sea and Aegean'.[78] This description identifies the multicultural heritage of Istanbul with former Ottoman territory. According to the application, Istanbul's status as ECoC will play an important role in 'shifting the agenda from one in which cultural homogeneity is regarded as the normative principle to one in which cultural diversity and heterogeneity are more openly accepted'.[79] The application boasts of Istanbul's 'contemporary experience of management of diversity' at the same time that it was implementing the removal of the Roma from Sulukule.[80]

The final assessment report by Ernst & Young also reveals the kind of events that were prioritised and implemented. The report highlighted what it deemed to be the significant successes of the year's programming, and cited four key areas: (1) 'an extensive programme of renovation and restoration of Istanbul's cultural and industrial heritage, including the four UNESCO World Heritage Sites on Istanbul's historic peninsula (which were at risk of losing their designation)'; (2) 'a number of high-profile cultural events including some featuring performers of international renown, such as the opening events and a number of international festivals'; (3) 'a large number of cultural events [that] show-cased the traditional and historical culture of Istanbul and of Turkey to a wider audience'; and (4) 'the commissioning and performance or exhibition of new artworks, including those developed by local artists and cultural institutions and/or specifically relating to contemporary Istanbul'.[81]

The first three categories of successes illustrate the specific dynamics of Otto-man cultural heritage and cultural memory at play in the ECoC programming, and also how the ECoC programming attempted to connect this heritage with international audiences. Examples of (1) included restoration efforts in historic neighbourhoods associated with both Ottoman and Byzantine heritage, such as Sultanahmet, Zeyrek and Süleymaniye; and restoration work on major his-torical monuments such as the Byzantine Theodosian land walls, Hagia Sophia and Topkapı Palace. Notably, a 'Museum of Byzantium' was also suggested for future development, but it does not appear that this plan ever materialised. Examples of (2) included the first ever U2 performance in Istanbul, the world premiere of Estonian composer Arvo Pärt's 'Adam's Lament', and the Second International Istanbul Ballet Competition.[82]

The most illustrative area of these successes was category (3). As the report emphasises: 'a large number of cultural events aimed to present the tradi-tional and historical culture of Istanbul and of Turkey to a wider audience'. As detailed above, this usually meant a focus on Ottoman Islamic heritage, most especially religious art such as calligraphy, Karagöz, the Ottoman fez and Turkish classical music (as described above). The report also included men-tion of events concerning non-Muslim minorities during the Ottoman period that were clearly staged to reinforce the narrative of Ottoman multicultural-ism. Such events included a Balkan Music festival and folk music in Turkish, Greek, Armenian and Ladino.[83]

In sum, the theme of the programming of the ECoC represented the AKP's neo-Ottomanism in its pursuit of its aim to brand Istanbul as a centre of imperial Ottoman cultural heritage and display elements of this cultural heritage to an international tourist audience during the ECoC. The Ottoman heritage highlighted in the programming illustrates the importance placed on the Ottoman past and specifically the presumed Sunni Muslim normativity of the height of Ottoman imperial power, despite its apparent commitment to multiculturalism and pluralism. Through this process of the reification of historical memory, the cultural capital and heritage of Istanbul is constructed specifically to reflect the hegemonic historical narrative of the AKP's neo-Ottomanism. At the same time, while the ECoC programming features multiculturalism as a major component of the artistic programming, in actuality multicultural neighbourhoods of Istanbul were being homogenised, or rather 'cleaned', of their diverse elements and diverse inhabitants, thereby eliminating the lived multiculturalism in the architectural public sphere in Istanbul.

The AKP strategy of positing an organic European connection to Istanbul along with the reduction of the city's cultural heritage to Sunni, Ottoman ideals exist in tension, but this combination is in fact implied in the description of Istanbul as a 'bridge' between 'East' and 'West'. Aside from the in-practice denial of multiculturalism in AKP sponsored urban renewal projects, even the AKP's discursive appeal to East–West multiculturalism has broken down in the post-Gezi period. Before Gezi Park, the AKP's attempt to align itself with the 'West' was also made evident by its pro-EU membership foreign policy. Yet during the Gezi Park protests, the West became the 'enemy' in Erdoğan's speeches and declarations. As will be discussed in more detail in Chapter 3, anti-Gezi discourse often blamed 'Western' interference for the uprisings. The AKP's relationship with the 'West' post-Gezi Park therefore remains conflicted and unresolved.

Evaluating Istanbul as EcoC

The Museumification of the City

Evaluating Istanbul's designation as ECoC from a variety of critical perspectives will shed light on the specific dynamics of this stage of the development of the AKP's neo-Ottomanism. At this early stage in its development, the AKP's neo-Ottomanism exhibited numerous tensions and ironies as it sought at one and the same time to orient itself towards Europe, while also retaining a distinctly Turkish Sunni vision of Ottoman Istanbul's cultural heritage and cultural memory. Analysing how the AKP reified Istanbul's public space as a kind of open-air museum, how it reinscribed Eurocentrism in this public space, and how it therefore politicised culture in Istanbul's public space reveals the complexities of the AKP's neo-Ottomanism at the moment when it was still attempting to turn towards Europe, while also beginning to exhibit the authoritarian and homogenising tendencies that would come to dominate its spatial politics over the course of the decade (as described in the following chapters).

One of the key ways that the formation and reformation of cultural capital take place in modern Turkish history is through museums, where cultural memory and cultural capital are meticulously constructed for public display and consumption. Universally, the construction of cultural capital is often accomplished by the cultural (re)imagining of history through archaeological attempts and the exhibition of state ideology via museum institutions. Museums can be seen as deliberate constructions of cultural memory created by the forces of power elites within society to control what story is told.

Museums have played this role throughout modern Turkish history. Wendy Shaw's work *Possessors and Possessed: Museums, Archeology, and the Visualization of History in the Late Ottoman Empire* analyzss how the Ottoman Empire used 'museums as an expression of the models of national mythmaking produced by Ottoman elites interested in constructing themselves as the guardians of ethnicity and in thereby fashioning a national identity'.[84] Her work analyses the idea of the myth-symbol complex that constructs narratives of ethnic identity. She also points to the shift in identities between the Ottoman Empire and the Turkish state identity of the new republic. In contrast to republican Turkish national identity, Ottoman identity was multi-ethnic, multilingual and multireligious: 'Ottomans were Turks by outside observation and by later designation, but in their own eyes they constituted a cosmopolitan Muslim elite.'[85] Within this conception of identity, Ottoman culture could openly admit of admixture and hybridity in a way republican Turkish culture would later struggle with.

The first museum in the Ottoman Empire could have been founded as early as 1723 or as late as 1846; the date is in fact contested.[86] The museum emerged along with many other European-influenced institutions to mark the utilitarianisms of modernity (prisons, universities, army, post office, archives, etc.). Though taken from the West, the Ottoman Empire did not adopt the meta-narrative of the European institution, that is, to collect and classify an area of objects; instead, the Ottoman museum portrayed a modern national identity that focused on illustrating local traditions that would satisfy contemporary needs.[87] Early displays consisted of military weapons and mannequins of Janissaries, with both types of artefact showcasing imperial superiority during a time of actual decline that the Ottomans experienced vis-à-vis the rapidly modernising and expansionistic European imperial powers.

This nascent form of museum acted as a place for reflection and allowed physical objects to be displayed while forming early political, nation-building identities. These museums were a project of Westernisation that exemplifies the 'Europeanesque' within Ottoman identity.[88] As Shaw explains, 'Like schools, museums provided for public spaces devoted to the construction and projection of the history, culture, and identity of the Ottoman state and its people. Both through its format and through its content, the museum could project a European framework with an Ottomanist and Islamic content and thus model the new state identity as simultaneously Western and Ottoman.'[89] From 1876 to 1909 museums continued to develop in the Ottoman Empire.[90] In Turkey, as elsewhere, the museum acts as a mediator and a medium in which a collective, public memory has created public history, marking how the conception of this history has changed over time. Museums have worth and cultural capital that gives them authority and power over collective memory that decides what is deemed worthy of inclusion, preservation and display. Museum curators act as powerful gatekeepers of the representation of a culture's past by programming this past and displaying it for the public.

Just as the nationalist Turkish Kemalist ideology created a homogenising view of the nation-state by using the medium of the museum, the AKP's neo-Ottoman view of the Ottoman Empire creates a homogenised and generalised view of the memory and history of the Ottoman Empire, which showcases a nostalgic, monolithic voice that collapses the entire empire and its diversity cleaned of political, social and cultural nuances, through the programming of the ECoC which renders Istanbul into an open-air museum. As described above, the ECoC application proposed events that capture the neo-Ottoman re-enactment trend, such as the Şenlikname parade, which is a 're-interpretation of the 17th century circumcision parade of Sultan Ahmet III'.[91] Another example of public neo-Ottoman re-enactment has been studied in Alev Çinar's work on how Islamists contest national definitions and performances of history by celebrating the Conquest of Istanbul Day (29 May 1453): this dimension of the AKP's construction of Istanbul's identity will be discussed in more detail in Chapter 5. In this case, neo-Ottomanism remembers the

Ottoman past by glorifying its founding events, thereby acting as a counter to traditional Kemalist secular historiography, for example, the official celebration of 29 October as Republic Day.[92]

Çinar states that 'Contestation of official history does not necessarily involve confrontation of its validity; rather, it unsettles the assumed naturalness and singularity'[93] ... [and thereby] 'the public performance of Ottoman–Islamic national identity emerges as a contestation of official national history.'[94] In other words, in the AKP's museumification of Istanbul, the secular Kemalist vision of the city and of Turkey's history in general is openly challenged in the public sphere. Yet it is also important to ask, to what extent is this commemoration of an idealised Ottoman past replacing the same essentialist vein of the homogenising efforts of the nascent nation-state? In what ways is neo-Ottomanism simply reconfiguring a past by using the same control of public memory and selective framing as the Kemalists, leading one to ask if neo-Ottomanism is simply the new nationalism in contemporary Turkey? Esra Özyürek found that in the 1990's Kemalist and Islamist views, histories and memories of the early republican era were in competition, but in the end both produced homogenising narratives.[95] The analysis in subsequent chapters will bear out the claim that the AKP's neo-Ottomanism is ultimately a form of hegemonic and homogenising nationalism, in this sense not unlike the secular nationalism that preceded it and that it attempts to resist.

The practice of reconstructing a new national past (and by extension future) must be founded on a suitable re-appropriation and reconstruction of the most immediate historical past. In other words, before Kemalist Turkish national cultural memory could conquer and displace Ottoman cultural memory, it first had to demonstrate the 'backwardness' and fundamentally irredeemable nature of the Ottoman past. Kemalist Turkey rendered Ottoman tradition into an essential, arcane and obsolete past; this notion is perfectly summed up in the Turkish word '*müzelik*', literally 'a museum thing'. This term denotes a useless object.[96] The meta-narrative of cultural memory is closely guarded and controlled by those with social, cultural and political power, and the items that are archived and programmed in cultural institutions are used to help to bolster support for the current administration and its ideological vision.

Ironically, through the ECoC designation, the AKP also transformed Istanbul as a city into a *müzelik* that acts as a museum piece in positive support of its social vision, rather than as a contrast to its social vision (as the Kemalists had depicted Ottoman tradition). The 'constructedness' of memory by political elites and its connection to changing social dynamics is precisely the dimension of memory most clearly at play in museums and historical preservation projects, and in this way the manipulation of Ottoman Istanbul's identity by the AKP during the ECoC process ironically mirrors the Kemalist manipulation of Ottoman Istanbul's identity. While secular Kemalist Turkish nationalism reified Ottoman Istanbul's identity in order to contrast itself to it, the AKP reified Ottoman Istanbul's identity in order to identify itself with it.

Aslı Iğsız's analysis of one project in particular sponsored by the ECoC, the 1923 Greek–Turkish Population Exchange Museum, shows how cultural diversity can be 'museumised', a process that 'disconnects the "objects of display" from history literally or metaphorically and transforms their meaning'.[97] As her insightful analysis reveals, when this process is applied by state or political actors to the experiences and cultural heritage of minority populations who have suffered repression and marginalisation, 'communities such as the Greeks, Armenians, Jews, and Roma are "celebrated" in these projects through exhibitions, music, or food, [and thus] are configured for display, divorcing them from history, depoliticizing and objectifying them'.[98] In other words, as we argue that the AKP has transformed the entirety of the city of Istanbul into a 'museum piece' through its manipulation of this public space in order to reflect its own hegemonic values, Iğsız's point establishes how this process affects and co-opts the memory of minority populations and their own cultural institutions in the city.

Reinscribing Eurocentrism

One of the most ironic outcomes of the ECoC designation was that the AKP's attempt to construct an authentic neo-Ottoman cultural identity for Istanbul reinforced a Eurocentric and even Orientalist vision of the city. Normative Eurocentrism emerged as a key feature of Istanbul's application for the status of ECoC, such as when it implied that Turkey was in need of yet further Westernisation and modernisation along the lines that had begun during the late Ottoman period:

> As of today, Istanbul needs practical instruments which will inform the manner in which its culture and political arena are shaped. There are many examples

of this culture dating from the period of Ottoman modernization known as the Tanzimat, when it served as a transforming force in terms of developments related to the concept of human rights and in the subordination of sovereignty to discourses about rights, facilitating harmony between urban renewal and the transformation of daily life.[99]

The ECoC programme must therefore be critically analysed as an organisation of power that creates an idea of the naturalness of 'Europeanness'. Yet this causes us to ask, what is 'Europeanness' and how does defining something as 'European' therefore otherise a different category of people? In the case of Istanbul's application to the EcoC, it was the artistic productions that were analysed as being either European or not European enough to be included or excluded from the ECoC programming. It is this rubric that creates delineations within the polyphony of cultures that reside in Istanbul that then asks those artists to delineate themselves and market themselves as European. Here it is therefore crucial to analyse this phenomenon from the point of view of Eurocentrism, or the idea that Europe stands as a symbolic elite or cultural legitimiser. The application notably stated that: 'Even if, in the strict geographical sense, only a small proportion of Turkey's territory is in Europe, this part nevertheless contains Istanbul, the country's metropolitan heart. Throughout history Istanbul has always looked toward Europe, economically and culturally . . .'[100] This quote stresses the importance of normative European identity in Istanbul and puts this normative sense of Europeanness at the heart of the city, even at the same time that the AKP sought to construct the city as a centre of neo-Ottoman cultural memory.

It is therefore necessary to call attention to the power forces involved with Eurocentrism instead of allowing it to maintain a neutral or normative position, yet the power and historical legacy of Eurocentrism is ignored in Istanbul's application and in the ECoC. Eurocentrism is being reinforced by the very application of Istanbul being a European Capital of Culture. Nancy Fraser's work, for example, has shed light on the problem of reification occurring in transcultural interaction, which drastically simplifies and reifies group identities.[101] With the ECoC designation the Eurocentric group identification is reified by titling Istanbul as a Capital of Culture for Europe even though Turkey has not been officially granted membership into the European Union.

Along similar lines, Liisa Malkki analyses the socio-political constructions of space and place by focusing on the metaphors people use to refer to kinship to root themselves in a geographical space.[102] The notions of 'East' and 'West' can be seen as the rootedness of categorisation that includes and excludes.[103] Malkki speaks of the tourist's desire for 'authenticity'.[104] In the 1990s Turkey utilised tourism and the potential of Istanbul as an exotic tourist destination for economic development: 'for Western eyes, Istanbul has emerged in the last decade as an outpost of "authenticity"'.[105] Is this not what the ECoC is constructing, an authentic 'Europe' through an essentialist lens? The ECoC selection process, therefore, represents a way to redraw the boundaries of Europe in cultural terms that are supported by political and social power forces.

The assumed normativity of 'the West' and its dichotomisation vis-à-vis 'the East' speaks to the cultural capital that Europe maintains not simply within Turkey but also on a global scale. The ECoC reproduces and legitimises culture deemed appropriate and 'up to par' with the West. In this case, we see a kind of 'internalised' or 'self-orientalisation' (like that mentioned above in Chapter 1) of the Turkish nation-state in its attempt to become deemed 'good enough' for Europe. But such efforts met with limited tangible reward. As the final report stated, it was not that this distinction gave Turkey huge sums of money to execute its programming for the ECoC year; instead final budget reports show that 95 per cent of the funds for Turkey came from the Turkish government, the Ministry of Finance to be exact.[106] The ECoC Application clearly states that financially the project will be led by the Turkish Ministry of Foreign Affairs with the support and participation of the Ministry of Tourism and Culture.[107]

This arrangement demonstrates the importance the Turkish government put on the ECoC label itself, irrespective of any tangible benefits it may or may not have received. It is clear, therefore, that it was not economic benefit that was obtained from Turkey's acceptance into the EcoC, but instead cultural and symbolic capital that reproduces the symbolic violence of Europe perceived as having a natural dominance over, as Stuart Hall would put it, the 'rest'.[108] Istanbul's application to the ECoC illustrates the immense cultural capital of merely possessing this distinction by stating, 'in cultural and in artistic terms it will be worth its weight in gold to the world as a European Capital of Culture'.[109] A few pages thereafter the application reads, 'The

European Capital of Culture programme is Istanbul's greatest undertaking to date, creating a platform that will generate discussions of new administrative models . . .'[110]

To further complicate this attempt at 'Europeanness', Carola Hein explores how the ECoC year simply took already planned and programmed artistic events in Istanbul and branded them as an 'EU brand and marketing opportunity'.[111] Furthermore, Hall shows how the notion of 'the West' is not based on geography, but instead is a result of the confluence of social, political and economic power.[112] With respect to Hall's point, it is clear that Turkey can be accepted by some as culturally 'Western', but not politically so, as the consistent failure of the EU accession process described above has demonstrated. This divide reveals the limits to Turkey's 'acceptance' into the global hegemonic concept of 'the West'. In 2002, for instance, French president Giscard d'Estaing predicted the fall of the European Union if Turkey were to be admitted.[113]

The European othering of Turkey has roots in its older discourse on the Ottoman Empire, and thus epitomises Edward Said's definition of 'Orientalism'. Specifically, Said challenges this line of orientalist writing in the works of Ottoman historian, Bernard Lewis. Said famously stated that Lewis' writings are 'steeped in the "authority" of the field . . . [his] work purports to be liberal objective scholarship but is in reality very close to propaganda *against* his subject material'.[114] Lewis' article 'Some Reflections on the Decline of the Ottoman Empire' fits well with Bourdieu's concept of symbolic violence where a sense of naturalness is believed to undergird the claim of Ottoman deterioration and decline due to technological backwardness. He uses Europe as the legitimate cultural vanguard, arguing that if the Ottomans had used Western tactics then it would have put them on a better or 'right path'.[115] Similarly, as is well known, Samuel Huntington's controversial work on 'The Clash of Civilizations' was based on Lewis' work and reinforces the binary of 'East' and 'West'.[116] These dynamics are clearly at the heart of Western European resistance towards Turkish attempts to fit into contemporary European identity or to position Ottoman cultural identity as part of European heritage.

In addition, even though the adoption of Istanbul as ECoC represents a normative acceptance of, and at least a temporary acceptance of Turkey into, the West, the orientalist division between 'East' and 'West' can be observed in the rationale for accepting Istanbul as an ECoC in the first place. According to the ECoC report, the city was thought to lack in cultural and creative industries: 'So the motivation centered on establishing Istanbul as a centre for the creation and exhibition of modern and contemporary culture.'[117] This statement implies the Eurocentric trope of the West as better and that its eastern counterparts suffer from being 'under-developed' and presumably lacking in 'modern and contemporary culture'. ECoC status was meant to 'generate transformative energy and build capacity; restore cultural and industrial heritage; address the urban and cultural dimensions of citizenship; function as a bridge connecting Europe to its East'.[118] This outlines how a Western organisation will transform Istanbul for the better, and does not speak to any way in which Istanbul might be understood as actually helping Europe.

In this scenario the ECoC is acting as an institution that signals and dictates what constitutes a 'cultivated public', as Bourdieu would call it, which inculcates Eurocentrism as a natural and legitimate entity to control Turkish cultural production.[119] The ECoC can also be analysed using the Bourdieuian concept of symbolic domination, where this market for 'Europeanness' is based on economic and political institutions supporting this 'official' view of culture. For instance, the ECoC application states that Anatolia is a 'cradle of western civilization'.[120] The ECoC as symbolic domination shows that this market for 'Europeanness' is based on economic and political institutions supporting this 'official' view of culture.[121] Bourdieu's analysis of symbolic domination originally addressed 'official' forms of language, but it is clear that this analysis can be extended to what is considered 'official' forms of cultural heritage and cultural memory. Ella Shohat's work cautions against essentialisms that revolve around a 'hierarchical discourse of "West is best"'.[122] In her words: 'Eurocentric versions of transnationalism covertly assume a telos toward which "traditional" cultural practices are presumed to be evolving.'[123] In regard to the ECoC case, we can see how Turkey must use the same rhetoric to 'integrate' or 'evolve' to fit European social and cultural norms, and to demonstrate its supposed organic historical connection with them.

Given the symbolic violence of Europe as a cultural legitimator, it is therefore necessary to ask why the AKP would want to participate in this Eurocentrism? As Pierre Bourdieu expands our ideas of capital he outlines the concept of cultural capital as something which is an 'embodied capital, external wealth converted into an integral part of the person, into a habitus, [that] cannot be transmitted instantaneously'.[124] Social value is also key in determining if something is considered to possess cultural capital. Cultural capital is a key component of the ECoC. Even as the AKP sought to reconstruct Istanbul's cultural capital using its own neo-Ottomanism, at this time in its history it still earnestly sought to conform itself to the cultural capital of Western Europe. A sense of power is displayed when the ECoC selection committee chooses what city to designate with the symbolic capital of the distinction European Capital of Culture. This sense of symbolic capital actually starts well before the selection process: it starts with the Turkish application to the ECoC and how Turkey markets itself to fit within the parameters of the ECoC.

The Politics of Culture and Governmentality

A critical approach to the ECoC designation also reveals how the politicisation of culture in this process was used by the AKP as a tool of social control and governmentality, in other words, how it began to reflect the dynamics of Erdoğanian neo-Ottomanism. Chris Barker defines cultural politics as a way to legitimate certain objects and events to create 'official' versions of culture. Therefore, all cultural representations are intrinsically political.[125] The political structure of society creates legitimate practices for culture. Foucault's concept of governmentality reveals how the 'art of governance' or governmentality has developed in a Western context over the centuries. A shift from a rule by sovereignty is replaced by economic rule.[126] Economy becomes a tool for governance whereby economy and agency dictate one's decisions.[127] 'Governmentality' describes how a citizen can become self-governing through social control. The citizen has internalised being watched and their production of self and self-monitoring emulates this observance. Governmentality is based on neo-liberal ideas of choice and freedom. Ultimately, governmentality, through self-discipline, creates an efficient way for a state to monitor its populace because the populace ends up monitoring themselves.

The state's use of cultural politics to govern a people or the control mechanisms put in place by the state to direct and dictate 'cultural heritage' can therefore be understood as a form of governmentality. In the case of the ECoC, this was accomplished through the Ministry of Tourism and Culture and the state's funding of the ECoC programming in Istanbul. In regard to the case of the Istanbul 2010 European Capital of Culture, the institutions involved in controlling the cultural capital exhibited, performed and displayed during that year were the pan-European organisation of European Capital of Culture as well as the Turkish government, as it was the main economic contributor for the year-long event (as described above). This nexus of power clearly shows the interlinkage of politics and culture in the case of the ECoC of Istanbul. Through the surveillance organisations that control taste and culture, a specific reading of a nation-state's cultural heritage is constructed as the official version of cultural memory. Istanbul's application for the ECoC began with five letters of support from Turkish and Istanbul-specific politicians as a legitimation tool for the application. One letter in particular by Prime Minister Recep Tayyip Erdoğan illustrates perfectly the interlinkage of politics and culture, where he states: 'Given that Turkey is a candidate State destined to join the European Union, Istanbul's designation as a European Capital of Culture will further the European political project, the European values, and the sense of European belonging.'[128]

In addition, the project of bettering Turkey from the perspective of civil society in the ECoC application reveals neoliberal rhetoric that Wendy Brown points to in her analysis of 'neoliberal governmentality'. According to Brown, this rhetoric creates an ideology based on market rationality while at the same time utilising democratic vocabulary.[129] In economic terms neoliberalism is tied to 'restructuring' finances of generally Third World countries to meet the demands of NAFTA-like plans or World Bank policies that aim at free trade and free market mentalities.[130] Istanbul's preparations for its status as ECoC can be viewed as a neoliberal restructuring of the cultural capital within Istanbul. In the case of Istanbul, the ECOC neoliberal governmentality is creating and 'extending and disseminating market values to all institutions and social action', in this case, revolving around the marketing and execution of 'cultural heritage' in Istanbul.[131] The normative claims of the ECoC being 'good' for civil society, while at the same time being a tourist revenue-generating project therefore result in a specifically neoliberal project of governmentality.

After the ECoC programming was completed, evaluations of the AKP's policies with respect to its implementation were seen to have met with significant resistance that revealed the problematic dynamics of the AKP's neo-Ottoman manipulation and construction of public space in Istanbul. Ernst

& Young was hired to provide a report on the outcome of Istanbul during the ECoC year using computer-aided telephone interviews (CATI) of 4,323 Istanbul residents along with a survey of fifty-nine Istanbul Chamber of Commerce members and interviews with employees from all departments of the ECoC Istanbul Agency. They found that a number of issues arose that negatively affected the ECoC's image and actual events. Specifically, Ernst & Young suggested that provisions should have been made for venues opened during the ECoC, local authorities should have actively involved local residents in the decision-making process so as to reduce the power of the ECoC central management and, most importantly, to 'avoid giving reason for the public to assign a political character to the organizing agency. It should remain independent and work in the interests of the whole community.'[132]

This report illustrates the issues embedded in the AKP-centred planning of the ECoC and the fact that locals and outside reporting agencies found that the events were too political in nature and seemed to be serving a political agenda instead of being arts for art's sake. The report detailed that the €288.5 million budget was used to put on '1,598 concerts; 763 exhibitions; 336 books, periodicals and catalogs; 1,127 stage performances; 1,201 conferences, seminars and symposiums and 735 workshops. In addition, eight museums and cultural centers were opened.'[133] Yet Ernst & Young pointed out that following the conclusion of the programme these statistics were no longer available and that no one monitored the output and effects of the ECoC programme, which led to media scrutiny of the ECoC Agency and the AKP regarding how this money was used and the outcome of its use.[134]

In another follow-up report done by the European Capital of Culture commission, Istanbul was rated and given poor marks because of the control the government exerted over the artistic process:

An executive body 'Istanbul 2010 European Capital of Culture Agency' was set up by law in 2007 to implement the ECoC programme. This agency enjoyed the strong political and financial commitment of the national government, as well as a significant degree of autonomy at least at the outset. Whilst the agency was successful in implementing a very extensive cultural programme and marketing campaign, certain features of the governance arrangements proved problematic and led to the overall impact of the ECoC being less than anticipated; as the government became the supplier of 95% of the funding, the state bodies exert increasing control over the ECoC to the frustration of the independent cultural operators, several of whom resigned their positions within the agency in 2009; the method of allocating and accounting for funding tended to follow conventional government procedures with the emphasis placed on accountability and value for money, which proved particularly problematic when applied to many of the cultural activities; the disbanding of the Artistic Committee hindered the pursuit of a single, coherent artistic vision and tended to discourage co-ordination across different strands of activity; the absence of a clear artistic vision also resulted in weak co-ordination between the cultural programme and the marketing campaign, with the latter not tending specifically to promote the former.[135]

This statement by the review of the ECoC revealed a heavy-handed, government controlled approach towards cultural heritage and cultural capital on the part of the AKP. Rather than empowering local artists and businesses, Istanbul's designation as ECoC became an opportunity for Erdoğan and AKP officials to be able to market and construct Istanbul's cultural identity in accordance with their own vision of neo-Ottoman identity.

Tensions and Ambiguities at the Beginning of Erdoğanian Neo-Ottomanism

This chapter has employed Bourdieu's concepts of cultural and symbolic capital to describe the designation of Istanbul as ECoC. From a cultural studies perspective, art and culture are intimately intertwined with politics. This chapter has therefore unpacked how the ideological basis of the ECoC process constitutes a form of Eurocentrism that employs both externally imposed orientalism and internalised orientalism. It also shows that the ECoC acted as a catalyst for the Sulukule gentrification project. The 'Ottoman style' townhouses that were built upon the Romani community are an example of the physical changes in the Turkish-built environment wrought by the AKP's neo-Ottomanism. The middle- to upper-middle class townhouses were built to benefit the Islamic bourgeoisie, while the original Romani inhabitants were displaced to TOKİ apartments on the periphery of the city centre.

The Sulukule project came at the beginning of the AKP's development of its distinctive vision neo-Ottomanism, what we have called 'Erdoğanian neo-Ottomanism', which in this case cleansed the city centre of Istanbul of 'devalued' cultures (the Roma community) and replaced them with an Otto-man-style townhouse-community that signified the cultural capital of the Islamic bourgeoise. The designation of Istanbul as ECoC caused a reorien-tation of the construction of the city's cultural heritage to look towards the Ottoman past through art and architectural events during 2010 which were to be on display for the international tourist. Yet in preparation for the ECoC, the Fatih municipality destroyed one of Istanbul's most historic neighbour-hoods, the Roma neighbourhood in Sulukule.

This lived experience of homogenising the city to create a specific architec-tural public sphere to greet international tourists stands in direct opposition to the multiculturalist discourses of the ECoC application, but is reinforced by the neo-Ottoman vision of Istanbul. As the ECoC application demon-strates, one of the distinguishing features of Erdoğanian neo-Ottomanism at this stage was the gap between its utilisation of multiculturalist rhetoric and its actual implementation of homogenising policies. This tendency to homogenise the Turkish public sphere through manipulations of the built environment that promote an ethnically Turkish, Sunni Muslim Ottoman identity is evidenced by the Sulukule gentrification project and the program-ming agenda in the official ECoC application. At the same time, the cultural capital from the AKP's rebranding of Istanbul attempts to present to the international community a view of Istanbul that programmes its Ottoman past while still claims that Istanbul's core identity is European. Ironically, then, the ECoC vision of Istanbul constitutes a form of Eurocentrism at the same time that it transforms the city into an open-air museum that displays the cultural heritage and cultural capital valued by the AKP's Erdoğanian neo-Otomanism.

Notes

1. This chapter has been adapted and revised from Dorroll, 'The Spatial Politics of Turkey's Justice and Development Party (AK Party)'.
2. For an overview of these changes, see Ahmad, *The Making of Modern Turkey*, 77–9; Ergun Ozbudun, 'The Nature of the Kemalist Political Regime', in Ergun Ozbudun and Ali Kazancigil (eds), *Ataturk: Founder of a Modern State* (London: Archon Press, 1982), 79–192.

3. Edel Hughes, *Turkey's Accession to the European Union: The Politics of Exclusion?* (New York: Routledge, 2011), 22. For a summary of key dates in the Turkish Republic's history of foreign policy relations with the EEC and then EU, see Özgül Erdemli, 'Chronology: Turkey's Relations with the EU', in Ali Çarkoğlu and Barry Rubin (eds), *Turkey and the European Union: Domestic Politics, Economic Integration and International Dynamics* (London: Frank Cass, 2003), 4–7.

4. Hughes, *Turkey's Accession to the European Union*, 23–6; Beken Saatçioglu, 'Turkey–EU Relations from the 1960s to 2010: A Critical Overview', in Belgin Akçay and Bahri Yılmaz (eds), *Turkey's Accession to the European Union: Political and Economic Challenges* (Lanham, MD: Lexington Books, 2012), 10–11.

5. Hughes, *Turkey's Accession to the European Union*, 26–30; Saatçioglu, 'Turkey–EU Relations from the 1960s to 2010', 12–16.

6. William Hale, 'Human Rights, the European Union and the Turkish Accession Process', in Ali Çarkoğlu and Barry Rubin (eds), *Turkey and the European Union: Domestic Politics, Economic Integration and International Dynamics* (London: Frank Cass, 2003), 103.

7. Ali Çarkoğlu, 'Who Wants Full Membership? Characteristics of Turkish Public Support for EU Membership', in Ali Çarkoğlu and Barry Rubin (eds), *Turkey and the European Union: Domestic Politics, Economic Integration and International Dynamics* (London: Frank Cass, 2003), 163, 176. The only major political party's voters who were majority opposed to EU membership was the far-right Islamist party, the Felicity Party (Saadet Partisi).

8. Çiğdem Nas, 'Europeanisation of Identity: The Case of the Rebuffed Candidate', in Çiğdem Nas and Yonca Özer (eds), *Turkey and the European Union: Processes of Europeanisation* (New York: Routledge, 2012), 34.

9. Nas, 'Europeanisation of Identity', 25.

10. Hughes, *Turkey's Accession to the European Union*, 119–47; Nas, 'Europeanisation of Identity', 36, 40.

11. Ayşe Banu Bıçakçı, 'Branding the City through Culture: Istanbul, European Capital of Culture, 2010', *International Journal of Human Sciences* 9:1 (2015), 994.

12. Fieldnotes from 2010 by Courtney Dorroll.

13. European Commission, 'European Capitals of Culture', available at: https://culture.ec.europa.eu/policies/culture-in-cities-and-regions/european-capitals-of-culture, last accessed 24 June 2022.

14. Kiran Klaus Patel (ed.), *The Cultural Politics of Europe: European Capitals of Culture and European Union since the 1980s* (London: Taylor & Francis, 2013), 3.

15. Banu Karaca, 'Europeanisation from the Margins? Istanbul's Cultural Capital Initiative and the Formation of European Cultural Policies', in Kiran Klaus Patel (ed.), *The Cultural Politics of Europe: European Capitals of Culture and European Union since the 1980s* (London: Taylor & Francis, 2013), 157–8.

16. Deniz Göktürk, Levent Soysal and İpek Tureli, 'Introduction: Orienting Istanbul: Cutlural Captial of Europe?' in Deniz Göktürk, Levent Soysal and İpek Tureli (eds), *Orienting Istanbul: Cultural Captial of Europe?* (London: Routledge, 2010), 13–14.

17. Verchihan Ziflioğu, 'Istanbul Tired of Oriental Viewpoints and Debates', *Hurriyet Daily News*, 22 January, 2010.

18. Ziflioğu, 'Istanbul'.

19. Hatice Ahsen Utku, 'İstanbul Concludes European Capital of Culture Stint with Achievements, Disputes', *Today's Zaman*, 2 January 2011.

20. Meryem Ilayda Altas, 'Atatürk Cultural Centre, Part of Istanbul's Essence, Reopens', *Daily Sabah*, 21 October, 2021, available at: https://www.dailysabah. com/arts/ataturk-cultural-center-part-of-istanbuls-essence-reopens/news, last accessed 26 July 2022.

21. Ernst & Young, *Istanbul 2010 European Capital of Culture Impact Assessment Report* (2011), 78–9.

22. Eda Beyazıt and Yasemin Tosun, 'Evaluating Istanbul in the Process of European Capital of Culture 2010', 42nd ISoCaRP Congress (2006), 10.

23. Turgay Koramaz and Elif Kisar-Koramaz, 'ECoC Istanbul: "A Commodity" for Consumers or "a Source" for All Citizens', *European Network on Housing Research* (2011), 1.

24. Koramaz and Kisar-Koramaz, 'ECoC Istanbul', 3.

25. Koramaz and Kisar-Koramaz, 'ECoC Istanbul', 9.

26. Zeynep Gunay, 'Conservation versus Regeneration?: Case of European Capital of Culture 2010 Istanbul', *European Planning Studies* 18:8 (2010), 1175.

27. Gunay, 'Conservation versus Regeneration?' 1184.

28. TOKİ houses are social housing projects that target low- and middle-income Turkish citizens that cannot afford housing.

29. Pelin Turgut, 'Constantinople's Gypsies Not Welcome in Istanbul', *Time*, 9 June, 2008, available at: http://content.time.com/time/world/article/0,8599, 1812905,00.html, last accessed 14 July 2022.

30. Pelin Pınar Ozden, 'An Opportunity Missed in Tourism-led Regeneration: Sulu-kule', *WIT Transactions on Ecology and the Environment: Sustainable Tourism III* 115 (2008), 141–52; Evrim Ülke Uysal, 'An Urban Social Movement Challenging Urban Regeneration: The Case of Sulukule, Istanbul', *Cities* 29 (2012), 14.

31. Uysal, 'An Urban Social Movement', 14.
32. Hacer Foggo, 'The Sulukule Affair: Roma Against Expropriation', *Roma Rights Quarterly* 4 (2007), 43.
33. *Sulukule UNESCO Report*, Sulukule Platform (Istanbul, 2008), available at: http://inuraistanbul2009.files.wordpress.com/2009/06/sulukule-unesco-report-xx.pdf, last accessed 26 July 2022, 6.
34. İpek Emeksiz, 'Istanbul's UNESCO Spot Still under Risk', *Hurriyet Daily News* 18 July 2010.
35. Funda Gençoğlu-Onbaşı, 'The Romani Opening in Turkey: Antidiscrimination?' *Turkish Studies* 13:4 (2012), 599.
36. Ayhan Simsek, 'Turkey's Kurdish Opening', *Deutsche Welle*, 19 November 2013.
37. Gençoğlu-Onbaşı, 'The Romani Opening', 604.
38. Gençoğlu-Onbaşı, 'The Romani Opening', 603.
39. Gençoğlu-Onbaşı, 'The Romani Opening', 604.
40. Quoted in Gençoğlu-Onbaşı, 'The Romani Opening', 605; Serkan Ocak, "Dokuz Sekizlik Roman Açılımı," *Radikal* 15 March, 2010.
41. Gençoğlu-Onbaşı, 'The Romani Opening', 605.
42. Gençoğlu-Onbaşı, 'The Romani Opening', 605; Ocak, "Dokuz Sekizlik."
43. Hülya Demir and Ahmet Yilmaz, 'Measurement of Urban Transformation Project Success Using the Analytic Hierarchy Process: Sulukule and Tepeüstü-Ayazma Case Studies, Istanbul', *Journal of Urban Planning and Development* June (2012), 176.
44. Rolien Hoyng, 'Place Brands, Nonbrands, Tags and Queries: The Networks of Urban Activism in the Creative City Istanbul', *Cultural Studies* 28:3 (2014), 514.
45. Kadri Gürsel, 'Crackdown Shatters AKP "Anti-corruption" Taboo', *Al-Monitor*, 19 December 2013, available at: https://www.al-monitor.com/originals/2013/12/corruption-crackdown-damages-akp.html, last accessed 14 July 2022.
46. Gürsel, 'Crackdown'.
47. Aslı Tunç, 'In Quest for Democracy: Internet Freedom and Politics in Contemporary Turkey', in Banu Akdenizli (ed.), *Digital Transformations in Turkey: Current Perspectives in Communication Studies* (Lanham, MD: Lexington Books, 2015), 195.
48. Gürsel, 'Crackdown'.
49. 'A whistleblower's Graft Tale: Losing Faith in Fatih', *Hürriyet Daily News*, 2013, available at: https://www.hurriyetdailynews.com/opinion/emre-deliveli/a-whistleblowers-graft-tale-losing-faith-in-fatih-59854, last accessed 15 July 2022.
50. Gürsel, 'Crackdown'.

51. 'Environment Minister Bayraktar Announces Resignation, Calls on PM Erdoğan to Quit', *Hürriyet Daily News*, 25 December 2013, available at: https://www.hurriyetdailynews.com/environment-minister-bayraktar-announces-resignation-calls-on-pm-erdogan-to-quit-60118, last accessed 15 July 2022.

52. 'Ertuğrul Günay: Bütün yüksek yapılar Başbakan'ın onayıyla inşa edildi', *T24*, 31 December 2013, available at: https://t24.com.tr/haber/ertugrul-gunay-butun-yuksek-yapilar-basbakanin-onayiyla-insa-edildi,247286, last accessed 15 July 2022.

53. Aslı Iğsız, 'From Alliance of Civilizations to Branding the Nation: Turkish Studies, Image Wars and Politics of Comparison in an Age of Neoliberalism', *Turkish Studies* 15:4 (2014): 694, 697.

54. ECoC Application (Istanbul), 'Candidate for 2010 European Capital of Culture: Istanbul: A City of the Four Elements', 2006, 11.

55. James Rampton, Nick McAteeer, Neringa Mozuraityte, Márta Levai and Selen Akçalı, 'Ex-post Evaluation of European Capitals of Culture: Final Report for the European Commission General Directorate for Education and Culture', Ecorys UK Ltd, August 2011, 5, available at: https://culture.ec.europa.eu/sites/default/files/files/capitals-culture-2010-report_en.pdf, last accessed 14 July 2022.

56. ECoC Application (Istanbul), 139.

57. ECoC Application (Istanbul), 51.

58. ECoC Application (Istanbul), 52.

59. Rampton et al., 'Ex-post Evaluation', vi.

60. European Commission, 'European Capitals of Culture'.

61. ECoC Application (Istanbul), 45.

62. Sakıp Sabancı Müzesi, 'Behind the Exhibition, *From Byzantion to Istanbul: 8000 Years of a Capital: Legendary Istanbul*', available at: https://www.sakipsabancimuzesi.org/en/exhibitions-and-events/online/16643, last accessed 15 July 2022.

63. Sakıp Sabancı Müzesi, 'Behind the Exhibition'.

64. Sakıp Sabancı Müzesi, 'Behind the Exhibition'.

65. Sakıp Sabancı Müzesi, 'Behind the Exhibition'.

66. Sakıp Sabancı Müzesi, 'Legendary Istanbul; Prof. Dr. Mehmet Özdoğan & Dr. Nazan Ölçer', available at: https://www.youtube.com/watch?v=hhgVsEpArrk, last accessed 15 July 2022; Sakıp Sabancı Müzesi, 'Efsane İstanbul Konuşmaları; Dr. Brigitte Pitarakis & Dr. Nazan Ölçer', available at: https://www.youtube.com/watch?v=hhgVsEpArrk, last accessed 15 July 2022.

67. Çağatay Anadol and Doğan Kuban, *From Byzantion to Istanbul:8000 Years of a Capital*, 5 June–4 September 2010 (Istanbul: Sabanci University, Sakip Sabanci Museum).

68. Sakıp Sabancı Müzesi, 'Behind the Exhibition'.
69. ECoC Application (Istanbul), 64.
70. Damon Syson, 'Istanbul Contrast Exhibition of Work by Dice Kayek', *Wallpaper**, 10 August 2010, available at: https://www.wallpaper.com/fashion/istanbul-contrast-exhibition-of-work-by-dice-kayek, last accessed 15 July 2022.
71. ECoC Application (Istanbul), 67.
72. 'Istanbul International Puppet Festival', *Istanbulview*, available at: https://www.istanbulview.com/istanbul-international-puppet-festival, last accessed 15 July 2022.
73. 'Istanbul International Puppet Festival'.
74. 'Istanbul International Puppet Festival'.
75. ECoC Application (Istanbul), 70.
76. ECoC Application (Istanbul), 23.
77. ECoC Application (Istanbul), 27.
78. ECoC Application (Istanbul), 36.
79. ECoC Application (Istanbul), 40.
80. ECoC Application (Istanbul), 40.
81. Rampton et al., 'Ex-post Evaluation', 78–9.
82. Rampton et al., 'Ex-post Evaluation', 78–9.
83. Rampton et al., 'Ex-post Evaluation', 78–9.
84. Wendy M. K. Shaw, *Possessors and Possessed: Museums, Archaeology, and the Visualization of History in the Late Ottoman Empire* (Berkeley: University of California Press, 2003), 2.
85. Shaw, *Possessors and Possessed*, 9–10.
86. Shaw, *Possessors and Possessed*, 31.
87. Shaw, *Possessors and Possessed*, 28.
88. Shaw, *Possessors and Possessed*, 18–21.
89. Shaw, *Possessors and Possessed*, 24.
90. Shaw, *Possessors and Possessed*, 24.
91. ECoC Application (Istanbul), 46.
92. Alev Çınar, 'National History as a Contested Site: The Conquest of Istanbul and Islamist Negotiations of the Nation', *Comparative Studies in Society and History* 43:2 (2001): 365.
93. Çınar, 'National History', 373.
94. Çınar, 'National History', 387.
95. Esra Özyürek, *Nostalgia for the Modern: State Secularism and Everyday Politics in Turkey* (Durham, NC: Duke University Press, 2006), 176.

96. Kimberly Hart, 'Weaving Modernity, Commercializing Carpets: Collective Memory and Contested Tradition in Örselli Village', in Esra Özyürek (ed.), *The Politics of Public Memory in Turkey* (Syracuse, NY: Syracuse University Press, 2007), 30.
97. Aslı Iğsız, 'Palimpsests of Multiculturalism and Museumization of Culture: Greco-Turkish Population Exchange Museum as an Istanbul 2010 European Capital of Culture Project', *Comparative Studies of South Asia, Africa, and the Middle East* 35:2 (2015): 326.
98. Iğsız, 'Palimpsests of Multiculturalism', 326.
99. ECoC Application (Istanbul), 54.
100. ECoC Application (Istanbul), 36.
101. Nancy Fraser, 'Rethinking Recognition', *New Left Review* 3 (2000): 108.
102. Liisa Malkki, 'National Geographic: The Rooting of Peoples and the Territorialization of National Identity among Scholars and Refugees', *Cultural Anthropology* 7:1 (1992), 27.
103. Malkki, 'National Geographic', 30.
104. Malkki, 'National Geographic', 36.
105. Göktürk, Soysal and Türeli, 'Introduction', 2–3.
106. Rampton et al., 'Ex-post Evaluation', 70–1.
107. ECoC Application (Istanbul), 179.
108. Stuart Hall, 'The West and the Rest: Discourse and Power', in Stuart Hall and Bram Gieben (eds), *Formations of Modernity* (Cambridge: Polity Press, 1992), 279.
109. ECoC Application (Istanbul), 23.
110. ECoC Application (Istanbul), 31.
111. Carolina Hein, 'The European Capital of Culture Programme and Istanbul 2010', in Deniz Göktürk, Levent Soysal and İpek Türeli (eds), *Orienting Istanbul: Cultural Capital of Europe?* (New York: Routledge, 2010), 264.
112. Hall, 'The West and the Rest', 277.
113. Göktürk, Soysal and Türeli, 'Introduction', 5.
114. Edward Said, *Orientalism* (New York: Random House, 1994), 316.
115. Bernard Lewis, 'Some Reflections on the Decline of the Ottoman Empire', *Studia Islamica* 9 (1958), 126.
116. Samuel P. Huntington, 'The Clash of Civilizations?' *Foreign Affairs* 73:3 (1993), 22–49.
117. Ex-post Evaluation (Istanbul), 67.
118. Ex-post Evaluation (Istanbul), 67.

119. Bourdieu, *The Field of Cultural Production*, 123.

120. Ex-post Evaluation (Istanbul), 61.

121. Pierre Bourdieu, *Language and Symbolic Power*, trans. Geno Raymond and Matthew Adamson (Cambridge: Polity Press, 1991), 50.

122. Ella Shohat, *Taboo Memories, Diasporic Voices* (Durham, NC: Duke University Press, 2006), 12.

123. Shohat, *Taboo Memories*, 15.

124. Pierre Bourdieu, 'The Forms of Capital', in John G. Richardson (ed.), *Handbook of Theory and Research for the Sociology of Education* (Westport, CT: Greenwood Press, 1986), 248.

125. Chris Barker, *The SAGE Dictionary of Cultural Studies* (Thousand Oaks, CA: Sage, 2004), 41.

126. Michel Foucault, 'Governmentality', in Aradhana Sharma and Akhil Gupta (eds), *Anthropology of the State: A Reader* (Oxford: Blackwell, 2006), 136.

127. Foucault, 'Governmentality', 140.

128. ECoC Application (Istanbul), 11.

129. Wendy Brown, *Edgework: Critical Essays on Knowledge and Politics* (Princeton, NJ: Princeton University Press, 2005), 49.

130. Brown, *Edgework*, 38.

131. Brown, *Edgework*, 40.

132. Ernst & Young, *Impact Assessment Report*, 59.

133. Ernst & Young, *Impact Assessment Report*, 55.

134. Ernst & Young, *Impact Assessment Report*, 55.

135. Rampton et al., 'Ex-post Evaluation', vii.

3

GEZI PARK, 2013: PROTESTING AND RESISTING THE AKP

Summary Background and Context: The Gezi Park Protest Movement

The largest public demonstration against AKP governance emerged during the late spring and early summer of 2013 in the middle of Istanbul at Gezi Park, an historic public green space in Taksim Square in the heart of Beyoğlu, the district of the city that has since the late Ottoman Empire been closely associated with Western European-oriented politics and culture. This area of Istanbul has since it was first constructed in the nineteenth century been central to a variety of identities considered threatening to conservative Islamic politics. At the time of its first development in the nineteenth century, it was the centre of Western-facing commerce and banking and the hub of a revival of non-Muslim (especially Greek Orthodox) cultural and economic prosperity; in the early days of the republic it was seen as a centre of the secularist classes who supported the Kemalist revolution; and in the years leading up to 2013 Gezi Park itself was a haven for the LGBTIQ community of the city.[1] The square has also contained prominent public monuments to these identities, including the massive Greek Orthodox Church of the Holy Trinity (completed in 1880), the Republic Monument (built in 1928) featuring two bronze statues of Atatürk, and the iconic modernist building of the Atatürk Culture Centre (built in 1969, renovated in 1978, demolished in 2018, and reconstructed in 2021).[2]

Figure 3.1 Gezi Park, July 2013. Photograph C. Dorroll.

The AKP government of the Istanbul municipality had for many years prior developed plans to destroy the park and replace it with a commercial space modelled after the Ottoman barracks that once existed on the site.[3] In 2009, the AKP government proposed a redevelopment plan for Taksim Square which included demolition of Gezi Park, and the plan was approved by the Istanbul municipality in 2011. Throughout 2012, local professional and community organisations united to oppose the plan, coalescing around a movement formed for this purpose called Taksim Solidarity (Taksim Dayanışması). The key demand of the movement was simple: to preserve the park and what it represented in the history of the city, and in particular to save it from commercialisation and retain its status as a public green space.[4] In late May 2013, some fifty environmentalist protestors physically occupied the park in order to prevent the destruction of its trees, and beginning on 27 May Turkish police violently evicted the protestors using water cannons, tear gas and pepper spray. Erdoğan himself quickly drew attention to the events as a moment where he resolutely refused to give in to opposition to his demands.[5]

Over the next few weeks, protestors assembled in massive numbers in Taksim Square and in urban areas around the country, uniting around a shared resistance (*direniş*) to Erdoğan's authoritarian style of governance and his recently proclaimed goal of transforming Turkish society via the cultivation of a 'pious generation' (*dindar nesil*) that would replace the kind of secular social classes previously dominant in Turkish society, and symbolised in Istanbul public space by Taksim Square.[6] The AKP's agenda and rhetoric in the years leading up to the protests had indicated a turn towards the forceful imposition of conservative morality in the public square, including restrictions on alcohol sales, the promotion of conservative gender roles and the stigmatisation of LGBTIQ identities.[7] From late May to June, some 2.5–3 million people in sevnty-nine of Turkey's eighty-one city municipalities protested in public in support of the Gezi movement. Over the course of the protests, some 10,000 protestors were wounded, 11 people (including a police officer in Adana) were killed, and some 900 protestors were detained.[8] The events profoundly polarised public opinion, and even produced one of the first public splits in AKP leadership. President Abdullah Gül called for restraint, including on the part of the police response, and personally announced in July that the development plans that would have destroyed the park had been cancelled.[9] In contrast, Prime Minister Erdoğan distinguished himself within his own party for taking a consistently hard-line and dismissive attitude towards the protestors' demands and towards the protestors themselves, famously dismissing them as 'looters' (*çapulcular*), claiming they were the manifestation of shadowy conspiracies against him and his constituents and that they did not represent the 'real Turkey'.[10]

Research on the protestors and their demands has shown that they consistently focused on the desire for 'freedom' (*özgürlük*). This meant in particular the freedom to live and express a diversity of lifestyles and identities threatened by AKP authoritarianism; and to create bonds of solidarity and community across multiple identities in order to transcend national/ethnic, gender, class and religious divides.[11] Well-educated youth in urban areas formed the core of the movement, which came to encompass such diverse ideological perspectives as environmentalists, secular Kemalists, leftists, labour and workers' rights activists, LGBTIQ rights activists, Alevi and Kurdish rights activists, devout Muslims opposed to AKP policies, and even football ultras.[12]

What united these groups was the concern that their perspectives and ways of life were being legally targeted by AKP authoritarianism, leading to a utopian political discourse of solidarity and freedom that focused on the right to live as one chooses alongside others who choose to live differently. As Susannah Verney, Anna Bosco and Senem Aydın-Düzgit aptly put it, the Gezi protests represented a reaction against a new style of AKP governance under Erdoğan that abandoned the party's initial commitments to human rights reform, and now instead exhibited 'a disdain for compromise, consensual politics and deliberation; a majoritarian understanding of democracy; a hierarchical and non-inclusive leadership; and a growing appetite to regulate private lives'.[13] In other words, the Gezi movement attempted to embody a pluralist and cosmopolitan form of Turkish national identity that was being threatened by the social vision of the AKP.

Though Gezi Park itself remains, subsequent events have served to vindicate the protestors' concern for Taksim Square and the authoritarian nature of the AKP crackdown on their movement. In 2021, a massive new mosque built on Taksim Square was opened, fulfilling a promise that Erdoğan had first made when campaigning for mayor of Istanbul in 1994.[14] In a deeply tragic end to the AKP's repression of the Gezi movement, one of the leading public backers of the movement, the philanthropist Osman Kavala was sentenced on 25 April 2022 to life in prison without parole for his support of the Gezi movement, on charges that his support for the Gezi movement amounted to sedition against the Turkish state. Seven other defendants were also sentenced to eighteen years in prison each.[15] The trial and verdict were widely seen in Turkey as the AKP's final judgement on Gezi and what it represented. Erdoğan publicly lauded the verdict, saying of Kavala: 'This man was the behind-the-scenes coordinator of the Gezi events, and our judiciary made its final decision on him.'[16]

This chapter explores the Gezi movement as a response to the AKP-led attempts to reshape the urban landscape in accordance with Erdoğanian neo-Ottomanism. Ultimately, the AKP's manipulation of the built environment does not constitute a sincere concern for the preservation of the Ottoman architectural heritage, but instead selectively exploits elements of it in order to create a constructed vision of the Ottoman past that is used in service of AKP policies, including their neoliberal economic interests. This chapter argues that at Gezi a *protest* public sphere formed to critically oppose Erdoğanian neo-Ottomanism's manipulation of the public sphere. Participant observation at Gezi Park and survey research of respondents at Boğaziçi University in Istanbul associated with or opposed to the protests will reveal the ways in which the Gezi Park incident dramatically exposed the disconnect between moralising social narratives of AKP policies and the AKP's exploitation of the built environment, a connection that constitutes the spatial politics of the AKP. As described above, Gezi Park was a public space created by secular Turkish nationalists and symbolised that identity's presence and prominence in the public sphere. Once the protests became a globally recognised symbol of opposition to AKP governance, as well as a space associated with plurality and difference, Gezi Park became a space that could not be re-appropriated and utilised by the AKP to further its own social and political agenda.

Finally, this chapter will explore the fraught relationship that the Gezi movement has with the past public space that it successfully occupied, which had become a haven for secular Turkish identities because it had decades beforehand seen the forcible displacement of non-Turks at the hands of secular Turkish nationalism. The Gezi movement therefore became a moment where the spatial politics of the AKP under Erdoğanian neo-Ottomanism met with resistance in the very public sphere they were seeking to dominate and manipulate. As will be described below, because the 'spirit of Gezi' represented a cosmopolitan, non-nationalist option for contemporary Turkish identity, it was seen as threatening and forcibly repressed by the AKP. Moreover, Gezi's cosmopolitanism can be interpreted as echoing the cosmopolitanism that had once existed in Taksim and surrounding neighbourhoods, shedding light on how in this same public space in Istanbul, cosmopolitan possibilities for Turkish identity have been repressed throughout the history of the republic – first in the past by secular Turkish nationalism, and then in the present by conservative religious Turkish nationalism under the AKP.

Critical Voices of the Protest Public Sphere

The protests of Gezi Park act as voices of what can be understood as the *protest* public sphere. The *architectural* public sphere that has been refashioned by the hegemonic AKP is directly being questioned by those involved in the protests. Gezi Park illustrates the uniting of various subaltern publics (anti-capitalist Muslims, Kurds, LGBTIQ individuals and Kemalists) to form a protest public sphere on the grounds of Gezi Park; when the park was banned and barricaded by Turkish police, the protests continued to be staged on Taksim Square and other parks throughout Turkey. This concept of the protest public sphere emerges from theoretical work that is critical of Habermas, such as Michael Warner and Nancy Fraser. Warner argued that the bourgeois public sphere theorised by Habermas creates a 'utopian universality' that only truly pertained to and was open to the white, literate male who owned property.[17] Our use of the concept of architectural public sphere shows that this public was constructed for the AKP Islamic bourgeoisie. As described in the first chapter, Nancy Fraser argued that multiple public spheres with varying power dynamics in fact exist, and this insight can be used to understand the significance of Gezi Park as an act of public resistance, forming a protest public sphere As Fraser states:

> Moreover, not only were there always a plurality of competing publics but the relations between bourgeois publics and other publics were always conflictual. Virtually from the beginning, counterpublics contested the exclusionary norms of the bourgeois public, elaborating alternative styles of political behavior and alternative norms of public speech. Bourgeois publics, in turn, excoriated these alternatives and deliberately sought to block broader participation.[18]

Our argument in this chapter is therefore that though the top-down architectural public sphere is dominated by those in power and does shape public space, it is not the *only* public sphere in existence. The protest public sphere at Gezi Park stands as a counter to the hegemonic urban plans of the AKP.

Telling the Story of Gezi Park

C. Dorroll started her research in Istanbul in mid-June 2013. Given the core significance of young people and students at the protests, as outlined above, C. Dorroll interviewed faculty, students and staff at the prominent Istanbul university, Boğaziçi University, about Gezi Park.[19] One particular interviewee described the initial days of the Gezi Park protests as having a 'festival like atmosphere'. Asked if there were any specific urban planning projects associated with the protests, they answered 'Turning the park into an army barracks and then a mall.'[20] When asked where they got most of their information regarding Gezi Park they replied:

> Mostly Facebook but with links to newspaper articles, blogs, etc. The 1st week of the protests all of the information came from Facebook and the first few days the information was all from people there and pictures they took. Later

on newspapers, blogs and the news stations started more coverage . . . Some of the news here was full of propaganda and bias toward Tayip's view. But some covered it relatively objectively.[21]

They went on to raise the issue of the polarising media coverage of Gezi Park:

. . . [The domestic news coverage was] angering. The lies and spin some of the news stations used was/is much like what happened in *1984*. For example, a nanny here on our campus, who only gets news from the biased news stations has a totally different view on what has happened. Tayip did a great job of controlling certain news stations and using it to his advantage. It is pretty scary actually.[22]

One interviewee was a former Boğaziçi undergraduate who was back on campus that summer and who had been part of the Gezi Park movement and intellectual conversations regarding the anti-capitalist movement in Turkey. This person was a Master's degree student in the sociology department of an American university, but was in Istanbul doing research that summer. This student described the Gezi Park protests as a real turning point in Turkish history. A critical mass of differing groups rallied together against the oppressive social policies of the AKP and the use of the police to brutalise protesters. These groups included, but were not limited to, LGBTIQ rights groups, anti-capitalist Muslims, Kurds, leftists, socialists and Kemalists. According to this student, the Gezi Park protests were not an issue that could be reduced to the conventional dichotomies of Turkish political debate, such as a secular–religious divide or a clash of ethnic nationalisms. They instead described how the protests transitioned from environmentalist activism to a broader demand for 'democracy'.[23]

As with the respondent above, Gezi Park has been informally labelled by some as having a 'festival atmosphere', especially with respect to the last few days in May before the brutal police efforts used to disperse the protestors. The first three days of the initial protest consisted of only a small group of young environmentalists protesting the destruction of one of Istanbul's last significant green spaces. The protesters set up tents and book areas for children. The atmosphere of the initial days was not unlike a small-scale carnival. People were milling around and clustered together in small groups. Even as the protests grew in numbers, the daylight hours still felt like a festival. Under the bright blue summer sky, people came to stand in the foreground to Gezi Park. It was difficult to distinguish between the protesters and the bystanders looking at the activities. During the day police stood about the protesters but were not known to unleash pepper spray or pressurised water. Perhaps this was because the area before Gezi was a popular shopping district and was usually full of tourists. There were people walking through the crowd of protesters, many performing the 'standing man' (*duran adam*) protest that consisted of silently standing still in one spot for hours on end in Taksim Square, the area directly before the then closed off Gezi Park. This act of protest was initiated by performance artist Erdem Gündüz, who on 17 June stood for 8 hours in the middle of Taksim Square facing the Turkish flag and the visage of Atatürk hanging on the Atatürk Culture Centre.[24] At the same time, there were opportunistic merchants in the Taksim area selling water, flags, tear-gas masks and light foods. Occasionally small groups would break out in chants that spread their individual agenda throughout the crowd.

Many of the protesters were also well-known performance artists, and this became clear to C. Dorroll during her visits to Taksim Square. There were numerous individuals dressed in provocative ways, such as artists dressed as justice, and others keeping watch over small memorials to protestors who had died in the clashes with police. One felt the presence of the hundreds of police officers and dozens of police vehicles (including numerous crowd-control armoured police vehicles, known as TOMA) surrounding the square. En route to Gezi Park one would see hundreds of police officers in Beşiktaş sleeping on the grass or in decommissioned public buses. The police officers were waiting until the early evening hours when the water cannons and tear gas would be unleashed on the protesters and the police in their riot gear would take action. It was at these times when the festival atmosphere eroded into mass chaos of protesters running into side streets and trying to go into hotels and restaurants. The attempts of the state to take control of the public sphere were extremely palpable to C. Dorroll during her observational research stints at the protest – luckily she did not have the misfortune to be caught up in acts of police brutality.

In the months following the protests, Judith Butler presented her thoughts on Gezi Park at Boğaziçi University on 6 September 2013. Her speech was titled 'Freedom of Assembly or Who Are the People?' She began by not directly referencing Gezi Park, but towards the end of the speech was reported to say 'Every claim we make to the public sphere is haunted by the prisons . . . Privatization and the prison work together to keep you out of the places where you know that you belong to each other.'[25] She was referring to the detention of and threat of detention to protesters, doctors, lawyers, human rights workers and journalists. Butler was speaking on the importance of the freedom of assembly and the importance of maintaining public spheres and not having them privatised. These comments were particularly salient to C. Dorroll, as they recalled the feelings she had seeing the heavy police presence at Taksim Square. It became clear to her that the AKP's efforts to control this corner of Istanbul's built environment and this section of Turkish public space had special resonance within their political objectives. This chapter explores these connections, asking why the AKP government responded with brutally to the protests? What made this particular building project so necessary to defend? The answer lies in their use of spatial politics. A challenge to their manipulation of the built environment in Istanbul translated into a challenge to their moral vision in general.

Gezi Park and the Gezi Movement

The Gezi Park protests began on 27–28 May 2013 with the occupation of the small green space known as Gezi Park, centrally located in the Taksim district of Istanbul.[26] Located behind a transportation hub and bus circle in Taksim Square, Gezi Park attracted little day to day attention until it became a site of protest. The park was originally constructed as part of the modernising city planning of Henri Prost.[27] Prost was commissioned in 1936 to redesign the city of Istanbul in accordance with modern, Western city planning, and one of the most famous remnants of this incomplete project is the green space now known as Gezi Park.

Originally named İnönü Esplanade (İnönü Gezisi), after the second president of the Republic of Turkey, Gezi Park was constructed on the former site of the Taksim Artillery Barracks. The barracks were originally constructed in 1808 as part of the military reforms of Selim III.[28] The barracks featured a wide area originally used as a military practice ground; however, as the Taksim district became more associated with entertainment and nightlife (as it remains today), this open arena enclosed within the walls of the barracks was used as a football field for major Turkish league matches.[29] The enclosure was used for this purpose from 1921 until its demolition began on 25 March 1940. Although the entirety of Prost's plan for the area left over after demolition of the barracks was never implemented, İnönü Esplanade, now known as Gezi Park, was completed on the site shortly after the demolition. It features a mix of stone pedestrian walkways shaded by rows of trees and rectangular areas of grass. The park was featured in the Victory Day celebrations of 30 August 1942, in fulfilment of its original design as a modernised space to represent the secularised and modernised values of the new Turkish Republic.[30]

It is interesting to note here this important role that the park played in its initial construction. As with all the rest of the Prost plans, it was intended to showcase the modern values of the secular Turkish Republic. It represented a kind of secular republican spatial politics forcibly rejecting the remains of the Ottoman past; the barracks were notable for their distinctively 'Islamic' architecture. As Birge Yıldırım puts it, in order to create 'the new secular spatial arrangement of the city the Islamic oriented Ottoman past was rejected.'[31] Prost's focus on public squares and wide avenues mainly suited for automobile transportation disrupted pre-modern and Ottoman patterns of public space. His designs were some of the most powerful examples of the assertion of early Turkish republican dominance over Ottoman cultural heritage (reflecting the general history described in the first chapter of this book).

The construction of the park resulted in collateral damage of another kind: the destruction of the multi-ethnic associations with the neighbourhood. As part of the general demolition for the new park, the centuries-old Surp Agop Armenian Cemetery was destroyed; this cemetery had in fact been gifted to the Armenian community of Istanbul by Sultan Süleyman the Magnificent (r. 1520–66). After a protracted legal battle in the 1930s, the cemetery was expropriated and destroyed to make room for development projects.[32] Gravestones that were not recovered by Armenians themselves became part of the stone foundation of Eminönü Square across the Golden Horn in the historical peninsula of Istanbul. They were also used to build the steps of Gezi Park.[33] Thirteen of these gravestones were actually uncovered during the protests, and became a rallying point for activism in support of Armenian rights. They spurred conversations among the Turkish activists themselves about Turkey's multi-ethnic heritage.[34]

On 31 October 2012, the city government announced the Taksim Pedestrianisation Project (Taksim Yayalaştırma Projesi), a redevelopment project for Taksim Square. On 8 November, the mayor of Istanbul Kadir Topbaş clarified that this project would include the destruction of Gezi Park and the rebuilding of the Ottoman barracks to be used as a shopping complex (AVM-alişveriş merkezi).[35] The initial protests were organised to oppose this project. Opponents of the project argued that it was yet another example of how neoliberal economic interests took precedence over environmental concerns or historic preservation in AKP-controlled areas whenever this was necessary.[36] The proposed design for the new complex would have completely disregarded the cosmopolitan eclecticism of the architectural style of the Ottoman barracks that had once stood there, which was designed by the renowned Ottoman royal architect, Armenian Krikor Balyan, and combined elements of 'Ottoman, Indian and "Moorish" design'.[37]

The first protests consisted of an occupation of the park by a small group of environmental activists in the group Taksim Solidarity (Taksim Dayanışması), beginning on 27–28 May 2013. This group of activists constructed tents and ad hoc living arrangements in the park in order to prevent destruction of the green space.[38] One of the participants in C. Dorroll's interviews claimed to have been present at this initial occupation. He remarked that 'on [the first day of the occupation], there were probably 1,000 people there, max. People set up tents and the event was only in Gezi park.'[39] The initial tent occupation featured a carnivalesque environment that served as a group of people going against the AKP-led urban renewal projects.

Taksim Solidarity was a movement created in 2012 to oppose the AKP's redevelopment plans in Taksim Square. Taksim Solidarity was formed by environmentalists and those that were part of the Turkish Chamber of Architects and Engineers (or TMMOB), the professional organisation that had authority over key elements of city planning and urban development. Chamber representative Mücella Yapıcı served as the spokesperson for Taksim Solidarity, and was detained by police between 8 July and 11 July 2013.[40] The Chamber of Architects also played a key role in the initial court case that temporarily halted the destruction of the park.[41] Here we see that the protests possessed both informal elements (the tent city and massive accumulation of protesters that took to the streets) and also formal elements (the Chamber of Architects going to court in order to stop the destruction of the park). In the aftermath of the protests, however, the Chamber of Architects attracted the wrath of the AKP government for its role in organising the protests. In a midnight session of parliament on 9 July 2013, the Chamber was stripped of its powers in municipal planning. According to the new law, 'the Ministry of Environment and Urban Planning will be "responsible for all the decisions related to the approval of urban projects, which were supervised by related chambers"'.[42] The Chamber's president, Mehmet Soğancı, quickly issued a statement declaring the move 'unconstitutional'.[43] On 10 July 2013, Chamber members demonstrated outside the parliament building, where they laid a black wreath that read: 'Resist, TMMOB: Turkey is with you'.[44]

What began as a small environmentalist and small interest group protest through an occupation of Gezi Park quickly became a much wider national movement after police moved in to brutally disperse the protestors and images of police brutality were shared rapidly on social media, which mobilised public protest movements around the country. On 28 May 2013, riot police attempted to disperse the peaceful protestors by force, using tear gas.[45] This incident produced the famous image of 'the woman in red', a young female protestor in a red dress being sprayed directly in the face with tear gas by a police officer.[46] After crowds returned in the following days, on 30 May 2013, police raided the park at dawn, burning down protestor tents. By this time, the police's treatment of the peaceful protestors had attracted wide attention and condemnation outside Taksim Square, and an estimated 10,000 people protested in Gezi Park that evening.[47]

At dawn on 31 May 2013, police again raided the park, using water cannon and tear gas to disperse the few hundred protestors gathered there. By 8 pm on the same day, an estimated 100,000 protestors had entered the neighbourhoods around Taksim, as the protests at Gezi Park became a national phenomenon.[48] Between 1 and 15 June 2013, Taksim Square and the surrounding Beyoğlu district became the scene of regular (and sometimes violent) clashes between the police and protestors, as demonstrators from all over the city attempted to defend the park from police encroachment. The last remaining occupiers of Gezi Park were removed from the park on 15 June 2013, after which Gezi activists created informal evening gatherings and conferences to discuss the future of the movement.[49] Police formed a perimeter around the park, preventing any future occupation of, or protest on, that site. Public acts of protests in Taksim continued, however, with the 'standing man' protests described above. Protestors repeated this form of protest throughout the succeeding days in Taksim Square and across the city, often stopping to stand in silence in front of any Turkish flag.

The Gezi protests also produced a new constellation of political slogans and discourse aimed at expressing the new 'spirit of Gezi' that challenged hegemonic nationalist and sectarian concepts. Protestors united around the slogan 'Diren!' (Resist!), using it as a major point of reference on Twitter, Facebook and other social media (which played a crucial role in the spread of the protests).[50] The Gezi protestors also appropriated terminology that Erdoğan used against them, calling them 'looters' (*çapulcu*).[51] The Gezi protestors used this term as a self-descriptive way to neutralise criticism projected at them. The identity markers of 'diren' and 'çapulcu' therefore became one of the primary ways to identify pro-Gezi viewpoints and participants.

Gezi Park protests carried different meanings for different social, political and ethnic groups, all with differing agendas. Different social groups imbued Gezi Park with distinctive meanings. For those protesting the AKP and who supported Gezi, Gezi Park exemplified a symbol of resistance, representing a celebration of difference, plurality and cosmopolitanism in the face of AKP social and political hegemony. For those that opposed the protesters, Gezi Park was an example of foreign intervention into Turkish domestic affairs. For some, the space would have remained utopian and festival-like, had the police not been brutal. Others saw the protests as an annoyance, a disturbance to the efforts of 'reform' by the AKP.

'A Movement of Diversities' and the 'Spirit of Gezi': Pro-Gezi Analyses of the Events

As described above, based on studies conducted at the protests by Turkish think tanks and researchers, it is possible to elaborate a reasonably accurate picture of the political leanings of the protestors and their demographic profile. The protestors tended to be young and relatively well educated; according to KONDA's interviews with 4,411 protestors between 6 June and 7 June 2013,

56 per cent had completed and undergraduate or MA degree, and the average age of the protestors was twenty-eight.[52] It is clear from other studies, such as that undertaken by the GENAR research group, that most protestors occupied the political left.[53] While the specific party affiliations of the protestors varied, it was clear that the protests were very anti-AKP.

The political allegiances and agendas of the protestors were far more complicated than a simple tendency towards the left, however. United against AKP social policies, once disparate interest groups came together in ways that created the incipient forms of social organisation and political identity in contemporary Turkey. This combination of interests was perhaps the most significant effect of the protests in general. Gezi Park represented for many a 'moment' of utopian pluralism and democracy yearned for by many of those opposed to the AKP's vision of society. As Yael Navaro-Yashin puts it, 'While the Turkish government wanted to break or re-orient memory, something unexpected took place instead. Spontaneously, and in the space of Gezi Park, that very site where the government had laid its eyes and channelled its interests, a social formation emerged, a movement of diversities.'[54] Put in the terms of our analysis, a protest public sphere emerged in the exact space of, and explicit opposition to, the AKP's attempts to construct a hegemonic public sphere.

The participation of various groups in the protests broke down long-standing barriers among different social groups in Turkish politics and society. Again, in the words of Navaro-Yashin, 'These protests have not allowed themselves to be placed in any known frameworks of analysis such as secularism versus Islam, modernists versus traditionalists, liberals versus conservatives, the bourgeoisie versus the working classes, left versus right, cosmopolitans versus nationalists, feminists versus sexist men, gay-rights activists versus homophobes.'[55] The protests, as Banu Karaca notes, through their varied entities that came together to protest the AKP, an expansion of sorts occurred within the political discourse in Turkey. Through the use of humour and irony they 'suspended the limits of what had been deemed legitimately sayable'.[56] Different groups were coming together and working together for the first time in Turkish history for a common goal, protesting the AKP urban renewal projects. It also broadened the discourse in each of these groups to be aware and inclusive of groups they might have previously seen as the 'other'.

Opposition to the AKP did not, in most cases, take the form of an anti-religious movement. The organisers of the events framed their resistance to the AKP in terms of resistance to moral policing and oppression, not as resistance to Islam itself. This means that, as Ateş Altınordu argues, 'to see the protests through the secular-vs.-religious framework is to overlook the complexity of what is actually going on'.[57] In an effort to prove that their grievances with the AKP government were not targeted at their fellow citizens who are pious Muslims, the protestors took several steps to show signs of respect for Muslim practices. On 4 June 2013, protest organisers announced that no alcohol should be consumed on the site of the protest in order to show respect for the Islamic holiday that day, Miraç Kandili, the commemoration of Muhammad's journey to heaven. Protestors also gave out traditional holiday sweets to those present to commemorate the holiday.[58]

Protestors associated with the Turkish Anti-Capitalist Muslims movement held *iftar* (fast-breaking dinners) during Ramadan in mid-July 2013.[59] This small but vocal movement, led by the opposition Muslim intellectual İhsan Eliaçık, represented the presence among the protestors of devout Muslims who objected to AKP rule on strictly religious grounds. Other protestors playfully appropriated traditional symbols of Turkish Islam, such as imagery associated with the great medieval Sufi poet Mevlana Jalal al-Din Rumi. The image of one protestor dressed in a black robe and a gas mask dancing the whirling dervish sema ritual, in imitation of the Mevlevi order but wearing a black robe instead of a white one, became a symbol of the blurring of the boundary between the secular and the religious in the protestors' performance of resistance.[60]

One internet meme, for instance, referenced a famous quote attributed to Rumi that invited everyone, whoever they were, to come to mystical prayer and experience closeness with God. Rumi's famous message of inclusivity was rewritten to read: 'Actually, I've thought a lot about it, Tayyip: Don't come!'[61] The respect for religion among non-religious groups has been demonstrated by widespread support for the freedom to wear the headscarf. The environment of Gezi showcases this new dynamic: 'a transformation is . . . taking place in the relationship between secular and religious citizens who together protest the authoritarian policies of the government and the violent practices of the police'.[62] At Gezi Park possibilities emerged for a new Turkish public sphere that demands the inclusion of the religious and non-religious and 'mutual respect for each other's freedoms'.[63]

C. Dorroll's personal interviews confirmed that pro-Gezi university students and personnel also described Gezi Park as a unique event in Turkish political history, describing it as a paradigmatic moment of social pluralism and cosmopolitanism. One protestor revealed that they had been planning to leave the country due to dissatisfaction with the trajectory of the current government; however, they decided to stay because 'the "spirit of Gezi" brought the good news that a large group of people had woken up. Now I have hope.'[64] The same interviewee specifically emphasised the capacity of the protests to unite previously divided political groups: 'people [at Gezi] set aside political allegiances for a single allegiance, they became a people with a single body'. Other interviewees made the same point. In the words of one interviewee, Gezi Park 'turned into a protest that expressed the complaints of people from every section of the opposition to the current government in power'.[65] The same respondent also made it clear that they were personally 'apolitical'.

Some interviewees even attempted to elaborate a new way of describing themselves that went beyond previously exclusivist categories of identity. One interviewee answered the question 'What is your nationality?' by remarking: 'neither Turk nor Kurd – Türkiye'.[66] This deliberately inclusive and cosmopolitan response represents a significant attempt to elaborate a Turkish identity that is free of ethnic categories, and was highly typical of Gezi discourse. This attempt to imagine a Turkish identity beyond hegemonic nationalist categories was a major feature of the ideological thrust of the protestors as a whole. In the words of another interviewee, because of Gezi Park, 'Everyone has now a story to tell.'[67] The protests enabled the possibility of a multiplicity of narratives of Turkish selfhood. The same interviewee also explicitly resisted being categorised as a particular nationality, remarking instead that they were Alevi, thereby using a religious marker of identity over that of a national marker of identity.

C. Dorroll's interviews also revealed that protests mobilised members of the Turkish electorate that were previously not motivated to engage in political action. One interviewee, like the individual mentioned above, described this as 'a kind of awakening' for this section of the apolitical population: 'I see these protests as a kind of awakening in that people who have never participated in demonstrations or took to the streets joined this . . . event.'[68] One interviewee actually described themselves in exactly these terms. In response to the question, 'Have the protests affected your life?' they responded by saying: 'Yes, definitely. My eyes were opened ☺ I was like an apolitical, careless person; now I'm much more interested in politics.'[69] Another interviewee remarked that 'these protests showed the power of (Turkey's youth) being able to be organized and that that the youth are not passive'.[70]

'They Are Being Used as the Cat's Paw of Foreign Countries': Anti-Gezi Analyses of the Events

Opponents of the Gezi Park protests centred their critique on the destructive behaviour of some of the protestors, the ideological leanings of the protestors, and the assertion that the protestors were wittingly or unwittingly serving the interests of foreign powers. Many pro-AKP commentators argued in essence that the protests began with good intentions but got out of hand and were infiltrated by elements hostile to Turkish interests. Other less generous pro-AKP critics alleged that the protests were a planned coup all along, and therefore had nothing to do with democratic self-expression. However, it is unclear where the line is drawn and what distinguished the 'initially legitimate protests' in contrast to the demonstrations that followed that were said to be destructive. Critics seem to have associated the entirety of the later protests (i.e., after roughly 31 May or 1 June 2013) with the destructive acts of some of the demonstrators. Critics also rejected the assertion of some protestors that they were defending themselves against what has been widely acknowledged as police brutality.

Writing in *Insight Turkey*, Tahir Abbas argued that 'the initial environmentalist protests were quickly superseded by the motivations of wider interest groups, which had specific anti-state motivations'.[71] Abbas acknowledged that the initial protests where inflamed by 'the [government's] mishandling of the initial resistance to the razing of Gezi Park'.[72] While Abbas' acknowledgement of mistakes on the part of the Turkish security authorities has been widely accepted, other commentators have been more inclined to view the protests as an unnecessary eruption of violence and disruption at best, and a planned attack on Turkish democracy at worst. Hatem Ete argued that the events at Gezi were characterised by 'the transformation of the democratic dissent of the first few days into the desire of ousting a democratically elected government'.[73] She argued that 'the Gezi protests can be defined as political events that began spontaneously with the aim of voicing certain demands in the public sphere, but which were soon hijacked by multiple internal and external actors with various motivations, and thus turned into an anti-AKP and anti-Erdoğan rally'.[74] As Atilla Yayla remarked, 'Having failed to outlaw the party in 2008, the [Kemalist] establishment would now attempt to succeed through street violence.'[75] Again, this line of criticism is somewhat unclear: it is difficult to understand what is meant when it is asserted that the Kemalist opposition to the AKP constitutes the 'establishment' since it had been out of power for over a decade during the eleven-year dominance of the AKP in the Turkish government.

Anti-Gezi commentators also question the interpretation that Gezi Park was a site of the de-politicisation of hegemonic Turkish nationalist identities and a space for genuine pluralism and the creation of an inclusive public sphere. They argue that anti-religious sentiment was in fact central to the protestors' motivations and that the protestors were manifestations of a deeply elitist Kemalist identity. Many anti-Gezi commentators have alleged that the protestors desecrated religious buildings and attacked religious individuals. In Yayla's words, 'protestors harassed devout Muslims, especially women, in many isolated events'.[76] Again, this criticism remains unclear: what exactly is the significance of events to the total identity of the protestors if they are admittedly 'isolated'?

According to anti-Gezi commentators, the protestors were not on the side of universally democratic values but rather were instead foot soldiers of the Kemalist elite who, eclipsed by the rise of the AKP, have lost their power. According to Ete, 'What the leftist liberals actually mean when they speak of democratization is that they want to be afforded privileged status in the new system.'[77] Ali Murat Yel and Alparslan Nas argued that the protestors 'were oriented around the politicization of Kemalist or Islamophobic impulses among the middle and upper-middle classes'.[78] Criticisms of the Gezi Park movement allege that democracy and pluralism were not really at issue at all, but that these terms were used as a cover for militantly secularist Kemalist agitation on the part of the upper classes. In contrast to the activists themselves, critics of Gezi do not see the movement as a moment of pluralism and the dismantling of political barriers. In fact, in the minds of anti-Gezi commentators, the protests represented just the opposite. They were instead the most radical reification and strengthening of the supposed Kemalist–Muslim divide in Turkey, with Kemalism understood here to be a militant secularism that is openly hostile to religion in all its forms and openly contemptuous of the religious lifestyle of the devoutly Muslim sectors of the Turkish population.

A number of C. Dorroll's interviewees who were anti-Gezi shared the assessment of these commentators. Those who were sympathetic to some of the aims of the protestors (but did not fully support the politics of the Gezi Park uprising) agreed that the initial protests had some merit, especially with respect to the outrage over police brutality. But these interviewees then argued that the protests were hijacked by extremist elements that had more sinister motives. These elements, in their view, aimed to destabilise Turkey or even serve the interests of foreign powers. In the words of one interviewee, 'At the beginning, [the protests were] a correct action but later on [were] ideological.'[79]

Other interviewees alleged that the international media sowed divisiveness and misinformation among the Turkish people for their own gain. As one interviewee put it, 'The media is misleading people and by doing so is inciting the people. And this is exactly what other countries want. They are the reason for the internal confusion. The goal is to weaken Turkey. And people are for this reason being used as a cat's paw.'[80] The same interviewee argued that the protests had nothing to do with environmentalism, but instead were due to 'the incitement of outside countries. It's a pointless protest.'

Another interviewee made the same assertion, arguing that the Gezi Park protestors 'are being used as the cat's paw of foreign countries'.[81] Another interviewee alleged that the Gezi protestors were actually composed of secularist nationalists attempting to thwart the democratic process in Turkey. They argued that the protestors were composed of Kemalist nationalists who had lost power under the AKP and were attempting to secure their previous hegemonic role.[82] They could not achieve a military coup, and so they instead turned to the protest movement to try and force the prime minister out of office. This response is a particularly clear example of the narrative discussed above, that the protestors are really composed of disaffected nationalists trying to recover their previous place of dominance by using undemocratic means.

Spatial Politics of the AKP and the Gezi Protests

Our analysis focuses on the AKP's building projects as forms of spatial politics because the AKP closely connects these projects with its political and social goals. According to Hammond and Angell, 'One of the signal accomplishments of Erdoğan and the AKP over the past decade has been the way the party has used infrastructure projects . . . to both ground their political authority and to naturalize a particular project of generating value.'[83] Hammond and Angell show how the AKP has used public work projects to emphasise the success of the party. This is a project of reshaping the Turkish public sphere to reflect the AKP's economic policy, a plan to 'restructure Istanbul's urban space under neoliberal terms'.[84] As Heghnar Watenpaugh puts it, 'For an architectural historian, it is no accident that both the great plans to remake Taksim, as well as the way protestors' speeches and actions often invoke history and architectural memory to buttress their arguments in the present.'[85]

The AKP project is also founded on a specific act of remembering the Ottoman past to the exclusion of the Kemalist nation-state identity; it is a way to remember Turkish identity 'through the lens of a glorious [Ottoman] past'.[86] Tahir Abbas' analysis points to the role of Ottoman nostalgia in the AKP project, but we argue that the AKP's neo-Ottomanism is more than simply nostalgia; it compromises spatial and aesthetic components that are much more deliberate than simply a wistful appropriation of 'a glorious past'. We therefore argue that this appropriation is not based on a genuine appreciation for Ottoman heritage or historic preservation, but is instead a mechanism used by the AKP to assert their political legitimacy. This is what we mean by the spatial politics of the AKP: the AKP's appropriation of the Ottoman architectural legacy is a strategic and selective one, put to the service of their neoliberal economic policy and their need to construct an image of moral and cultural authenticity.

The protests at Gezi Park and the AKP's response to them were an important example of the dynamics of the spatial politics of the AKP. These events, like those discussed in other case studies in this book, reveal that AKP's manipulation of the built environment is not just an incidental manifestation of their political success or their economic might, but is more importantly a specific strategy of linking their moralising social policies with a neo-Ottoman architectural aesthetic: it connects the neo-Ottoman architectural imaginary with the moral imaginary of the AKP, and this connection constitutes what has been termed the 'spatial politics' of the AKP. In the hands of the AKP, architecture becomes more than simply an aesthetic experience or project. The manipulation of public space, and the repression of alternative configurations of public space such the Gezi movement, enact the moral and physical imaginary of the AKP's programme. The AKP's social vision is composed of a conservative programme of social values and loyal devotion to the paternalistic Turkish state, analogous to loyalty to the patriarchal family structure. Furthermore, this neo-Ottoman past actively forgets the multi-ethnic and multireligious aspects of Ottoman society. This neo-Ottoman imaginary combines a Sunni Turkish Muslim conception of the Ottoman past with the social conservatism and nationalist paternalism of the AKP.

Numerous commentators and scholars have discussed the attempts of the AKP to create a new narrative of Turkish nationhood and selfhood centred around a socially conservative moralised subjectivity. As Nilüfer Göle argues, 'New decrees and moralizing discourses have aroused the suspicion that government was intending to intervene in secular ways of life.'[87] These 'moralizing discourses' include statements on the part of the prime minister on the obligation of women to have children and the criticism of alcohol consumption, in addition to a now famous incident where a security personnel member at an Ankara subway station publicly chided a couple over the station's loudspeaker for kissing in public. AKP legislation that was announced just before the protests that would restrict alcohol sales and advertisement also played into the reaction against AKP moralising.[88] The socially conservative politics of the AKP were also on display in Erdoğan's patriarchal masculine persona, which he emphasised in his way of relating to the protestors and their demands.[89] Erdoğan's 'patriarchal authoritarian masculinity' can also be seen as one of the pillars of his success among some sectors of the Turkish electorate.[90]

The Gezi protests reveal the connection between the moralising politics of the AKP and the manipulation of the built environment in Turkey. The oppositional discourse of the protestors to the building projects in Gezi Park reveal their awareness of the AKP's use of architectural motifs and imaginaries to consolidate their control over Turkish social policy and their assertion of the dominance of their moral values in the Turkish public sphere. Gezi Park is one of the turning points in the history of the AKP's spatial politics because it clearly exposes the connection between the AKP's moralising social agenda and their understanding of neo-Ottoman cultural memory and cultural capital. The construction of the Ottoman barracks at Gezi Park is not simply a nostalgic harkening back to the Ottoman Empire; it is an assertion of the manifest superiority of the AKP's social values over the supposed degenerate secularism exemplified in the neighbourhood culture of Beyoğlu and Taksim.

The interviews that C. Dorroll conducted at Boğaziçi University demonstrate the link between the neo-Ottoman architectural imaginary of the AKP and its conservative moral imaginary. They therefore illustrate this book's argument for the existence of the spatialised political strategies of the AKP, a link that might otherwise have gone unnoticed were it not for the public voices of the protestors, the existence of which is a reaction to precisely the moralising dimensions of AKP politics and their building programme. This is why the Gezi Park protests combined protests against the destruction of the park with protests against the moralising conservative social policies of the AKP. This combined reaction reveals the link between these two components of AKP political action, a link that was felt so profoundly by disaffected members of the Turkish electorate that it touched off the largest popular movement in decades in Turkey.

Protestors used a range of discursive modes to signify their critique of the AKP's moralising politics. These ranged from accusations that the AKP government, and Prime Minister Erdoğan in particular, is dictatorial, to outright criticism of the AKP's attempt to impose a set of moral norms on the diverse Turkish populace. One Gezi supporter accused the AKP of 'making decisions on a whim' and described the Turkish people under the AKP as 'being governed with a mentality that is more divisive, more pressured, and more exploitative with each passing day'.[91] Another supporter argued that under the AKP a significant portion of the Turkish populace was placed in a subaltern position, or otherwise put, dismissed: 'People went to the protests to be listened to and to let their voices be heard. If their voices had been listened to, it would have not have affected Turkey this negatively.'[92] Another interviewee described one reason for the protests as 'Erdoğan's way of governance (authoritarian non-democratic).'[93] Another Gezi supporter described one of these reasons as 'the ever increasing authoritarian attitude of the PM [Prime Minister]'.[94]

The supporters of the Gezi protests that C. Dorroll interviewed focused even more intently on the moralising social politics of the AKP as the initial cause of the protests. A number of interviewees accused the AKP government of intrusion into the private affairs and lifestyles of citizens. When asked what they thought the main reasons for the protests were, one interviewee included in their response 'the intervention of the state [into the] private issues of citizens'.[95] Another made the very same point, citing the government's 'intervention into private issues'.[96] The same interviewee also pointed to the AKP's 'intolerance towards different lifestyles'. Another interviewee cited as reason for the protest 'the current government's not showing respect to any thinking other than their own, and not taking society into account'.[97] Another accused the AKP of 'behaviours that violate the boundaries of personal rights and freedoms'.[98]

One interviewee cited the alcohol restrictions as an example of the kind of actions that precipitated the protests.[99] Another summarised the approach of the AKP as 'imposing a sharia-based lifestyle'.[100] These responses reveal an important dimension of the Gezi Park protestors' objections to the AKP. They use the terminology 'lifestyle' and 'private life' to indicate the attempts of the government to insert their own moral agenda into the Turkish public sphere and to issue legislation that encourages a conservative Islamic lifestyle in opposition to the lifestyle of secular liberal classes. Their use of the term 'lifestyle' indicates the protestors' understanding that the politics of the AKP are aimed at the cultivation of a conservative moral subjectivity and public sphere. Their choice to make this criticism on the site of a future AKP neo-Ottoman building project indicates their acknowledgement of the connection between the moralistic policies of the AKP and their utilisation of architecture, the link that constitutes the spatial politics of the AKP. One interviewee made this connection explicit when they described the proposed neo-Ottoman barracks as a 'symbol' of the AKP's agenda; they further pointed out that the 'Gezi Protests were against these symbolic stances toward history'.[101]

One interviewee's lengthy but highly interesting response to the question about the main reasons for the Gezi Park protests summarises the moralising dimension of the AKP's politics:

Because Tayyıp has increasingly been trying to take away the 'Islam light [lite]' that makes Turkey a great place to live. It is a place where conservatives and liberals live peacefully together, but Tayyıp has put a wedge between that. Also, for years I thought he was an OK guy because I saw how he cleaned up Istanbul and kept it out of economic crisis but when he took away the outside seating at restaurants in Beyoğlu, I paused, then he put away one of my neighbour's husband and another's father away for conspiracy to overthrow the government (and also took away their rights as family men which means their families cannot see them) and I was concerned. Then he established the drinking laws and said people could go home after 10:00 and 'drink themselves to death' and I was angered and then the bullying and machismo at Gezi Park pushed me over the edge.[102]

This response is particularly illuminating on a number of levels. Its terminology alludes to the same dimension of lifestyle that other interviewees used, particularly the term 'Islam lite', which refers to a specific type of Islam that does not interfere in individuals' personal decisions about their day-to-day lives. It also implies that this form of lifestyle was a major component of Turkish society until the conservative social politics of the AKP. This response reveals the protestors' acknowledgement that the moralising social politics of the AKP were a deliberate shift away from a previous Turkish moral subjectivity. Further, this response connects the AKP's manipulation of the urban environment with their conservative moralising social policies. In the list of events that caused him to become anti-AKP, the interviewee connected Erdoğan's sudden ban on outdoor seating in certain parts of Istanbul with the alcohol restrictions instituted by his party.

In short, the Gezi protestors' discourse reveals and allows us to describe the connection between the AKP's social policies and the physical spaces that they build in order to help instantiate these policies. This discourse reveals the spatial politics of the AKP, which is the attempt by the AKP to utilise an architectural imaginary to enact their social and political agenda. For the AKP, architecture is not merely a demonstration of their political power success or their social values; it is in fact a means to turn the latter into a reality. The construction of a neo-Ottoman architectural public sphere corresponds with, and is meant to actually enable, the creation of a new Turkish moral subjectivity and public sphere.

The Denial of Cosmopolitan Pasts and Futures

As described above, the Gezi Park protest movement was a turning point in the history of the AKP's governance because it became the first main public site of protest against the AKP's spatial politics specifically, as it zeroed in on the AKP's attempts to manipulate the urban landscape as emblematic of its attempt to shape the whole of contemporary Turkish national identity to fit its conservative Sunni Muslim social vision. The Gezi movement therefore became an enduring symbol of resistance to Erdoğan's goal of transforming Turkish society to fit a homogeneous conception of conservative, Turkish Sunni Muslim identity. In even broader terms, the Gezi movement was understood by its participants (as illustrated above) as not simply an act of negative resistance to Erdoğan's AKP, but also the positive elaboration of vision of social pluralism that had been elusive throughout Turkey's modern nationalist history. The Gezi movement's occupation and attempted transformation of public space was meant to initiate a broader, and consciously unprecedented, transformation in Turkish society.

At the same time, the significance of the Gezi movement in the context of Istanbul's urban landscape can be fully understood only when set against the backdrop of the history of the urban spaces that it occupied. Taking into account this backdrop reveals how selective Erdoğan's vision of neo-Ottomanism is (a point that will only be further reinforced in the final two chapters of this book), and also reveals how urban space in this exact area was a site of contestation over Turkish national identity long before the Gezi movement emerged. As described above, the Gezi movement took place in the Taksim area, focusing on İstiklal Caddesi and the neighbourhoods immediately surrounding it. Approximately 100–150 years before, these exact areas were the centre of the most religiously plural areas of modern Istanbul. These same areas had been targeted decades before by secular Turkish nationalists because of the threat they posed to a homogeneous Turkish national identity. Since the middle of the nineteenth century, the public space of Gezi has, in fact, been the site of social visions and ways of life that homogenising Turkish nationalism (initially secular Kemalism, and now Erdoğanian neo-Ottomanism) has seen as threatening.

In the nineteenth century, the contemporary municipal district of Beyoğlu was known as Pera, when it formed an adjoining suburb of the historical centre of the city. Prior to the nineteenth century, the only neighbourhood in this area (which lies north of the old city across the Golden Horn) was Galata, an ancient district that had been inhabited by West European traders in the

Byzantine period. The centre of Istanbul, as it had been in Constantinople, remained in the walled old city of what is now the Fatih municipal district. However, in the nineteenth century Galata became the centre of the new international banking and business classes of the modern Ottoman economy (especially following the 1838 Anglo-Ottoman commercial treaty), leading to massive urban growth in the area and giving rise to an entirely new urban space that both economically and physically was oriented towards Western European models.[103] Pera quickly became highly diverse in religious and ethnic composition, including indigenous Muslim Turks, Armenian Orthodox Christians and Sephardic Jews. The largest group and the one that quickly came to dominate economic and social life of this new, westward-looking district were indigenous Greek Orthodox Christians, the non-Muslim population of the Ottoman Empire whose forbearers had once been the masters of the city when it was the Byzantine capital of Constantinople.

Drawn to the immense economic opportunity offered in the new district, Greek Orthodox Christians from elsewhere in Istanbul and around the empire migrated in large numbers to Pera (or Stravrodromi as it was and is known in Greek) throughout the nineteenth century, quickly establishing the district as the centre of not only Western-style reformist intellectual culture in general, but of the cultural and economic renaissance of the Ottoman Greek Orthodox in particular.[104] In 1804, the first Greek Orthodox church since the Byzantine period was built in Pera, the Church of the Presentation of the Virgin Mary of Stavrodromi (also known as the Church of the Panagia in Pera), and the monumental and well-known Church of the Holy Trinity that to this day towers over Taksim Square was completed in 1880 (Figure 3.2).[105] Greek schools, other churches and community institutions rapidly expanded throughout the district in the nineteenth century, which remained the centre of Greek life in the city into the early republican period. At the same time, the Ottoman government implemented several wide-ranging reforms between 1839 and 1876 (known as the Tanzimat, or 'reordering', period in Ottoman history) that guaranteed religious freedom and social equality for non-Muslims in the empire, also contributing to the revitalisation of Greek culture and prosperity in the city.[106]

At the same time, the experiences of Greek Orthodox Christians in Istanbul during this period were marked by a tense dual reality. At the same time that

Figure 3.2 Holy Trinity Greek Orthodox Church, Taksim Square, July 2013.
Photograph C. Dorroll.

they experienced remarkable social and economic advancement, they fell under
intense and often violent prejudice by the Ottoman authorities following the
Greek War of Independence in 1821–32, which led to the breaking away of
mainland Greece from the empire and the establishment of the independent
Kingdom of Greece in 1832.[107] On Easter Sunday, 1821 (10 April), the holiest
day of the year in the Orthodox community, Patriarch Gregory V (the ecclesiastical leader of all Orthodox in the Ottoman Empire) was hanged in public
by the Ottoman authorities in retaliation for the rebellion, despite the fact that
Gregory had been unequivocally and vocally pro-Ottoman from the beginning
of the war.[108] This event marked the beginning of modern Turkish prejudice and
violence against the indigenous Greek community, which (as will be described in
detail in the last chapter of this book) takes the form of persistent suspicion of
disloyalty and resulting collective punishment, discrimination and mass violence
against the Greek community.

For this reason, important scholars of this history such as Amy Mills, Nora
Fisher-Onar and İlay Romain Örs have offered important critiques on the

common nostalgia associated with inter-ethnic and inter-religious harmony in nineteenth-century 'Belle Époque' Istanbul. As Fisher-Onar notes, while nineteenth-century Pera certainly exhibited ideals of urban cosmopolitanism, such principles were clearly not always realised in practice, and their idealisation is often more reflective of contemporary neoliberal imaginaries than actual historical conditions.[109] As Romain Örs points out, such contemporary nostalgia both fails to account for how such a supposedly ideal social pluralism could have given rise to the violent nationalisms that destroyed it, and also fails to ask difficult questions about structural violence and discrimination that afflicts the present-day indigenous Greek community in Istanbul.[110] And as Mills notes: 'Although Istanbul's multicultural urban landscape conveys an image of the city's history as cosmopolitan, the implied harmony of this image is immediately fractured by any study of the contentious and violent making of the built environment itself.'[111]

At the same time, the lived reality of ethnic and religious pluralism in such areas of Istanbul as Pera/Beyoğlu offered, then and now, a vision of Turkish society whose cosmopolitan potential is intolerable to the social imaginary of homogenising Turkish nationalism. As Romain Örs puts it, the identity of the Greeks of Istanbul (as Greek-speakers and Orthodox Christians indigenous to the pluralist environment of the late Ottoman Empire and therefore neither to the ethnic nationalism of either modern Greece or Turkey) demonstrates 'that there is a wider cultural sense of "belonging" based on a cosmopolitan notion beyond the nation, which is overshadowed, impoverished, and often targeted by nationalist ideology'.[112] For this reason, manifestations of such pluralist or cosmopolitan visions, whether in historical Pera or at Gezi, have been targeted with violence by the nationalist state. In 1914, the population of Istanbul was approximately 900,000 people, and some 23 per cent were Istanbul Greeks, or over 200,000 people.[113] Today, no more than 2,500 members of this community survive, representing some 0.02 per cent of the city's population of about 15 million.[114] After the population exchange of 1923, the community was reduced to around 100,000 in the early republican period, when the Taksim area remained the centre of Greek life in the city.[115]

While the Taksim area of Istanbul was also the centre of Greek life in the late Ottoman Empire and the early republic, it was also the site of mass violence that dealt a fatal blow to this community's long-term survival in the nationalist republic. In late August 1955, rumours spread in Turkey that Greek Cypriots were planning to attack the Turkish minority on the island of Cyprus; the Turkish Prime Minister Adnan Menderes supported this rumour in the widely read newspaper *Hürriyet* on 25 August, even going as far as to threaten reprisals on the Greek community in Istanbul. On the afternoon of 6 September, Turkish state radio alleged that the historic home of Mustafa Kemal Atatürk in the Greek city of Thessaloniki had been bombed, and shortly thereafter massive crowds suddenly emerged throughout Istanbul that rapidly transformed into a pogrom targeting non-Muslim homes, businesses and property.[116] One of the largest staging areas for the rioters was Taksim Square.[117]

Throughout the night and early morning of 6 and 7 September 1955, rioters destroyed over 1,000 homes, over 4,000 shops, and dozens of pharmacies, factories, restaurants and other business; in addition to dozens of churches and schools owned by Greeks and other non-Muslims. Hundreds of women were raped, countless beaten and injured, and one priest – the ninety-year old Fr. Chrysanthos Mantas – was burned alive in Balıklı monastery; the bishop of Pamphilos was also murdered.[118] Taksim and other neighbourhoods in Beyoğlu were decimated, and appeared the next day as if they had been a war zone, though the rioters had avoided any property owned (or perceived to be owned) by Muslim Turks. Subsequent investigation confirmed that the violence had been organised by Turkish state actors, and that local police had been instructed to allow the violence to pass unchallenged. Menderes himself was later convicted of inciting the violence.[119]

The events of 1955 produced a feeling of fear and insecurity among indigenous Greeks and other non-Turkish Muslim minorities in the republic, and over the next few decades thousands more would be expelled by the Turkish government or forced to migrate due to extreme social hostility and discrimination.[120] The period between 1964 and 1974 in particular saw mass deportations of Greeks from Istanbul on various pretexts (such as the Greeks who were indigenous to Ottoman Istanbul and protected legal residents of the Turkish Republic, but who possessed Greek nationality because their ancestors lived in Ottoman-ruled mainland Greece before the Greek War of Independence).[121] In other words, beginning with the 1955 pogrom and in the decades that followed, the centre of cosmopolitan and pluralist social visions and histories within the urban landscape of Istanbul was violently dismantled by violence promoted by the nationalist Turkish state – a dynamic that would be echoed decades later at Gezi Park.

However, the Gezi movement's relationship with the past of the urban area that it inhabits is deeply ironic in a way that illuminates just how profound an impact the reshaping of urban and pubic space can have. It is true that the cosmopolitan and pluralist ideals of the Gezi movement centred in contemporary Beyoğlu echoed the non-nationalist and cosmopolitan lifestyle of the Greeks who once lived in this part of the city. Yet at the same time, as Romain Örs points out, the class of urban, secular, liberal Turks in Beyoğlu who formed the core of the Gezi movement often remain unaware that their residence in that neighbourhood was made possible by the fact that Greeks and other non-Turkish minorities were expelled from the country or forced to leave due to the fear of violence and discrimination in the wake of the 1955 pogrom.[122]

Ironically, therefore, while being passionately opposed to exclusionary nationalisms, the secular Turkish liberalism represented by the Gezi movement has been socially advantaged by the effect these nationalisms have had on the urban landscape of Istanbul. Indeed, as emphasised above, Taksim and the neighbourhoods immediately next to it (such as Gümüşsuyu and Talimhane, not to mention the neighbourhoods around İstiklal Caddesi) were up until this time known for being primarily upper-middle and upper-class Greek areas. Secular, liberal Turks moved into these areas in the 1980s and 1990s (when they came to be seen as newly fashionable places to live) by purchasing the now low-priced homes of Greeks who had fled Turkey or been forcibly expelled by the Turkish government in previous decades, often having their property taken by the state or having been forced to abandon it.[123]

Finally, considering the views of present-day indigenous Istanbul Greeks on the Gezi movement powerfully illustrates the pluralist and cosmopolitan potential of the movement, in spite of the deeply fraught history of the urban landscape of Taksim. As Özgür Kaymak discovered in her comprehensive ethnographic research on the life histories and contemporary experiences of non-Muslim minorities in Istanbul, support for the Gezi movement among these populations was very high, regardless of age group. Kaymak also notes that voting patterns of non-Muslims in Istanbul changed radically after Gezi. Prior to the Gezi protests, the majority of non-Muslim minorities in Istanbul had voted for the AKP, and had in fact voted for centre-right parties in the decades previously, due to their antipathy to the secular Kemalist Cumhuriyet Halk Partisi (CHP; Republican People's Party) that was associated with the Turkish nationalism that had so badly harmed their communities throughout the twentieth century. The democratising and liberalising message of the early AKP was also a cause for cautious optimism among these communities. After the crackdown at Gezi, however, these communities began to vote (if reluctantly) for leftist and liberal anti-AKP parties such as the CHP or the Halkların Demokratik Partisi (HDP; Democratic People's Party), as they considered the AKP's response to Gezi to indicate dangerous authoritarianism led by Erdoğan and his supporters.[124]

Anna Maria Beylunioğlu's important recent research has also shown that it was precisely the rise of the AKP's conservative Sunni Islamic nationalism in the wake of Gezi that altered minority populations' attitudes towards the AKP.[125] Meaningful steps towards reform in the discriminatory treatment of minorities by the Turkish state (including in property law) occurred during the first decade or so of AKP administration: 'However, the government's increasing emphasis on the superiority of Islamic values after the AKP's authoritarian turn in 2011 and the failure to cement a legal framework for religious freedom based on equality and human rights has placed a brake on the prospect of transformation.'[126] According to Beylunioğlu's insightful summary of the AKP's ideological shift in its attitude towards pluralism and cosmopolitanism, 'a particular selective blending of EU norms and Ottoman models has given way over time to a more chauvinistic approach implying the superiority of Islamic values'.[127] As she points out, the proposal to reconvert Hagia Sophia into a mosque also reinforced the nature of the AKP's ideological shift (as will be discussed in much greater detail in Chapter 5).[128]

The transformative potential of a pluralist and cosmopolitan vision at Gezi was felt strongly by many Istanbul Greeks who supported the movement, and it was precisely this potential that the AKP under Erdoğan saw as threatening to its neo-Ottoman social vision. Many non-Muslim participants in the Gezi protests described Gezi as a space where they did not experience the normal tension and discrimination to which they had become accustomed around ethnic Turks.[129] Younger generations of Istanbul Greeks in particular saw Gezi as a chance to 'claim the freedoms' rightfully owed to them, and older generations often supported the movement in spite of their traditional hesitance to participate publicly in politics or protest for fear of backlash.[130] The inspirational power found in the glimpse of another way of being a citizen of the Republic of Turkey that emerged, and was then destroyed, at Gezi is perhaps best summarised by the statement of a seventy-year-old Istanbul Greek woman: 'I saw heaven at Gezi.'[131]

Notes

1. Sinan Erensü and Ozan Karaman, 'The Work of a Few Trees: Gezi, Politics, and Space', *International Journal of Urban and Regional Research* 41:1 (2017): 27; Jeremy F. Walton, '"Everyday I'm *Çapulling!*": Global Flows and Local Frictions of Gezi', in Isabel David and Kumru F. Toktamış (eds), *'Everywhere Taksim': Sowing the Seeds for a New Turkey at Gezi* (Amsterdam: Amsterdam University Press, 2015), 46–50.

2. Walton, '"Everyday I'm *Çapulling!*"', 47–8; Timur Hammond, 'The Politics of Perspective: Subjects, Exhibits, and Spectacle in Taksim Square, Istanbul', *Urban Geography* 40:7 (2019), 1047–48.

3. Hayriye Özen, 'An Unfinished Grassroots Populism: The Gezi Park Protests in Turkey and their Aftermath', *South European Society and Politics* 20:4 (2015), 539–40;

4. Erensü and Karaman, 'The Work of a Few Trees', 27; Özen, 'An Unfinished Grassroots Populism', 540.

5. Özen, 'An Unfinished Grassroots Populism', 540.

6. Kaan Ağartan, 'Politics of the Square: Remembering Gezi Protests Five Years Later', *New Perspectives on Turkey* 58 (2018), 202. On Erdoğan's own description of this transformational vision beginning in the spring of 2013, see 'Dindar nesil yetiştireceğiz', *Yeni Şafak*, 28 February 2016; available at: https://www.yenisafak.com/gundem/dindar-nesil-yetistirecegiz-2424175, last accessed 15 June 2022.

7. Ağartan, 'Politics of the Square', 202; Philip Dorroll, *Islamic Theology in the Turkish Republic* (Edinburgh: Edinburgh University Press, 2021), 188–95.

8. Isabel David and Kumru F. Toktamış, 'Introduction: Gezi in Retrospect', in Isabel David and Kumru F. Toktamış (eds), *'Everywhere Taksim': Sowing the Seeds for a New Turkey at Gezi* (Amsterdam: Amsterdam University Press, 2015), 15, 20.

9. David and Toktamış, 'Introduction: Gezi in Retrospect', 15.

10. David and Toktamış, 'Introduction: Gezi in Retrospect', 15; Hammond, 'The Politics of Perspective', 1043.

11. Gülseli Baysu and Karen Phalet, 'Beyond Muslim Identity: Opinion-based Groups in the Gezi Park Protest', *Group Processes and Intergroup Relations* 20:3 (2017),

351, 361; Özen, 'An Unfinished Grassroots Populism', 541; Özden Melis Uluğ and Yasemin Gülsüm Acar, "Names Will Never Hurt Us": A Qualitative Exploration of Çapulcu Identity through the Eyes of Gezi Park Protestors', *British Journal of Social Psychology* 58 (2019): 720–3.

12. Ağartan, 'Politics of the Square', 202; Baysu and Phalet, 'Beyond Muslim Identity', 351; Erensü and Karaman, 'The Work of a Few Trees', 30.

13. Verney, Bosco and Aydın-Düzgit, 'The AKP on the Road to Presidentialism', 6.

14. 'Istanbul's Taksim Mosque Opens After Decades of Lgal Wrangling', *Daily Sabah*, 28 May 2021, available at: https://www.dailysabah.com/turkey/istanbul/istanbuls-taksim-mosque-opens-after-decades-of-legal-wrangling, last accessed 15 June 2022; Hammond, 'The Politics of Perspective', 1039–54.

15. 'Turkish Court Sentences Osman Kavala to Life in Prison', *Ahval*, 22 April 2022, available at: https://ahvalnews.com/turkey-democracy/turkish-court-sentences-osman-kavala-life-prison, last accessed 15 June 2022.

16. 'ECHR Ruling on Jailed Philanthropist Kavala No Longer Applies, says Erdoğan', *Ahval*, 28 April 2022, available at: https://ahvalnews.com/erdogan-kavala/echr-ruling-jailed-philanthropist-kavala-no-longer-applies-says-erdogan, last accessed 15 June, 2022.

17. Michael Warner, *Publics and Counterpublics*, 2nd edn (Brooklyn: Zone Books, 2002), 382.

18. Nancy Fraser, 'Rethinking the Public Sphere: A Contribution to the Critique of Actually Existing Democracy', *Social Text* 25/26 (1990), 61.

19. Where respondents and interlocutors used English, all responses have been recorded using the spelling, grammar, etc. exactly as they were spoken or written.

20. Ethnographic Interviews conducted at Boğaziçi University in Istanbul regarding Gezi Park, 22 July 2013(1).

21. Ethnographic Interviews conducted at Boğaziçi, 22 July 2013 (1).

22. Ethnographic Interviews conducted at Boğaziçi, 22 July 2013 (1).

23. Ethnographic Interviews conducted at Boğaziçi, 22 July 2013 (2).

24. 'Timeline of Gezi Park Protests', *Hürriyet Daily News*, 6 June 2013, available at: https://www.hurriyetdailynews.com/timeline-of-gezi-park-protests--48321, last accessed 8 July 2022.

25. Laura Moth, 'What Judith Butler Did Not Say in Istanbul', *Today's Zaman Blog*, 17 September 2013.

26. Nilüfer Göle, '"Gezi": Anatomy of a Public Square Movement', *Insight Turkey* 15: 3 (2013), 7; Timur Hammond and Elizabeth Angell, 'Is Everywhere Taksim?: Public Space and Possible Publics', Special Issue *JADMAG 'Resistance Everywhere': The*

Gezi Protests and Dissident Visions of Turkey, eds Anthony Alessandrini, Nazan Üstündağ and Emrah Yıldız 1:4 (2013): 68; Ayşe Parla, 'Protest and the Limits of the Body', Hotspots, *Fieldsights*, 31 October 2013, available at: https://culanth.org/fieldsights/protest-and-the-limits-of-the-body, last accessed 8 July 2022.

27. Birge Yıldırım, 'Transformation of Public Squares of Istanbul between 1938–1949', Proceedings of the 15th International Planning History Society Conference, 15–18 July 2012, available at: http://www.usp.br/fau/iphs/abstracts-and-papers.html, last accessed 11 July 2022.

28. Yıldırım, 'Transformation', 6.

29. Yıldırım, 'Transformation', 6.

30. Yıldırım, 'Transformation', 7.

31. Yıldırım, 'Transformation', 4.

32. Alice von Bieberstein and Nora Tataryan, 'The What of Occupation: "You Took Our Cemetery, You Won't Have Our Park!"' Hotspots, *Fieldsights*, 31 October 2013, available at: https://culanth.org/fieldsights/the-what-of-occupation-you-took-our-cemetery-you-wont-have-our-park, last accessed 8 July 2022.

33. von Bieberstein and Tataryan, 'The What of Occupation'.

34. von Bieberstein and Tataryan, 'The What of Occupation'; Heghnar Watenpaugh, 'Learning from Taksim Square: Architecture, State Power, and Public Space in Istanbul', *Huffington Post*, 14 August 2013, available at: https://www.huffpost.com/entry/learning-from-taksim-squa_b_3443505, last accessed 11 July 2022.

35. Hammond and Angell, 'Is Everywhere Taksim?'; 'Timeline of Gezi Park Protests'.

36. Bengi Akbulut, '"A Few Trees in Gezi Park": Resisting the Spatial Politics of Neoliberalism in Turkey', in L. Anders Sandberg, Adrina Bardekjian and Sadia Butt (eds), *Urban Forests, Trees, and Greenspace: A Political Ecology Perspective* (London: Routledge, 2014), 227–41.

37. 'Taksim through Time', *Stambouline*, 30 May 2013, available at: https://www.stambouline.info/2013/05/taksim-through-time.html?showComment=1369998152505, last accessed 11 July 2022.

38. Hammond and Angell, 'Is Everywhere Taksim?'; Yael Navaro-Yashin, 'Editorial – Breaking Memory, Spoiling Memorization: The Taksim Protests in Istanbul', Hotspots, *Fieldsights*, 31 October 2013, available at: https://culanth.org/fieldsights/editorial-breaking-memory-spoiling-memorization-the-taksim-protests-in-istanbul, last accessed 8 July 2022.

39. 8 July 2013 (2b).

40. William Armstrong, 'Gezi Continues to Dominate Agenda in Turkey', *Turkish Review* 3:5 (2013): 526.

41. Aslı Iğsız, 'Brand Turkey and the Gezi Protests: Authoritarianism, Law, and Neo-liberalism (Part One)', *Jadaliyya*, 12 July 2013, available at: https://www.jadaliyya.com/Details/29078, last accessed 8 July 2022.

42. Iğsız, 'Brand Turkey and the Gezi Protests'.

43. Armstrong, 'Gezi', 526.

44. 'NGO Members March against Government Bill to Sideline Chambers in Urban Planning', *Hürriyet Daily News*, 10 July 2013, available at: https://www.hurriyet-dailynews.com/ngo-members-march-against-government-bill-to-sideline-chambers-in-urban-planning-50472, last accessed 8 July 2022.

45. 'Timeline of Gezi Park Protests'.

46. See in Eylem Aydın (ed.), *Çapulcunun Gezi Rehberi* (Istanbul: Hemen Kitap, 2013).

47. 'Timeline of Gezi Park Protests'.

48. 'Timeline of Gezi Park Protests'.

49. Parla, 'Protest and the Limits of the Body'; 'Timeline of Gezi Park Protests'; Saira Zuberi, 'Her Yer Taksim! Feminist and LGBTQI Engagement in the Gezi Park Protests', *Thomson Reuters Foundation News*, 26 July 2013, available at: https://news.trust.org/item/20130726185721-m7dvq, last accessed 8 July 2022.

50. *Çapulcunun Gezi Rehberi*, 55.

51. *Çapulcunun Gezi Rehberi*, 9, 121.

52. Ömer Çaha, 'Gezi Park Demos: Democratic Protests or Revolt?' *Turkish Review* 3:5 (2013), 533.

53. Çaha, 'Gezi Park Demos', 533; Coşkun Taştan, 'The Gezi Park Protests in Turkey: A Qualitative Field Research', *Insight Turkey* 15:3 (2013), 28.

54. Navaro-Yashin, 'Editorial'.

55. Navaro-Yashin, 'Editorial'.

56. Navaro-Yashin, 'Editorial'.

57. Ateş Altınordu, 'Occupy Gezi, Beyond the Religious–Secular Cleavage', *The Immanent Frame*, 10 June 2013, available at: https://tif.ssrc.org/2013/06/10/occupy-gezi-beyond-the-religious-secular-cleavage, last accessed 8 July 2022.

58. Altınordu, 'Occupy Gezi'.

59. Mustafa Akyol, 'Why Turkey Has Anti-Capitalist Muslims', *Al-Monitor*, 17 July 2013, available at: https://www.al-monitor.com/originals/2013/07/turkey-anti-capitalist-muslims-gezi-social-justice-activism.html, last accessed 11 July 2022; Fehim Taştekin, 'Turkey's Gezi Park Protestors Regroup for Ramadan', *Al-Monitor*, 4 July 2013, available at: https://www.al-monitor.com/originals/2013/07/turkey-gezi-park-protesters-observe-ramadan-iftars.html, last accessed 8 July 2022.

60. *Çapulcunun Gezi Rehberi*, 11.
61. *Çapulcunun Gezi Rehberi*, 52.
62. Altınordu, 'Occupy Gezi'.
63. Altınordu, 'Occupy Gezi'.
64. 8 July 2013 (2).
65. 8 July 2013 (3).
66. 8 July 2013 (7).
67. 10 July 2013 (3).
68. 8 July 2013 (14).
69. 8 July 2013 (11).
70. 8 July 2013 (8).
71. Tahir Abbas, 'Political Culture and National Identity in Conceptualising the Gezi Park Movement', *Insight Turkey* 15:4 (2013), 19.
72. Tahir Abbas, 'Political Culture', 22.
73. Hatem Ete, 'The Political Reverberations of the Gezi Protests', *Insight Turkey* 15:3 (2013), 19.
74. Ete, 'Political Reverberations', 21.
75. Atilla Yayla, 'Gezi Park Revolts: For or Against Democracy?' *Insight Turkey* 15:4 (2013), 9.
76. Yayla, 'Gezi Park Revolts', 9.
77. Ete, 'Political Reverberations', 21–2.
78. Ali Murat Yel and Alparslan Nas, 'After Gezi: Moving towards post-Hegemonic Imagination in Turkey', *Insight Turkey* 15:4 (2013), 179.
79. Ethnographic Interviews conducted at Boğaziçi, 8 July 2013 (12).
80. Ethnographic Interviews conducted at Boğaziçi, 8 July 2013 (6).
81. Ethnographic Interviews conducted at Boğaziçi, 8 July 2013 (1).
82. Ethnographic Interviews conducted at Boğaziçi, 8 July 2013 (12).
83. Hammond and Angell, 'Is Everywhere Taksim?'
84. von Bieberstein and Tataryan, 'The What of Occupation'.
85. Watenpaugh, 'Learning from Taksim Square'.
86. Abbas, 'Political Culture', 24.
87. Göle, 'Gezi', 10.
88. Göle, 'Gezi', 10.
89. Can Açıksöz and Zeynep Korkman, 'Erdoğan's Masculinity and the Language of the Gezi Resistance', *Jadaliyya*, 22 June 2013, available at: https://www.jadaliyya.com/Details/28822, last accessed 11 July 2022.
90. Açıksöz and Korkman, 'Erdoğan's Masculinity'.

91. Ethnographic Interviews conducted at Boğaziçi, 8 July 2013 (2).
92. Ethnographic Interviews conducted at Boğaziçi, 8 July 2013 (3).
93. Ethnographic Interviews conducted at Boğaziçi, 10 July 2013 (3).
94. Ethnographic Interviews conducted at Boğaziçi, 8 July 2013 (14).
95. Ethnographic Interviews conducted at Boğaziçi, 8 July 2013 (13).
96. Ethnographic Interviews conducted at Boğaziçi, 8 July 2013 (14).
97. Ethnographic Interviews conducted at Boğaziçi, 8 July 2013 (5).
98. Ethnographic Interviews conducted at Boğaziçi, 8 July 2013 (2).
99. Ethnographic Interviews conducted at Boğaziçi, 10 July 2013 (1).
100. Ethnographic Interviews conducted at Boğaziçi, 10 July 2013 (3
101. Ethnographic Interviews conducted at Boğaziçi, 8 July 2013 (13).
102. Ethnographic Interviews conducted at Boğaziçi, 22 July 2013 (1).
103. Ayşe Özil, 'Skyscrapers of the Past and their Shadows: A Social History of Urbanity in Late Ottoman Istanbul', *International Journal of Turkish Studies* 21:1/2 (2015), 82–4; Alexis Alexandris, *The Greek Minority of Istanbul and Greek–Turkish Relations: 1918–1974* (Athens: Centre for Asia Minor Studies, 1992), 31–2.
104. Özil, 'Skyscrapers of the Past and their Shadows', 84–94; Méropi Anastassiadou, 'Greek Orthodox Immigrants Of and Modes of Integration Within the Urban Society of Istanbul (1850–1923)', *Mediterranean Historical Review* 24:2 (2009), 151–67.
105. The most current and comprehensive information about these churches can be found at the official website of the Beyoğlu Rum Ortodoks Kiliseleri ve Mektepleri Vakfı, the Beyoğlu Greek Orthodox Churches and Schools Foundation, available at: http://www.stavrodromion.org/en.
106. Alexandris, *The Greek Minority of Istanbul and Greek–Turkish Relations*, 30; Paschalis Kitromilides, 'The Ecumenical Patriarchate', in Lucian Leustean (ed.), *Orthodox Christianity and Nationalism in Nineteenth-Century Southeastern Europe* (New York: Fordham University Press, 2014), 31.
107. Akgönül, *Türkiye Rumları*, 42.
108. Kitromilides, 'The Ecumenical Patriarchate', 29.
109. Nora Fisher-Onar, 'Between neo-Ottomanism and Neoliberalism: The Politics of Imagining Istanbul', in Nora Fisher-Onar, Susan C. Pearce and E. Fuat Keyman (eds), *Istanbul: Living with Difference in a Global City* (New Brunswick, NJ: Rutgers University Press, 2018), 10.
110. İlay Romain Örs, 'Cosmopolitanist Nostalgia: Geographies, Histories, and Memories of the Rum Polites', in Nora Fisher-Onar, Susan C. Pearce, and

E. Fuat Keyman (eds), *Istanbul: Living with Difference in a Global City* (New Brunswick, NJ: Rutgers University Press, 2018), 82–4, 93.

111. Amy Mills, 'Becoming Blind to the Landscape: Turkification and the Precarious National Future in Occupied Istanbul', *Journal of the Ottomand an Turkish Studies Association* 5:2 (2018), 99–100.

112. İlay Romain Örs, 'Beyond the Greek and Turkish Dichotomy: The *Rum Polites* of Istanbul and Athens', *South European Society and Politics* 11:1 (2006), 81.

113. Stanford J. Shaw, 'The Population of Istanbul in the Nineteenth Century', *International Journal of Middle East Studies* 10:2 (1979), 265–77.

114. Alexis Alexandris, 'İstanbul'un Rum Azınlığının Son Göçü (1964–1974): İstanbul'daki Yunan Uyrukluların Sınırdışı Edilemeleri', in İlay Romain Örs (ed.), *İstanbullu Rumlar ve 1964 Sürgünleri: Türk Toplumun Homojenleşmesinde bir Dönüm Noktası* (Istanbul: İletişim Yayınları, 2019), 161.

115. Alexandris, *The Greek Minority of Istanbul and Greek–Turkish Relations*, 191–2. See also Aslı Iğsız's important analysis of these events in *Humanism in Ruins: Entangled Legacies of the Greek–Turkish Population Exchange* (Stanford, CA: Stanford University Press, 2018).

116. Alexandris, *The Greek Minority of Istanbul and Greek–Turkish Relations*, 256–7. See also for a summary of events Ali Tuna Kuyucu, 'Ethno-religious "Unmixing" of "Turkey": 6–7 September Riots as a Case in Turkish Nationalism', *Nations and Nationalism* 11:3 (2005), 362.

117. Speros Vryonis Jr, *The Mechanism of Catastrophe: The Turkish Pogrom of September 6–7, 1955, and the Destruction of the Greek Community of Istanbul* (New York: Greekworks.com, 2005), 125.

118. Alexandris, *The Greek Minority of Istanbul and Greek–Turkish Relations*, 257–9. Patricularly powerful eyewitness accounts of the destruction in Taksim and along İstiklal Caddesi can be found in Vryonis, *The Mechanism of Catastrophe*, 125–53; Rifat N. Bali (ed.), *6–7 Eylül 1955 Olayları: Tanıklar-Hatıralar II* (Istanbul: Libra Yayıncılık, 2020), 33–7, 53–4.

119. Alexandris, *The Greek Minority of Istanbul and Greek–Turkish Relations*, 263–70.

120. Akgönül, *Türkiye Rumları*, 223; Özgür Kaymak, *İstanbul'da Az(ınlık) Olmak: Gündelik Hayatta Rumlar, Yahudiler, Ermeniler* (Istanbul: Libra Yayıncılık, 2017), 45–6. While this chapter focuses on this history as it relates to the urban space around Taksim in particular, a longer historical treatment is provided in the final chapter of this book, as it concerns the longer historical identity of the indigenous Greek community of Istanbul.

121. Akgönül, *Türkiye Rumları*, 251; Alexandris, *The Greek Minority of Istanbul and Greek-Turkish Relations*, 281; Alexandris, 'İstanbul'un Rum Azınlığının Son Göçü', 141–65.

122. İlay Romain Örs, *Diaspora of the City: Stories of Cosmopolitanism from Istanbul and Athens* (New York: Palgrave Macmillan, 2018), 72

123. Kaymak, *İstanbul'da Az(ınlık) Olmak*, 118, 142.

124. Kaymak, *İstanbul'da Az(ınlık) Olmak*, 267–73.

125. Anna Maria Beylunioğlu, 'Recasting the Parameters of Freedom of Religion in Turkey: Non-Muslims and the AKP', in Bahar Başer and Ahmet Erdi Öztürk (eds), *Authoritarian Politics in Turkey: Elections, Resistance, and the AKP* (London: I. B. Tauris, 2017), 141.

126. Beylunioğlu, 'Recasting the Parameters', 143.

127. Beylunioğlu, 'Recasting the Parameters', 152.

128. Beylunioğlu, 'Recasting the Parameters', 151.

129. Kaymak, *İstanbul'da Az(ınlık) Olmak*, 260–1.

130. Kaymak, *İstanbul'da Az(ınlık) Olmak*, 261, 263. Kaymak also notes, however, that not all Istanbul Greeks felt the same about the protests, and that many still retained a sense of wariness or political apathy.

131. Quoted in Kaymak, *İstanbul'da Az(ınlık) Olmak*, 263.

4

THE STATION OF THE MARTYRS, 2017: MEMORIALISATION AND CONSOLIDATION OF THE AKP

Summary Background and Context: The 2016 Coup Attempt

On 15 July 2016, Turkey experienced one of the most severe national traumas in its recent history when a rogue group of military officers attempted to violently overthrow the elected civilian AKP government, leading to the death of some 250 innocent persons, mostly civilians, who resisted to stop the coup. This chapter will analyse this crucial turning point in Turkey's recent political history through a study of how the AKP utilised neo-Ottomanism as a way to address trauma and to construct spaces of healing, remembrance and national identity. This chapter will focus in particular on the Monument to the Martyrs of 15 July (15 Temmuz Şehitler Makamı) in order to uncover how the AKP has restructured public space in Istanbul in response to the events of 15 July 15, utilising neo-Ottomanism to create spaces of refuge that address social trauma, and to incorporate the memories of those martyred into the sacred national epic (*destan*) of the Turkish Republic and its centuries-old Sunni Islamic heritage.

From the evening of 15 July to the morning of 16 July 2016, rogue members of the Turkish armed forces unsuccessfully attempted to forcibly overthrow the elected government of Recep Tayyip Erdoğan. A small group of conspirators deployed ground troops, tanks, fighter jets and attack helicopters in order to gain control of the Turkish government and media, but were foiled by mass civilian resistance, resistance within the armed forces and its high chain of command, and resistance from the AKP itself and all other elected opposition parties. Some 250 people, mostly civilians, died resisting the coup attempt, as troops and attack helicopters fired on civilian crowds. It was the bloodiest attempted military intervention in the history of the Turkish Republic, and was the only such intervention to be stopped by direct civilian resistance. It remains one of the most traumatic national events in the country's history.

Beginning at approximately 10:30 pm local time, coup forces occupied and closed the two open bridges spanning the Bosphorus, the Bosphorus Bridge and Fatih Sultan Mehmet Bridge, the first signal of what was to come.[1] As events unfolded, Turkish citizens frantically shared social media images and messages enabling civilians around the country to be immediately apprised of what was happening and how events developed, minute by minute. Shortly before 11 pm, gunshots were heard in Ankara and fighter jets and attack helicopters were seen flying over the capital, with attack helicopters seen flying low over Istanbul. By 11 pm, Prime Minister Binali Yıldırım informed the public that an attempted coup was underway. At 11:25 pm, coup plotters within the military emailed a statement to be read over the country's media channels, claiming that the Turkish armed forces had taken control of the country in the name of the protection of the democratic order.

The chief of staff of the Turkish armed forces, Hulusi Akar, was taken hostage along with other high-ranking military commanders in Ankara at 11:47 pm. Just after midnight on 16 July, the coup plotters announced the preparation of a new constitution, and continued to claim total control of the situation, though presidential sources and supporters claimed otherwise. A turning point in the night's events occurred at 12:26 am. After narrowly escaping capture or assassination, President Erdoğan used FaceTime on his personal iPhone to call CNN Türk news anchor Hande Fırat as she was broadcasting live. She held the phone facing the camera, and he addressed the Turkish nation, calling for them to resist the coup. Civilian resistance was decisively galvanised, and massive crowds took to the streets to stop the coup by confronting armed soldiers and tanks in the streets, most famously on the Bosphorus Bridge. At the direction of the Diyanet, mosques throughout the country broadcast prayers and messages of support to civilian resistors around the country.[2] Over the next few hours, attack helicopters and soldiers fired on civilians; and fighter jets bombarded the Turkish parliament building, with lawmakers sheltering inside.

By the early hours of the morning, however, the coup plot had been averted and the civilian-led government was back in control of the country. The quick response of Erdoğan and the civilian leadership proved decisive. Yıldırım and Erdoğan's addresses to the Turkish people, combined with the immediate disavowal of the coup attempt by every elected Turkish political party (whether allied with the AKP or not) and the immediate disavowal of the coup plotters by General Ümit Dündar, commander of the 1st Army, ensured that every sector of the Turkish government and civil society would resist.[3] Dündar and the rest of the Turkish military high command's resistance to the coup attempt, their mobilisation of loyal forces against the coup plotters, and their pledging support of the elected government likely prevented further military units mobilising on behalf of the coup plotters. In the end, some 8,500 Turkish military personnel were involved, but this represented only 1.5 per cent of the total personnel of the Turkish armed forces.[4] Most of all, the bravery of ordinary civilians and their willingness to confront armed military forces (without being armed themselves) halted the advance of the coup plotters, the first time such a direct confrontation had ever occurred between civilians and soldiers in the Turkish Republic, with civilians emerging victorious.[5]

This united front combined with the hastiness of the coup's attempted execution ensured that it would not succeed. As later analyses uncovered, the coup plotters moved ahead with the hastily organised plot, even though it was clear that public opinion would be against such a move, because it was clear that the AKP civilian leadership was planning purges within the military command that could have implicated the coup plotters.[6] In addition, the coup plotters had initially intended to carry out their attempt in the early morning hours of 16 July when fewer members of the public could have known about it; but they were forced to move their plans forward by several hours – during a time when Istanbul and Ankara were still extremely active – because Turkish intelligence had penetrated their encrypted communications networks and discovered that something was in motion.[7]

It became clear within a few hours of the attempt, and has been confirmed by numerous further analyses, that the plot was organised by a small group of military officers loyal to the charismatic Turkish Sunni Muslim preacher and religious leader Fethullah Gülen.[8] Gülen's movement, dubbed the Hizmet ('service') movement by its followers, began in the 1970s and 1980s as Gülen's charismatic preaching and leadership amassed a following of conservative Sunni Muslim believers seeking to raise the social profile and influence of Islam in the Turkish Republic. Gülen's movement was part of the broader revival of conservative piety in Turkey since the 1980s that sought an 'Islamised national order', a broader goal which he furthered through the expansion of much-needed social and education services in Turkey and abroad (most especially science education and the construction and maintenance of education facilities such as college-prep centres and dormitories within Turkey designed to support pious Turks' entrance and success in higher education).[9]

Gülen's goal of nurturing religious piety among Turkish youth and the broader promotion of conservative Turkish Islamic values meshed well with the AKP's agenda in its early years, and the two movements worked in tandem for the first decade of AKP administration.[10] The AKP leadership eventually realised, however, that the movement had as its goal not simply social or political influence, but the total capture of the state with its own operatives, a goal that Gülen himself had set out before the inner circle of his followers in videos leaked to the Turkish press (an event which precipitated his fleeing to the United States, where he has lived since 1999).[11] In 2012, the AKP moved to close down the key educational centres run by the movement (the college-prep centres, or *dershaneler*), and in December 2013 the movement struck back initiating corruption probes against the AKP in Istanbul (where, as in much of the rest of the country, Gülenist personnel had largely taken control of the national police forces and academies).[12] As Caroline Tee notes regarding the Gülenist-led corruption probes of December 2013: 'By going public with a raft of toxic allegations it was clear that the Gülenists intention was to unseat now-President Erdoğan and precipitate a change in the Turkish administration.'[13]

The movement was designated by the AKP as a 'parallel structure' (*parallel yapı*) within the state that needed to be rooted out, a designation vindicated by the events of 15 July.[14] At the same time, the extremely wide scope of the AKP government's efforts to root out the coup plotters has been criticised. While analyses of the coup have made clear that it was indeed Gülenist officers and members of Gülen's inner circle (including likely even Gülen himself) who were responsible for the coup, it has also been made clear that the large majority of Gülen's pious followers never had any knowledge of the workings of this inner circle and had no intent of taking part in violence.[15] Nevertheless, the coup has provided the AKP an opportunity to crack down on opposition of all kinds and strengthen its authoritarian governance. Between July 2016 and September 2021, 'public prosecutors in Turkey have launched terror investigations against over 1.5 million people'.[16] During the same period, a total of 208,833 verdicts based on the anti-terrorism statute of the Turkish penal code (Article 314) were delivered by public prosecutors. Over the two-year-long state of emergency implemented after the coup attempt, some 80,000 people were imprisoned and over 150,000 people were fired from state positions. Turkey's political climate has therefore changed decisively as a result of the coup events.

Turkey's social climate was transformed to an equally great extent. One important study by Zeynep Şimşir and Bulent Dilmaç conducted during the months immediately following the coup attempt revealed that the many people in Istanbul and Ankara who had heard or witnessed scenes of violence experienced symptoms of post-traumatic stress disorder consistent with exposure to warfare.[17] Those interviewed for this study reported feelings of despair, fear, vulnerability and closeness to death; they also reported feelings of renewed attachment to family, spirituality, prayer, worship and to the Turkish homeland itself (themes that will be discussed in detail below).[18]

Also in response to the intense social trauma of 15 July, the AKP government in the years since the coup attempt has emphasised the importance of the category of the civilian martyr in Turkish civic life, holding up the sacrifices of those who resisted the coup attempts and their families as model citizens worthy of remembrance. These practices of remembrance have been incorporated into children's school curricula, and have become a key component of Turkish civic culture in recent years.[19] In addition, official public ceremony associated with these practices of remembrance have featured a notably strong focus on Islamic identity: as Nadav Solomonovich has pointed out, the annual national holiday instituted by the AKP to commemorate the martyrs of 15 July is the first instance of a 'deliberately "Islamized"' public holiday in the history of the Turkish Republic.[20] This chapter's analysis will therefore focus on how public architecture and ceremony have contributed decisively to the AKP's response to this national trauma, and how this response has consolidated the AKP's hegemonic conception of Turkish national identity.

Description of the Monument to the Martyrs of 15 July

The Monument to the Martyrs of 15 July (15 Temmuz Şehitler Makamı) is located adjacent to the grounds of Nakkaştepe National Garden (Nakkaştepe Millet Bahçesi), at the end of the 15 July Martyrs' Bridge on the Asian side of Istanbul (15 Temmuz Şehitler Köprüsü). Completed in 1973, this massive suspension bridge (frequently referred to as 'the first bridge', birinci köprü) was the first to connect the European and Asian sides across the Bosphorus, and stretches from the neighbourhood of Ortaköy on the European side to the neighbourhood of Beylerbeyi on the Asian side. The bridge's first name was simply 'The Bosphorus Bridge' (Boğaziçi Köprüsü), and it was officially renamed as the 15 July Martyrs' Bridge by a cabinet decision on 25 July, ten days after the coup attempt, and in recognition of the sacrifices made by ordinary citizens on the bridge itself.[21] The bridge rises 64 m (210 ft) above water level, is 33.4 m (109 ft) wide and 1,560 m (5,118 ft) long.[22]

When it was first opened, the bridge was the fourth-largest suspension bridge in the world, and it retained this status until 2012 (it is currently the third-largest in Europe, and the seventh-largest in the world).[23] The bridge was considered a major engineering triumph, fulfilling a goal that had long been considered impossible: connecting the Asian and European sides of Istanbul by a single bridge stretching between them. The official opening ceremony took place on 30 October 1973, fifty years and one day after the founding of the Turkish Republic, marking the occasion and the bridge itself as a major sign of Turkish national development and pride.[24] Two other suspension bridges across the Bosphorus have been built since then, both to the north travelling up the strait: the Fatih Sultan Mehmet Bridge, completed in 1988; and the Yavuz Sultan Selim Bridge, completed in 2016 (also referred to unofficially as the second and third bridge, respectively).

The first point to be made about the monument is that, by virtue of its location at the end of this bridge, it stands in a crucial place in the urban space of Istanbul. For decades, the 'first bridge' has symbolised the city of Istanbul itself, having been depicted countless times in popular and official media as emblematic of the great city that spans Europe and Asia, East and West. A single image of the first bridge is enough to refer to the entire identity of the city of Istanbul. The location of the monument, therefore, serves not only to commemorate the specific historic events on the night of 15 July, but also places these events and their symbolism quite literally at the centre of Istanbul itself – in the heart of its central thoroughfare, the Bosphorus strait, and all that the strait symbolises in the urban history of the city that stretches back nearly 2,000 years.

The monument sits on top of a small hill that rises from the end of the bridge on the Asian side. The flow of some six lanes of traffic leaving and departing the bridge continues endlessly just beneath the hill.[25] The grassy areas immediately surrounding the monument are impeccably maintained despite their immediate proximity to one of the busiest roads in the entire city (with the very expansive green spaces of Nakkaştepe National Garden situated immediately to the west of the monument grounds, which also include a small museum[26] and other buildings). The main path leading up to the monument is lined with greenery and mature cypress trees, which are also planted prominently around the monument itself. Exactly 250 mature cypress trees and exactly 250 roses were planted at the time of the construction of the monument to symbolise the 250 citizens who were killed during the coup attempt.[27] Additionally, a stand with a QR code was placed in front of each of the 250 roses, which when scanned using a designated smart phone app provides details on the each of the 250 martyrs whose lives and sacrifice are commemorated at the site.[28] The Turkish flag is also flown prominently in a number of places around the site.

The monument itself has a simple but striking design. It is an open-air geodesic dome composed of interlocking lattice work of pure, white stone. The structure sits atop a solid slab of white stone, and thus forms an actual *makam* – or, 'station' as used in the archaic English sense of 'place' or 'location'. Thus, the most literal and accurate translation of the actual name of the monument – *15 Temmuz Şehitler Makamı* – is 'The Station of the Martyrs of 15 July'. The fact that the term *makam* was used instead of words that have the more direct and common meaning of 'monument' – such as *abide* or *anıt* – is highly significant. The building is therefore specifically meant to not only commemorate the lives of the martyrs of 15 July, but to more specifically proclaim and embody their literal 'place' both in the sense of where they stood, but also their higher 'station' in the world itself and in the history of the Turkish nation. As will be discussed in detail below, the actual, eternal 'station of the martyrs' is Paradise, as promised in Islamic sacred belief about those who sacrifice themselves for the greater good of the Muslim community.

The interior of the dome is not monumental, but offers space enough for several dozen people to stand underneath it at the same time. It covers approximately 130 m² (approx. 1,400 ft²). The architect who designed the monument, Hilmi Şenalp, describes the dome as 'crystalline geodesic', and he emphasises that the interlocking arms that make up the dome symbolise the interlocking of national unity that prevented the coup plotters from succeeding in their attempt.[29] The space between the arms is several feet wide, meaning that the 'interior' space of the dome is exposed to the light, air and outside elements. A fountain, very much like those often found in mosque courtyards, stands in the middle of the interior space. The central elements of the interior space underneath the dome are three upright stone tablets inset into the latticed arms of the dome, again in pure white, engraved with the names of the 250 martyrs of 15 July. According to Şenalp, this list of names is meant to be the focal point of the entire monument.[30] Finally, on the outward face of the monument, stands a stone panel engraved with a poem written by Abdullah Akın to mark the occasion of the erection of the monument (as will be discussed in more detail below).[31]

Discussion of one final element of the physical structure will lead into consideration of its sacred meaning. At the very top of the interior space of the dome, where the arms forming the dome interlock to form a pentagon, five panels within the pentagon that look down directly on those standing below all have the same Arabic text carved into them: *huwwa al-shahid* ('He is the All-Witnessing'). The term 'All-Witnessing' is one of the ninety-nine names of God (in Arabic, al-asma al-husna') a list of descriptions God uses to describe God's self in the Qur'an, and which therefore have special theological significance in Islamic tradition. These names signify specific attributes of God that God specifically chose to reveal to human beings, and therefore are believed to reveal important information about who God is.

In the Islamic tradition, works and treatises describing the individual meaning of the ninety-nine names of God are some of the most popular and enduring genres of religious literature. Contemplation of the meaning of the names of God is both an intellectual and spiritual activity that illumines the mind of the believer with deeper information about God's actions in the world, and about how individual personal conduct should be moulded to reflect, in our own limited way, these divine virtues. The meaning of the divine name

'All-Witnessing' refers to God's seeing of all things that happen in the world, whether they are immediately apparent to us or not; God knows the seen and the unseen.[32] The name has two senses: that God is Witness to all things happening and existing in the cosmos; and that God on the Day of Judgement will bear witness to – that is, tell and know the truth about – all that human beings have committed in their lives so that they might be judged by their actions: 'He will bear witness to mankind on the day of resurrection from what He knows and has seen concerning them.'[33] The Arabic term used here, *shahid*, is also the term in Arabic and Turkish for 'martyr' (in Turkish, *şehit*), meaning one who witnesses to the truth through their ultimate sacrifice (which is, in fact, the same etymological origin of the word in English, which derives from the Greek for 'witness').

This sacred inscription therefore opens up the Islamic sacred meaning of the monument. The structure is a 'witness' to those who were themselves witnessed to the truth by sacrificing themselves for it – in this case, those who sacrificed themselves for the Turkish nation and its sacred principles. The use of a divine name to convey this sense of martyrdom/witnessing furthermore emphasises that God also knows the truth of what happened on 15 July 15: that the Turkish nation was attacked by internal enemies whose true intentions cannot be hidden, and who will be judged by God their Creator for these deeds on Judgement Day. The name of God as the All-Witnessing watches over everyone who enters into the monument, as God watches over and protects the nation of Turkey, as evidenced by the triumph of national will and sacrifice on 15 July 2016.

Architecture and Sacred Space: A *Türbe* for the Turkish Nation

The significance of the Martyr's Monument within the phenonon of Erdoğanian neo-Ottomanism's impact on the city of Istanbul has to do with the way the monument uses neo-Ottomanism as a means to cultivate a sacred space of rest, tranquillity and healing from trauma. The monument reveals an important nuance in the way that Erdoğanian neo-Ottomanism impacts the physical space of the city of Istanbul because it shows how this kind of neo-Ottomanism can function as both a political discourse of power inscribed by architectural means, and also as a means of healing, comfort and commemoration in the context of national and personal trauma. The monument places within the bustling and chaotic urban landscape of the city a space of intentional quiet, serenity and remembrance. It achieves this effect in much the same way that other forms of Erdoğanian neo-Ottomanism function: by utilising aspects of Turkish Sunni Islamic tradition.

This is not to say that the neo-Ottomanism of the monument is not also political, but rather to highlight through this example how Erdoğanian neo-Ottomanism can also function to transform the urban space of Istanbul in order to foster experiences that may seem unexpected in this context, such as remembrance, tranquillity and healing. As Timur Hammond has argued regarding the monument, this structure is part of spatial practices designed to 'link people, events, and places together in relations of responsibility and obligation', producing a 'memorial public'.[34] Architectural spaces and public practices involving memorialisation and remembrance associated with traumatic events are not a-political, but the way in which they participate in spatial politics is distinctly different from other architectural sites, sacred spaces, and public spaces and events. The social and political effects they produce are derived from their role in building strength and solidarity in the face of trauma.

The effects of rest and healing at the monument are achieved by the monument's use of specifical elements of Turkish Sunni Islamic religious tradition, especially from the Ottoman period, to construct a space that recalls eternal Paradise, the reward promised to faithful Muslim believers – especially martyrs – after all the troubles and pain experienced in this life. This is the specific place, or 'station' (*makam*) of the martyrs being alluded to in the name of the monument, 15 Temmuz Şehitler Makamı, most literally translated as 'the station/location of the martyrs of July'. The name of the monument refers to itself as the place of the martyrs in this life, in other words, the physical place where they are commemorated, and the physical place where they fell (the bridge itself). At the same time, the name equally means the eternal place of the martyrs, where they now reside and will forever reside – in Paradise.

It is not only the name of the monument that refers to Paradise, but the key elements of the physical design of the monument do so as well. As the architect Hilmi Şenalp explained, he designed the monument to recall and resemble a *türbe*, the small, domed tombs of Ottoman-era saints and holy persons where Turkish Muslim believers often say special prayers on behalf of the souls of the persons buried or commemorated at the site (as will be discussed below, this is exactly how Erdoğan and those around him treated the monument when it was first opened).[35] Şenalp described his design as specifically traditional, not 'a modern memorial', but, rather a space that takes as its inspiration the unique features of Turkish Islamic cultural tradition and civilisation.[36] He stresses that the monument was specifically designed to look towards 'our future' in a way that is fitting to 'our spirit' and 'our cultural heritage' (*kültürel birikimimiz*).[37]

The importance of Ottoman tradition itself is in fact key to understanding Şenalp's architectural work overall, which can be understood as one of the pioneers of the neo-Ottoman style in contemporary Turkey. As Kishwar Rizvi's analysis has shown, Şenalp and his firm Hassa Mimarlık have been 'one of the most important disseminators' of Turkish neo-Ottoman architectural style.[38] Şenalp's work is 'an exploration in cultural continuity' that 'celebrates the classical period of Ottoman art and history as the epitome of Turkish civilization'.[39] As Coşkun Yılmaz puts it, Şenalp's style is specifically attentive to the 'form and spirit of tradition' and is consciously aware of his 'constructive identity' as an architect.[40]

Moreover, in Şenalp's work 'the history of Turkish architecture becomes . . . a nationalist proclamation that distinguishes itself from the earlier paradigm of Kemalist secular republicanism'.[41] In other words, Şenalp's designs are explicitly oriented towards what this book describes as Erdoğanian neo-Ottomanism: the restructuring of public space in Istanbul in order to reflect conservative nationalist values and the pre-eminence of the Turkish Sunni identity. Şenalp's most famous projects are neo-Ottoman mosques sponsored by the Turkish government and built outside Turkey as symbols of Turkish national culture and influence. These include the Tokyo Mosque and Cultural Centre (completed in 2000), the Ertuğrul Gazi Mosque complex in Ashgabat, Turkmenistan (completed in 1997–8), and the Şehitlik Mosque in Berlin (completed in 2005), which will be discussed in more detail at the end of this book.[42]

Şenalp's own words on the Martyrs' Monument capture its function as a sacred space that points towards Paradise, in the manner of a traditional Ottoman tomb and place of pilgrimage: 'The dome, in symbolizing eternity and the universe in its entirety, expresses that the martyrs are not in fact "dead", that together with eternal life they have attained to divine blessings.'[43] Not only the size and shape of the structure, but also the structuring of the environment around it reinforces the association with the traditional Ottoman sacred tomb (*türbe*). As described above, the site stands at the top of a small hill, as do many Ottoman-era saint's tombs that served as places of pilgrimage. The gardens and greenery around the space (such as the roses and cypress trees) recall the gardens often present around Ottoman-era sacred buildings.

As Jale Necdet Erzen has noted, sacred architecture in the Ottoman tradition commonly featured water and gardens specifically designed to recall the gardens of Paradise promised to the believers in the Qur'an: 'Gardens of Eden with rivers running below, abiding therein. That is the recompense of one who purifies himself.'[44] Fountains and rose gardens in particular were used in Ottoman architecture for this purpose, and as noted above, these two elements are featured prominently in the Martyrs' Monument: the fountain at the centre, and the 250 roses planted to recall the 250 martyrs. In addition, in Ottoman Islamic poetic imagery, the cypress tree is often associated with eternal life, as it is evergreen, and is often also paired with imagery of the waters of life as described in Islamic depictions of Paradise.[45] The 250 mature cypress trees planted at the site of the monument to signify the 250 martyrs therefore also strongly recalls the eternal life and bliss promised to those who sacrificed their lives for the good of the Muslim community.

In addition, the poem written to commemorate the dedication of the monument on 15 July 2017 exemplifies the monument's use of Ottoman and Turkish Sunni Islamic tradition to create a restful and healing space that points towards Paradise and eternal life. Etched on a stone panel facing outward on the exterior of the structure, the 'Epitaph of the Station of the Martyrs' (Şehitler Makamı Kitabesi) was composed by the poet Abdullah Akın and is written in a traditional Ottoman poetic meter (*ebced*) whereby the letters add up to the year 2016 as calculated in the Islamic calender (1438 Hicri).[46] Like the architect Şenalp, Akın describes his poetry's style as the eschewal of secular modernism and the embracing of tradition, or in his words, 'classical' (*klasik*) style. Akın sees his work as a struggle against the decline of the knowledge of the Ottoman language and tradition among Turks of younger generations, lamenting that 'we have broken off from the ancient language'. He relates how he felt a great loss at not being able to read the inscriptions on Ottoman-era buildings, and so 'felt a great responsibility' to learn how to do so. As Ottoman courses were not common at the time, this proved to be a difficult task on one's own, and he was in fact tutored in Ottoman translation by the architect Hilmi Şenalp.[47]

As influences for his consciously traditional style, Akın cites major figures in the Ottoman tradition such as Yeni Şehirli Avni (1826–84), Fuzuli (d. 1556), Baki (1526–1600), Kazım Paşa (1821–90) and Leskofçalı Galip (1828–67). Testifying to the deeply Islamic religious and spiritual dimension of his poetry, he cites in particular the influences of Ottoman Sufi poets such as Niyazi Mısri (1618–94), Hasan Sezai (d. 1738), Osman Şemsi Efendi (1814–93), Cemalettin Uşaki (d. 1751), Abdullah Selahaddin Uşaki (1705–83); and, as he emphasises, hundreds of others could be added to this list.[48] In other words, it is important to note that Akın's poetic contribution to the monument is grounded in the same kind of Ottoman and Turkish Sunni tradition that underlies the neo-Ottomanism of the architecture and physical space of the monument.

Also, like the monument's physical design, Akın's poem points clearly towards the place of the martyrs in Paradise and the immense sanctity of their deeds and memory. Strikingly, he attributes the successful composition of the poem itself to the supernatural power of the martyrs: 'The intercession [himmet] of the martyrs caused the poem on the epitaph to be written.'[49] The term 'himmet' has very strong associations with Ottoman Islamic tradition, as it is a technical term in Sufi spirituality referring specifically to the power of Sufi saints to provide supernatural assistance to themselves or others through the power and permission of God.[50] This assertion further strengthens the association of the monument with the traditional form of a Sufi saint's tomb, where prayers for the souls of the departed may be offered, and miracles at the hands of the saints in Paradise may still occur.

The poem[51] is written in the modern Turkish alphabet and language but in an archaic Ottoman idiom, thus rendering the text both legible to the common Turkish reader but in a register that emphasises its traditional Islamic sanctity. For example, in the usage of common words with modern Turkish equivalents, the poem consistently prefers Ottoman terms such as 'mekan' or 'mevki', Arabic-derived words for 'place', instead of the far more common modern Turkish 'yer'. The poem praises the martyr's unhesitating self-sacrifice that will forever be the pride of the Turkish nation and homeland, and one of the epic victories that characterise Turkish national history. He uses, again, strikingly Ottoman terms to describe what the martyrs achieved, which was the continued preservation of 'religion and state' (*din ü devlet*), a classical Ottoman formulation for the medieval Islamic ideal of governance whereby the Sunni Islamic faith and the earthly government of the sultan cooperate harmoniously to ensure the well-being and justice of all under the empire's dominion, both in this life and the next.[52]

The poem places special emphasis on the place of the martyrs in Paradise: 'May your station [*makam*] be the highest paradise; God's Most Beloved – the Prophet Muhammad – your close companion; your place side by side with the martyrs of Karbala.' It also cites Qur'anic verses related to the rewards of the faithful in Paradise as revelation of the proper glory that they have received, and will enjoy, in Paradise for all eternity: 'May "garments of fine green silk and rich brocade" be glad tidings of your very garments, with the grace of "their Lord shall give them to drink" may your portion attain to perfect happiness.'[53] The poem closes with a reference to one of the ninety-nine names of God, 'the Eternally Living (al-Hayy)', which Akın emphasises is a reference to the fact that martyrs never truly die, but enjoy eternal life, as described in Qur'an 2:154: 'And say not of those who are slain in the way of God, "They are dead". Nay, they are alive, but you are unaware.'[54]

To sum up, the Monument to the Martyrs of 15 July is a particularly dense and evocative architectural embodiment of the neo-Ottoman transformation of public space in Istanbul under AKP leadership. The monument incorporates all of the crucial elements in Erdoğanian neo-Ottoman identity, including Turkish nationality, Sunni Islamic faith, and Ottoman (and Seljuk) heritage and tradition. Indeed, rather than simply being alluded to in this monument, these concepts receive dramatic emphasis in order to highlight how different this construction of Turkish identity is from other possible constructions of Turkish national identity (such as secular Kemalism or cosmopolitanism). The architect and poet involved in the project place special emphasis on the importance of tradition (*gelenek*) itself, and the need to reconnect with the authentic Turkish Islamic past that has been denied to the current generations of Turkish Muslims by the legacy of secular Kemalism. History, legacy and sacred precedent receive special emphasis and dignity at the monument, and notions of progress or innovation are de-emphasised or simply absent.

The role of Islam in this identity construction is equally powerful. Qur'anic verses hover above the space of the monument that quite literally witness to

God's own ever-present witnessing of all that happens in the world, including the events of 15 July 2016. The monument itself was constructed to resemble a sacred tomb (*türbe*), and recalls in a variety of ways the station of the martyrs in the gardens of Paradise promised in the Qur'an to them and to any others who sacrifice themselves for the sake of the Muslim community. These elements of tradition and faith come together to produce a public edifice that transforms the mundane spot of urban territory at the base of a busy suspension bridge into a restful haven devoted to memory and healing, forever calling to mind how this small spot in the vast urban landscape of Istanbul was forever transformed into an intensely sacred space when ordinary citizens gave their lives there to defend their nation from a violent assault.

Having outlined the significance of the space and monument itself, it is also necessary to briefly mention here the ways in which the AKP and Erdoğan himself have made clear just how important this place was and is to their interpretation of Turkish national identity. According to the AKP major of Istanbul at the time the monument was conceived and constructed, Kadir Topbaş, Erdoğan himself first suggested the idea to use the bridge as a site for a monument dedicated to the martyrs of 15 July. He and Topbaş worked together to designate the exact location for the monument, and Erdoğan personally approved the architectural designs for it which were presented to him by the architect.[55] Topbaş placed special emphasis on the fact that Erdoğan went personally with him to the bridge to determine the exact location of the monument, displaying therefore a strong personal interest in the development and success of the project.[56]

It is also worthwhile noting that in this interview where Topbaş discussed the significance of the monument from the AKP's perspective, he utilised the neo-Ottoman emphasis on Turkish Islamic tradition and its significance for Turkish national identity itself, as described by Şenalp and Akın above. Topbaş drew special attention to the fact that the monument was designed according to 'our traditional [*geleneksel*] dome, cupola style'.[57] Moreover, according to Topbaş, this anchoring in traditional Turkish Islamic architectural style was an indicator of the future direction of the Turkish nation itself: 'The Republic of Turkey will live forever, we will walk together into the future as a nation.' In the context of Turkey's future, he strongly emphasised the importance of memory, especially the need to always keep alive the memory of the martyrs of

15 July whose decisive sacrifice ensured the continued life and security of the Turkish nation.[58]

Public Ceremony and Sacred Time: A *Destan* for the Turkish Nation

As noted above, Coşkun Yılmaz insightfully articulated the significance of Hilmi Şenalp's architectural style as a project that always remained conscious of his 'constructive identity' as an architect. In other words, the monument that Şenalp designed was meant not simply to express the individual vision of its designer, but rather to reveal and memorialise the cultural characteristics that make up the structural edifice of Turkish national history. In Şenalp's work, Turkish national history is interpreted as a kind of architecture: a mighty fortress that shelters the Turkish people, protecting them from their enemies and lifting them to glory, whose strength and integrity is composed of key moments of heroic sacrifice and achievement that are to the Turkish national narrative what keystones, foundations, buttresses and other key architectural features are to a monumental building.

The elaborate and highly meaningful ceremonies that accompanied the opening of the monument, occurring on the first anniversary of the coup attempt, reveal exactly how – through the medium of this particular monument – the events of 15 July were to be incorporated into the AKP's historical narrative of Turkish national identity. The occasion of the opening of the Martyr's Monument became the moment where the importance of not only this particular architectural edifice was publicly manifested and cemented in the urban landscape of Istanbul. It also served as the moment when Erdoğan and the AKP gave full expression to their vision of how these events fit into the larger sacred narrative of Turkish national history.

The concept that Erdoğan and the AKP used to fit the events of 15 July into the narrative of Turkish national history is the concept of *destan*. In modern Turkish, the term *destan* refers to ancient or traditional folk epics associated with Turkic-speaking peoples, and originally derived from oral narratives.[59] The oral tradition of Turkic epic literature originating in Central Asia is the oldest form of literature produced by Turkic-language speaking peoples, and is associated in modern Turkey with the ancient and venerable origins of the Turkish nation. A wide range of folk and epic poetry recounting heroic exploits, romance, natural grandeur and spiritual devotion comprise this genre, the most famous example of which is *The Book of Dede Korkut*.[60] This epic, which likely dates to the tenth century, includes legends associated with the migration of the Oğuz Turks from Central Asia to Anatolia. Because the Ottoman dynasty was derived from the Oğuz Turkic lineage, and because contemporary Turks are inheritors of the Ottoman legacy, this text has acquired the status of the Turkish national epic, and it exemplifies the heroism, bravery and sacrifice that are so strongly emphasised in the neo-Ottoman interpretation of Turkish history and national identity.

This is the deep historical legacy that is directly referred to when the concept of *destan* is invoked. The events of 15 July are consistently referred to as a new Turkish national heroic epic – a *destan* – that both constitute a sacred narrative in and of themselves, and can also be seen as another key moment in the ongoing *destan* that is Turkish national history; put another way, these events are the latest epic building block in the ongoing construction of the glorious architecture of Turkish national history and identity. The ceremonies associated with the first annual commemoration of the events of 15 July – dramatically culminating in the opening of the Martyrs' Monument – were clearly designed to articulate and reinforce the epic quality and significance of this most recent *destan* in Turkish history.

In the most basic sense, the term *destan* is simply one of the most common words used to describe the 15 July coup attempts in all types of AKP media and political discourse, including when referring to the significance of the Martyrs' Monument. The phrase 'the epic of 15 July' (15 Temmuz Destanı) was highlighted in every possible venue at the first annual commemoration of the event, and serves as a semi-official title for the events that is used frequently in AKP government settings, such as in the official communications of the Office of the Presidency of the Turkish Republic.[61] In his interview describing the construction and significance of the Martyrs' Monument, Topbaş stated that on 15 July 'as a nation, another great epic of heroism [*kahramanlık destanı*] was written'.[62]

The poet Abdullah Akın who wrote the epitaph for the Martyrs' Monument, also referred to the events of 15 July as a *destan*, and even referred to his poem as a kind of miniature *destan*, meaning to encapsulate the perspective of a single heroic participant in the larger epic narrative of 15 July.[63] As described above, his poem does indeed faithfully reflect many of the central themes of traditional heroic epic: the brave selfless actions of the heroes; the gratefulness of their people for such sacrifices; and their glorification in the memory of the people and in Paradise as promised by God. The sacred significance of this new national epic is also highlighted in official Diyanet discourse. In the main publication devoted to 15 July sponsored by the Diyanet's publishing house – *In the Words of the Veterans of 15 July* – then President of Religious Affairs Mehmet Görmez described 15 July as a *destan* of the scale and significance of the Seljuk Turks' victory over the Byzantines in Anatolia at the Battle of Manzikert in 1071 or the Battle of Gallipoli in 1915.[64] In the former event, the homeland of the Turkish nation was secured in battle; in the latter event, that same homeland was defended from the almost overwhelming power of foreign invaders. In AKP discourse, the epic of 15 July is as significant as these great turning points in Turkish national history.

In the AKP discourse on 15 July, two focal points emerge that structure any such epic narrative: the hero and the villain. In his interpretation of the Martyrs' Monument, Yılmaz effectively summarised the terms by which these focal points are described by AKP discourse on 15 July. As he puts it, the events were an 'epic of heroism and attempted betrayal'.[65] In this epic the hero that emerges is the common Turkish people – the *halk* – who rose up against those who betrayed the nation– the *hainler*. This dichotomy between the heroic people and the evil traitors – the *halk* vs. the *hainler* – structures the entirety of the AKP's description of these events, and it is this recurrent discursive dichotomy that gives the AKP discourse on the events a clearly epic structure, intentionally designed to mirror the traditional Turkish genre of the *destan*.

An analysis of the first annual commemoration of the attempted coup of 15 July, which culminated in the dedication and opening of the Martyrs' Monument described above, clearly reveals a process by which the AKP used public space and performance to incorporate the narrative of 15 July as a national epic after the patten of Turkish Islamic tradition, in keeping with Erdoğan's distinctive form of neo-Ottomanism as described throughout this book. An entire week of events was planned under the aegis of the Office of the Presidency (and therefore under the guidance of Erdoğan himself), and these events set out in dramatic and public detail the specifics of how the AKP has incorporated the events of 15 July into its neo-Ottoman construction of Turkish identity and this identity's inscription onto the urban landscape of

Istanbul. Significantly, the climax of this entire week-long programme was the dedication and opening of the Martyrs' Monument, which took place late on the evening of 15 July 2017, exactly one year (to the very hours) from the 15 July coup attempt.

The themes discussed above (and throughout this book) book-ended the entire week's programme, emphasising the specifically Islamic sacred significance of the *destan* of 15 July. The week's programme commenced on Tuesday, 11 July with visits to the tombs of those martyred during the coup attempt, where prayers and blessings were offered on behalf of those who had perished. Following the midday prayers on that day, a special programme was held throughout the entire country that made clear the importance of Turkish Sunni Islamic tradition in the remembrance and significance of the 15 July coup attempt. The reading of the Mevlid-i Şerif took place simultaneously in the Great Mosques and Ottoman Imperial Mosques (*Ulu Camiler* and *Selatin Camileri*) in all eighty-one provinces of the country.[66]

The Mevlid-i Şerif is the common name for the sacred praise poem by Süleyman Çelebi (d. 1422) that hymns the life, virtues and miracles of the Prophet Muhammad.[67] For centuries its recitation has been a key feature of many sacred occasions, including the annual celebration of the birth of the Prophet Muhammad (Mevlid Kandili), and it is one of the most well-known and beloved texts in the Turkish Sunni tradition. The term 'Great Mosques' refers to a particular category of monumental mosques in Turkish Islamic history that have particular historical significance and were dedicated to holding the Friday mass congregational prayer and sermon.[68] Mosques with this designation in Turkey include Afyon Ulu Camii (c. 1272), Aksaray Ulu Camii (1408–9), Arslanhane Camii in Ankara (1290), Birgi Ulu Camii in Izmir province (1312), Bursa Ulu Camii (1396–9), Diyarbakır Ulu Camii (1092), Doğanhisar Ulu Camii in Konya province (1548), Edirne Ulu Camii (1414), Erzurum Ulu Camii (1179), Kayseri Ulu Camii (1134–43) and Mardin Ulu Camii (1176).[69] The term 'Selatin Camileri' refers to monumental mosques personally commissioned by Ottoman sultans, and includes famous examples in Istanbul such as Fatih Camii (1463–70), Bayezid Camii (1501–6), Sultanahmet Camii (1609–16) and Süleymaniye Camii (1550–7).

It is therefore difficult to overstate the symbolic power of this countrywide ritual programme to inaugurate the week of remembrance for the first annual commemoration of the events of 15 July. One of the most sacred ritual texts in Turkish Islamic history was read simultaneously in the most ancient and grand mosques around the country, a selection of sites that specifically focused on mosques from the Seljuk and Ottoman periods (rather than mosques built in the modern period). This event clearly connects the national epic of the heroism of the martyrs of 15 July with the entirety of Turkish Sunni Islamic history, specifically as it is founded in public spaces and architectural masterpieces still standing in all corners of the Turkish Republic. With this gesture, the *destan* of 15 July is placed securely in the entire epic narrative of the Turkish people, as worthy of sacred remembrance and commemoration of the most glorious moments in the history of Turkish Islamic civilisation.

Over the following days, further national programming included exhibits, commemorative events and academic panels. The heroism and sacrifice of the common people – the *halk* – who resisted the coup attempt that day was the main focus, including special memorials and events for close relatives of the martyrs. The identity of the enemies and national betrayers defeated that day – the *hainler* – was also highlighted through a special AKP meeting and presentation of the official analysis and report of the events – *The 15 July Victory of the National Will Research Report*.[70] This document clearly defines the enemy faced by the Turkish people in the epic struggle of 15 July: the Gülenist Terror Organisation (Fetullahçı Terör Örgütü, or FETÖ) which planned, led and unsuccessfully attempted to overthrow the elected government of Recep Tayyip Erdoğan, thus engaging in an act of national betrayal (*ihanet*) that was committed against the whole of the Turkish people (*halk*).[71]

The report emphasises Erdoğan calling the Turkish people to resistance during the night of the coup, especially focusing on his statement: 'I have never, even until today, recognized any power above the power of the people [*halk*].'[72] The document stresses that it is the Turkish people who resisted the coup attempt who are the true heirs and continuators of the long tradition of Turkish Islamic identity, which the coup plotters only abused to their own advantage: 'FETÖ . . . masked itself in the faith of Islam and in the historical glory that our people have longed for.'[73] The events of 15 July were therefore not only a betrayal of the national democratic will, but also a betrayal of Turkish national history and identity itself, whose tradition of epic heroism is represented in the actions of the Turkish people.

Similarly, official Diyanet discourse has continued to prioritise the theological condemnation of FETÖ as central to its mission. The official Diyanet Friday sermon addressing the two-year anniversary of the coup attempt (published on 13 July 2018) emphasised FETÖ's treacherous exploitation of authentic Turkish Islamic tradition, and likened its treachery to one of the most despised sins in the Qur'an: *fasād*, or in Turkish 'fesat' – wreaking violent havoc upon the Earth.[74] The official Diyanet Friday sermons for the next two years of commemoration (2019 and 2020) were also devoted to the subjects of national betrayal (*ihanet*) and the exploitation of Islam by FETÖ.[75] The Diyanet has continued to publish books and studies focusing on the threat of FETÖ to authentic Islam in Turkey, including the widely read and distributed report, *FETÖ in its Own Words: An Organized Exploitation of Religion*.[76]

The week's programme culminated in the events held in Istanbul on the evening and night of 15 July 2017, one year from the 2016 coup attempt. These events took place at the 15 July Martyrs' Bridge and ended with the climactic opening of the Martyrs' Monument. The programme for that day read as follows:

- 6:30 pm: National Unity March across the bridge.
- 8:00 pm: National Unity March arrival at the ceremony grounds.
- 8:35 pm: Performance by Ottoman military band (*mehter*).
- 9:15 pm: President Erdoğan's honouring of the martyrs' relatives and those who participated in the resistance (*gaziler*).
- 9:30 pm: Qur'anic recitation and prayer of supplication (*dua*).
- 10:05 pm: Screening of the 15 July documentary.
- 10:30 pm: Reading of the names of the 250 martyrs and projection of lights in their honour.
- 10:45 pm: President Erdoğan's remarks.
- 11:30 pm: Official opening of the Martyrs' Monument.
- 11:45 pm: Video projection in Saraçhane.
- 12:13 am (16 July): Throughout Turkey, reciting of the funerary prayer (*sela*) and the beginning of democracy vigils with President Erdoğan's call.[77]

The programme then continued in Ankara with events marking the phases of the coup attempt in the early morning hours of 16 July 2016; and ended with morning prayers at 4:50 am at the Mosque of the Nation (Beştepe Millet Camii).[78]

The ceremony focused specifically on the opening of the Martyrs' Monument, dramatically reinforcing the themes of Islamic sanctity and neo-Ottoman identity as described above. Accompanied by other AKP officials and Turkish political figures, Erdoğan led the opening ceremony by prominently participating in prayers of supplication offered for the martyrs commemorated at the site. The prayers were intoned by the mufti of Istanbul, Hasan Kamil Yılmaz. Images of the ceremony show the assembled group of dignitaries and honoured guests gathered around the fountain in the centre of the monument mirroring the way in which pilgrims might pray for the souls of holy figures and saints at a traditional Turkish Islamic *türbe*. These public prayers therefore fully inaugurated the space as a public architectural manifestation of the sacred Islamic dimension of neo-Ottomanism used in service of the healing of national trauma and the memorialising of national heroism.[79]

Monument to a Faithful Nation: God and Homeland

As described above, the AKP under Erdoğan's leadership has used neo-Ottoman constructions of public space and architecture in Istanbul as a way to address the nationality produced by the 15 July coup attempt, in the process reinforcing and deepening its commitment to a neo-Ottoman vision of Turkish national identity. In this effort, Turkish Sunni Islamic tradition became both building blocks in a national identity and epic narrative, and also a means to produce spaces of healing and tranquillity in the midst of national trauma. The projects described above that are central to this effort are the renaming of the first Bosphorus Bridge to the 15 July Martyrs' Bridge (15 Temmuz Şehitler Köprüsü), the construction of the Monument to the Martyrs of 15 July (15 Temmuz Şehitler Makamı), and the elaborate and meaningful discourses and ceremonies associated with these public events and buildings. One concept in particular is found prominently in all of the AKP's discourses, ceremonies, public events and monuments associated with 15 July: religious faith, or *iman*.

Erdoğan and the AKP have consistently attributed the success of the resistance to the coup attempt to one key feature that decisively distinguishes their neo-Ottoman vision of Turkishness from secular Kemalism: religious faith. Time and again in the years since 2016, Erdoğan and the AKP have reiterated that the reason why the everyday Turkish people were able to stand up to the might of tanks and armed soldiers was because they were armed with *iman*, a quality that implicitly sets them apart from secular Kemalist understandings of Turkishness and connects them in the AKP imaginary with the Ottoman Turkish Islamic heritage. Those who resisted the coup attempt were the truest possible examples of Turkish national identity because they were those who exhibited the utmost level of unwavering faith in God and selfless love for the Turkish homeland (*vatan*).

As Behlül Özkan's important work has demonstrated, the term *vatan* – homeland – is particularly significant to Turkish nationalism. Turkish nationalism since its emergence in the wake of the Ottoman collapse was founded on allegiance to a clearly delineated territorial homeland, the territory of the modern Republic of Turkey. In Turkish nationalism, 'the concept of homeland is the dominant symbol that portrays the contested and unfixed association between people and place as obvious, commonsensical, and agreed upon'.[80] The importance of this term to Erdoğan and the AKP's response to the coup attempt further reinforces the importance of Turkish nationalism to their conception of identity. As has been described throughout this book, Erdoğan and the AKP's neo-Ottomanism is composed of a synthesis of Turkish nationalism, social conservativism and Sunni Ottoman Islamic heritage. Each of these elements emerges clearly to the fore in their response to the attempted coup, and the synthesis of these elements is particularly clear in the discourse of faith and homeland.

The discourse of faith and homeland emerged immediately after the events of 15 July themselves. In the official Diyanet sermon for Friday, 22 July 2016, *iman* is placed at the centre of the success of the Turkish people's resistance to the coup attempt, quoting Qur'an 3:139: 'Do not falter and do not grieve, for you will be ascendant if you are believers.' In this sermon appears a phrase and argument that emerges in numerous other ceremonial, architectural and discursive contexts associated with the AKP: 'This terrible experience has shown us this: There can be no force greater than hearts full with love of God and love for the homeland!'[81] From this great love for and faith in God flows all of the Turkish national characteristics described in detail in the analyses above, including fidelity to tradition and national unity: 'We have unchanging values, an immense experience over 14 centuries.'

The Turkish homeland is above all a land of sacrifice and selflessness in the service of God and the community of Muslims: 'This nation is the children of martyrs.' Islam, the Turkish state, and the Turkish nation are connected as a single heroic tradition that appeals to God for its success: 'Save us from every kind of internal and external enemy who would threaten the survival of our religion, our state, our nation.' The title of the sermon itself even uses the exact architectural language that figures so prominently in the Martyrs' Monument and in Erdoğanian neo-Ottomanism more broadly: the day after 15 July is described as 'Milletçe Kenetlenme ve Geleceğimizi İnşa Etme Günü': 'the day of the interlocking as a nation and the construction of our future'.[82]

Then president of religious affairs Mehmet Görmez strongly emphasised the importance of faith in God when interpreting the significance of the events of 15 July. He was strongly convinced that it was nothing other than 'divine power' (*ilahi kudret*) that rendered the Turkish people victorious that night because at that moment of existential threat, the only support the Turkish nation had was 'the faith that it had in God and the love it had for the homeland'. He repeated the key argument that had emerged in proclamations immediately after the events: '15 July showed us that there can be no force greater than hearts full of love of God and love for the homeland.' Observing the victory of the faithful Turkish people that night, 'the whole world was witness to the roots of our culture and identity', that is, faith in God and love for homeland.[83]

Erdoğan's remarks delivered immediately before opening the Martyrs' Monument on the evening of 15 July 2017, perfectly summarise this understanding of Turkish national identity and its manifestation in the heroic struggle of the Turkish people on the night of 15 July 2016. He emphasised that the *iman* of the resistors was stronger than all the modern weaponry arrayed against them, and asked: 'Who can enslave a nation that takes on tanks with *takbir*s [the act of proclaiming 'God is Great', i.e., Allahu Akbar!]?'[84] He argued that a nation is precisely a group of people that share a tradition and a history, that have the same 'pasts, values, and dreams'. The Turkish nation in particular has, in its thousands of years of history, faced enemies and betrayals countless times before, and has emerged victorious in the face of all of them. As he put it: 'In this country, the hill of the martyrs was never, will never lie empty! The land that our martyrs laid down on is clear, the flag that they held is clear, the faith [*iman*] in their hearts is clear, the profession of faith on their tongues is clear. And what is clear of those who martyred them? Only their betrayals [*ihanetler*].'[85]

Erdoğan stressed that keeping the memory of 15 July alive is 'our greatest responsibility to history'.[86] As in the past, the Turkish people must remain ever-vigilant against the enemies that might beset them (a theme that will be taken up in the next chapter as well). But the Turkish people can receive healing, strength and comfort from the fact that they will, rooted in their faith in God and love for their homeland, emerge victorious over these enemies as their ancestors have always done throughout their history. Reflecting on this legacy, at the very end of his remarks before he then prayed for the souls of the martyrs at the newly opened monument in their honour, Erdoğan offered his own version of a famous Kemalist slogan: 'I thank God that He made me a member of a nation like this.'[87]

Notes

1. Timeline of events from 'Turkey Attempted Coup: Timeline of Events', *TRT World*, 15 July 2016, available at: https://www.trtworld.com/turkey/turkey-coup-attempt-timeline-of-events-144495, last accessed 23 May 2022.
2. M. Hakan Yavuz and Rasım Koç, 'The Gülen Movement vs. Erdoğan: The Failed Coup', in M. Hakan Yavuz and Bayram Balcı (eds), *Turkey's July 15 Coup: What Happened and Why* (Salt Lake City, UT: University of Utah Press, 2018), 88.
3. Mujeeb Khan, 'The July 15th Coup: A Critical Institutional Framework for Analysis', in M. Hakan Yavuz and Bayram Balcı (eds), *Turkey's July 15 Coup: What Happened and Why* (Salt Lake City: University of Utah Press, 2018), 52.
4. Yaprak Gürsoy, *Between Military Rule and Democracy: Regime Consolidation in Greece, Turkey, and Beyond* (Ann Arbor: University of Michigan Press, 2017), 196.
5. Gürsoy, *Between Military Rule and Democracy*, 196.
6. Gürsoy, *Between Military Rule and Democracy*, 198; Yavuz and Koç, 'The Gülen Movement vs. Erdoğan', 86.
7. Khan, 'The July 15th Coup', 52.
8. M. Hakan Yavuz and Bayram Balcı, 'Introduction: The Gülen Movement and the Coup', in M. Hakan Yavuz and Bayram Balcı (eds), *Turkey's July 15 Coup: What Happened and Why* (Salt Lake City: University of Utah Press, 2018), 12.

9. Caroline Tee, *The Gülen Movement in Turkey: The Politics of Islam and Modernity* (London: I. B. Tauris, 2016), 1. Tee's study is the most authoritative and comprehensive recent treatment of the movement and its history.

10. Caroline Tee, 'The Gülen Movement and the AK Party: The Rise and Fall of a Turkish Islamist Alliance', in M. Hakan Yavuz and Bayram Balcı (eds), *Turkey's July 15 Coup: What Happened and Why* (Salt Lake City: University of Utah Press, 2018), 150–72.

11. Tee, 'The Gülen Movement and the AK Party', 159–60; Yavuz and Balcı, 'Introduction', 8.

12. Ergun Özbudun, 'AKP at the Crossroads: Erdoğan's Authoritarian Drift', in Susannah Verney, Anna Bosco and Senem Aydın-Düzgit (eds), *The AKP since Gezi Park: Moving to Regime Change in Turkey* (New York: Routledge, 2020), 17–19; Tee, 'The Gülen Movement and the AK Party', 152; Yavuz and Koç, 'The Gülen Movement vs. Erdoğan', 84.

13. Tee, 'The Gülen Movement and the AK Party', 152.

14. M. Hakan Yavuz, 'The Three Stages of the Gülen Movement: From Pietistic Weeping to Power-Obsessed Structure', in M. Hakan Yavuz and Bayram Balcı (eds), *Turkey's July 15 Coup: What Happened and Why* (Salt Lake City: University of Utah Press, 2018), 20, 38.

15. Yavuz and Koç, 'The Gülen Movement vs. Erdoğan', 79.

16. 'Turkish Prosecutors Launched over 1.5 Million Terror Probes between 2016–2020, Justice Ministry', *Ahval*, 21 September 2021, available at: https://ahvalnews.com/terror-charges/turkish-prosecutors-launched-over-15-million-terror-probes-between-2016-2020-justice, last accessed 23 May 2022. See also Akay Zilan, 'Ülkede her an terörist olabilirsiniz', *BirGün* 19 September 2021, available at: https://www.birgun.net/haber/ulkede-her-an-terorist-olabilirsiniz-359165, last accessed 23 May 2022.

17. Zeynep Simsir and Bulent Dilmac, 'Experiences of Post-traumatic Growth in Witnesses to the July 15 Coup Attempt in Turkey', *Illness, Crisis, and Loss* 29:3 (2021), 222.

18. Simsir and Dilmac, 'Experiences of Post-traumatic Growth', 227, 232, 234, 236.

19. Pınar Melis Yelsalı Parmaksız, 'The Transformation of Citizenship Before and After the 15 July Coup Attempt', in Nikos Christofis (ed.), *Erdoğan's New Turkey: Attempted Coup Coup d'État and the Acceleration of Political Crisis* (New York: Routledge, 2020), 113, 120–1; Nadav Solomonovich, '"Democracy and National Unity Day" in Turkey: The Invention of a New National Holiday', *New Perspectives on Turkey* 64 (2021): 66–7.

20. Solomonovich, '"Democracy and National Unity Day" in Turkey', 60.
21. 'Bosphrous Bridge, Ankara's Main Square to be Renamed after July 15', *Hürriyet Daily News*, 26 July 2022, available at: https://www.hurriyetdailynews.com/bosphorus-bridge-ankaras-main-square-to-be-renamed-after-july-15-102081, last accessed 2 May 2022.
22. 'Boğaz Köprüsü Ne Zaman Yapıldı? Yüksekliği Ve Uzunluğu Nedir?' *Milliyet*, 16 November 2021, available at: https://www.milliyet.com.tr/egitim/bogaz-koprusu-ne-zaman-yapildi-yuksekligi-ve-uzunlugu-nedir-6643282, last accessed 2 May 2022.
23. 'Boğaz Köprüsü Ne Zaman Yapıldı?'
24. '15 Temmuz Şehitler Köprüsü', official website of the Üsküdar municipality, available at: https://www.uskudar.bel.tr/tr/main/pages/15-temmuz-sehitler-koprusu/36, last accessed 2 May 2022.
25. For extensive aerial drone footage of the monument from the air, see '15 Temmuz Şehitler Makamı'na ziyaretçi akını havadan görüntülendi', *Demiören Haber Ajansı*, 15 July 2020, available at: https://www.youtube.com/watch?v=thmVMm3ia3U, last accessed 2 May 2022; and for a virtual tour of the site, see '360 Video – 15 Temmuz Şehitler Makamı, Sanal Tur, Vr gezi', Ahmed Nafi Akbaba, available at: https://www.youtube.com/watch?v=oIh94k7v0f4, last accessed 2 May 2022. Due to the very high degree of security sensitivity at the site, obtaining photographs was not deemed feasible due to any risks it might have incurred to the photographer. A very detailed sense of the physical site can be obtained through the media mentioned here.
26. The museum was opened on 15 July 2019, three years after the coup attempt and two years after the opening of the Martyr's Monument: '"Hafıza 15 Temmuz" Müzesi Açıldı', official website of the Istanbul Governorate, available at: http://www.istanbul.gov.tr/hafiza-15-temmuz-muzesi-aciliyor#, last accessed 3 May 2022.
27. Coşkun Yılmaz, '15 Temmuz Şehitler Makamı', *Üsküdar Kültür, Sanat ve Medeniyet Dergisi* 4:1 (2017): 74.
28. Ezgi Çapa, Topbaş, '15 Temmuz Şehitler Abidesi'ni inceledi', *Demiören Haber Ajansı*, 12 July 2017; 'İbb Başkanı Topbaş, '15 Temmuz Şehitler Abidesi'nde İncelemelerde Bulundu', *Haberler.com*, 12 July 2017, available at: https://www.haberler.com/guncel/ibb-baskani-topbas-15-temmuz-sehitler-abidesi-nde-9824004-haberi, last accessed 2 May 2022.
29. Yılmaz, '15 Temmuz Şehitler Makamı', 74.
30. Yılmaz, '15 Temmuz Şehitler Makamı', 75.

31. İlker Nuri Öztürk, 'Şehitler kitabesi kendini yazdırdı', *Yeni Şafak*, 23 July 2017, available at: https://www.yenisafak.com/gundem/sehitler-kitabesi-kendini-yazdirdi-2761228, last accessed 3 May 2022.

32. The great Sunni scholar, mystic and theologian Abu Hamid al-Ghazali (1058/9–1111) authored the paradigmatic treatise in this genre, and his interpretations of the names are widely considered standard. For his treatment of the name 'All-Witnessing', in English, see Al-Ghazali, *The Ninety-Nine Beautiful Names of God*, trans. David B. Burrell and Nazih Daher (Cambridge: Islamic Texts Society, 1992), 123; and in the original Arabic, see Abu Hamid al-Ghazali, *Al-Maqsad al-Asna fi Sharh Ma'ani Asma' Allah al-Husna*, ed. Fadlou A. Shehadi (Beirut: Dar el-Machreq, 1971), 137.

33. Al-Ghazali, *The Ninety-Nine Beautiful Names of God*, 123.

34. Timur Hammond, 'Making Memorial Publics: Media, Monuments, and the Politics of Commemoration Following Turkey's July 16 Coup Attempt', *Geographical Review* 110:4 (2020): 536.

35. Yılmaz, '15 Temmuz Şehitler Makamı', 73.

36. Yılmaz, '15 Temmuz Şehitler Makamı', 73.

37. Yılmaz, '15 Temmuz Şehitler Makamı', 73.

38. Kishwar Rizvi, *The Transnational Mosque: Architecture and Historical Memory in the Contemporary Middle East* (Chapel Hill: University of North Carolina Press, 2015), 56.

39. Rizvi, *The Transnational Mosque*, 57.

40. Yılmaz, '15 Temmuz Şehitler Makamı', 73.

41. Rizvi, *The Transnational Mosque*, 57.

42. On these projects, see Rizvi, *The Transnational Mosque*, 33–67; Martin Klapetek, 'Şehitlik Mosque and the Islamic Cemetery at Columbiadamm: Islam in Public Space', *Studia Religiologica* 52:1 (2019), 63–77.

43. Quoted in Yılmaz, '15 Temmuz Şehitler Makamı', 74.

44. Qur'an 22:76 (*Study Qur'an* translation, ed. and trans. Seyyid Hossein Nasr, Caner K. Dagli, Maria Massi Dakake, Joseph E. B. Lumbard and Muhammad Rustom. New York: HarperOne, 2015); Jale Necdet Erzen, 'Reading Mosques: Meaning and Architecture in Isla', *Journal of Aesthetics and Art Criticism* 69:1 (2011), 126–7.

45. Gönül Tekin, 'The Motif of "Cypress-River-Beloved One-Garden" in Nevā'ī's and Aḥmed Pāşā's Poetry and its Archetype', *Oriente Moderno* 76:2 (1996), 465, 468, 483.

46. Öztürk, 'Şehitler kitabesi kendini yazdırdı'; Yılmaz, '15 Temmuz Şehitler Makamı', 76. See also Mustafa İsmet Uzun, 'Ebced', *İslam Ansiklopedisi* (Ankara: Türkiye Diyanet Vakfı, 1994), 68–70.

47. Öztürk, 'Şehitler kitabesi kendini yazdırdı'.

48. Öztürk, 'Şehitler kitabesi kendini yazdırdı'.

49. Öztürk, 'Şehitler kitabesi kendini yazdırdı'.

50. Mehmet Demirci, 'Himmet', *İslam Ansiklopedisi* (Ankara: Türkiye Diyanet Vakfı, 1998), 56–7.

51. The full text of the poem can be found in Yılmaz, '15 Temmuz Şehitler Makamı', 76; Öztürk, 'Şehitler kitabesi kendini yazdırdı'.

52. Marinos Sariyyanis, 'Ruler and State, State and Society in Ottoman Political Thought', *Turkish Historical Review* 4 (2013): 91–2, 96, 104.

53. Both quotes are from Qur'an 76:21 (*Study Qur'an* translation).

54. Öztürk, 'Şehitler kitabesi kendini yazdırdı' (*Study Qur'an* translation).

55. Reported by Topbaş in a live interview to Haberler.com shortly before the monument was completed and opened in July 2017; see 'Topbaş, 15 Temmuz Şehitler Abidesi'ni İnceledi', Haberler.com, available at: www.dailymotion.com/video/x5tc9hs, last accessed 15 May 2022; see also 'Topbaş, 15 Temmuz Şehitler Abidesi'ni İnceledi', Haberler.com, 12 July 2017, available at: https://www.haberler.com/guncel/topbas-15-temmuz-sehitler-abidesi-ni-inceledi-9824329-haberi, last accessed 15 May 2022.

56. 'Topbaş, 15 Temmuz Şehitler Abidesi'ni İnceledi' [Haberler.com].

57. 'Topbaş, 15 Temmuz Şehitler Abidesi'ni İnceledi' [Haberler.com].

58. 'Topbaş, 15 Temmuz Şehitler Abidesi'ni İnceledi', memurlar.net, 12 July 2022, available at: https://www.memurlar.net/haber/680582/topbas-15-temmuz-sehitler-abidesi-ni-inceledi.html, last accessed 15 May 2022.

59. Talat S. Halman, *A Millennium of Turkish Literature: A Concise History*, ed. Jayne L. Warner (Syracuse, NY: Syracuse University Press, 2011), 57.

60. Halman, *A Millennium of Turkish Literature*, viii, 8–10.

61. See the elaborate narrative of events provided by the Communication Ministry of the Office of the Presidency of the Republic of Turkey at: https://www.iletisim.gov.tr/turkce/stratejik_iletisim_calismalari/detaylar/15-temmuz-destani, last accessed 15 May 2022.

62. 'Topbaş, 15 Temmuz Şehitler Abidesi'ni İnceledi', *Demiören Haber Ajansı*, 12 July 2017.

63. Öztürk, 'Şehitler kitabesi kendini yazdırdı'.

64. Mehmet Görmez, 'Takdim', in *15 Temmuz Gazilerin Dilinden* (Istanbul: DİB Yayınları, 2017), 15.

65. Yılmaz, '15 Temmuz Şehitler Makamı', 72.

66. 'Cumhurbaşkanlığı Himayesinde 15 Temmuz'un Birinci Yılına Özel Anma Programı', 10 July 2017, Office of the Presidency of the Republic of Turkey,

available at: https://www.tccb.gov.tr/haberler/410/78862/cumhurbaskanligi-himayesinde-15-temmuzun-birinci-yilina-ozel-anma-programi.html, last accessed 15 May 2022.

67. On this text, see A. Necla Pekolcay, 'Mevlid', *İslam Ansiklopedisi* 29 (Ankara: Türkiye Diyanet Vakfı, 2004), 485–6; Süleyman Chelebi, *The Mevlidi Sherif*, trans. F. Lyman MacCallum (London: John Murray, 1943); Süleyman Çelebi, *Vesilatü'n Necat* (Ankara: Diyanet İşleri Başkanlığı Yayınları, 2017).

68. Nusret Çam, 'Ulucami', *İslam Ansiklopedisi* 42 (Ankara: Türkiye Diyanet Vakfı, 2012), 81–2.

69. In addition to the list provided in *İslam Ansiklopedisi*, see also the publication provided by the Atatürk Culture, Language and History High Council of the Office of the Presidency of the Republic of Turkey: Mustafa Cambaz, *Türküye Ulucamileri Fotoğraf Serisi* (Istanbul: Atatürk Kültür Merkezi Başkanlığı, 2016).

70. *15 Temmuz Milli İradenin Zaferi Araştırma Raporu* (Ankara: AK Parti Sosyal Politikalar Başlanlığı, 2017).

71. *15 Temmuz Milli İradenin Zaferi Araştırma Raporu*, 32.

72. *15 Temmuz Milli İradenin Zaferi Araştırma Raporu*, 52–3.

73. *15 Temmuz Milli İradenin Zaferi Araştırma Raporu*, 48.

74. 'Milletçe Yeniden Doğuş: 15 Temmuz', Diyanet İşleri Başkanlığı, 13 July 2018. The sermon quotes Qur'an 2:11–12 on the subject of *fesat*: 'And when it is said unto them, "Do not work corruption upon the earth", they say, "We are only working righteousness". Nay, it is they who are the workers of corruption, though they are unaware' (*Study Qur'an* translation).

75. '15 Temmuz'u Anmak, İhanet Anlamak', Diyanet İşleri Başkanlığı, 12 July 2019; '15 Temmuz ve Birlik Ruhu', Diyanet İşleri Başkanlığı, 10 July 2020. On the particular significance of these annual sermons, see also Solomonovich, '"Democracy and National Unity Day" in Turkey', 64.

76. *Kendi Dilinden FETÖ: Örgütlü Bir Din İstismarı* (Ankara: Diyanet İşleri Başkanlığı Yayınları, 2017).

77. On the 'democracy vigils' held throughout Istanbul that day, see also Adem Demir, Kaan Bozdoğan, Sefa Mutlu, Muhammed Gencebay Gür, Mehmet Ali Derdiyok, Lale Bildirici and Halil Demir, 'İstanbul'da 'demokrasi nöbetleri' başladı', *Anadolu Ajansı*, 16 July 2017, available at: https://www.aa.com.tr/tr/15-temmuz-darbe-girisimi/istanbulda-demokrasi-nobetleri-basladi/862478, last accessed 16 May 2022.

78. 'Cumhurbaşkanlığı Himayesinde 15 Temmuz'un Birinci Yılına Özel Anma Programı'.

79. 'Cumhurbaşkanı Erdoğan, 15 Temmuz Şehitler Anıtı'nı açtı', *Vatan*, 16 July 2017, available at: https://www.gazetevatan.com/gundem/cumhurbaskani-erdogan-15-temmuz-sehitler-anitini-acti-1085065, last accessed 16 May 2022.

80. Özkan, *From the Abode of Islam to the Turkish Vatan*, 105.

81. 'Gün, Milletçe Kenetlenme ve Geleceğimizi İnşa Etme Günüdür', Diyanet İşleri Başkanlığı, 22 July 2016.

82. 'Gün, Milletçe Kenetlenme ve Geleceğimizi İnşa Etme Günüdür'.

83. Görmez, 'Takdim', 16–17; see also Solomonovich, '"Democracy and National Unity Day" in Turkey', 64.

84. '15 Temmuz'u Unutmamak ve Unutturmamak Tarihimize Karşı En Büyük Sorumluluğumuzdur', Office of the Presidency of the Republic of Turkey, 15 July 2017, available at: https://www.tccb.gov.tr/haberler/410/79932/istanbuldaki-15-temmuz-demokrasi-ve-mill-birlik-gunu-anma-toreni-basladi.html#:~:text=%C4%B0stanbul'da%2015%20Temmuz%20Demokrasi,kar%C5%9F%C4%B1%20da%20en%20b%C3%BCy%C3%BCk%20sorumlulu%C4%9Fumuzdur, last accessed 16 May 2022.

85. Quoted in Yılmaz, '15 Temmuz Şehitler Makamı', 77.

86. '15 Temmuz Unutulmayacak', *Üsküdar Kültür, Sanat ve Medeniyet Dergisi* 4:1 (2017): 80.

87. '15 Temmuz Unutulmayacak'.

5

THE RECONVERSION OF HAGIA SOPHIA, 2020: FINAL CONQUEST AND VICTORY OF THE AKP

Summary Background and Context: Hagia Sophia

The monumental building of Hagia Sophia in Istanbul is one of the most significant architectural structures and achievements in global history. When it was constructed almost 1,500 years ago, it was the largest church ever built, and retained this status for centuries. Hagia Sophia was built by the Byzantine emperor Justinian I (r. 527–65), beginning in 532 and completed in 537. The building was designed by renowned architects Anthemius of Tralles and Isidore of Miletus, and was the third structure on the site to bear the name Hagia Sophia. The foundations for the first church of Hagia Sophia were commissioned by Constantine himself, with the building being completed under his son, Emperor Constantius II in 360. This church was destroyed by fire in 404, and replaced by a second church of the same name under Emperor Theodosius II in 415. This building was destroyed in the Nika riots against Justinian's reign in 532.[1] The present structure was built between 532 and 537 and took the same name as the two churches that preceded it, and represented the sheer might of Byzantine imperial dominion. The original dome collapsed during an earthquake in 558 and was rebuilt in 562. The structure completed in 537 and the second dome completed in 562 are what survive to the present day. Throughout the Byzantine period Hagia Sophia represented the ecclesiastical centre of Eastern Orthodox Christian religious culture and tradition, and has retained its spiritual importance within this tradition to the present day.

Figure 5.1 Hagia Sophia, January 2022. Photograph Vural Yazıcıoğlu.

After the Ottoman emperor Mehmet II (r. 1444–6, 1451–81) conquered Constantinople in 1453 and converted it to the capital of his empire, Hagia Sophia was converted into the Ottoman imperial mosque, now known in Turkish as Ayasofya.[2] Hagia Sophia retained its status at the centre of Ottoman imperial and religious culture until the end of the empire and the rise of the Turkish Republic in 1922–3. Upon its conversion into the Ottoman imperial mosque, significant physical changes were made to the interior and exterior of the building by Mehmet II. These included the removal of crosses, icons and relics from the interior, and the addition of two minarets to the exterior (only persons of the imperial Ottoman lineage were permitted to add more than one minaret to a mosque); Mehmet also built the first *medrese* attached to Hagia Sophia.[3] The mosaics on the lower floor were quickly plastered over, while those in the upper floor seem to have remained uncovered into the sixteenth century, and various others in the narthex and galleries were not covered until even later. The mosaics that were on display during Hagia Sophia's time as a public museum were first uncovered by the American archaeologist Thomas Whittemore in 1931.[4] Muslim relics associated with Muhammad and Mehmet's victory banners were added to the interior, and Mehmet instructed the preacher of the Friday sermon to read the sermon with sword in hand. Mehmet also established an enormous sacred monetary endowment (*waqf* or *vakıf*) for the building composed of his own personal share of the city's property after the conquest.[5]

After Mustafa Kemal Atatürk founded the Republic of Turkey in 1923, the status of the building of Hagia Sophia was again reconsidered in the light of the newly ascendent political ideology, in this case, a form of Westernising secularism that wished to disassociate itself from both Muslim and Christian religious tradition. In 1934, Hagia Sophia was closed to worship and reopened as a museum. This decision would become a rallying point for conservative Muslim opposition to Kemalist secularism in the decades to come, including among circles that led to the creation of the AKP. Under Erdoğan's leadership, the decision was finally made to reconvert the museum back into a mosque. In June 2020, just weeks before the decision to reconvert the museum of Hagia Sophia back into the mosque of Hagia Sophia was finalised and then implemented in July, the well-regarded Turkish polling and research firm Metropoll published their findings that the Turkish populace remained starkly divided over the question of whether or not Hagia Sophia should be reconverted back into a mosque. According to the poll, 46 per cent of respondents felt that Hagia Sophia should be reconverted back into a mosque, while 43 per cent felt that it should remain a museum. Responses to this question exhibited stark partisan divides: for instance, 70.7 per cent of AKP voters felt that Hagia Sophia should be reconverted back into a mosque, and only 21.6 per cent felt that it should remain a museum; for CHP voters, the numbers were entirely reversed, with 21.8 per sent supporting Hagia Sophia's reconversion and 67.6 per cent opposing it.[6]

In other words, while clearly a deeply politicised issue, the decision to reconvert Hagia Sophia back into a mosque did enjoy substantial support from AKP voters in particular, support that Erdoğan knew he could count on when implementing this decision. On 10 July 2020 the 10th chamber of the *Danıştay* (the highest Turkish administrative court) in Ankara issued a ruling that invalidated the 24 November decision to convert the mosque of Hagia Sophia into a museum. President Erdoğan quickly signed presidential decree number 2729 ordering 'the opening of Hagia Sophia to Muslim worship [*ibadet*]', meaning, the formal reconversion of the museum of Hagia Sophia into the grand mosque of Hagia Sophia, 'Ayasofya-i Kebir Cami-i Şerifi'. The date for the first congregational Friday prayer service was set for 24 July 2020.

This chapter analyses the shift from Hagia Sophia's status as a museum to a mosque in the summer of 2020 as the paradigmatic example of the public dominance and triumphalism of the AKP's nationalist vision under Erdoğan. As Istanbul's most recognisable architectural monument, it is impossible to overstate the significance of Hagia Sophia to the spatial politics of the AKP in Istanbul. The shift in its status marks the high point of the AKP's use of architecture and public space to exclude multicultural or pluralistic narratives of Turkish national identity. This chapter will describe the complex historical and contemporary significance of the physical building of Hagia Sophia in order to explain why it was that Erdoğan and the AKP saw it as absolutely necessary to their spatial political vision to reconvert the museum of Hagia Sophia into the Grand Mosque of Hagia Sophia. This chapter will chart in detail the history of the spatial politics of the building of Hagia Sophia, focusing on the historical significance, political and social discourse, public ceremony and physical changes related to the reconversion of the museum of Hagia Sophia into the mosque of Hagia Sophia.

As will be detailed in this chapter, due to its complex religious history, Hagia Sophia can be used to represent an alternative, non-nationalist and cosmopolitan vision of Istanbul's identity that is inclusive of its association with both Christianity and Islam, Greek–Byzantine and Ottoman–Turkish cultural and religious history. It was for this reason that Erdoğan and the AKP saw it as absolutely necessary to reconvert the Hagia Sophia, as explicitly an act of ultimate victory over alternative non-Muslim and non-Turkish claims and visions of belonging to the city of Istanbul. The reopening ceremony, political rhetoric and physical changes to the building itself made by the AKP all epitomise the phenomenon of Erdoğanian neo-Ottomanism. Moreover, analysing the reactions and statements of the most prominent local and global representatives of the indigenous Greek Orthodox community of Istanbul provides the full context for Erdoğan and the AKP's actions, clearly revealing the marginalising and otherising dynamics at the heart of the AKP's spatial politics under Erdoğan.

The Church of Hagia Sophia: History and Significance of the Byzantine Imperial Cathedral

Prior to its conversion into a mosque after the conquest of Istanbul in 1453, Hagia Sophia was one of the most significant Christian buildings in the world. As an unparalleled architectural and artistic achievement, an ecclesiastical centre, and a potent symbol of Eastern Orthodox Christian religiosity, Hagia Sophia has played a role in the history of Eastern Christianity that is incomparable to any other physical space. As this chapter argues, the AKP and Erdoğan's decision to reconvert Hagia Sophia back into a mosque in July 2020 represented an assertion of homogeneous and conservative Turkish Sunni nationalism over and against what Hagia Sophia represented in its original usage as a Byzantine Christian cathedral. Therefore, a consideration of the history of this building and its development as the focal point of medieval Byzantine and subsequently Eastern Orthodox Christian religious identity is critical for understanding the context of, and reaction to, this decision.

Hagia Sophia represented the unrivalled power of the emperor who commissioned it, Justinian I (r. 527–65). Commonly reckoned to have presided over one of the imperial high points of the Eastern Roman Empire – usually referred to as Byzantium – Justinian's intense ambition is intentionally reflected in the sheer size of Hagia Sophia. Seeing the structure for the first time, one is immediately struck by the size of the central dome, the focal point of the structure (see Figure 5.4). The dome rises 56.6 m (186 ft) into the air, with a diameter of 31.87 m (105 ft), making it far taller than medieval Christian cathedrals in Western Europe, for instance. The interior of the building is massive, at 255,800 cubic m (2,753,408 ft), with space to hold around 16,000 people.[7] The structure remains impressive almost 1,500 years after it was built. At the time of its construction, however, it would have been truly astonishing – one of the largest religious structures ever constructed in human history. The church of Hagia Sophia was clearly intended by Justinian to radically surpass any existing monument in his empire, standing as a testament to his renewed imperial might and the centrality of the Christian faith to the identity of the society that he ruled.

Despite its singular achievement, however, Hagia Sophia was the result of previous centuries of engineering advancement and artistic experimentation. The design of Anthemius and Miletus can be interpreted as one of the crowning achievements of the by then centuries-long tradition of Roman engineering experimentation and innovation.[8] Moreover, as Slobodan Ćurčić has argued, Hagia Sophia can be understood as the dramatic climax of previous decades of architectural experimentation and confidence in the sixth century, engendered by Justinian's long and successful reign.[9] The signature element of Hagia Sophia, its monumental dome, had precedents in Byzantine and Constantinopolitan architecture, such as the massive but no longer extant Myrelaion Rotunda, which was probably part of a fifth-century palace complex.[10]

No contemporary documents (such as technical or financial records) related to the construction of Hagia Sophia survive to the present, though they surely at one time were part of the imperial Byzantine archive (Byzantine documents from these periods often do not survive in large numbers, due to the devastation wrought during the sack of the city in 1204 by Latin Crusaders, and the Ottoman conquest in 1453).[11] The written testimonies of Hagia Sophia that do survive are passages in other literary genres, most notably the contemporary work of the historian Procopius (d. c. 565). In his work titled

Figure 5.2 Hagia Sophia interior, January 2022. Photograph Vural Yazıcıoğlu.

Figure 5.3 Hagia Sophia interior, January 2022. Photograph Vural Yazıcıoğlu.

'On Buildings' (*De aedificiis*, I.1.20–65), written c. 544, or some two decades after Hagia Sophia's construction, Procopius elaborated the 'official propaganda' of the Byzantine state concerning its imperial cathedral.[12] Procopius' account draws attention to the pious devotion driving Justinian's command to erect such an extraordinary religious edifice, his active role in its construction and the divine wonder that it was designed to evoke: it is a space that 'boasts of an ineffable beauty' where the interior design channels light so effectively that '[y]ou might say that the [interior] space is not illuminated by the sun from the outside, but that the radiance is generated within, so great an abundance of light bathes the shrine all round'.[13]

Contemporary accounts also stress the magnificence of the great dome, which due to the ingenuity of the placement of the supporting columns and attendant structures, appears to hang in mid-air without support. As Procopius put it, 'All of these elements, marvellously fitted together in mid-air, suspended from one another and reposing only on the parts adjacent to them, produce a unified and most remarkable harmony in the work.'[14] The poem of Paulus Silentiarius recited in 563 also draws attention to the seemingly

airborne quality of the dome and its arches, while describing in rich detail
the opulence of the interior, most especially the colourful variety of the most
expensive marbles drawn from throughout the empire: 'Yet who, even in the
thundering strains of Homer, shall sing the marble meadows gathered upon
the mighty walls and spreading pavement of the lofty church?'[15]

Hagia Sophia served as the imperial cathedral of the Byzantine Empire
from the moment of its construction to the end of the empire, a time spanning almost an entire millennium. Because the Byzantine tradition was central
to the development of the whole of the Eastern Christian tradition, this means
that Hagia Sophia is not simply an impressive example of Byzantine architecture, but more importantly one of the most significant places in all of Christian
history, most especially Eastern Orthodox Christian history. This fact is crucial
to understanding its legacy into the present, and the ways in which Erdoğan's
AKP set their own political identity over and against this legacy.

The Christian denomination now referred to as the Eastern Orthodox
Church is the ecclesiastical descendent of the official church of the Eastern
Roman, or Byzantine Empire, a medieval imperial state whose political history

Figure 5.4 Hagia Sophia dome and upper galleries, January 2022. Photograph Vural Yazıcıoğlu.

Figure 5.5 Hagia Sophia *mihrab* (with view of covered mosaic icons at the top), January 2022. Photograph Vural Yazıcıoğlu.

is usually dated from the reign of Constantine (306–37) to its definitive end with the conquest of its capital, Constantinople ('the city of Constantine') by Mehmet II in 1453.[16] Prior to the Great Schism of 1054, the two largest linguistic and cultural halves of the Christian world – the Latin and the Greek – formed a single communion, or denomination. After 1054, the Western, Latin-speaking tradition of the Roman imperial church – centred in the episcopal see of Rome – developed into the communion now known as Roman Catholicism, with the subsequent development of the Protestant churches from the sixteenth century onward.

The Greek-speaking tradition of the Roman imperial church – comprising the episcopal sees of Antioch, Jerusalem, Alexandria and Constantinople – developed into the Byzantine imperial church, with pride of place given to the episcopal see or patriarchate of Constantinople as the Byzantine imperial capital. Peoples who were converted to Christianity by representatives of this imperial tradition, such as the Rus under Prince Vladimir I (r. 980–1015), remained under the ecclesiastical jurisdiction of Constantinople until its capture in 1453, after which time jurisdictions formerly under Constantinople began to develop into independent (or autocephalous) churches that remained in communion with one another.

Thus, the contemporary Eastern Orthodox Church comprises a complex network of local jurisdictions of varying levels of formal dependence on one another, which nonetheless comprise a united denomination by virtue of their mutual recognition as members of the same church. Other Eastern Christian churches with similar historical roots, but denominational identities distinct from the Eastern Orthodox, include the Oriental Orthodox Churches (most notably the Armenian, Syriac, Coptic, Ethiopian and Eritrean churches). When totalled together, in 2017 the Pew Research Center estimated the global number of Orthodox Christians (Eastern and Oriental) to be some 12 per cent of global Christianity, at some 260 million people.[17] Despite their status as the historical second half of Christian religious tradition, Eastern Christians have declined in numbers relative to Western Christians (i.e., Roman Catholics and Protestants) over the course of the past few centuries, especially as a result of the high levels of modern population growth in nations that were once colonised by Western Christian empires.[18]

The significance of Hagia Sophia for Eastern Orthodox Christian identity and tradition can be assessed in two dimensions: the physical space itself and its religious meaning; and Hagia Sophia's status as the symbol of the Ecumenical Patriarchate of Constantinople. With respect to the religious significance of the building itself, Hagia Sophia was designed to symbolise and encapsulate in monumental form the essential tenets of the Christian faith. The name Hagia Sophia (Ἁγία Σοφία) literally means 'Holy Wisdom', referring to the wisdom of God, the omnipresent and omnipotent order that underlies the whole cosmos. At the same time, as one of the greatest modern Eastern Orthodox theologians, Georges Florovsky, argued, the name Hagia Sophia is also a reference to Jesus Christ. Greek patristic and Byzantine theologians, from as early as the second century, interpreted references to Divine Wisdom in the Hebrew Bible as references to the second person of the Holy Trinity, the Son, Jesus Christ.[19] This interpretation was based on significant New Testament passages that describe Christ as the Wisdom of God, such as 1 Corinthians 1:24.[20] The term Hagia Sophia therefore calls to mind the central tenet of Eastern Orthodox Christian religious tradition, that in accordance with God's infinitely wise plan for the universe, God became incarnate in order to save and transform the whole cosmos. The theological associations of this name underscore the function of the building as a physical manifestation of the total cosmic vision of Byzantine Christianity.[21]

The elaborate Byzantine liturgical worship and hymnody that took place inside Hagia Sophia also played a key role in the development of Eastern Orthodox liturgy, the central form of religious practice in this tradition which is composed of melodic chant and focuses on the central rite of the Eucharist. The design of Hagia Sophia was meant to maximise the aesthetic possibilities of this liturgical tradition, thus heightening the sense of the worshipper crossing the boundary between the earthly and the heavenly. Bissera Pentcheva's recent work has explored in-depth the complex and innovative liturgical practices developed in Hagia Sophia, and in her words, 'the liturgy of the Great Church explored venues where the aural and visual could be pushed beyond the limits of language and interpretation'.[22]

The sheer immensity of the interior space produced spectacular acoustic reverberations, and the liturgical chant composed over the centuries for use in the space exploited this quality in order to produce an overwhelming sonic experience for the thousands of worshippers in attendance that would have been 'enveloping, resonant, and non-intimate' in character.[23] The choirs that performed the chant for the various worship services conducted throughout the week, culminating in the Divine Liturgy celebrating the Eucharist every Sunday, were composed of dozens of professional singers, and were stationed around a raised marble platform in the middle of the sanctuary, the *ambo*, which would have been surrounded by the vast numbers of congregants. The *ambo* was ascended by the Patriarch of Constantinople in order to extend blessings to the crowd, and by the deacons for readings from the Scriptures. The central rites of the Divine Liturgy were performed by the priests at the main altar at the east end of the sanctuary. In total, including singers, priests, door keepers and others, the cathedral employed some 500 people to perform the liturgy every Sunday, in addition to the presence of thousands of worshippers.[24] As Pentcheva points out, this almost millennium-long tradition of liturgy in Hagia Sophia came to an abrupt and violent end with the conquest of 1453, though in recent years attempts have been made to recreate what these hymns might have sounded like using advanced recording technology.[25]

Accounts of the considerable spiritual impact of experiencing worship in Hagia Sophia became prominent elements of Eastern Orthodox religious tradition. The most famous and widely circulated of these accounts is the legend recounted in the early twelfth-century Russian *Primary Chronicle* telling how the prince of the Rus, Vladimir I of Kiev (c. 958–1015), chose Byzantine Christianity as the official religion for his then pagan realm, resulting in the 'Baptism of Rus' and the founding of the Russian Orthodox Church (currently the largest of the Eastern Orthodox jurisdictions). According to the legend, Vladimir had been visited by emissaries from the Muslim Bulgars, the Jewish Khazars, German (i.e., Western or Latin) Christians and Byzantine (Greek) Christians in 986, each eager to convert the Rus to their respective faith. Since each described their faith in glowing terms, Vladimir's advisers recommended that he send his own emissaries to experience each group's worship to determine which was best. After attending worship services conducted by each group, Vladimir's emissaries returned with the strong recommendation to adopt the religion of the Byzantines, because their experience of worship in Hagia Sophia was so transcendent that they 'knew not whether [they] were in heaven or on earth'.[26] This legend remains one of the most widely familiar and recognisable elements of modern Eastern Orthodox popular religious culture, widely reproduced and retold in both formal and informal contexts.[27]

The second dimension of Hagia Sophia's significance in Eastern Orthodox tradition concerns its status as the historical location and symbol of the Ecumenical Patriarch of Constantinople (after the capture of Hagia Sophia in 1453, the patriarchal headquarters would eventually be relocated to the Fener neighbourhood, centred on the patriarchal church of St George, and is now commonly referred to as 'the Phanar'). As the Eastern Roman Empire gradually developed into a distinct polity (known in modern parlance as Byzantium), the Patriarchate of Constantinople as the episcopal see of the imperial capital (the 'New Rome'), grew in prominence relative to the other ancient eastern patriarchates (in Jerusalem, Antioch and Alexandria). In the sixth century, the Patriarch of Constantinople acquired the title of 'Ecumenical', referring to its ecclesiastical jurisdiction over the entirety of the territory of the Eastern Roman Empire.[28] As Byzantium expanded its territory and imperial sphere of influence, the ecclesiastical jurisdiction of the Ecumenical Patriarchate grew along with it. By the ninth century, some 500–600 archbishops, metropolitans and bishops fell under the jurisdiction of the see of Constantinople, as the Ecumenical Patriarch oversaw missionary efforts that resulted in the expansion of Byzantine Christianity (modern Eastern Orthodoxy) into the cultures that it now calls home today (such as Russia, Bulgaria, Serbia and elsewhere).[29]

As the cathedral of the Ecumenical Patriarchate, Hagia Sophia thus represents the history of Eastern Orthodoxy itself, as the spring from which flowed the previous fifteen hundred years of its history. Hagia Sophia's association with the office of the Ecumenical Patriarchate of Constantinople is a key reason for the continuing attachment many Eastern Orthodox feel to this sanctuary. Past holders of the episcopal see of Constantinople were responsible for the most foundational components of Eastern Orthodox Christian religious belief and practice. The extent of these contributions would require entire volumes to detail in their entirety, so only two of the most notable examples will be discussed briefly here: St Gregory of Nazianzus, known as 'Gregory the Theologian' (329–391), archbishop of Constantinople from 379 to 381); and St John Chrysostom (347–407), archbishop of Constantinople from 398 to 404. The importance of these two saints remains highly significant to the current identity of the Ecumenical Patriarchate of Constantinople. In 1204, during the Latin Crusader sack of Constantinople, the relics of these two saints were looted from Hagia Sophia and taken to Rome. In 2004, Pope John Paul II returned these relics to the care of Ecumenical Patriarch Bartholomew, and they remain a central element of the immense sanctity of the patriarchal church of St George in Istanbul.[30]

Gregory of Nazianzus is recognised as one of the most influential theologians in the history of the Christian Church due to his status as the first to fully elaborate the doctrine of the Holy Trinity in the terms that it has been understood in Christian theology ever since.[31] Gregory wrote the treatises that elaborated this doctrine as orations he delivered while archbishop of Constantinople from 379 to 381.[32] Gregory also served as chair (and subsequently passionate defender) of the Ecumenical Council of Constantinople, whose creed (the Nicene-Constantinopolitan Creed) to this day retains its status as the guarantor of doctrinal orthodoxy for millions of Christians worldwide. John Chrysostom, archbishop of Constantinople from 398 to 404, is chiefly remembered for the vast library of homilies that he composed, which combined with Gregory's theological orations comprise some of the most widely circulated texts in Byzantine and Eastern Orthodox history. The present-day weekly worship service of the Eastern Orthodox Church, the Divine Liturgy of John Chrysostom, retains his name because the text of the central Eucharistic rite was authored by John himself (and has been the text regularly used for this purpose since approximately the year 1000).[33] In other words, these two saints exemplify the incalculable importance of the Ecumenical Patriarchate and the city of Constantinople to the history of Eastern Orthodoxy. The historical association of the church of Hagia Sophia with this ecclesiastical office means that this present building is weighted with immense religious meaning for the Eastern Orthodox tradition.

Finally, the physical space of the present Hagia Sophia itself also witnessed and hosted countless significant events in the history of this particular Christian tradition, including, to name only two examples, the Fifth and Sixth Ecumenical Councils which confirmed and elaborated foundational elements of Christian dogmatic theology.[34] Perhaps the most striking visible remnant of the centrality of Hagia Sophia to Orthodox Christian religious history is the mosaic icon of Mary the Mother of God and the infant Christ, installed in 867 in the apse to celebrate the restoration of the veneration of holy images, or icons, which retain their status as the most fundamental element of Eastern Orthodox material piety and worship art.[35] As will be described in more detail later in this chapter, the view of this mosaic has been obstructed by a white curtain since the reconversion of Hagia Sophia to a mosque in 2020.

The Mosque of Hagia Sophia: History and Significance of the Ottoman Imperial Mosque

As Anna Bigelow argues, the key to understanding Hagia Sophia's complex legacy is its status as 'a site of mutually exclusive universalisms', meaning that the church of Hagia Sophia, and then the mosque of Hagia Sophia, both embodied absolute claims to imperial and religious authority. As this chapter will later argue, it is important to introduce an important nuance to this claim by recognising that in the context of the modern Turkish Republic, there is a profound asymmetry between the power and social status of the communities who make these respective claims, that is, Greek Orthodox Christians and Turkish Sunni Muslims.[36] As Gülrü Necipoğlu points out, 'the original construction of Hagia Sophia signified the triumph of Christianity over paganism under Justinian; its second consecration as Mehmed II's royal mosque represented the final victory of Islam that had been predicted by 'various signs' that could be discerned in Islamic history and tradition that foretold the rise of the Ottoman Empire.[37]

When analysing why the restoration of the mosque of Hagia Sophia could elicit such strong support among large sectors of the Turkish voting populace, Bigelow and Necipoğlu's insight is crucial: Hagia Sophia embodies deeply held views of Turkish Islamic faith and history that Erdoğan shares with his constituency. In other words, there is a pious Turkish Islamic narrative of Hagia Sophia that places this building at the centre of what it means to be a faithful, traditional Turkish Muslim. This narrative is deeply rooted in the Ottoman history of Hagia Sophia, and exploring it will reveal the reason why the reconversion of the museum of Hagia Sophia into the mosque of Hagia Sophia resonated so strongly with the AKP's supporters in particular, and many pious Turkish Muslims in general. In addition, as Spyros Sofos has shown, the deep emotional attachment that many Turkish Muslims feel for Hagia Sophia is also rooted in attachment to national sovereignty and personal freedom. The reconversion of the museum of Hagia Sophia into the mosque of Hagia Sophia represents a kind of 'restitution' of the rights and religious identity of pious Turkish Muslims after decades of repressive Kemalist secularism.[38]

Simply put, the imperial mosque of Hagia Sophia played a crucial role in the formation of Ottoman Turkish Islamic tradition and piety, analogous to the role that (as Hagia Sophia) it played in the formation of Eastern Orthodox Christian tradition and piety in its original form as a church (as described above). Attachment to Hagia Sophia as a public, sacred Islamic space is deeply felt by many Turkish Muslims because this space was one of the nuclei of the formation of the spiritual traditions that Turkish Muslims identify as distinct to their practice of Sunni Islam. The first to place Hagia Sophia in the central role of Ottoman piety was, of course, Mehmet II himself, who, according to his court historian Tursun Beg, was awestruck when he first entered the building after conquering Constantinople. Due to the overwhelming divine wonder that he felt in this space, Mehmet ordered then and there that Hagia Sophia would become the imperial mosque the Ottoman dynasty.[39] The incorporation of Hagia Sophia into Ottoman Islamic tradition can be examined in two dimensions: its spiritual incorporation and its architectural incorporation.

The spiritual incorporation of Hagia Sophia into Ottoman Islamic tradition was accomplished by numerous signs and wonders, and the reconstruction of a sacred history of the building that asserted that it was destined to become a mosque from the time it was constructed in the sixth century. Mehmet II himself miraculously rediscovered the burial place along the walls of the city of Abu Ayyub al-Ansari, the standard bearer of the Prophet Muhammad who died during the first siege of Constantinople attempted by Arab armies between 674 and 678.[40] The sacred tomb (*türbe*) of Abu Ayyub al-Ansari became central to the piety of the Ottoman dynasty from that point onward and continues to be one of the most sacred locations of the city in Turkish Sunni practice. Mehmet II also commissioned the histories of Hagia Sophia written by the mystic and scholar Akşemseddin (d. 1459), upon whom Mehmet relied for spiritual guidance. Akşemseddin delivered the sermon for the first Friday prayers held in Hagia Sophia after the conquest, and he elaborated a sacred narrative of Hagia Sophia where the supernatural Muslim saint al-Khidr appears to Justinian in a dream and directs him to build Hagia Sophia.[41]

The spiritual incorporation of Hagia Sophia into Ottoman Islamic tradition only deepened over time, as the sanctuary and the theological schools attached to it (*medreses*) became central to the development of the Ottoman Islamic intellectual tradition. One of the most important institutional contexts for Sunni Muslim intellectual life in the Ottoman Empire was its vast and highly bureaucratised system of Islamic higher education, the *medrese* system, where formal centres of Islamic learning were ranked and graded according to criteria of prestige and imperial patronage, with professional scholars rising through the ranks of this system by obtaining teaching appointments at increasingly prestigious *medreses* throughout their career.[42] At the top of this system stood the most prestigious of schools and the imperial mosques to which they were attached, and one of the foremost among these was Hagia Sophia. Appointment as a professor at the Hagia Sophia *medrese* was awarded as one of the highest academic and spiritual honours in the Ottoman Empire. Contemporary histories of Ottoman Islamic intellectual life, such as Taşköprülüzade's sixteenth-century biographical history of Ottoman scholars, *Shaqa'iq al-Nu'maniyya*, record appointments to professorships as among the crowning achievements of the careers of particularly distinguished scholars.[43] One particularly prominent example was Molla Hüsrev (d. 1480), who was appointed by Mehmed II as the second imperial judge of Istanbul in addition to his professorship at Hagia Sophia. Molla Hüsrev was one of the founding figures of the Ottoman Turkish Islamic tradition and a renowned authority in Islamic sacred law and legal theory (*fiqh* and *usul al-fiqh*), Arabic language, literature, poetry and calligraphy; his works on sacred law in particular remained key texts throughout the Ottoman period.[44] Hagia Sophia retained this sacred status among devout Turkish Muslims well into the republican period, many of whom interpreted it as a symbol of the highest theological and ethical ideals of their faith.

Perhaps the strongest example of this interpretation of Hagia Sophia's significance is a book written by Ömer Nasuhi Bilmen (1883–1971) explaining the spiritual significance of the conquest of Constantinople and its conversion from a Christian to an Islamic imperial capital, including the conversion of Hagia Sophia into a mosque. Bilmen was one of the most influential Sunni theologians and scholars in the history of modern Turkey – his comprehensive Islamic catechism (*Büyük İslâm İlmihali*), first published in Istanbul in 1947–8 is one of the most widely read religious books in the entire modern Turkish language, with a record-breaking over 2.5 million copies printed. Bilmen led a distinguished academic and public service career, having been steeped in traditional Ottoman Islamic learning, teaching, scholarship and then serving in Islamic academic roles in the republican period, including serving as the fifth director of the Directorate of Religious Affairs, the highest public religious office in the Turkish Republic.[45] Few others represent the traditional mainstream of Ottoman, and then Republican Turkish, Sunni Muslim piety as well as Bilmen, and therefore his interpretation of the conquest of Constantinople very effectively illuminates the building's significance for pious Turkish Sunni Muslims in the republican period (whose pious sentiments in this regard Erdoğan would later instrumentalise in his reconversion of Hagia Sophia into a mosque).

In 1939, the Turkish government began preparations for a 500-year anniversary celebration of the conquest of Constantinople that would be held in 1953. These preparations focused on the repair and restoration of major imperial Ottoman structures in Sultanahmet, the central area of the historical peninsula, including Topkapı Palace and sites associated with Mehmet II.[46] In the context of this significant state-sponsored celebration of the Ottoman Islamic identity of Istanbul, Bilmen published his own book in 1953 explaining and celebrating the spiritual significance of the conquest of Constantinople.[47] The book represents a distillation of the theological tradition of Turkish Ottoman Sunnism that Bilmen argues is embodied in the event of the conquest and conversion of Constantinople from a Christian to a Muslim city. It is rooted in the classical Ottoman Islamic scholastic tradition, and is presented as a deliberately non-political treatise that teases out the spiritual significance of 1453 for Turkish Muslims living in the present day. Bilmen's book is therefore written to be clearly distinct from the overtly Turkish Islamic nationalist calls for the reconversion of Hagia Sophia and the overthrowing of Turkish secularism (that will be discussed later in this chapter), and is best understood as a summary of the general pious sentiment among many Turkish Muslims that Turkish Islamic nationalist movements instrumentalise in service of their own specific political projects, such as Erdoğan's AKP.

Bilmen's book is composed of three parts: the first is a traditional Ottoman-style learned interpretation of the Qur'anic Surah al-Fath (The Victory; associated here with Islam's victory over Arabian polytheism); the second is a comparative-religion style argument for the exaltedness and truth of Islam in contrast to other world religions; and the third is a summary of the events of the conquest of Constantinople, including a hagiographical depiction of the life and character of Mehmed II. The argument of the book is that a properly spiritual contemplation of the events of 1453 reveals the true meaning of Islam's superiority (*galebe*), which is its theological truth and virtuous ethical ideals. Bilmen does not read the Islamic religious significance of 1453 in political terms, or as the beginning of political Turkish nationalist mythos that needs to be revived in the present day. Rather, he uses his interpretation of these events to call his fellow Turkish Muslims to spread and strengthen the faith of Islam through peaceful virtuous deeds.

Bilmen arrives at this reading of 1453 by utilising the theological and spiritual tools of the Ottoman Islamic scholastic tradition, the very tradition that was nurtured in the *medrese* of Hagia Sophia and across the Ottoman Empire. He argues that Islam is superior to other faiths because it alone presents the purest doctrinal truth of religion, that is, belief in the One God and the Prophecy of Muhammad through whom the final divine message of the Qur'an was revealed.[48] This constitutes the true essence of Islam's superiority and historical advancement toward predominance over other worldviews. Bilmen summarizes the Islamic religious worldview by utilizing a schema deeply rooted in Ottoman Islamic intellectual tradition, the three-fold division of Islam into creed, worship, and ethics/human relationships.[49] The creed of Islam is belief in the One God who created the entirety of the cosmos *ex nihilo*, and whose attributes alone represent complete perfection. The worship of Islam is composed of the basic ritual duties of the five pillars and the system of ritual purification associated with them. The ethics of Islam are rooted in the individual cultivation of virtues, leading to social flourishing and harmony. These individual virtues include most of all humility, loving kindness and compassion. The social values that are based on these individual virtues include justice, equality and uprightness.[50]

Bilmen then applies this conventional Ottoman summary of the Islamic faith to his spiritual interpretation of 1453. What present-day Turkish Muslims should learn from the example of 1453 is that 'their own beautiful actions' are the way that Islam should be peacefully spread across the world, through the two methods of virtuous deeds and scholarly effort.[51] He argues explicitly that the extent to which Muslims adhere to these exalted ethical ideals of their faith is the exact extent to which Islam will spread in the world. In the context of the highly secular society of Republican Turkey, Bilmen therefore calls for Turkish Muslims to return to their spiritual roots and virtues as a way to strengthen the faith of Islam in the modern world.[52] Bilmen's interpretation of the events of 1453 perfectly captures the deep spiritual resonance of Hagia Sophia the Ottoman cathedral mosque for millions of pious Turkish Sunni Muslims: before the rise of even the republic itself, this structure was imbued and associated with the highest values of the religious and cultural tradition of Turkish Sunnism.

The second dimension of Hagia Sophia's importance in Ottoman Islamic tradition is its physical presence, and the architectural incorporation of Hagia Sophia into Ottoman Islamic tradition was equally as significant as its spiritual incorporation. Beginning with Mehmet II as described above, successive sultans engaged in projects to continually restore, renovate and strengthen the massive and aging building.[53] The most recent of these efforts that are still clearly visible in the present space were modifications made by Abdülmecid I,

who commissioned the Italian artists Gaspare and Giuseppe Fossatti to restore
and repair the structure between 1847 and 1849. This included the instal-
lation of the eight large calligraphic roundels by the renowned calligrapher
Kazasker Mustafa İzzet Efendi, and the uncovering, cleaning and recovering
of the mosaics. Abdülmecid was reportedly critical of the methods of covering the mosaics employed by previous sultans, and even wanted the mosaics
outside the prayer hall to remain visible, but succumbed to pressure to re-cover
them. He asked that the mosaics be re-covered in such a way that they could be
publicly displayed when public opinion and sensibilities allowed it.[54] Kazasker
Mustafa İzzet Efendi also restored the calligraphic inscription on the interior
of the great dome, Qur'an 24:35, the famous Verse of Light:

> God is the Light of the heavens and the earth. The parable of His Light is a
> niche, wherein is a lamp. The lamp is in a glass. The glass is as a shining star
> kindled from a blessed olive tree, neither of the East nor of the West. Its oil
> would well-nigh shine forth, even if no fire had touched it. Light upon light.
> God guides unto His Light whomsoever He will, and God sets forth parables
> for mankind, and God is Knower of all things.[55]

Finally, in the sense of physical and public space, the significance of Hagia
Sophia for Ottoman and Turkish Islamic tradition is difficult to overstate.
Hagia Sophia quickly became paradigmatic for Ottoman mosque design, and
thus its influence is quite literally visible in nearly every Ottoman and modern
Turkish mosque, where the domed design, whether large or small, is a product of the direct influence of Hagia Sophia's distinctive monumental dome.[56]
Classical Ottoman mosque design was a direct imitation of the aesthetic
of Hagia Sophia, where a central dome became standard as 'the central element of a mosque'.[57] Indeed, every dome on a Turkish mosque is in fact a
public, architectural reminder of the extent to which Hagia Sophia transformed into the paradigmatic Hagia Sophia of Ottoman Turkish Islamic tradition. The spiritual and physical appeal of Hagia Sophia to Turkish Sunni
Muslims is therefore deeply rooted and, making it uniquely powerful and
intuitively available to the political mobilisation of Turkish Islamism in the
twentieth century and then the conservative Turkish Islamic nationalism of
Erdoğan's AKP.

The Movement to Reconvert the Museum of Hagia Sophia to the Mosque of Hagia Sophia

Soon after the 1934 decision by Mustafa Kemal Atatürk to convert the Hagia Sophia mosque into the museum of Hagia Sophia, a movement within the Turkish Islamist opposition to Kemalism developed to reconvert the museum back into the status of a mosque. The discourse used by the various figures in this movement foreshadowed the discourse that would be used by the contemporary AKP under Erdoğan to legitimate his own decision to accomplish this reconversion. In stark contrast to the highly theological, widely popular, but spiritually apolitical, piety surrounding Hagia Sophia that was epitomised in Bilmen's book discussed above, this movement is bound up with the roots of the modern republican-era Turkish political Islamism from which the AKP initially sought to distance itself when it was first founded.

Erdoğan reached back into these not only conservative nationalist but also Islamist discourses when we argued for the legitimacy of his decision to reconvert the museum of Hagia Sophia into the mosque of Hagia Sophia. In addition, these twentieth-century Islamist discourses also contained the basic contours of the explicitly anti-Greek Orthodox ideology that would also re-emerge in Erdoğan and the AKP discourse surrounding the reconversion. A brief analysis of the discourse of the twentieth-century Turkish Islamist movement to reconvert Hagia Sophia into a mosque is therefore the last piece of the historical contextual puzzle that needs to be examined in order to understand the full significance of Erdoğan's 2020 decision, and the changes that it brought about both within Hagia Sophia and in the urban landscape of Istanbul more broadly.

The first Islamist figure who is widely remembered for calling for the reconversion of Hagia Sophia was Osman Yüksel Serdengeçti (1917–83).[58] Born Osman Zeki in Akseki, he changed his surname to 'serdengeçti' after he began to publish an anti-Kemalist journal of the same name, which is an Ottoman-era term for a soldier who volunteered for front-line duty against the enemy, out of piety and patriotism. Coming from a family of educated Ottoman Muslim intellectuals, Serdengeçti was the son of Selim Yüksel, a local mufti, and the nephew of Ahmet Hamdi Akseki, the distinguished Ottoman theologian and third director of the Directorate of Religious Affairs. While in his last year of undergraduate education at Ankara University, Serdengeçti was arrested for participating in a student protest and imprisoned in Istanbul where he was tortured. Freed three months later, these experiences shaped his view of politics and religion for the rest of his life. The cover motto of his opposition journal, which resulted in his frequent arrest and imprisonment, epitomised the essential elements of the kind of conservative Turkish Islamic nationalism that would be central to Erdoğan's own ideology: 'the journal for those who run to God, the nation, and the fatherland'.

In 1952, Serdengeçti published a piece calling for the reconversion of Hagia Sophia into a mosque. A case was then opened against him in 1953 by the Ankara Heavy Penal Court, and he was indicted on 17 January under a statute that carried a maximum penalty of execution. Though he was subsequently exonerated, his story became crucial to the memory of the twentieth-century movement to reconvert Hagia Sophia, and was frequently recalled in the lead-up to the 2020 decision.[59] A poem he wrote to Hagia Sophia opens with a line that aptly summarises the fusion of conservative Islam and Turkish ethnic nationalism that would develop over the twentieth century and later be fully utilised by Erdoğan: Serdengeçti describes Hagia Sophia as 'the light of Islam' and 'the pride of Turkishness'.[60]

In the following decades, the leading figures of the Turkish Islamist movement would make such calls central to their political message and ethos. In a 1968 article, Necip Fazıl Kısakürek (1904–83), perhaps the most prominent Islamist intellectual in modern Turkish history, argued forcefully for the reconversion of Hagia Sophia into a mosque in order to avenge the humiliation of Ottoman territorial loss and defeat.[61] Kısakürek was also one of the most significant influences on Erdoğan himself, who has publicly praised him and proudly acknowledge his influence and personal importance on many occasions.[62] As Umur Uzer has shown, Kısakürek's specifically anti-Western, antisemitic, and anti-Christian version of Turkish Islamic nationalism is a foundational element of the AKP's conception of Turkish identity under Erdoğan's leadership.[63] Unlike Bilmen, for Kısakürek, the meaning of Hagia Sophia is explicitly political: it represents the rightful political dominance of the Turkish Muslim nation over its imperial lands, whose destiny has been repressed and denied by the secularist Kemalist state. In his typically provocative rhetorical style, Kısakürek describes Hagia Sophia as 'the axis pin of the pincers of Islam's assault' through the military power of the Ottoman Empire.[64]

Kısakürek describes the conversion of the mosque Hagia Sophia into the museum of Hagia Sophia as a victory of Christianity over Islam, a shameful declaration of the superiority of the former over the latter, a manifestation of Western imperialism against Muslim Turkey, which has been aided and abetted by 'cosmopolitans', Jews, and Masons.[65] As will be seen later in this chapter, Kısakürek's language of conservative Turkish Islamic nationalism powerfully anticipates the discourses that Erdoğan and the AKP would use to justify and legitimate their 2020 decision. Finally, Kısakürek also described the conversion of Hagia Sophia into a museum as 'the greatest of betrayals to Turkish history, its sanctity, its spirit'.[66] As will also be demonstrated below, the language of 'betrayal' (*ihanet*) here directly links the call to reconvert Hagia Sophia to specifically anti-Greek Orthodox discourse with roots in the late Ottoman period, and this discourse of 'betrayal' would be utilised by Erdoğan himself in the context of the 2020 decision.

Also in 1968, the equally prominent Islamist writer Sezai Karakoç (1933–2021) made a similar argument. He likened the conversion of Hagia Sophia into a museum to its being buried, entombed, fallen into sleep or a feverish coma that prolongs the painful throes of death.[67] In an appeal to the kind of popular spiritual attachment described above in Bilmen's book, Karakoç argues that reconverting it into a mosque reflects the authentic desire of the Turkish people. Moreover, he frames this call in the context of the demands of Turkish religious nationalism: he declares that 'as a believing nation', if Hagia Sophia museum is reconverted back into a mosque, God will no doubt grant victory and power to the Turkish nation.[68]

Similar calls remained a common feature of Turkish Islamic oppositional politics in the ensuing years and decades. Hasan Hüseyin Ceylan, a former Refah Partisi MP from Ankara, recalled that one of his key memories of his student days was hearing Kısakürek's call for Hagia Sophia's reconversion at a conference in 1973 dedicated to that theme, declaring: 'Let the chains be broken, let Hagia Sophia be opened!'[69] Ceylan later published a book in 1993 titled *Ayasofya İhaneti* (*The Betrayal of Hagia Sophia*), which marshalled a wide range of historical and political arguments for reconversion, and mentioned Serdengeçti as one of the earliest figures in this important movement. In 1991, an area dedicated for Muslim prayer was opened in the side of the building, and in 2013 the former MP from Kayseri, Yusuf Halaçoğlu, introduced a resolution for the reconversion of Hagia Sophia museum into a mosque. In 2015, the then director of the Ministry of Culture and Tourism, Yalçın Topçu, publicly supported the calls for reconversion. On 1 July 2016, the first call to prayer in eighty-five years was broadcast from the museum of Hagia Sophia.[70] In the years leading up to the 2020 decision, protests led by conservative right-wing and Islamist political activists and the distribution of literature calling for the reconversion became frequent and visible around the building itself.

Finally, and importantly for the analysis below, explicitly anti-Greek Orthodox tropes continued to be central to the discourse of this movement. For instance, a 1970 political advert in the newspaper *Bugün* published on the anniversary of the conquest of Constantinople (29 May) depicted a massive and fearsome Greek Orthodox priest, emphasising a sinister-looking beard and the flowing black robes often worn by Greek Orthodox clergy, towering over Hagia Sophia and reaching menacingly towards it with a wild look in his eye. The caption read: 'Hagia Sophia must be made a mosque again, against those who wish to resuscitate Byzantium!' and 'The insistence on keeping Hagia Sophia a museum is nothing other than serving Greek imperialism.'[71]

Along similar lines, a piece written by the Ankara University political historian Fahir Armaoğlu and reprinted by Ceylan in his 1993 book epitomises the anti-Greek Orthodox dimensions of the rhetoric used by the Hagia Sophia reconversion movement, and was likely included in Ceylan's comprehensive polemical book for this reason. Armaoğlu wrote that the conversion of Hagia Sophia into a museum amounted to 'bowing to the wishes of Greek Orthodoxy' and 'declaring fealty not to Islam but to Christianity'.[72] The conversion was, therefore, above all an affront to Turkey's 'sovereignty and independence', which Armaoğlu argues is existentially threatened by the presence of the Greek Orthodox community within the Turkish Republic.[73] Armaoğlu describes the Ecumenical Patriarchate of Constantinople (whose significance to Eastern Orthodoxy as a whole is described in detail above and who remains resident in Istanbul) as a 'cancerous tumour' whose influence threatens to overwhelm Turkish sovereignty and ethnic identity itself. This is because, according to Armaoğlu, the Greek Orthodox of Turkey harbour the desire for revenge over the conquest of Constantinople in 1453, and 'for them Ayasofya is the greatest representative of' Greek irredentism.[74] In short, Armaoğlu argues that the Greek Orthodox of Turkey are always on the brink of betrayal of the Turkish nation.

The discourse of the Hagia Sophia reconversion movement is significant because, as will be seen below, it was fully reappropriated by Erdoğan in the context of his 2020 decision and developed far beyond its original confines as an opposition ideology set against Kemalist secularism. Erdoğan's decision to reconvert Hagia Sophia can be interpreted as the culmination of all his efforts to transform Istanbul to reflect and fit his political vision. With this reconversion, the ideology and discourse of modern conservative Turkish Islamic nationalism reaches a striking peak, as it attempts to achieve complete dominance over all other possible identities and historical imaginaries associated with Istanbul. As will be described below, the specifically anti-Greek Orthodox dimension of this discourse is crucial because the Greek Orthodox identity is the other major claimant to the religious and historical legacy of Hagia Sophia: it is therefore demonised and depicted as a conquered enemy in order to justify the legitimacy of the reconversion, and of the dominance of the conservative Turkish Sunni nationalist reading of the city of Istanbul itself.

The Reconversion of Hagia Sophia and its Spatial Politics and Impact

Shortly after signing the decree to reconvert Hagia Sophia into a mosque, Erdoğan delivered a prepared speech on the significance of this transformation that has now been officially designated the 'Hagia Sophia Manifesto' and is featured prominently on the official Turkish government website devoted to the mosque of Hagia Sophia.[75] This manifesto not only draws on all of the reconversion movement discourses described above, but also fully expresses Erdoğan's political vision of conservative Turkish Sunni nationalism, the political vision that he and his AKP followers have inscribed on the landscape of Istanbul over the past decade. This text therefore deserves close scrutiny, as it reveals how Erdoğan's reconversion of Hagia Sophia represents the pinnacle of his project to utilise the urban landscape of Istanbul to represent his political programme and his vision of Turkish identity.

Erdoğan begins the speech by immediately grounding the legitimacy of his decision in the legacy of Mehmet II, arguing that the sacred monetary trust (*vakfiye*) that he established for the conversion, preservation and maintenance of the structure of Hagia Sophia for its use specifically as a mosque and intellectual centre means that the contemporary Turkish nation-state is completely within both its national and religious rights to reconvert the building into a mosque.[76] He makes it absolutely clear that the inviolable basis for his deci-sion is Turkish national sovereignty, which makes the decision incontrovert-ible. Therefore, any opinion to the contrary is simply an act of support for 'the infringement of our independence'.[77] That the initial emphasis of Erdoğan's manifesto is national sovereignty is highly significant. It represents the extent to which the mere presence of alternative, non-Turkish Sunni identities associated with Istanbul and its physical space represent, in his view, an existential threat to his vision of Turkishness. If Hagia Sophia is not rendered fully Turkish, its deeply cosmopolitan and/or Greek Orthodox associations threaten the Turk-ishness of Istanbul, and thus of the nation itself.

After making this crucial opening argument, Erdoğan then re-emphasises the sacred Ottoman roots of his decision. He refers to a copy of the Ottoman-era *vakfiye* document that is hanging behind him as he speaks (*vakfiyename*), calling it the fundamental root and basis (*asıl*) of his decision. By referring to both Turkish national sovereignty and Ottoman Islamic heritage as equally foundational for his decision, he reveals how his conception of Turkish iden-tity sees these two identities – the non-national, imperial Ottoman Islamic, and the national, ethnic Turkish – as identical, the latter leading naturally to the former in an irreversible, sacred historical process. The reconversion of the museum of Hagia Sophia into the mosque of Hagia Sophia therefore repre-sents the reunion of this organic tradition that was violently ripped asunder by the inauthentic Western secularism of the Kemalist state.[78] He therefore goes on to say that opposition to his decision simply represents hostility towards Islam itself, which he says is 'climbing with each passing day', in other words, here attempting to associate opposition to his decision with the rise of global Islamophobia.[79]

Using language that we will see reappear in the sermon delivered at the 24 July Friday prayer, Erdoğan depicts the original conquest of Constantinople in 1453 in miraculous terms, arguing simplistically that Mehmet II guaranteed the lives and freedom of the conquered Byzantines. He also includes the point that 'look-ing with tolerance on members of other faiths' is a key part of Islamic ethics.[80] He declares that it was the prayers of the saintly Mehmet II himself that rendered the physical space sacred for Muslims, then and there transforming it into a mosque. As will be recalled from previous analyses above, this is exactly the argument that was made in Ottoman sources regarding the legitimate sanctity of the space as a mosque. Importantly, he also gestures towards the kind of popular piety surrounding Hagia Sophia that was described above via Bilmen's book, saying that he has felt a special love for Hagia Sophia since he was a boy.

Erdoğan then uses language that, as will be made clear in the final section of this chapter, is rooted specifically in anti-Greek Orthodox sentiment in modern Turkey. He describes the decision to convert the Ottoman imperial mosque of Hagia Sophia into a museum as 'the betrayal [*ihanet*] of history'. As will be made clear below, the threat of betrayal is exactly how anti-Greek Orthodox discourse has, since the beginning of the republic, consistently referred to the 'threat' of indigenous Greek Orthodox in Turkey as always harbouring the potential to betray the Turkish nation. He cites word-for-word an equally revealing quote from the early republican journalist and writer Peyami Safa (1899–1961): 'Ayasofya's transformation into a museum did not fend off Christianity's designs on Istanbul; on the contrary, it emboldened them, incited and exacerbated them.'[81] This is a clear reference to the Turkish nationalist fear of a lurking Greek Orthodox irredentism that would subsume the whole of the Turkish nation, and that is so potent and threatening that the mere recognition of the building of Hagia Sophia as having a dual religious heritage associated with it (by transforming it into a museum that emphasised both its Byzantine Orthodox and Turkish Sunni identities) amounts to collaboration with, or submission to, this ever-present Greek Orthodox threat to Turkishness.

Erdoğan closed his speech with an appeal to Turkey's status as a leader in global Muslim politics, declaring that the 'resurrection of Hagia Sophia' (*Ayasofya'nın dirilişi*) portends the eventual liberation of the mosque of Al-Aqsa (the Dome of the Rock) in Jerusalem, and must be seen as a symbol of hope for all who suffer oppression around the world.[82] This argument attempts to frame the significance of Erdoğan's decision as reaching far beyond the issue of Turkey's national sovereignty or Islamic heritage, positioning the Turkish state, nation and people under Erdoğan as leaders of the global Muslim community, the entirety of the *umma*. Echoing the rhetoric of the reconversion movement, Erdoğan appeals here to a broader, transnational conception of Islamist nationalism that places Turkey at the helm of liberationist anti-Western and anti-imperialist politics. Finally, it is worth noting that Erdoğan also quotes Serdengeçti's poem, whose life and work was so important to the reconversion movement, as described above.[83]

Reactions to Erdoğan's decision from across the Turkish political spectrum were swift. Most major political figures rushed to support the decision, including many of the major opposition parties. The only opposition party to offer immediate criticism was the HDP. The outspoken Istanbul HDP and long-time human rights activist Hüda Kaya was highly critical of the decision, linking it with sectarianism and arguing that it contravened common sense.[84] Kaya had already been roundly criticised and mocked in the Turkish press two days previously, after she stated on a television news programme that rather than being converted into a mosque, Hagia Sophia should be converted back into a church because the space properly belongs to those who originally built it. Many media responses to this suggestion were truly shocked and outraged, with one headline simply asking, 'Are you the party of Greece?'[85] Assistant general chairman of the HDP Garo Paylan also criticised the decision shortly after it was announced, arguing that it would needlessly increase tensions between Christians and Muslims.[86] CHP responses were largely muted or indifferent, avoiding direct criticism of the decision itself.[87]

Positive responses were far more common on the part of Turkish politicians and public figures. For example, through official statements on Twitter, Mansur Yavaş, the AKP mayor of Ankara; Devlet Bahçeli, chairman of the MHP; Ahmet Davutoğlu, the former prominent AKP politician and prime minister who, in 2019, was founder of the opposition Gelecek Partisi (GP; Future Party); and Meral Akşener, founder of the opposition İyi Parti (İYİ; Good Party), all expressed their support for the decision. Particularly strong support came naturally from AKP politicians, many of whom used rhetoric reminiscent of the reconversion movement described above. For example, the AKP general chair of the parliament Numan Kurtulmuş tweeted: 'The chains have been broken, Hagia Sophia has been opened,' in a direct reference to language used by prominent Islamist activists such as Kısakürek, as described above. Finally, the director of the Directorate of Religious Affairs, Ali Erbaş, tweeted an image of tulips blooming in front of Hagia Sophia, stating simply: 'Thanks be to God'.

The formal ceremonies that accompanied the first Friday prayer after the reconversion decision further reinforced the extent to which Erdoğan envisioned the reclaiming of the museum of Hagia Sophia as the Grand Mosque of Hagia Sophia as emblematic of his entire programme to define contemporary Turkish identity in his own conservative Sunni Turkish nationalist terms. At approximately noon that day, Erdoğan entered the sanctuary first. After a series of Qur'an recitations performed by Diyanet specialists, Erdoğan read the first chapter of the Qur'an, Surat al-Fatiha, and then the first five verses of the second chapter of the Qur'an.[88] At the end of this special Diyanet programme, Ali Erbaş, director of the Directorate of Religious Affairs, delivered the Friday sermon, titled 'The Emblem of Victory, the Entrustment of the Conqueror'. In this sermon, Erbaş further emphasised the arguments and rhetoric Erdoğan used in the speech that he gave on 10 July and analysed above. When combined together, these two documents form a powerful summary of the AKP's political ideology under Erdoğan's leadership.

Erbaş describes the reconversion of Hagia Sophia as the culmination of a centuries-long process of God bestowing special imperial and sacred authority on the Turkish people and their state. He places special emphasis on the Prophetic Hadith that Constantinople would someday be conquered for Islam, and describes the Turkish conquest of Anatolia and eventually of Istanbul not as an instance of 'violent overpowering, but rather revitalisation; not destruction, but rather the building-up' of a new and glorious Turkish-Islamic civilisation that is based on the control of territory that has been given as a sacred trust (*emanet*) by God to the believing Turkish people and state.[89] On these lands, the national homeland (*vatan*) of the Turks developed into the mighty empire of the Ottomans and the nation-state over which Erdoğan and the AKP preside today. Erbaş calls to mind and offers blessings upon the saintly persons associated with Ottoman Istanbul, including Ayyub al-Ansari, Akşemseddin and Mehmet II himself. In addition, he quotes extensively – but notably without explicit attribution – the words of the Islamist ideologue mentioned above, Necip Fazıl Kısakürek, whose activism and discourse was so important to the twentieth-century reconversion movement among the anti-Kemalist conservative nationalist and Islamist opposition.[90]

As with Erdoğan's speech on 10 July, Erbaş grounds the political and legal legitimacy of the reconversion decision in sacred and inviolable Ottoman precedent. By rendering Hagia Sophia a mosque with a sacred endowment (*vakıf*), Mehmet II ensured that it was meant to remain a mosque in perpetuity, 'until the Day of Judgement'.[91] Violation of this endowment by transforming the Ottoman Grand Mosque of Hagia Sophia into a museum was therefore not only illegal, but quite literally defiance of the will of God. Hagia Sophia belongs not only to the Turkish nation, but to the whole global Muslim community – the *umma* – as a sacred right. Also like Erdoğan, Erbaş depicts the conquest of Istanbul in highly idealised and miraculous terms, claiming that Mehmet II ordered and established full religious liberty for all of his subjects. Like Erdoğan, he also argues that the reconversion of Hagia Sophia is a sign of hope for all oppressed Muslims in the world, presages the eventual liberation of Jerusalem, and epitomises the Muslim duty to strive for peace, justice and mercy across the world and on behalf of all human beings.[92]

The primary message of his sermon, as with Erdoğan's, remained domestic, however, and is well summarised by his statement: 'The opening of Hagia Sophia to worship is the firm resolve to construct, with the spiritual power taken from its roots, a secure future for our glorious nation that above all else holds onto the love of faith and homeland.'[93] As was widely noticed and reported in local and global media, Erbaş ascended the pulpit carrying a ceremonial sword, in imitation of a custom founded by the Ottoman conqueror of Constantinople, Mehmet II. This highly symbolic act had the effect of reconnecting the ceremony with Ottoman precedent, including the affirmation of Turkish Sunni Muslim dominance in social, political and public space. After the sermon, the congregational Friday prayer was performed, and thereafter Erdoğan again read Surat al-Fatiha. His wife Emine Erdoğan led the prayers in the women's section of the mosque. After the conclusion of the prayers and the attendant ceremony, Erdoğan and his retinue then visited the sacred tomb of Mehmet II, where they offered individual prayers on behalf of Mehmet II.[94] A final indicator of the immense sanctity attached to this event by Erdoğan is the fact that he celebrated its significance on its one-year anniversary, stating in a tweet that Hagia Sophia's resurrection constitutes 'the symbol of the reascendence of the sun of our civilization'.

Prior to this event on 24 July 2020, a number of physical changes to the interior of the worship space were made that would render it suitable for Muslim worship, many of which were meant to re-institute Ottoman-era changes to the space that had been removed or downplayed upon its transformation into a museum. Exterior changes to the building were minimal, the most notable being simply replacing the sign at the entrance that referred to the building as 'Ayasofya Müzesi' (Hagia Sophia Museum) to 'Ayasofya-i Kebir Cami-i Şerifi' (the Grand Mosque of Hagia Sophia). The interior changes were much more striking and in some ways compromised the original features of the building outlined above that were specifically designed to fit the acoustic and liturgical dimensions of Byzantine Orthodox worship, but can be described as relatively minor. The major changes to the space that had been made during the Ottoman period described above remained during its period as a museum, and so the formal changes required to reconvert the space into a mosque were relatively minimal, as the mass covering of mosaics and the destruction of liturgical structures had already taken place centuries ago.

At the same time, the specific changes made to the interior of the space, though not physically substantial, possessed immense significance politically and ideologically. These changes were very specifically designed to embody the conservative nationalist values of Erdoğanian neo-Ottomanism and to inscribe them on the most prominent of all architectural spaces in Istanbul, the Hagia Sophia. The most obvious and striking change was the laying of green carpet that covered the entirety of the worship space, as is customary in spaces considered ritually pure for Muslim prayer (see Figures 5.2 and 5.3). Notably, the famous section of circular marble designs (the *omphalion*) where Byzantium emperors are often said to have been crowned remains uncovered and visible. In addition, massive chandeliers were hung throughout the space, again highly typical for the interior of grand Ottoman mosques (see Figure 5.4).

The most urgent matter was to attend to the more a thousand-year-old mosaic icon of the Virgin Mary and infant Christ in the apse, along with other figural icons near it in the apse space, that therefore remained visible in the worship space (installed in 867 where the Byzantine altar would have been, and whose significance is described above). Because the prominent visibility of such an image could be considered idolatrous in a Muslim sacred space, the icon needed to be covered in some way. The solution found was to drape white curtains over these mosaics so that they are not visible when facing them straight ahead, but can be seen from a side angle (see Figure 5.5). This was in fact the very same solution that was devised and implemented by Sultan Ahmet I as far back as the seventeenth century.[95] In addition, at the time of writing the upper galleries were closed to the public for restoration, where some of the most significant extant examples of Byzantine sacred mosaics in the world are located, including the monumental Deësis depicting Christ, the Virgin Mary and John the Baptist, and installed shortly after the Byzantines retook Constantinople from Crusader occupation in 1261. The mosaics on the lower floor, however, which are located outside the worship space proper, remain uncovered and open to the public.

Additional calligraphic panels were also added to the space, especially in the area near the prayer niche, or *mihrab*, indicating the direction of prayer towards Mecca, which is located in the space where the Byzantine altar would have been. The most prominent of these added calligraphic panels (which appears to have been added shortly after the first prayer was held) is one that was personally donated by Erdoğan himself.[96] This panel can be considered one of the most significant modifications to the space of Hagia Sophia in terms of the spatial politics of Erdoğanian neo-Ottomanism because it seamlessly brings together an appeal to Ottoman Islamic tradition, Sunni Muslim piety, and the need to render them victorious and dominant in the public social space of Istanbul (see Figures 5.6 and 5.7).

Figure 5.6 Hagia Sophia calligraphic panel donated by President Recep Tayyip Erdoğan, January 2022. Photograph Vural Yazıcıoğlu.

Figure 5.7 Hagia Sophia *mihrab* (with calligraphic panel donated by President Recep Tayyip Erdoğan on the left), January 2022. Photograph Vural Yazıcıoğlu.

The panel was painted by noted calligrapher Mehmet Özçay, and is located immediately to the left of the *mihrab*, making it clearly visible and highly prominent in the worship space. The panel is composed of the entirety of verses 159–60 from the third chapter of the Qur'an, al-'Imran; but the centred and enlarged selection from these verses is: 'If God helps you, none shall overcome you.' The significance of the selection of this line is very clear: as in Erdoğan's Hagia Sophia manifesto, and Erbaş' sermon, the argument is made that the Turkish nation's divinely ordained destiny is being brought to fulfilment by the ascendence of Erdoğan's conservative nationalist neo-Ottomanism. His success and legitimacy is attributed to God above all else, inscribed in the heart of the architectural landmark that more than others represents the whole of Istanbul's historical and contemporary identity.

Erdoğanian Neo-Ottomanism's Reconquest of Constantinople

One of the major arguments of this chapter is that the full meaning of the spatial politics of Erdoğan's reconversion of Hagia Sophia cannot be fully understood without analysing this event in the context of the history and present situation of the Greek Orthodox minority in the Turkish Republic, specifically the Greek Orthodox population indigenous to the city of Istanbul, hereafter referred to as Istanbul Greeks or the indigenous Greek Orthodox of Istanbul.[97] As descendants of Greek-speaking Orthodox Christians indigenous to the former Ottoman Empire, their identity is deeply connected with the legacy of the Orthodox Christian Byzantine Empire, the culture and religious community that built Hagia Sophia and who first built the city of Constantinople, after its conquest in 1453 the Ottoman capital, and now the republican-era city of Istanbul.[98] Membership and participation in Eastern Orthodox Christianity is also therefore a defining feature of Istanbul Greek identity, and the Ecumenical Patriarchate is widely seen among this community as a central representative and guardian of its interests and culture.[99] Importantly, members of the Istanbul Greek community have for generations insisted that their deepest sense of attachment is to 'The City' itself, meaning, the identity of being from the supranational, multi-ethnic, multireligious, urban fabric of Ottoman Istanbul, stretching as far back as the Byzantine imperial capital of Constantinople.[100] Neither Greece nor Turkey exclusively, but rather, 'The City' itself constitutes the homeland of this community in their own understanding.

Therefore, as persons indigenous to the territory of the present Turkish Republic, but who are neither Muslim nor ethnic Turks, their distinctly non-nationalist form of belonging to the urban landscape of Istanbul is radically different from that of the conservative Turkish Islamic nationalism of Erdoğanian neo-Ottomanism. Their identity has in fact been troubling to secular Turkish nationalism from the beginning of the republic. As İlay Romain Örs puts it, Istanbul Greek identity is troubling to various forms of Turkish nationalism because it shows that 'there is a wider cultural sense of "belonging" based on a cosmopolitan notion beyond the nation, which is overshadowed, impoverished, and often targeted by nationalist ideology'.[101] This discomfort to nationalist ideology has resulted in the indigenous Greek minority experiencing successive waves of mass violence, structural inequality and forced migration that has reduced their numbers to an alarming extent in their homeland of Istanbul. In 1914, the total population of Istanbul was approximately 900,000 people. Of this total population, almost 23 per cent were Istanbul Greeks, or over 200,000 people (about 61 per cent were Muslim).[102] In the present day, this number is no more than 2,500 out of nearly 15 million residents of Istanbul – no more than 0.02 per cent of the city's total population.[103]

The most notable events that have resulted in the near-total destruction of this community occurred in successive waves throughout the twentieth century. The 1923 population exchange began this process by reducing the number of Istanbul Greeks to approximately 100,000 persons.[104] The highly prejudicial wealth tax of 1942–4 that devastated the livelihoods of thousands[105]; the violent pogrom of 6–7 September 1955 (described above in Chapter 3); the forced migration (*sürgün*) of 1964 as a response to events in Cyprus[106]; successive waves of migration, property seizures by the state from the 1970s to the present day[107]; and a general climate of hostility and structural inequality[108] has resulted in the almost total destruction of this community.

The Istanbul Greek claim to Hagia Sophia represents exactly the kind of Istanbul identity that Erdoğanian neo-Ottomanism is designed to reject and replace: a non-nationalist, multi-ethnic, multireligious urban space that appeals neither to Byzantine nor Ottoman superiority, but situates itself within both of these cultural legacies in various cosmopolitan ways. It is therefore no coincidence that Erdoğan's rhetoric concerning the urgent necessity to reconvert Hagia Sophia reproduces tropes specifically deployed against the Istanbul Greek minority throughout the republican period. Erdoğan's explicit deployment of the trope of 'betrayal' (*ihanet*) described above is in fact the exact crime and lurking social danger that Istanbul Greeks have been accused of by successive Turkish governments in order to justify their mass repression and expulsion. This rhetoric began after the Greek War of Independence in 1821, and only intensified throughout the republican period.[109] In other words, when Erdoğan describes the reconversion of Hagia Sophia as, above all else, righting the historical wrong of 'betrayal' to rightful possession of Hagia Sophia by Sunni Turkish identity, he is basing this argument and rhetoric on the most common anti-Greek trope deployed by many Turkish nationalist administrations before him, all concerned with the threat that such an identity poses to their conception of Turkish identity.

The responses to the reconversion of Hagia Sophia from the Ecumenical Patriarch of Constantinople, Bartholomew I, and the Archbishop of the Greek Orthodox Archdiocese of America, Elpidophoros I, dramatically illustrate the significance of the context described above. Bartholomew, as the current Patriarch of Constantinople, is the direct inheritor, and present representative of, the episcopal see that has held so much significance in the Eastern Orthodox tradition globally, as described at the beginning of this chapter. And as also emphasised above, he is considered by the indigenous Istanbul Greek Orthodox to be the leading representative of their community, its history and values, and its present interests. Elpidophoros is also one of the most prominent global representatives of Bartholomew, as his diocese – the Greek Orthodox Archdiocese of America – falls directly under the ecclesiastical jurisdiction of the Ecumenical Patriarchate, and thus Bartholomew's authority.

Moreover, both Bartholomew and Elpidophoros are members of the Istanbul Greek community (and also remain citizens of the Turkish Republic). Bartholomew (who ascended the throne of the Ecumenical Patriarchate in 1991) was born in 1940 in the village of Aghioi Theodoroi on the island of Imvros (now known as Gökçeada) as part of the once-prominent indigenous Greek community there.[110] Due to all of the factors described above, the indigenous Greek community on Imvros that Bartholomew grew up in has all but vanished. In 1920, there were 9,000 indigenous Greeks on the island, making up the predominant part of the population and the culture of Imvros. By 2000, only some 300 remained, and in the present day, this number is very likely approaching zero.[111] In other words, the most prominent religious leader of the world's Eastern Orthodox Christians, and whose position as such is the very position once housed in Hagia Sophia itself, is also a member of one of the populations most disastrously affected by the repression of minorities in Republican Turkey.

Archbishop Elpidophoros, also a member of the indigenous Greek community, is from Istanbul itself. He spent the first ten years of his life there, from 1967 to 1977, when his family migrated to Thessaloniki in Greece. He returned to Istanbul in 1994, and resided and served in various capacities in the Ecumenical Patriarchate until 2019 when he departed for New York to assume the office of Archbishop of the Greek Orthodox Archdiocese of America.[112] Both Bartholomew and Elpidophoros proudly claim their identity as Istanbul Greek, and envision it as deeply rooted in their homeland, the complex and cosmopolitan space described above that is thoroughly indigenous to the Turkish Republic, but is also exactly the kind of space forcibly erased and eclipsed by the spatial politics of Erdoğan's neo-Ottoman political project.

At the landmark conference on indigenous Greek identity held in Istanbul in 2006, Patriarch Bartholomew delivered opening remarks in Turkish where he said: 'with respect to rights and responsibilities, as Rum we are neither guests nor foreigners nor migrants in Istanbul. We know well where we come from.'[113] Similarly, in an interview given to the Turkish newspaper *Hürriyet* shortly after his election as Archbishop of the Greek Orthodox Archdiocese of America, under the Ecumenical Patriarchate of Constantinople, Archbishop Elpidophoros combined a critique of the Turkish state's abuses of the human rights of the indigenous Greek Orthodox of Turkey with a description of his childhood memories of inter-religious harmony in the Bakırköy neighbourhood, including the joys of sharing festive practices during Ramadan and the Paschal season. Elpidophoros describes Istanbul as 'our homeland' and the place to which he feels the deepest attachment.[114]

In a sermon he delivered on 30 June 2020, Bartholomew cautioned that the reconversion of Hagia Sophia into a mosque would only increase tensions between Christians and Muslims globally. He stressed the universal and cosmopolitan dimension of Hagia Sophia, saying that this structure belongs 'to all of humanity', and is a 'symbolic place of encounter, dialogue, solidarity and mutual understanding between Christianity and Islam'.[115] In an official message posted on 28 August 2020, which directly challenged Erdoğan's reinscribing of Ottoman identity onto the architectural space of Hagia Sophia, he emphasised that Hagia Sophia's architecture had been specifically designed to proclaim Christian theological convictions, and that therefore this structure will always stand for these convictions, regardless of its current use. In his own rather striking words, 'The only use of Hagia Sophia, which respects and exemplifies its true mission, is its use as a Christian house of worship.'[116] He further argued that the religious particularity in Hagia Sophia's architectural design still implied a universal dimension: 'The church of the Holy Wisdom of God, as an architectural expression of the salvation of mankind and all of creation in Christ, belongs to all of humanity.'[117]

In a 10 July 2020 tweet, Elpidophoros expressed concerns about the potential consequences the decision could have for the Ecumenical Patriarchate and the indigenous Greeks within Turkey specifically, making clear that he feared a resulting 'negative turn from respect for religious freedom'. In the same message he argued that the reconversion of Hagia Sophia constituted 'the worst example of religious chauvinism'. Even more significantly, in a sermon delivered on 19 July 2020, he officially declared a form of liturgical counter-programming to the public ceremonies that were going to be held at Hagia Sophia on 24 July by the Diyanet (and described in detail above).[118] He declared 24 July 2020 an official day of mourning throughout the Greek Orthodox Archdiocese of America. At every Greek Orthodox church in the United States on that day the following actions would be performed: the tolling of the bells in lamentation; the lowering of all flags to half-mast; and the chanting of the Akathist hymn to the Virgin Mary in the evening. One of the most ancient liturgical rites in the Greek Orthodox Church, this extended hymn is an appeal to the Virgin Mary for protection and intercession in times of crisis, composed in Byzantine Constantinople for that purpose. To emphasise the specific role of the Akathist in this day of mourning, Elpidophoros highlighted the verses in his sermon that call upon the Virgin Mary as the 'only hope of the hopeless', 'the repository of the Wisdom of God', and 'the treasury of His Foreknowledge'.[119]

On the day of the reconversion, 24 July 2020, Elpidophoros tweeted a statement that epitomised both the significance of that day when read from the perspective of the indigenous Greek Orthodox of Turkey, and the erasure of non-Turkish Sunni identity that was specifically envisioned in the project of Erdoğanian neo-Ottomanism: 'Hagia Sophia is the embodiment of our Orthodox Christian faith. We mourn its conversion to a mosque. Every culture is worthy of respect, and Ἁγία Σοφία [Hagia Sophia in the original Greek], the epitome of the Byzantine achievement, should have been left as a place of cultural intersection and religious harmony.' He personally delivered a sermon on 24 July at the Archdiocesan Cathedral of the Holy Trinity in New York, where, like Bartholomew, he emphasised that the Orthodox Christian identity of Hagia Sophia's architectural space could not be eclipsed by the reconversion. In his words, 'The painted walls of Ἁγία Σοφία shall never be silenced, for they speak of the presence of God in this world; they speak of the mercy of God; and they speak of love of God for every human person.'[120] He directly addressed the curtain covering the apse mosaic icon by saying: 'The celestial vision in the apse of Ἁγία Σοφία, of the Theotokos [Birthgiver of God] Mary holding her Son, our Lord Jesus Christ, has spoken to untold millions through the centuries. Now, she will be veiled in an act of desecration, because it is the Mother of God who makes the space sacred.'[121]

Finally, in an encyclical that he wrote for the one-year anniversary of the 24 July day of mourning, Elpidophoros made the stakes and significance of Hagia Sophia's reconversion even clearer when he declared that:

> One year ago today, the Great Church of Holy Wisdom, our Ἁγία Σοφία, was unnecessarily seized and given over to an alien purpose. This was a grim day for all people of good will and equanimity, because Hagia Sophia is much more than a sacred space. It is the vision and embodiment of the substance of our Orthodox Christian Faith. As a cultural icon, the Great Church could have been left as a museum. And although this is less than any of us would desire, at least it respected the integrity of the space. But for this past year, in a city which has abundant places for Islamic worship, it was misappropriated and done so in order to send a message to religious minorities, and to appeal to misplaced nationalistic fervor.[122]

Combining a consideration of the *ihanet* discourse in Erdoğan and the AKP's discourse surrounding the reconversion with Bartholomew and Elpidophoros' reactions and statements therefore provides the full context and meaning of the spatial politics of Erdoğan's reconversion of the museum of Hagia Sophia into the mosque of Hagia Sophia. This reconversion was the paramount example of the inscribing of Erdoğan's conservative Turkish Sunni nationalist identity on the architectural space of Istanbul. This act was not only a declaration of these politics via the architectural space of Hagia Sophia. It was also the deliberate erasure of a non-national, multireligious, ethnically cosmopolitan Istanbul identity that Hagia Sophia could have represented (and does represent for some such as the Istanbul Greeks), but was deemed a truly existential threat to Muslim Turkishness by Erdoğan and the AKP under his leadership.

Notes

1. Bissera V. Pentcheva, 'Liturgy and Music at Hagia Sophia' *Oxford Research Encyclopaedia of Religion*, 5 April 2016, available at: https://doi.org/10.1093/acrefore/9780199340378.013.99, last accessed 9 February 2022; Slobodan

Ćurčić, 'Design and Structural Innovation in Byzantine Architecture before Hagia Sophia', in Robert Moore and Ahmet Ş. Çakmak (eds), *Hagia Sophia from the Age of Justinian to the Present* (Cambridge: Cambridge University Press, 1992), 16.

2. To avoid confusion, the original name 'Hagia Sophia' will be used throughout in reference to the building, whether its status being discussed is a church, mosque or museum.

3. Gülrü Necipoğlu, 'The Life of an Imperial Monument: Hagia Sophia after Byzantium', in Robert Moore and Ahmet Ş. Çakmak (eds), *Hagia Sophia from the Age of Justinian to the Present* (Cambridge: Cambridge University Press, 1992), 203.

4. Necipoğlu, 'The Life of an Imperial Monument', 204, 218, 225.

5. Necipoğlu, 'The Life of an Imperial Monument', 204.

6. 'Son Ayasofya anketi sonuçları açıklandı', Yeniçağ, 11 July 2020, available at: https://www.yenicaggazetesi.com.tr/son-ayasofya-anketi-sonuclari-aciklandi-akp-chp-iyi-parti-mhp-saadet-partisi-288960h.htm, last accessed 18 February 2022.

7. Pentcheva, 'Liturgy and Music at Hagia Sophia'.

8. William C. MacDonald, 'Roman Experimental Design and the Great Church', in Robert Moore and Ahmet Ş. Çakmak (eds), *Hagia Sophia from the Age of Justinian to the Present* (Cambridge: Cambridge University Press, 1992), 14.

9. Ćurčić, 'Design and Structural Innovation', 17.

10. Ćurčić, 'Design and Structural Innovation', 25, 31.

11. Cyril Mango, 'Byzantine Writers on the Fabric of Hagia Sophia', in Robert Moore and Ahmet Ş. Çakmak (eds), *Hagia Sophia from the Age of Justinian to the Present* (Cambridge: Cambridge University Press, 1992), 41.

12. Mango, 'Byzantine Writers on the Fabric of Hagia Sophia', 43.

13. Cyril Mango, *The Art of the Byzantine Empire, 312–1453: Sources and Documents* (Toronto: University of Toronto Press, 1986), 74.

14. Mango, *The Art of the Byzantine Empire*, 75.

15. Mango, *The Art of the Byzantine Empire*, 85; on the interior decoration, see also Pentcheva, 'Liturgy and Music at Hagia Sophia'.

16. For up-to-date summaries of Eastern Orthodox Christian history and religious culture, see Paul Ladouceur, *Modern Orthodox Theology: Behold, I Make All Things New* (London: T. & T. Clark, 2019); John Anthony McGuckin, *The Eastern Orthodox Church: A New History* (New Haven, CT: Yale University Press, 2020); Eve Tibbs, *A Basic Guide to Eastern Orthodox Theology: Introducing Beliefs and Practices* (Grand Rapids, MI: Baker Academic, 2021).

17. Pew Research Center, 'Orthodox Christianity in the 21st Century' (2017), available at: https://www.pewresearch.org/religion/2017/11/08/orthodox-christianity-in-the-21st-century, last accessed 27 July 2022, 6–7.

18. Pew Research Center, 'Orthodox Christianity in the 21st Century', 6–7.

19. Georges Florovsky, 'The Hagia Sophia Churches', Résumés des Rapports et Communications, Sixième Congrès International d'Études Byzantines, Paris, 1940, 255–60; reprinted in *The Collected Works of Georges Florovsky, vol. 4: Aspects of Church History* (Belmont, MA: Nordland, 1975), 131–2.

20. Florovsky, 'The Hagia Sophia Churches', 132.

21. John Meyendorff, *Byzantine Theology: Historical Trends and Doctrinal Themes* (New York: Fordham University Press, 1979), 142, 151–2.

22. Pentcheva, 'Liturgy and Music at Hagia Sophia'.

23. Pentcheva, 'Liturgy and Music at Hagia Sophia'.

24. Pentcheva, 'Liturgy and Music at Hagia Sophia'.

25. Pentcheva describes the process of 'auralisation', whereby 'the measured aural response of a particular space . . . is imprinted on a recorded or live performance that contains minimal other room acoustics'. In 2013, the choral group Capella Romana used this technique and produced an album of hymns based on late Byzantine hymnal texts that would have been used in Hagia Sophia, thus giving a sense of what these hymns might have sounded like when sung with the reverberation and echo of the original space.

26. *The Russian Primary Chronicle: The Laurentian Text*, trans. and ed. Samuel Hazzard Cross and Olgerd O. Sherbowitz-Wetzor (Cambridge, MA: Mediaeval Academy of America, 1953), 111; see also Thomas Hopko, 'Vladimir I', in Lindsay Jones (ed.), *Encyclopedia of Religion*, 2nd edn (New York: Macmillan Reference, 2004), 9631–2; Scott Kenworthy, 'Vladimir of Kiev, Prince', in George Thomas Kurian (ed.), *Encyclopedia of Christian Civilization* (Oxford: Wiley-Blackwell, 2011), 2468–9.

27. See, for example, the official church history teaching text from the Orthodox Church in America, Volume Three of the catechetical series *The Orthodox Faith*, by Fr. Thomas Hopko, *Church History*, rev. and expanded David C. Ford (Yonkers, NY: St. Vladimir's Seminary Press, 2016), 119.

28. Archimandrite Nikodemos Anagnostopoulos, *Orthodoxy and Islam: Theology and Muslim–Christian Relations in Modern Greece and Turkey* (New York: Routledge, 2017), 18.

29. Anagnostopoulos, *Orthodoxy and Islam*, 19–20.

30. 'Relics of Holy Church Fathers Restored to their Original Resting Place: A Positive Step Towards Reconciliation and Unity Between the Orthodox and Roman-Catholic Churches', 27 November 2004, Greek Orthodox Archdiocese of America

news service, available at: https://www.goarch.org/whats-new/-/asset_publisher/
rlvS19snJYAk/content/relics-of-holy-church-fathers-restored-to-their-original-
resting-place-a-postive-step-towards-reconciliation-and-unity-between-the-orthodox-
and-roman-/pop_up?_101_INSTANCE_rlvS19snJYAk_viewMode=print&_101_
INSTANCE_rlvS19snJYAk_languageId=en_US, last accessed 15 February 2022.

31. Brian Daley, SJ, *Gregory of Nazianzus* (New York: Routledge, 2006), 16.
32. Daley, *Gregory of Nazianzus*, 15–17.
33. Hugh Wybrew, 'Liturgies and the Fathers', in Ken Parry (ed.), *The Wiley-Blackwell Companion to Patristics* (Chichester: Wiley-Blackwell, 2019), 388.
34. Anagnostopoulos, *Orthodoxy and Islam*, 20.
35. On this mosaic, see Robin Cormack, 'The Mother of God in the Mosaics of Hagia Sophia at Constantinople', in Maria Vassilaki (ed.), *Mother of God: Representations of the Virgin in Byzantine Art* (Milan: Skira, 2000), 107–23.
36. Anna Bigelow, 'Hagia Sophia's Tears and Smiles: The Ambivalent Life of a Global Monument', in Nora Fisher-Onar, Susan C. Pearce, and E. Fuat Keyman (eds), *Istanbul: Living with Difference in a Global City* (New Brunswick, NJ: Rutgers University Press, 2018), 113.
37. Necipoğlu, 'The Life of an Imperial Monument', 200.
38. Spyros A. Sofos, 'Space and the Emotional Topography of Populism in Turkey: The Case of Hagia Sophia', *Cogent Social Sciences* 7:1 (2021), 7.
39. Necipoğlu, 'The Life of an Imperial Monument', 197.
40. Necipoğlu, 'The Life of an Imperial Monument', 200.
41. Orhan F. Köprülü and Mustafa İsmet Uzun, 'Akşemseddin', in *İslam Ansiklopedisi* (Ankara: Türkiye Diyanet Vakfı, 1989), 299–302. The key aspects of Akşemseddin's narrative are summarised in David-John Williams, 'The Use of Memory to Re-Found Hagia Sophia', *Koinonia: The Journal of the Anglican and Eastern Churches Association* 74 (2020): 15–19. See also Patrick Franke, 'Khidr in Istanbul: Observations on the Symbolic Constructions of Sacred Space in Traditional Islam', in George Stauth (ed.), *Yearbook of the Sociology of Islam 5: On Archaeology of Sainthood and Local Spirituality in Islam: Past and Present Crossroads of Events and Ideas.* (Bielefeld: transcript Verlag, 2015), 36–56.
42. A summary of current research on this system, and an analysis of its main institutional and theological contours, can be found in Dorroll, *Islamic Theology in the Turkish Republic*, 18–27.
43. Aḥmad ibn Muṣṭafā Taşköprülüzade, *al-Shaqāʾiq al-Nuʿmāniyya fī ʿUlamāʾ al-Dawla al-ʿUthmāniyya* (Beirut: Dār al-Kitāb al-ʿArabī, 1975), 97–8, 293, 297–8, 371–2, 382. See also Dorroll, *Islamic Theology in the Turkish Republic*, 26–7.

44. Ferhat Koca, 'Molla Hüsrev', *İslam Ansiklopedisi* (Ankara: Türkiye Diyanet Vakfı, 2005), 252–4.

45. Rahmi Yaran, 'Ömer Nasuhi Bilmen', *İslam Ansiklopedisi* (Ankara: Türkiye Diyanet Vakfı, 1992), 162–3.

46. Pınar Aykaç, 'The Commission for the Preservation of Antiquities and its Role in the Appropriation of Istanbul's Diverse Heritage as National Heritage (1939–1953)', *New Perspectives on Turkey* 62 (2020), 85, 94–5.

47. Ömer Nasuhi Bilmen, *Surei fethin Türkce tefsiri ve itilâyi İslâm ile Istanbulun tarihçesi* (Istanbul: Burhaneddin Erenler Matbaası, 1953). The edition cited here is a 2020 reprint that was reissued in the context of the build-up to the reconversion of Hagia Sophia: *Fetih Sûresi Tefsiri* (Istanbul: Ravza Yayınları, 2020).

48. Bilmen, *Fetih Sûresi Tefsiri*, 171–3.

49. These categories are variously phrased in Ottoman sources; Bilmen identifies them as *Akâide*, *İbadetler* and *Ahlâkıyat/Muamelat*, respectively; Bilmen, *Fetih Sûresi Tefsiri*, 182.

50. Bilmen, *Fetih Sûresi Tefsiri*, 182–9.

51. Bilmen, *Fetih Sûresi Tefsiri*, 194.

52. Bilmen, *Fetih Sûresi Tefsiri*, 193–4.

53. For a summary of these efforts, see Necipoğlu, 'The Life of an Imperial Monument', 205–21.

54. Necipoğlu, 'The Life of an Imperial Monument', 281.

55. *Study Qur'an* translation.

56. Metin Ahunbay and Zeynep Ahunbay, 'Structural Influence of Hagia Sophia on Ottoman Mosque Architecture', in Robert Moore and Ahmet Ş. Çakmak (eds), *Hagia Sophia from the Age of Justinian to the Present* (Cambridge: Cambridge University Press, 1992), 180.

57. Ahunbay and Ahunbay, 'Structural Influence of Hagia Sophia on Ottoman Mosque Architecture', 194.

58. The biographical information in this section is from Ferman Karaçam, 'Osman Yüksel Serdengeçti', *İslam Ansiklopedisi* (Ankara: Türkiye Diyanet Vakfı, 2009), 555–6.

59. 'Osman Yüksel Serdengeçti, "Ayasofya açılsın" dediği için idamla yargılanmıştı', *Yeni Akit*, 10 June 2020, available at: https://www.yeniakit.com.tr/haber/osman-yuksel-serdengecti-ayasofya-acilsin-dedigi-icin-idamla-yargilanmisti-1286857.html, last accessed 1 January 2022.

60. Hasan Hüseyin Ceylan, *Ayasofya İhaneti* (Istanbul: Dünya Bizim, 2020), 149.

61. Necip Fazıl Kısakürek, 'Ayasofya', *İslam Medeniyeti*, 15 May 1968, 11.

62. Yavuz, *Nostalgia for the Empire*, 85–90.

63. Uzer, 'Conservative Narrative', 276, 281, 285.

64. Kısakürek, 'Ayasofya', 11.

65. Kısakürek, 'Ayasofya', 11–12.

66. Kısakürek, 'Ayasofya', 12.

67. Sezai Karakoç, 'Ayasofya, ne kadar sabırlısın!', *İslam Medeniyeti*, 15 May 1968, 36.

68. Karakoç, 'Ayasofya, ne kadar sabırlısın!', 36.

69. Ceylan, *Ayasofya İhaneti*, 9; reprint and expansion of Hasan Hüseyin Ceylan, *Ayasofya İhaneti* (Ankara: Rehber Yayıncılık, 1993).

70. Bigelow, 'Hagia Sophia's Tears and Smiles', 124.

71. In Serhat Arvas, *Kılıç Hakkı Ayasofya: Tarihi ve Önemi* (Istanbul: IQ Kültür Sanat Yayıncılık, 2018), 104.

72. Fahir Armaoğlu, 'Ayasofya İbadete Açılmalıdır!', *Tercüman*, 27 April, 1988; reprinted in Ceylan, *Ayasofya İhaneti* (2020), 63.

73. Ceylan, *Ayasofya İhaneti*, 63.

74. Ceylan, *Ayasofya İhaneti*, 64.

75. See at: https://www.ayasofyacamii.gov.tr/tr/ayasofya-manifestosu, last accessed 26 February 2022.

76. The first published version of this text was printed in the AKP political magazine *Türkiye Bülteni*, which is the version being cited here. The contemporary online 'manifesto' version is posted on the website noted above. 'Cumhurbaşkanımız Danıştay'ın Ayasofya Kararının Ardından Saat 20.53'te Millete Sesleniş Konuşması Yaptı', *Türkiye Bülteni* 18:144 (2020), 50.

77. 'Cumhurbaşkanımız', 50–1.

78. 'Cumhurbaşkanımız', 51.

79. 'Cumhurbaşkanımız', 51.

80. 'Cumhurbaşkanımız', 51.

81. 'Cumhurbaşkanımız', 53.

82. 'Cumhurbaşkanımız', 53.

83. 'Cumhurbaşkanımız', 53.

84. 'Ayasofya'nın ibadete açılacak olmasına siyasilerden ilk yorumlar', *T24*, 10 July 2020, available at: https://t24.com.tr/haber/ayasofya-da-ibadetin-yolunun-acil-masina-siyasilerden-ilk-yorumlar,889901, last accessed 26 February 2020.

85. 'HDP'li vekil Ayasofya'nın kilise olmasını istedi', *En Son Haber*, 8 July 2020, available at: https://www.ensonhaber.com/ic-haber/hdpli-vekil-ayasofyanin-kilise-olmasini-istedi, last accessed 26 February 2022.

86. 'İlk yorumlar'.

87. Yavuz Baydar, 'Conversion of Hagia Sophia Will Deal Another Blow to the Foundations of Secular Turkey', *Ahval*, 10 July 2020, available at: https://ahvalnews.com/
hagia-sophia/conversion-hagia-sophia-will-deal-another-severe-blow-foundations-
secular-turkey-yavuz, last accessed 26 February 2022.

88. 'Ayasofya-i Kebir Cami-i Şerifi, 86 Yıl Sonra Kılınan Cuma Namazıyla İbadete
Açıldı', *Türkiye Bülteni* 18:144 (2020), 54–9.

89. 'Diyanet İşleri Başkanı Erbaş, yeniden ibadete açılan Ayasofya-i Kebir Cami-i
Şerifi'nde ilk hutbeyi irad etti', available at: https://www.diyanet.gov.tr/tr-TR/
Kurumsal/Detay/29715/diyanet-isleri-baskani-erbas-yeniden-ibadete-acilan-
ayasofya-i-kebir-cami-i-serifinde-ilk-hutbeyi-irad-etti, last accessed 1 March 2020.

90. 'Diyanet İşleri Başkanı Erbaş'.

91. 'Diyanet İşleri Başkanı Erbaş'.

92. 'Diyanet İşleri Başkanı Erbaş'.

93. 'Diyanet İşleri Başkanı Erbaş'.

94. 'Diyanet İşleri Başkanı Erbaş'.

95. Necipoğlu, 'The Life of an Imperial Monument', 218.

96. Kaan Bozdoğan, 'Cumhurbaşkanı Erdoğan Ayasofya Camisi'ne hat levhası bağışladı',
Anadolu Ajansı, 8 December 2020, available at: https://www.aa.com.tr/tr/turkiye/
cumhurbaskani-erdogan-ayasofya-camisine-hat-levhasi-bagisladi/2069104#, last
accessed 3 March 2020.

97. This population refers to itself in Greek as the Ρωμιοί – the Romioi – or 'Romans',
that is, the term by which the Byzantines referred to themselves as inhabitants of
the Roman Empire (the term 'Byzantine' for the Eastern Roman Empire from
Constantine to 1453 is a term invented by Western historiography). In Turkish,
this term is written as *Rum*, or in the case of the Greeks of Istanbul, *İstanbullu
Rumlar*. The term also was used in the Ottoman period to denote any subject
who was a member of the Eastern Orthodox Church, as these were all placed
under the direct administration of the Ecumenical Patriarch of Constatninople,
who was designated the official mediator between this subject population and
the Ottoman central government. It was even at times used by the Ottoman
sultans to refer to themselves as inheritors of the Byzantine imperium. On this
terminology, see Alexandris, *The Greek Minority of Istanbul and Greek–Turkish
Relations*, 17; Samim Akgönül, 'Rum Nedir? Kim Der, Kime Der, Niye Der?' in
Hakan Yücel (ed.), *Rum Olmak, Rum Kalmak* (Istanbul: İstos Yayınları, 2016),
31; Nurdan Türker, *I Have No Country, I have a Homeland: Istanbul Romiois:
Place–Memory–Migration*, trans. Arda Akbaş and Fatima Sakarya (Berlin: Peter
Lang, 2020), 47.

98. On the importance of Byzantium for Istanbul Greek identity, see Kaymak, *İstanbul'da Az(ınlık) Olmak*, 213; İlay Romain Örs, '"Şehrin" Diasporası: Atina'da Yaşayan İstanbullu Rumlar', in *İstanbul Rumları: Bugün ve Yarın* (Istanbul: İstos Yayınları, 2012), 194.

99. On the importance of Eastern Orthodoxy and the Ecumenical Patriarchate to Istanbul Greek identity, see Alexandris, 'İstanbul'un Rum Azınlığının Son Göçü', 162; Aslı Tunç and Ariana Ferentinou, 'Identities In-between: The Impact of Satellite Broadcasting on Greek Orthodox Minority (Rum Polites) Women's Perception of Their Identities in Turkey', *Ethnic and Racial Studies* 35:5 (2012), 919; Türker, *I Have No Country*, 119–20, 123–4, 228.

100. On the importance of 'The City' to Istanbul Greek identity, see Örs, 'Beyond the Greek and Turkish Dichotomy'; Örs, *Diaspora of the City: Stories of Cosmopolitanism from Istanbul and Athens*, 72, 104; Türker, *I Have No Country*, 177, 233; Tunç and Ferintinou, 'Identities In-between', 916, 918.

101. Örs, 'Beyond the Greek and Turkish Dichotomy', 81.

102. Shaw, 'The Population of Istanbul in the Nineteenth Century', 265–77.

103. Alexandris, 'İstanbul'un Rum Azınlığının Son Göçü', 161.

104. Alexandris, *The Greek Minority of Istanbul and Greek–Turkish Relations*, 87.

105. Alexandris, *The Greek Minority of Istanbul and Greek–Turkish Relations*, 232–3; Akgönül, *Türkiye Rumları*, 97.

106. Akgönül, *Türkiye Rumları*, 164, 251; Alexandris, *The Greek Minority of Istanbul and Greek–Turkish Relations*, 281–3; Alexandris, 'İstanbul'un Rum Azınlığının Son Göçü', 141–65; Örs, *Diaspora of the City*, 138.

107. Akgönül, *Türkiye Rumları*, 319, 345.

108. Kaymak, *İstanbul'da Az(ınlık) Olmak*, 207, 250, 254–5.

109. On the trope of the ever-present threat of indigenous Greek betrayal of the Turkish nation, see Akgönül, *Türkiye Rumları*, 22, 43, 61, 252; Alexandris, *The Greek Minority of Istanbul and Greek–Turkish Relations*, 316; Kaymak, *İstanbul'da Az(ınlık) Olmak*, 195–6, 228; Mills, 'The Cultural Politics of Ethnic Nationalism', 1184; Ceren Sözeri, 'Kıbrıs Meselesinin Rehineleri: Basının Gözüyle 1964 Sürgünleri', in Hakan Yücel (ed.), *Rum Olmak, Rum Kalmak* (Istanbul: İstos Yayınları, 2016), 71, 77.

110. For details of his life, see Greek Orthodox Archdiocese of America, 'Biography of His All Holiness Patriarch Bartholomew', available at: https://www.goarch.org/-/biography-ecumenical-patriarch, last accessed 3 March 2020.

111. Hakan Yücel and Süheyla Yıldız, 'İstanbul'da ve İmroz'da Rum Olmak, Atina'da Rum Kalmak', *Alternatif Politika* 6:2 (2014), 154.

112. Specific dates provided to the authors courtesy of the Greek Orthodox Arch-diocese of America. For further biographical information, see Greek Orthodox Archdiocese of America, 'Biography of His Eminence Archbishop Elpidopho-ros of America', available at: https://www.goarch.org/archbishop/biography, last accessed 3 March 2020.

113. 'İstanbul Patriği Bartholomeos'un Konferansı Açış Konuşması', *İstanbul Rumları: Bugün ve Yarın* (Istanbul: İstos Yayınları, 2012), 14.

114. İpek Yezdani, 'Bakırköy'den ABD'ye başpiskopos', *Hürriyet*, 13 June 2019, available at: https://www.hurriyet.com.tr/gundem/bakirkoyden-abdye-baspis-kopos-41242370, last accessed 8 June 2022.

115. 'Ecumenical Patriarch Bartholomew: The Conversion of Hagia Sophia into a Mosque Will Sow Discord between Christians and Muslims', *Agenzia Fidez*, 1 July 2020, available at: http://www.fides.org/en/news/68248-ASIA_TURKEY_Ecumenical_Patriarch_Bartholomew_the_conversion_of_Hagia_Sophia_into_a_mosque_will_sow_discord_between_Christians_and_Muslims, last accessed 3 March 2020.

116. Order of St. Andrew the Apostle: Archons of the Ecumenical Patriarchate in America, 'His All-Holiness Offers Uplifting Message regarding Hagia Sophia', 28 August 2020; available at: https://www.archons.org/-/hah-thanks-order-hagia-sophia-support, last accessed 3 March 2020.

117. Order of St. Andrew the Apostle, 'His All-Holiness Offers Uplifting Message'.

118. 'Holy Eparchial Synod Designates July 24 as a Day of Mourning', *Orthodox Observer*, available at: https://www.goarch.org/-/july-24-day-of-mourning, last accessed 3 March 2020.

119. 'Holy Eparchial Synod Designates July 24 as a Day of Mourning'.

120. 'Homily for the National Day of Mourning over Ἁγία Σοφία', *Orthodox Observer*, available at: https://www.goarch.org/news/archbishop/homilies/-/asset_publisher/JjmOoSCoGGMm/content/day-of-mourning-homily?_101_INSTANCE_JjmOoSCoGGMm_languageId=en_US, last accessed 3 March 2020.

121. 'Homily for the National Day of Mourning over Ἁγία Σοφία'.

122. 'Archiepiscopal Encyclical on the Day of Mourning for Hagia Sophia', Prot. No. 186/2021, *Orthodox Observer*, available at: https://www.goarch.org/-/agia-sophia-day-of-mourning, last accessed 3 March 2020.

CONCLUSION

... to read the present in terms of the past by writing the past in terms of the present.

Lamont Lindstrom[1]

Summary of Arguments

This book has analysed four case studies in Istanbul in order to illustrate key turning points in a specific decade of Erdoğan's rule (2010–20).[2] This decade was a crucial moment in Turkish history that revealed not only his personal power, but also speaks to how those at the margins worked against his view of the city where he and the AKP attempted to build and shape their vision of an ideal Turkish identity. Our analysis used architecture and public space as our text, utilising a close reading of that text as well as incorporating historical and ethnographic details to contextualise the scene within which it emerged and was 'written' on the landscape of Istanbul. While this analysis is not meant to epitomise or stand in for all of Turkey's experiences under the AKP administration, analysing this unique historical moment in this way reveals an important technique of Erdoğan's administration, and specifically how he utilises Ottoman history as a tool for creating his own power within the context of Istanbul.

We have termed this technique 'Erdoğanian neo-Ottomanism', meaning the AKP's use of the power of the state to shape the urban landscape in their social and ideological image. Within this story one can also see a powerful example of a global trend in modern nationalism, where those in power create meaning in the space they inhabit and those on the margins push back as they are being pushed out. In the age of the neoliberal and neo-Ottoman hegemony of the AKP, the physical space and place of Turkey is shifting to showcase the ideologies of the ruling power. All the cases under examination stand as examples of the shaping of the built environment according to AKP economic, social and political ideals, and we also see embedded the reactions of those affected by this specific use of space. By analysing specific examples of spatial politics, this project attempts to map how the AKP inscribes their power on the built landscape over and against the protests of certain counter groups in Turkey. A key argument of this book is that the AKP's utilisation of the Ottoman past is driven not only by economic motives, but is animated by the specific cultural ideology that we call Erdoğanian neo-Ottomanism.

The arguments in this book began by linking the spatial politics of Erdoğan's AKP with certain key trends and precedents in modern Turkish history, most especially how the spatial politics of the AKP in contemporary Istanbul are the latest in a series of attempts by hegemonic elites to shape the public sphere in modern Turkey using the tools of cultural capital and cultural memory. The application, preparation and implementation of Istanbul as the European Capital of Culture in 2010 represented an early and ambiguous phase in the development of the neo-Ottomanism of the AKP under Erdoğan. It represented at one and the same time the desire of Turkey to look towards and become integrated with Western Europe, while at the same time the authoritarianism and anti-pluralism of Erdoğanian neo-Ottomanism began to emerge as well in the ways in which the city was shaped by the AKP during these events, as they destroyed local multicultural heritage and emphasised the Ottoman Turkish dimensions of Istanbul's identity.

The ambiguities and tensions in the Turkish–European relationship on display in the ECoC would be resolved in the direction of authoritarianism and anti-Westernism at Gezi Park, when Erdoğan led the AKP's crackdown on this pro-pluralist and pro-multicultural uprising. After Gezi, Erdoğanian neo-Ottomanism emerged as a fully-fledged ideology and form of spatial politics enacted by the AKP in the city of Istanbul whereby Erdoğan and the AKP sought to shape the city in their own image as a space that promoted and reflected conservative Sunni Turkish Islamic identity. Ironically, a very similar project of homogenising nationalism had occurred decades before at the hands of secular Turkish nationalists in and around Gezi Park, as revealed in the histories and experiences of the indigenous Greek Orthodox from this part of Istanbul, which had once been the centre of their community. Again, the AKP's spatial politics emerge as a more recent version of Turkish state dynamics going back to the early years of the republic. The practices of memorial and remembrance after the violent coup attempt of 2016 showed the ways in which Erdoğanian neo-Ottomanism can serve as a response to social trauma, while at the same time further reinforcing the hegemonic nationalism of the AKP under Erdoğan. The reconversion of Hagia Sophia into a mosque in 2020 epitomised the absolute dominance of Erdoğan and the AKP's vision of Turkish identity in Istanbul's public space, representing the culmination of the authoritarian transformation of the decade. Yet even then, voices of resistance from indigenous Greek Orthodox leaders from Istanbul dramatically highlighted and pushed back against the political and ideological dimensions of Erdoğan and the AKP's use of Ottoman heritage within the landscape of the city of Istanbul.

Who Has the Right to the City? Art, Religion and Cultural Heritage

When analysing the urban landscape in contemporary Turkey under AKP rule, it is important to follow David Harvey and ask: who has the right to the city?[3] Our project stands as an ethnography and textual analysis of the conflict of an idealised architectural public sphere that supports the policies and social vision of the AKP and those who protested against the construction of this public sphere. Habermas famously described the public sphere as form of opposition to the government, an idealised, utopian space that was supposed to be constituted by public opinion voiced without the involvement of the government. Our work, however, shows how governments cannot be taken completely out of the public sphere narrative when we use architecture as our text. Just as Michael Warner elaborated on the nature of the text with respect to the public sphere, in that he defined the public sphere as any readable text, we have built on his argument to use architecture as the text by which to analyse a public sphere. We have also used Nancy Fraser's idea of counter publics to illustrate what we call the protest public sphere that emerged in Turkey to oppose the manipulation of public space by the AKP. It is not our purpose, however, to characterise these former spaces as romanticised, idealised places. In fact, many of these areas were in need of repair and restoration; yet it was the systematic displacement of subaltern populations that indicated that those with politics similar to the AKP, those with a certain level of financial resources and the proper cultural capital were considered to possess more of a right to these redeveloped spaces. Our book reveals the multiplicity of differing publics that can exist at similar times under differing power dynamics.

In this book, art and religion are viewed as tools that are used to produce cultural heritage. Art and religion can be both a medium to display power and can also be used as a resistance mechanism. In certain forms they are utilised by the architectural public sphere, as in the AKP's manipulation of the built environment as described above in the cases of the ECoC, Gezi Park, the Martyrs' Monument and Hagia Sophia. These are examples of official heritage, the construction of which marked key turning points in the AKP's consolidation of its power over the crucial decade of 2010–20. Art is also a tool used to resist narratives of official heritage, as described above in the resistance displayed at Gezi Park and the reaction of indigenous Greek Orthodox leaders to the reconversion of Hagia Sophia. In these cases, this resistance and reaction sheds crucial light on the nature of Erdoğanian neo-Ottomanism itself, as they precisely identify the goal of this ideological project: to erase plural and cosmopolitan pasts, presents and possible futures; and replace these with a homogeneous and religiously conservative definition of what it means to be a true and authentic Turkish citizen.

With questions of cultural capital and heritage one must therefore ask: whose version of heritage is being displayed? Where are these heritage motifs occurring? When are these heritage memories on display? And, finally, who is given the power to display his or her cultural heritage? Whose art is on display and whose religion is allowed to worship in which spaces? We must also remember that heritage is not static: it changes with changes in political power, which themselves are of course not static. How heritage in the Turkish city is understood and framed is continually subject to the goals and ideologies of existing power regimes. Heritage is also a commodity, something produced for outside consumption typically in order to financially enrich the vision of the elites. The production of heritage and the production of political elites are in line with political place-making and remaking.

This book has analysed a specific moment in Turkish contemporary history by looking at components of cultural heritage as texts of power, and the subsequent protests generated by this use of heritage as acts of asserting one's rights to try to reclaim and retain existing people's rights to the city landscape. This project looks at the specific ways in which Ottoman heritage was framed and presented in an effort to establish an interpretation of Ottoman tradition that supports the cultural vision of Erdoğanian neo-Ottomansim with respect to how the city and country should be displayed to outsiders and insiders. At the heart of each case study lies the tension between rebuilding and restoration, and modernisation and historicisation. We analysed who has the power to project the vision of Istanbul, how history is currently being framed by people in power positions and whose history and heritage is being silenced.

Erdoğanian Neo-Ottomanism beyond the Nation

In order to open a future conversation on the dynamics of Erdoğan's neo-Ottomanism as described in this book, as a closing reflection it is helpful to consider how this neo-Ottomanism functions and exists in contexts beyond the borders of the modern Turkish nation-state. As we have described above, Erdoğanian neo-Ottomanism is a form of conservative Turkish Islamic nationalism. It is therefore important to ask, how does this ideology shift in the contexts beyond the Turkish nation? What does Erdoğan's neo-Ottomanism look like and what does it do when it refers to elements of Ottoman heritage that once were part of the Ottoman Empire, but are now located beyond the borders of the Republic of Turkey? On the one hand, this neo-Ottomanism abroad can function in precisely the opposite way that it does in Turkey: by serving and uplifting the marginalised where Turks are ethnic minorities, instead of acting as a force for marginalisation of non-Turks. On the other hand, this neo-Ottomanism abroad can also reveal the radical limitations and expose its own highly constructed and political nature when set against a non-Turkish cultural backdrop.

The case of Şehitlik Camii (Martyrs' Mosque) in Berlin reveals how neo-Ottoman memory can serve to protect and foster the interests of a marginalised community, exactly opposite of how it functions under Erdoğan within Turkey itself. Situated in Columbiadamm in the Neukölln district, an area of Berlin inhabited by multigenerational Turkish and other non-German ethnic residents, Şehitlik Camii was built between 1999 and 2005 by the architect Hilmi Şenalp (who designed the Martyrs' Monument described in Chapter 4 above, and who is renowned for his neo-Ottoman architectural and artistic style). The mosque is built in a deeply traditional neo-Ottoman style, with every detail corresponding to traditional imperial Ottoman mosque design. It was funded by Diyanet İşleri Türk-İslam Birliği (Türkisch-Islamische Union der Anstalt für Religion e.V.; the Turkish-Islamic Union for Religious Affairs), an umbrella organisation founded and funded by the Turkish state to serve the needs of the Turkish minority in Germany, the largest minority in Germany's post-war history. It was built next to a Muslim cemetery that dates to 1866 (hence, the name of the mosque), which was built and expanded in successive years for Muslim residents of Berlin, including Ottoman soldiers who died in the city after receiving treatment there during the First World War.[4]

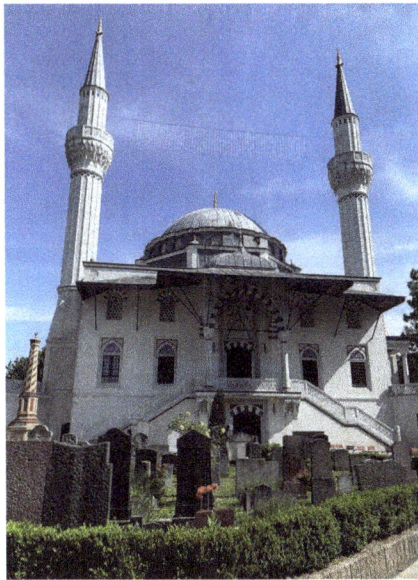

Figure C.1 Şehitlik Mosque, Berlin, June 2022. Photograph P. Dorroll.

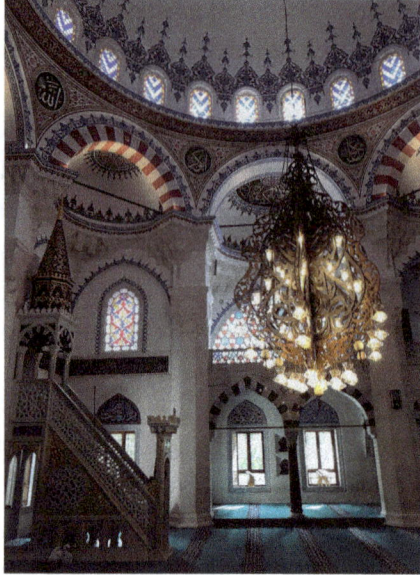

Figure C.2 Şehitlik Mosque interior, Berlin, June 2022. Photograph P. Dorroll.

Figure C.3 Şehitlik Mosque dome, Berlin, June 2022. Photograph P. Dorroll.

Today, the mosque is a key institution in the life of the Turkish minority in Berlin, who have for decades struggled with the effects of social and economic marginalisation, and even violence, suffered as a result of being an ethnic minority in a state that for most of the twentieth century officially treated them as foreigners, non-citizens and dangerous outsiders.[5] In this context, the deep traditionalism of the neo-Ottoman design of the mosque is clearly meant to embody the pride these residents had in their cultural roots and religious practice.[6] As Martin Klaptek puts it, in this case neo-Ottoman architectural style represents 'an accentuation of the uniqueness of the community'.[7] The mosque and the community services that it provides have long served as an institutional pillar of this marginalised community, and its design reflects exactly the opposite of what neo-Ottomanism under Erdoğan represents in Turkey today: an assertion of the value of multiculturalism and the defence of the rights and uniqueness of religious and ethnic minorities.

At the same time, neo-Ottomanism abroad can reveal and 'accentuate' the highly constructed and political nature of its own ideology. As Jeremy Walton's ground-breaking research has revealed of neo-Ottomanism beyond Turkey, 'sites of renascent Ottoman memory – especially those outside of Turkey – undermine and contradict the premises of Neo-Ottomanism in unanticipated ways'.[8] Walton discusses the case of the New Mosque (Yeni Camii) in Thessaloniki, built in 1902 by Salonica's *dönme* community, a distinctive Ottoman religious group that both practiced Islam and also remained followers of the seventeenth-century Salonica Jewish messianic figure Sabbatai Zevi. Though it represents a uniquely Ottoman form of religious and cultural heritage, the mosque has been ignored by those in the Turkish government who would otherwise be highly interested in reviving Ottoman architectural heritage. Walton therefore terms the mosque 'a site of amnesia', where the highly diverse, cosmopolitan, and even syncretistic and heterodox elements of Ottoman Islamic heritage are ignored or forgotten by contemporary Erdoğanian neo-Ottomanism because they challenge the homogenising assumptions and goals of this ideology (as outlined in detail above in this book).[9]

In 2013, approximately fifty students from the indigenous Turkish minority of northern Greece travelled from the city of Komotini (Gümülcine in Turkish) to the mosque in order to perform prayers there. But as Walton notes, this group did so in a manner that was natural to them, that is, in the standard Sunni Hanafi practice descended from imperial Ottoman tradition.[10] This event ironically encapsulates both the dynamic described above – where Ottoman memory is used in service of minority communities – at the same time that this practice itself contributes to the erasure and forgetting of the memory of another marginalised community, the *dönme*, whose memory cannot be reconciled with official discourses of Erdoğanian neo-Ottoman cultural memory.

Other Ottoman-era sites abroad are treated very differently by the Turkish state under Erdoğan's AKP. In his analysis of the restoration and promotion of the tomb (*türbe*) of Murad I, Behar Sadriu demonstrates that the contemporary Turkish state's interest in this Ottoman-era site reveals it to be 'a site of ongoing, contemporary hagiographical construction – a hagiography of Sultan Murad I and the Ottomans, commissioned by contemporary Turkey, which guards this memory'.[11] Now located in the village of Mazgit in Kosovo, the shrine complex was originally built during the Ottoman period to commemorate the Ottoman victory at the Battle of Kosovo in 1389. It was ignored by the Turkish government during the early years of the republic, and has not seen much interest by the local population.[12]

In 2005, however, the Turkish Directorate of Religious Affairs renovated the site, and, in 2010, turned the adjacent inn building into a museum that focuses on the life of Murad I and the Battle of Kosovo. Significantly, in 2010, Erdoğan visited the tomb, accompanied by leaders of the Kosovar Muslim community, and also prayed at there, an act of piety deeply connected with Ottoman Sunni tradition (as described above in Chapter 4). Photographs and descriptions of this official visit are also featured in the museum's exhibition.[13] Strikingly, Erdoğan referred to this tomb, though located in the territory of another state, as an *emanet* – a sacred trust – in the care of the Turkish nation and the Turkish people.[14] As noted above, this was the exact term – *emanet* – that the head of the Directorate of Religious Affairs Ali Erbaş used to describe the relationship between the modern Turkish state and Hagia Sophia. The neglect of sites such as Yeni Camii in Thessaloniki, in favour of sites such as this, again reveals the constructed nature of Erdoğan's neo-Ottomanism as it declares Ottoman sites identified with Turkish Sunni Islamic tradition as authentic sites of modern Turkish cultural heritage, while neglecting or forgetting sites that are connected with other versions of the Ottoman past.

One final example reinforces the highly politicised nature of Erdoğan's neo-Ottomanism, however natural or neutral it appears to some in its domestic context. Lerna Yanık and Jelena Subotić's analysis of the tomb (also a *türbe*) of the Ottoman-era Bektashi saint Gül Baba focuses on how such sites can be used by states to increase their international status and strengthen explicitly political alliances and interests. Gül Baba was a dervish who was a companion of Süleyman the Magnificent during his campaigns in Hungary, who died in battle and was buried in the Rózsadomb district of contemporary Budapest in the sixteenth century.[15] From 2016 to 2018, the Turkish and Hungarian government (under fellow authoritarian Viktor Orbán) collaborated to fund and direct a major restoration of the site. The renovations were unveiled by Erdoğan during a state visit in order to strengthen economic ties between the two countries.

Interestingly, the fact that Gül Baba was not an orthodox Sunni Muslim did not exclude him from being claimed by Erdoğan's consideration of Ottoman heritage in this explicitly political context where economic interests were at the forefront. Orbán has often cited Turkey under Erdoğan as a model for the kind of state and society he is attempting to build in Hungary: one that is consciously opposed to the liberal West, proudly authoritarian and even explicitly anti-democratic.[16] This example reinforces how deeply political Erdoğan's vision of neo-Ottomanism is, insofar as it can embrace contradiction and inconsistency when necessary in order to serve his specific political objectives.

Therefore, in the final analysis, the mere continued existence of remnants of the bewildering complexity and plurality of Ottoman society, itself a centuries-long experience and tradition, call into question the hegemonic narrative of Erdoğanian neo-Ottomanism. Not only living persons themselves, but also the very kinds of architectural remnants that appear to be so deeply valued by Erdoğan and the AKP, can at times undermine the present-day ideologies and spatial politics that support their devotion to these architectural remnants in the first place. The physical and spatial objects of Erdoğanian neo-Ottoman devotion are more complex in their own nature than they are allowed to be in the AKP's ideology. In other words, it appears that Ottoman tradition itself has the capacity to resist its political utilisation, and that the voices of the past are never fully willing to harmonise themselves with the commands issued by the present.

Notes

1. Lamont Lindstrom, 'Leftamap Kastom: The Political History of Tradition on Tanna (Vanuatu)', *Mankind* 13:4 (1982), 317.
2. Parts of this conclusion are from Dorroll, 'The Spatial Politics of Turkey's Justice and Development Party (AK Party)'.
3. David Harvey, 'The Right to the City', *New Left Review* 53 (2008), 23–40, available at: https://newleftreview.org/issues/ii53/articles/david-harvey-the-right-to-the-city, last accessed 8 June 2022.
4. Rizvi, *The Transnational Mosque*, 34–6.
5. On the history of this population, see David Horrocks and Eva Kolinsky (eds), *Turkish Culture in German Society Today* (Oxford: Bergahn, 1996).
6. Rizvi, *The Transnational Mosque*, 39.
7. Klapetek, 'Şehitlik Mosque and the Islamic Cemetary at Columbiadamm', 74.
8. Jeremy F. Walton, 'Geographies of Revival and Erasure: Neo-Ottoman Sites of Memory in Istanbul, Thessaloniki, and Budapest', *Die Welt des Islams* 56 (2016): 511.
9. Walton, 'Geographies of Revival and Erasure', 523.
10. Walton, "Geographies of Revival and Erasure', 524.
11. Behar Sadriu, 'Shrine Diplomacy: Turkey's Quest for a post-Kemalist Identity', *History and Anthropology* 30:4 (2019), 426.
12. Sadriu, 'Shrine Diplomacy', 422–6.
13. Sadriu, 'Shrine diplomacy', 428.
14. Sadriu, 'Shrine diplomacy', 429.
15. Lerna K. Yanık and Jelena Subotić, 'Cultural Heritage as Status Seeking: The International Politics of Turkey's Restoration Wave', *Cooperation and Conflict* 56:3 (2001), 255.
16. Yanık and Subotić, 'Cultural Heritage as Status Seeking', 257.

BIBLIOGRAPHY

15 Temmuz Milli İradenin Zaferi Araştırma Raporu (2017), Ankara: AK Parti Sosyal Politikalar Başklanlığı.

'15 Temmuz Şehitler Köprüsü', Official Website of the Üsküdar Municipality, available at: https://www.uskudar.bel.tr/tr/main/pages/15-temmuz-sehitler-koprusu/36, last accessed 2 May 2022.

'15 Temmuz Şehitler Makamı'na ziyaretçi akını havadan görüntülendi' (2020), Demiören Haber Ajansı, 15 July, available at: https://www.youtube.com/watch?v=thmVMm3ia3U, last accessed 2 May 2022.

'15 Temmuz'u Anmak, İhanet Anlamak' (2019), *Diyanet İşleri Başkanlığı*, 12 July.

'15 Temmuz'u Unutmamak ve Unutturmamak Tarihimize Karşı En Büyük Sorumluluğumuzdur' (2017), Office of the Presidency of the Republic of Turkey, 15 July, available at: https://www.tccb.gov.tr/haberler/410/79932/istanbuldaki-15-temmuz-demokrasi-ve-mill-birlik-gunu-anma-toreni-basladi.html#:~:text=%C4%B0stanbul'da%2015%20Temmuz%20Demokrasi,kar%C5%9F%C4%B1%20da%20en%20b%C3%BCy%C3%BCk%20sorumlulu%C4%9Fumuzdur, last accessed 16 May 2022.

'15 Temmuz Unutulmayacak' (2017), *Üsküdar Kültür, Sanat ve Medeniyet Dergisi* 4:1, 79–83.

'15 Temmuz ve Birlik Ruhu' (2020), Diyanet İşleri Başkanlığı, 10 July.

'2023 Siyasi Vizyon', *AK Parti*, available at: https://www.akparti.org.tr/parti/2023-siyasi-vizyon, last accessed 26 July 2022.

'A Whistleblower's Graft Tale: Losing Faith in Fatih' (2013), *Hürriyet Daily News*, n.d., available at: https://www.hurriyetdailynews.com/opinion/emre-deliveli/a-whistleblowers-graft-tale-losing-faith-in-fatih-59854, last accessed 15 July 2022.

Abbas, Tahir (2013), 'Political Culture and National Identity in Conceptualising the Gezi Park Movement', *Insight Turkey* 15:4, 19–27.

Açiksöz, Can and Zeynep Korkman (2013), 'Erdoğan's Masculinity and the Language of the Gezi Resistance', *Jadaliyya*, 22 June, available at: http://www.jadaliyya.com/pages/index/12367/Erdoğan%E2%80%99s-masculinity-and-the-language-of-the-gezi, last accessed 7 June 2022.

Ağartan, Kaan (2018), 'Politics of the Square: Remembering Gezi Protests Five Years Later', *New Perspectives on Turkey* 58, 201–17.

Ahmad, Feroz (2002), *The Making of Modern Turkey*. New York: Routledge.

Ahunbay, Metin and Zeynep Ahunbay (1992), 'Structural Influence of Hagia Sophia on Ottoman Mosque Architecture', in Robert Moore and Ahmet Ş. Çakmak (eds), *Hagia Sophia from the Age of Justinian to the Present*. Cambridge: Cambridge University Press, 179–94.

Akbaba, Ahmed Nafi, '360 Video – 15 Temmuz Şehitler Makamı, Sanal Tur, Vr gezi', available at: https://www.youtube.com/watch?v=oIh94k7v0f4, last accessed 2 May 2022.

Akbulut, Bengi (2014), '"A Few Trees in Gezi Park": Resisting the Spatial Politics of Neoliberalism in Turkey', in L. Anders Sandberg, Adrina Bardekjian and Sadia Butt (eds), *Urban Forests, Trees, and Greenspace: A Political Ecology Perspective*. London: Routledge, 227–41.

Akgönül, Samim (2007), *Türkiye Rumları: Ulus-Devlet Çağından Küresselleşme Çağına Bir Azınlığın Yok Oluç Süreci*. Istanbul: İletişim Yayınları.

Akgönül, Samim (2013), *The Minority Concept in the Turkish Context: Practices and Perceptions in Turkey, Greece, and France*. Leiden: Brill.

Akgönül, Samim (2016), 'Rum Nedir? Kim Der, Kime Der, Niye Der?', in Hakan Yücel (ed.), *Rum Olmak, Rum Kalmak*. Istanbul: İstos Yayınları, 21–38.

Akinsha, Konstantin, Grigorij Kozlov and Sylvia Hochfield (2007), *The Holy Place: Architecture, Ideology, and History in Russia*. New Haven, CT: Yale University Press.

Akyol, Mustafa (2013), 'Why Turkey Has Anti-Capitalist Muslims', *Al-Monitor*, 17 July, available at: https://www.al-monitor.com/originals/2013/07/turkey-anti-capitalist-muslims-gezi-social-justice-activism.html, last accessed 11 July 2022.

Alexandris, Alexis (1992), *The Greek Minority of Istanbul and Greek–Turkish Relations: 1918–1974*. Athens: Centre for Asia Minor Studies.

Alexandris, Alexis (2019), 'İstanbul'un Rum Azınlığının Son Göçü (1964–1974): İstanbul'daki Yunan Uyrukluların Sınırdışı Edilemeleri', in İlay Romain Örs (ed.), *İstanbullu Rumlar ve 1964 Sürgünleri: Türk Toplumun Homojenleşmesinde bir Dönüm Noktası*. Istanbul: İletişim Yayınları.

AlSayyad, Nezar (2014), *Traditions: The 'Real', the Hyper, and the Virtual in the Built Environment*. London: Routledge.

Altınordu, Ateş (2013), 'Occupy Gezi, Beyond the Religious–Secular Cleavage', *The Immanent Frame*, 10 June, available at: https://tif.ssrc.org/2013/06/10/occupy-gezi-beyond-the-religious-secular-cleavage, last accessed 8 July 2022.

Anadol, Çağatay and Doğan Kuban, *From Byzantion to Istanbul: 8000 Years of a Capital*, 5 June–4 September 2010. Istanbul: Sabanci University, Sakip Sabanci Museum.

Anagnostopoulos, Archimandrite Nikodemos (2017), *Orthodoxy and Islam: Theology and Muslim–Christian Relations in Modern Greece and Turkey*. New York: Routledge.

Anastassiadou, Méropi (2009), 'Greek Orthodox Immigrants Of and Modes of Integration Within the Urban Society of Istanbul (1850–1923)', *Mediterranean Historical Review* 24:2, 151–67.

Anderson, Benedict (1983), *Imagined Communities: Reflections on the Origin and Spread of Nationalism*. New York: Verso, 2006.

'Archiepiscopal Encyclical on the Day of Mourning for Hagia Sophia', Prot. No. 186/2021, *Orthodox Observer*, available at: https://www.goarch.org/-/agia-sophia-day-of-mourning, last accessed 3 March 2020.

Armaoğlu, Fahir (1988), 'Ayasofya İbadete Açılmalıdır!', *Tercüman*, 27 April, in Hasan Hüseyin Ceylan, *Ayasofya İhaneti*. Istanbul: Dünya Bizim, 2020, 63–4.

Armstrong, William (2013), 'Gezi Continues to Dominate Agenda in Turkey', *Turkish Review* 3:5, 522–7.

Arvas, Serhat (2018), *Kılıç Hakkı Ayasofya: Tarihi ve Önemi*. Istanbul: IQ Kültür Sanat Yayıncılık.

Asad, Talal (1993), *Genealogies of Religion: Discipline and Reasons of Power in Christianity and Islam*. Baltimore, MD: Johns Hopkins University Press.

Asad, Talal (2005), *Formations of the Secular: Christianity, Islam, Modernity*. Palo Alto, CA: Stanford University Press.

Aslan, Senem (2021), 'Public Tears: Populism and the Politics of Emotion in AKP's Turkey', *International Journal of Middle East Studies* 53:1, 1–17.

'Ayasofya-i Kebir Cami-i Şerifi, 86 Yıl Sonra Kılınan Cuma Namazıyla İbadete Açıldı' (2020), *Türkiye Bülteni* 18:144, 54–9.

'Ayasofya'nın ibadete açılacak olmasına siyasilerden ilk yorumlar' (2020), *T24*, 10 July, available at: https://t24.com.tr/haber/ayasofya-da-ibadetin-yolunun-acilmasina-siyasilerden-ilk-yorumlar,889901, last accessed 26 February 2020.

Aydın, Eylem (ed.) (2013), *Çapulcunun Gezi Rehberi*. Istanbul: Hemen Kitap.

Aykaç, Pınar (2020), 'The Commission for the Preservation of Antiquities and its Role in the Appropriation of Istanbul's Diverse Heritage as National Heritage (1939–1953)', *New Perspectives on Turkey* 62, 75–99.

Baban, Feyzi (2007) 'The Public Sphere and the Question of Identity in Turkey', in E. Fuat Keyman (ed.), *Remaking Turkey: Globalization Alternative Modernities and Democracy*. Lanham, MD: Lexington Books, 75–99.

Bali, Rifat N. (ed.) (2020), *6–7 Eylül 1955 Olayları: Tanıklar-Hatıralar II*. Istanbul: Libra Yayıncılık.

Banu Bıçakçı, Ayşe (2015), 'Branding the City through Culture: Istanbul, European Capital of Culture, 2010', *International Journal of Human Sciences* 9:1, 993–1006.

Barker, Chris (2004), *The SAGE Dictionary of Cultural Studies*, Thousand Oaks, CA: Sage, 41.

Başer, Bahar and Ahmet Erdi Öztürk (eds) (2017), *Authoritarian Politics in Turkey: Elections, Resistance, and the AKP*. London: I. B. Tauris.

Bastéa, Eleni (1999), *The Creation of Modern Athens: Planning the Myth*. Cambridge: Cambridge University Press.

Baydar, Yavuz (2020), 'Conversion of Hagia Sophia Will Deal Another Blow to the Foundations of Secular Turkey', *Ahval*, 10 July, available at: https://ahvalnews.com/hagia-sophia/conversion-hagia-sophia-will-deal-another-severe-blow-foundations-secular-turkey-yavuz, last accessed 26 February 2022.

Bayraktaroğlu, Arın (2002), 'The Media: Change and Impact', *Turkish Transformation* 123–40.

Baysu, Gülseli and Karen Phalet (2017), 'Beyond Muslim Identity: Opinion-based Groups in the Gezi Park Protest', *Group Processes and Intergroup Relations* 20:3, 350–66.

Bender, Thomas and Alev Cinar (2007), *Urban Imaginaries Locating the Modern City*. Minneapolis: University of Minnesota Press.

Berkes, Niyazi ([1964] 1999), *The Development of Secularism in Turkey*. Montreal: McGill University Press; reprinted New York: Routledge.

Beyazıt, Eda and Yasemin Tosun (2006), 'Evaluating Istanbul in the Process of European Capital of Culture 2010', 42nd ISoCaRP Congress.

Beylunioğlu, Anna Maria, 'Recasting the Parameters of Freedom of Religion in Turkey: Non-Muslims and the AKP', in Bahar Başer and Ahmet Erdi Öztürk (eds), *Authoritarian Politics in Turkey: Elections, Resistance, and the AKP*. London: I. B. Tauris, 141–56.

Bieberstein, Alice von and Nora Tataryan, 'The What of Occupation: "You Took Our Cemetery, You Won't Have Our Park!"' (2013), Hotspots, *Fieldsights*, 31 October, available at: https://culanth.org/fieldsights/the-what-of-occupation-you-took-our-cemetery-you-wont-have-our-park, last accessed 8 July 2022.

Biehl, Kristen Sarah (2020), 'A Dwelling Lens: Migration, Diversity and Boundary-Making in an Istanbul Neighbourhood', *Ethnic and Racial Studies* 43:12, 2236–54.

Bigelow, Anna (2018), 'Hagia Sophia's Tears and Smiles: The Ambivalent Life of a Global Monument', in Nora Fisher-Onar, Susan C. Pearce and E. Fuat Keyman (eds), *Istanbul: Living with Difference in a Global City*. New Brunswick, NJ: Rutgers University Press.

Bilmen, Ömer Nasuhi (1953), *Surei fethin Türkce tefsiri ve itilâyi İslâm ile Istanbulun tarihçesi*. Istanbul: Burhaneddin Erenler Matbaası.

Bilmen, Ömer Nasuhi (2020), *Fetih Sûresi Tefsiri*. Istanbul: Ravza Yayınları.

Blasing, John Konuk (2019), 'Hegemonic Discourses Clash in the Stadium: Sport, Nationalism, and Globalization in Turkey', *International Journal of Middle East Studies* 51:3, 475–8.

'Boğaz Köprüsü Ne Zaman Yapıldı? Yüksekliği Ve Uzunluğu Nedir?' (2021), *Milliyet*, 16 November, available at: https://www.milliyet.com.tr/egitim/bogaz-koprusu-ne-zaman-yapildi-yuksekligi-ve-uzunlugu-nedir-6643282, last accessed 2 May 2022.

'Bosphrous Bridge, Ankara's Main Square to be Renamed after July 15' (2022), *Hürriyet Daily News*, 26 July, available at: https://www.hurriyetdailynews.com/bosphorus-bridge-ankaras-main-square-to-be-renamed-after-july-15-102081, last accessed 2 May 2022.

Bourdieu, Pierre (1977), *Outline of a Theory of Practice*, trans. Richard Nice. Cambridge: Cambridge University Press, 1977.

Bourdieu, Pierre (1984), *Distinction: A Social Critique of the Judgment of Taste*, trans. Richard Nice. Cambridge, MA: Harvard University Press.

Bourdieu, Pierre (1986), 'The Forms of Capital', in John G. Richardson (ed.), *Handbook of Theory and Research for the Sociology of Education*. Westport, CT: Greenwood Press, 241–58.

Bourdieu, Pierre (1991), *Language and Symbolic Power*. Cambridge, MA: Harvard University Press.

Bourdieu, Pierre (1993), *Field of Cultural Production: Essays on Art and Literature*. New York: Columbia University Press.

Bozdoğan, Kaan (2020), 'Cumhurbaşkanı Erdoğan Ayasofya Camisi'ne hat levhası bağışladı', *Anadolu Ajansı*, 8 December, available at: https://www.aa.com.tr/tr/turkiye/cumhurbaskani-Erdoğan-ayasofya-camisine-hat-levhasi-bagisladi/2069104#, last accessed 3 March 2020.

Bozdoğan, Sibel (2001), *Modernism and Nation Building: Turkish Architectural Culture in the Early Republic*. Seattle, WA: University of Washington Press.

Bozoğlu, Gönül (2020), 'A Great Bliss to Keep the Sensation of Conquest Alive!: The Emotional Politics of the Panorama 1453 Museum in Istanbul', in Chiara de Cesari and Ayhan Kaya (eds), *European Memory in Populism*. London: Routledge, 91–111.

Braude, Benjamin (1982), 'Foundation Myths of the Millet System', in Benjamin Braude and Bernard Lewis (eds), *Christians and Jews in the Ottoman Empire: The Functioning of a Plural Society*. New York: Holmes & Meier, 69–87.

Brown, Wendy (2005), *Edgework: Critical Essays on Knowledge and Politics*. Princeton, NJ: Princeton University Press.

Çağaptay, Soner (2016), *Islam, Secularism, and Nationalism in Modern Turkey: Who is a Turk?* London: Routledge.

Çağaptay, Soner (2018), *Erdoğan's Empire: Turkey and the Politics of the Middle East*. London: I. B. Tauris.

Çaha, Ömer (2013), 'Gezi Park Demos: Democratic Protests or Revolt?' *Turkish Review* 3:5, 532–5.

Çam, Nusret (2012), 'Ulucami', *İslam Ansiklopedisi* 42. Ankara: Türkiye Diyanet Vakfı, 80–1.

Cambaz, Mustafa (2016), *Türküye Ulucamileri Fotoğraf Serisi*. Istanbul: Atatürk Kültür Merkezi Başkanlığı.

Çapa, Ezgi, 'Topbaş, 15 Temmuz Şehitler Abidesi'ni inceledi', *Demiören Haber Ajansı*, 12 July 2017.

Çarkoğlu, Ali (2003), 'Who Wants Full Membership? Characteristics of Turkish Public Support for EU Membership', in Ali Çarkoğlu and Barry Rubin (eds), *Turkey and the European Union: Domestic Politics, Economic Integration and International Dynamics*. London: Frank Cass, 161–83.

Çarkoğlu, Ali and Gözde Yavuz (2010), 'Press–Party Parallelism in Turkey: An Individual Level Interpretation', *Turkish Studies* 11:4, 613–24.

Çelebi, Süleyman (2017), *Vesilatü'n Necat*. Ankara: Diyanet İşleri Başkanlığı Yayınları.

Celik Rappas, Ipek A. and Sezen Kayhan (2018), 'TV Series Production and the Urban Restructuring of Istanbul', *Television & New Media* 19:1, 3–23.

Ceylan, Hasan Hüseyin (1993), *Ayasofya İhaneti*. Ankara: Rehber Yayıncılık.

Ceylan, Hasan Hüseyin (2020), *Ayasofya İhaneti*. Istanbul: Dünya Bizim.

Chelebi, Süleyman (1943), *The Mevlidi Sherif*, trans. F. Lyman MacCallum. London: John Murray.

Çinar, Alev (2001), 'National History as a Contested Site: The Conquest of Istanbul and Islamist Negotiations of the Nation', *Comparative Studies in Society and History* 43:2, 364–91.

Clark, Janine (2004), *Islam, Charity and Activism: Middle Class Networks and Social Welfare in Egypt, Jordan and Yemen*. Bloomington: Indiana University Press.

Çolak, Yilmaz (2006), 'Ottomanism vs. Kemalism: Collective Memory and Cultural Pluralism in 1990s Turkey', *Middle Eastern Studies* 42:4, 587–602.

Cormack, Robin (2000), 'The Mother of God in the Mosaics of Hagia Sophia at Constantinople', in Maria Vassilaki (ed.), *Mother of God: Representations of the Virgin in Byzantine Art*. Milan: Skira.

'Cumhurbaşkanı Erdoğan, 15 Temmuz Şehitler Anıtı'nı açtı' (2017), *Vatan*, 16 July, available at: https://www.gazetevatan.com/gundem/cumhurbaskani-Erdoğan-15-temmuz-sehitler-anitini-acti-1085065, last accessed 16 May 2022.

'Cumhurbaşkanımız Danıştay'ın Ayasofya Kararının Ardından Saat 20.53'te Millete Sesleniş Konuşması Yaptı' (2020), *Türkiye Bülteni* 18:144, 50–3.

'Cumhurbaşkanlığı Himayesinde 15 Temmuz'un Birinci Yılına Özel Anma Programı' (2017), Office of the Presidency of the Republic of Turkey, 10 July, available at: https://www.tccb.gov.tr/haberler/410/78862/cumhurbaskanligi-himayesinde-15-temmuzun-birinci-yilina-ozel-anma-programi.html, last accessed 15 May 2022.

Ćurčić, Slobodan (1992), 'Design and Structural Innovation in Byzantine Architecture before Hagia Sophia', in Robert Moore Ahmet Ş. Çakmak (eds), *Hagia Sophia from the Age of Justinian to the Present*. Cambridge: Cambridge University Press.

Daley, Brian, SJ (2006), *Gregory of Nazianzus*. New York: Routledge.

David, Isabel and Kumru F. Toktamış (eds) (2015), *'Everywhere Taksim': Sowing the Seeds for a New Turkey at Gezi*. Amersterdam: Amsterdam University Press.

David, Isabel and Kumru F. Toktamış (2015), 'Introduction: Gezi in Retrospect', in Isabel David and Kumru F. Toktamış (eds), *'Everywhere Taksim': Sowing the Seeds for a New Turkey at Gezi*. Amsterdam: Amsterdam University Press, 15–24.

Degirmenci, Koray (2010), 'Homegrown Sounds of Istanbul: World Music, Place, and Authenticity', *Turkish Studies* 11:2, 251–68.

Demir, Adem et al. (2017), 'İstanbul'da 'demokrasi nöbetleri' başladı', *Anadolu Ajansı*, 16 July, available at: https://www.aa.com.tr/tr/15-temmuz-darbe-girisimi/istanbulda-demokrasi-nobetleri-basladi/862478, last accessed 16 May 2022.

Demir, Hülya and Ahmet Yilmaz (2012), 'Measurement of Urban Transformation Project Success Using the Analytic Hierarchy Process: Sulukule and Tepeüstü-Ayazma Case Studies, Istanbul', *Journal of Urban Planning and Development* 138:2, 173–82.

Demirci, Mehmet (1998), 'Himmet', *İslam Ansiklopedisi*. Ankara: Türkiye Diyanet Vakfı, 56–7.

Deringil, Selim (1999), *The Well-Protected Domains: Ideology and the Legitimation of Power in the Ottoman Empire, 1876–1909*, London: I. B. Tauris.

'Dindar nesil yetiştireceğiz' (2016), *Yeni Şafak*, 28 February, available at: https://www.yenisafak.com/gundem/dindar-nesil-yetistirecegiz-2424175, last accessed 15 June 2022.

'Diyanet İşleri Başkanı Erbaş, yeniden ibadete açılan Ayasofya-i Kebir Cami-i Şerifi'nde ilk hutbeyi irad etti', *T.C. Cumhurbaşkanlığı Diyanet İşleri Başkanlığı*, available at: https://www.diyanet.gov.tr/tr-TR/Kurumsal/Detay/29715/diyanet-isleri-baskani-erbas-yeniden-ibadete-acilan-ayasofya-i-kebir-cami-i-serifinde-ilk-hutbeyi-irad-etti, last accessed 1 March 2020.

Dönmez, Rasim Özgür (2015), 'Nationalism in Turkey under Justice and Development Party Rule: The Logic of Masculinist Protection', *Turkish Studies* 16:4, 554–71.

Dorroll, Courtney (2015), 'The Spatial Politics of Turkey's Justice and Development Party (AK Party): On Erdoğanian neo-Ottomanism', PhD dissertation, University of Arizona Library, available at: https://repository.arizona.edu/handle/10150/556854, last accessed 8 June 2022.

Dorroll, Courtney (2016), 'Hamamönü: Reconfiguring an Ankara Neighborhood', *Journal of Ethnography and Folklore* 1/2, 55–86.

Dorroll, Courtney (Forthcoming), 'Between Memory and Forgetting and Purity and Danger: The Case of the Ulucanlar Prison Museum', in Catharina Raudvere and Petek Onur (eds), *Neo-Ottoman Imaginaries in Contemporary Turkey: Gendered Discourses, Agencies, and Visions*. London: Palgrave Macmillan.

Dorroll, Philip (2016), 'Post-Gezi Islamic Theology: Intersectional Islamic Feminism in Turkey', *Review of Middle East Studies* 50:2, 157–71.

Dorroll, Philip (2021), *Islamic Theology in the Turkish Republic*. Edinburgh: Edinburgh University Press.

Duben, Alan (2011), 'İstanbul: Music, Cultural Authenticity, and Civility', *New Perspectives on Turke*, 45:3, 237–45.

Duru, Asli (2019), '"A Walk Down the Shore": A Visual Geography of Ordinary Violence in Istanbul', *Environment and Planning* 37:6, 1064–80.

Duru, Deniz Neriman (2015), 'From Mosaic to Ebru: Conviviality in Multi-Ethnic, Multi-Faith Burgazadası, Istanbul', *South European Society & Politics* 20:2, 243–63.

'ECHR Ruling on Jailed Philanthropist Kavala No Longer Applies, says Erdoğan' (2022), *Ahval*, 28 April, available at: https://ahvalnews.com/erdogan-kavala/echr-ruling-jailed-philanthropist-kavala-no-longer-applies-says-erdogan, last accessed 15 June 2022.

Eckardt, Frank and Kathrin Wildner (2015), *Public Istanbul: Spaces and Spheres of the Urban*. Bielefeld: transcript Verlag.

ECoC Application (Istanbul) (2006), 'Candidate for 2010 European Capital of Culture: Istanbul: A City of the Four Elements', 1–173.

'Ecumenical Patriarch Bartholomew: The Conversion of Hagia Sophia into a Mosque Will Sow Discord between Christians and Muslims' (2020), *Agenzia Fidez*, 1 July, available at: http://www.fides.org/en/news/68248-ASIA_TURKEY_Ecumenical_Patriarch_Bartholomew_the_conversion_of_Hagia_Sophia_into_a_mosque_will_sow_discord_between_Christians_and_Muslims, last accessed 3 March 2020.

Eligür, Banu (2010), *The Mobilization of Political Islam in Turkey*. Cambridge: Cambridge University Press.

Emeksiz, İpek (2010), 'Istanbul's UNESCO Spot Still under Risk', *Hurriyet Daily News*,18 July.

'Environment Minister Bayraktar Announces Resignation, Calls on PM Erdoğan to Quit' (2013), *Hürriyet Daily News*, 25 December, available at: https://www.hurriyetdailynews.com/environment-minister-bayraktar-announces-resignation-calls-on-pm-erdogan-to-quit-60118, last accessed 15 July 2022.

Ercan, Müge Akkar (2010), 'Searching for a Balance Between Community Needs and Conservation Policies in Historic Neighbourhoods of Istanbul', *European Planning Studies* 18:5, 833–59.

Erdemli, Özgül (2003), 'Chronology: Turkey's Relations with the EU', in Ali Çarkoğlu and Barry Rubin (eds), *Turkey and the European Union: Domestic Politics, Economic Integration and International Dynamics*. London: Frank Cass, 4–7.

Erdi-Lelandais, Gülçin (ed.) (2014), *Understanding the City: Henri Lefebvre and Urban Studies*. Newcastle: Cambridge Scholars.

Erensü, Sinan and Ozan Karaman (2017), 'The Work of a Few Trees: Gezi, Politics, and Space', *International Journal of Urban and Regional Research* 41:1, 19–36.

Ergin, Murat and Yağmur Karakaya (2017), 'Between neo-Ottomanism and Otto-mania: Navigating State-Led and Popular Cultural Representations of the Past', *New Perspectives on Turkey* 56, 33–59.

Ernst & Young (2011), *Istanbul 2010 European Capital of Culture Impact Assessment Report*.

Erol, Sibel (2011), 'The Chronotope of Istanbul in Orhan Pamuk's Memoir Istanbul', *International Journal of Middle East Studies* 43:4, 655–76.

'Ertuğrul Günay: Bütün yüksek yapılar Başbakan'ın onayıyla inşa edildi', *T24*, 31 December, available at: https://t24.com.tr/haber/ertugrul-gunay-butun-yuksek-yapilar-basbakanin-onayiyla-insa-edildi,247286, last accessed 15 July 2022.

Erzen, Jale Necdet (2011), 'Reading Mosques: Meaning and Architecture in Isla', *Journal of Aesthetics and Art Criticism* 69:1, 125–31.

Ete, Hatem (2013), 'The Political Reverberations of the Gezi Protests', *Insight Turkey* 15:3, 15–25.

Ethnographic Interviews Conducted at Boğaziçi University, Istanbul, regarding Gezi Park, 8 July–2 August 2013.

'EU Restarts Talks with Turkey after Three Years' (2013), *BBC News*, 5 November, available at: http://www.bbc.com/news/world-europe-24825002, last accessed 7 June 2022)

European Commission, 'European Capitals of Culture', available at: https://culture.ec.europa.eu/policies/culture-in-cities-and-regions/european-capitals-of-culture, last accessed 24 June 2022.

'Exploring the Impact for Istanbul of being a European Capital of Culture' (2011), *Performance: Think Tank for Business Performance & Innovation* 4.4.

Findley, Carter Vaughn (2010), *Turkey, Islam, Nationalism, and Modernity: A History, 1789–2007*. New Haven, CT: Yale University Press.

Fisher-Onar, Nora (2009), 'Echoes of a Universalism Lost: Rival Representations of the Ottomans in Today's Turkey', *Middle Eastern Studies* 45:2, 229–41.

Fisher-Onar, Nora (2018), 'Between neo-Ottomanism and Neoliberalism: The Politics of Imagining Istanbul', in Nora Fisher-Onar, Susan C. Pearce and E. Fuat Keyman (eds), *Istanbul: Living with Difference in a Global City*. New Brunswick, NJ: Rutgers University Press, 1–22.

Fisher-Onar, Nora, Susan C. Pearce and E. Fuat Keyman (eds) (2018), *Istanbul: Living with Difference in a Global City*. New Brunswick, NJ: Rutgers University Press.

Florovsky, Georges (1940), 'The Hagia Sophia Churches', Résumés des Rapports et Communications, Sixième Congrès International d'Études Byzantines, Paris,

255–60; reprinted in *The Collected Works of Georges Florovsky, vol. 4: Aspects of Church History*. Belmont: Nordland, 1975.

Foggo, Hacer (2007), 'The Sulukule Affair: Roma Against Expropriation', *Roma Rights Quarterly* 4, 41–7.

Foucault, Michel (2006), 'Governmentality', in Aradhana Sharma and Akhil Gupta (eds), *Anthropology of the State: A Reader*. Oxford: Blackwell, 131–43.

Franke, Patrick (2015), 'Khidr in Istanbul: Observations on the Symbolic Constructions of Sacred Space in Traditional Islam', in George Stauth (ed.), *Yearbook of the Sociology of Islam 5: On Archaeology of Sainthood and Local Spirituality in Islam: Past and Present Crossroads of Events and Ideas*. Bielefeld: transcript Verlag.

Fraser, Nancy (1990), 'Rethinking the Public Sphere: A Contribution to the Critique of Actually Existing Democracy', *Social Text* 25/26, 56–80.

Fraser, Nancy (1992), 'Rethinking the Public Sphere: A Contribution to the Critique of Actually Existing Democracy', in C. Calhoun (ed.), *Habermas and the Public Sphere*. Cambridge: Polity Press, 109–42.

Fraser, Nancy (2000), 'Rethinking Recognition', *New Left Review* 3, 107–20.

Gellner, Ernest (1983), *Nations and Nationalism*. Cornell, NY: Cornell University Press.

Gençoğlu-Onbaşı, Funda (2012), 'The Romani Opening in Turkey: Antidiscrimination?' *Turkish Studies* 13:4, 599.

Genis, Serife (2007), 'Producing Elite Localities: The Rise of Gated Communities in Istanbul', *Urban Studies* 44:4, 771–98.

Gentile, Emilio ([2001] 2006), *Politics as Religion*, trans. George Staunton. Princeton, NJ: Princeton University Press.

Gerber, Haim (2002), 'The Public Sphere and Civil Society in the Ottoman Empire', in Miriam Hoexter, Shmuel N. Eisenstadt and Nehemia Levtzion (eds), *The Public Sphere in Muslim Societies*. Albany: State University of New York Press, 65–82.

al-Ghazālī, Abu Ḥāmid (1971), *Al-Maqṣad al-Asnā fī Sharḥ Ma'ānī Asmā' Allah al-Ḥusnā*, ed. Fadlou A. Shehadi. Beirut: Dar el-Machreq.

al-Ghazālī, Abu Ḥāmid (1992), *The Ninety-Nine Beautiful Names of God*, trans. David B. Burrell and Nazih Daher. Cambridge: Islamic Texts Society.

Ghulyan, Husik (2019), 'The Spatialization of Islamist, Populist, and Neo-Ottoman Discourses in the Turkish Capital Under AKP Rule', *New Perspectives on Turkey* 61, 125–53.

Goknar, Erdag (2006), 'Orhan Pamuk and the "Ottoman" Theme', *World Literature Today* 80:6, 34–8.

Göktürk, Deniz, Levent Soysal and İpek Türeli (2010), 'Introduction: Orienting Istanbul: Cultural Capital of Europe?' in Deniz Göktürk, Levent Soysal and İpek Türeli (eds), *Orienting Istanbul: Cultural Capital of Europe?* New York: Routledge, 1–24.

Göle, Nilüfer (2013), '"Gezi": Anatomy of a Public Square Movement', *Insight Turkey* 15:3, 7–14.

Görmez, Mehmet (2017), 'Takdim', *15 Temmuz Gazilerin Dilinden*. Istanbul: DİB Yayınları.

Greek Orthodox Archdiocese of America (2004), 'Relics of Holy Church Fathers Restored to their Original Resting Place: A Positive Step Towards Reconciliation and Unity Between the Orthodox and Roman-Catholic Churches', Greek Orthodox Archdiocese of America News Service, 27 November, available at: https://www.goarch.org/whats-new/-/asset_publisher/rlvS19snJYAk/content/relics-of-holy-church-fathers-restored-to-their-original-resting-place-a-postive-step-towards-reconciliation-and-unity-between-the-orthodox-and-roman-/pop_up?_101_INSTANCE_rlvS19snJYAk_viewMode=print&_101_INSTANCE_rlvS19snJYAk_languageId=en_US, last accessed 15 February 2022

Greek Orthodox Archdiocese of America (2020), 'Biography of His All Holiness Patriarch Bartholomew', available at: https://www.goarch.org/-/biography-ecumenical-patriarch, last accessed 3 March 2020.

Greek Orthodox Archdiocese of America (2020), 'Biography of His Eminence Archbishop Elpidophoros of America', available at: https://www.goarch.org/archbishop/biography, last accessed 3 March 2020.

Gulyan, Husik (2019), 'The Spatialization of Islamist, Populist, and neo-Ottoman Discourses in the Turkish Capital under AKP Rule', *New Perspectives on Turkey* 61, 125–53.

Gunay, Zeynep (2010), 'Conservation versus Regeneration?: Case of European Capital of Culture 2010 Istanbul', *European Planning Studies* 18:8, 1173–86.

Gürsel, Kadri (2013), 'Crackdown Shatters AKP "Anti-corruption" Taboo', *Al-Monitor*, 19 December, available at: https://www.al-monitor.com/originals/2013/12/corruption-crackdown-damages-akp.html, last accessed 14 July 2022.

'Gün, Milletçe Kenetlenme ve Geleceğimizi İnşa Etme Günüdür' (2016), Diyanet İşleri Başkanlığı, 22 July.

Gül, Murat (2009), *The Emergence of Modern Istanbul: Transformation and Modernisation of a City*. London: I. B. Tauris.

Gürsoy, Yaprak (2017), *Between Military Rule and Democracy: Regime Consolidation in Greece, Turkey, and Beyond*. Ann Arbor: University of Michigan Press.

Habermas, Jürgen (1962), *The Structural Transformation of the Public Sphere: An Inquiry into a Category of Bourgeois Society*, trans. T. Burger and F. Lawrence. Cambridge: Polity Press, 1989.

'"Hafıza 15 Temmuz" Müzesi Açıldı', Official Website of the Istanbul Governorate, available at: http://www.istanbul.gov.tr/hafiza-15-temmuz-muzesi-aciliyor#, last accessed 3 May2022.

Hale, William (2003), 'Human Rights, the European Union and the Turkish Accession Process', in Ali Çarkoğlu and Barry Rubin (eds), *Turkey and the European Union: Domestic Politics, Economic Integration and International Dynamics*. London: Frank Cass, 101–19.

Hall, Stuart (1992), 'The West and the Rest: Discourse and Power', in Stuart Hall and Bram Gieben (eds), *Formations of Modernity*. Cambridge: Polity Press, 276–320.

Halman, Talat S. (2011), *A Millennium of Turkish Literature: A Concise History*, ed. Jayne L. Warner. Syracuse, NY: Syracuse University Press.

Hammond, Timur (2019), 'The Politics of Perspective: Subjects, Exhibits, and Spectacle in Taksim Square, Istanbul', *Urban Geography* 40:7, 1039–54.

Hammond, Timur (2020), 'Making Memorial Publics: Media, Monuments, and the Politics of Commemoration Following Turkey's July 16 Coup Attempt', *Geographical Review* 110:4, 536.

Hammond, Timur (2020), 'Papering, Arranging, and Depositing: Learning from Working with an Istanbul Archive', *Area (London 1969)* 52:1, 204–12.

Hammond, Timur and Elizabeth Angell (2013), 'Is Everywhere Taksim?: Public Space and Possible Publics', Special Issue *JADMAG 'Resistance Everywhere': The Gezi Park Protests and Dissident Visions of Turkey*, eds, Anthony Alessandrini, Nazan Üstündağ and Emrah Yıldız 1:4, 68–72.

Hart, Kimberly (2007), 'Weaving Modernity, Commercializing Carpets: Collective Memory and Contested Tradition in Örselli Village', in Esra Özyürek (ed.), *The Politics of Public Memory in Turkey*. Syracuse, NY: Syracuse University Press, 16–39.

Hart, Kimberly (2019), 'Istanbul's Intangible Cultural Heritage as Embodied by Street Animals', *History and Anthropology* 30:4, 448–59.

Harvey, David (1996), *Justice, Nature, and the Geography of Difference*. Oxford: Blackwell.

Harvey, David (2008), 'The Right to the City', *New Left Review* 53, 23–40, available at: https://newleftreview.org/issues/ii53/articles/david-harvey-the-right-to-the-city, last accessed 8 June 2022.

'HDP'li vekil Ayasofya'nın kilise olmasını istedi' (2020), *En Son Haber*, 8 July, available at: https://www.ensonhaber.com/ic-haber/hdpli-vekil-ayasofyanin-kilise-olmasini-istedi, last accessed 26 February 2022.

Hechter, Michael (2000), *Containing Nationalism*. Oxford: Oxford University Press.

Hefner, Robert (2011), 'Shari'a Politics: Law and Society in the Modern Muslim World', in Robert Hefner (ed.), *Shari'a Politics: Islamic Law and Society in the Modern World*. Bloomington: Indiania University Press, 1–54.

Hein, Carolina (2010), 'The European Capital of Culture Programme and Istanbul 2010', in Deniz Göktürk, Levent Soysal and İpek Türeli (eds), *Orienting Istanbul: Cultural Capital of Europe?* New York: Routledge, 253–67.

Heraclides, Alexis (2012), '"What Will Become of Us Without Barbarians?" The Enduring Greek–Turkish Rivalry as an Identity-Based Conflict', *Journal of Southeast European and Black Sea Studies* 12:1, 115–34.

Hintz, Lisel (2018), *Identity Politics Inside Out: National Identity Contestation and Foreign Policy in Turkey*. Oxford: Oxford University Press.

'Holy Eparchial Synod Designates July 24 as a Day of Mourning' (2020), *Orthodox Observer*, 19 July, available at: https://www.goarch.org/-/july-24-day-of-mourning, last accessed 3 March 2020.

'Homily for the National Day of Mourning over Ἁγία Σοφία' (2020), *Orthodox Observer*, 24 July, available at: https://www.goarch.org/news/archbishop/ homilies/-/asset_publisher/JjmOoSCoGGMm/content/day-of-mourning- homily?_101_INSTANCE_JjmOoSCoGGMm_languageId=en_US, last accessed 3 March 2020.

Hopko, Thomas (2004), 'Vladimir I', in Lindsay Jones (ed.), *Encyclopedia of Religion*, 2nd edn. New York: Macmillan Reference.

Hopko, Thomas (2016), *The Orthodox Faith, vol. 3: Church History*, rev. and expanded David C. Ford. Yonkers, NY: St. Vladimir's Seminary Press.

Horrocks, David and Eva Kolinsky (eds) (1996), *Turkish Culture in German Society Today*. Oxford: Bergahn.

Houston, Christopher (2020), *Istanbul, City of the Fearless: Urban Activism, Coup d'État, and Memory in Turkey*. Oakland: University of California Press.

Hoyng, Rolien (2014), 'Place Brands, Nonbrands, Tags and Queries: The Networks of Urban Activism in the Creative City Istanbul', *Cultural Studies* 28:3, 494–517.

Hudson, Leila (2006), 'Late Ottoman Damascus: Investments in Public Space and the Emergence of Popular Sovereignty', *Critique: Critical Middle Eastern Studies* 15:2, 151–69.

Hudson, Leila (2008), *Transforming Damascus: Space and Modernity in an Islamic City*. New York: I. B. Tauris.

Hughes, Edel (2011), *Turkey's Accession to the European Union: The Politics of Exclusion?* New York: Routledge.

Huntington, Samuel P. (1993), 'The Clash of Civilizations?' *Foreign Affairs* 73:3, 22–49.

'İbb Başkanı Topbaş, '15 Temmuz Şehitler Abidesi'nde İncelemelerde Bulundu' (2017), *Haberler.com*, 12 July, available at https://www.haberler.com/guncel/ibb-baskani-topbas-15-temmuz-sehitler-abidesi-nde-9824004-haberi, last accessed 2 May 2022.

Iğsız, Aslı (2013), 'Brand Turkey and the Gezi Protests: Authoritarianism, Law, and Neoliberalism (Part One)', *Jadaliyya*, 12 July, available at: https://www.jadaliyya.com/Details/29078, last accessed 8 July 2022.

Iğsız, Aslı (2014), 'From Alliance of Civilizations to Branding the Nation: Turkish Studies, Image Wars and Politics of Comparison in an Age of Neoliberalism', *Turkish Studies* 15:4, 689–704.

Iğsız, Aslı (2015), 'Palimpsests of Multiculturalism and Museumization of Culture: Greco-Turkish Population Exchange Museum as an Istanbul 2010 European Capital of Culture Project', *Comparative Studies of South Asia, Africa, and the Middle East* 35:2, 324–45.

Iğsız, Aslı (2018), *Humanism in Ruins: Entangled Legacies of the Greek–Turkish Population Exchange*. Stanford, CA: Stanford University Press.

Ilayda Altas, Meryem (2021), 'Atatürk Cultural Center, Part of Istanbul's Essence, Reopens', *Daily Sabah*, 21 October, available at: https://www.dailysabah.com/arts/ataturk-cultural-center-part-of-istanbuls-essence-reopens/news, last accessed 26 July 2022.

Imber, Colin (1987), 'The Ottoman Dynastic Myth', *Turcica* 19, 7–27; reprinted in Colin Imber (1996), *Studies in Ottoman History and Law*. Istanbul: Isis Press, 305–22.

'Istanbul International Puppet Festival', *Istanbulview*, available at: https://www.istanbulview.com/istanbul-international-puppet-festival, last accessed 15 July 2022.

'İstanbul Patriği Bartholomeos'un Konferansı Açış Konuşması' (2012), *İstanbul Rumları: Bugün ve Yarın*. Istanbul: İstos Yayınları, 13–16.

'Istanbul's Taksim Mosque Opens after Decades of Legal Wrangling' (2021), *Daily Sabah*, 28 May, available at: https://www.dailysabah.com/turkey/istanbul/istanbuls-taksim-mosque-opens-after-decades-of-legal-wrangling, last accessed 15 June 2022.

Jones, Paul (2011), *The Sociology of Architecture*. Liverpool: Liverpool University Press.

Kadıoğlu Polat, Defne (2021), 'No One Is Larger than the State: Consent, Dissent, and Vigilant Violence during Turkey's Neoliberal Urban Transition', *Journal of Southeast European and Black Sea Studies* 21:2, 189–211.

Karaca, Banu, 'Europeanisation from the Margins? Istanbul's Cultural Capital Initiative and the Formation of European Cultural Policies', in Kiran Klaus Patel (ed.), *The Cultural Politics of Europe: European Capitals of Culture and European Union since the 1980s*. London: Taylor & Francis, 157–76.

Karaçam, Ferman (2009), 'Osman Yüksel Serdengeçti', *İslam Ansiklopedisi*. Ankara: Türkiye Diyanet Vakfı, 555–6.

Karakaya, Yagmur (2020), 'The Political Staging of Nostalgia: Neo-Ottomanism in Contemporary Turkey', *Nostalgia Now* London: Routledge, 131–46.

Karakoç, Sezai (1968), 'Ayasofya, ne kadar sabırlısın!', *İslam Medeniyeti*, 15 May.

Karal, Enver Ziya (1994), 'The Principles of Kemalism', in Ali Kazangıcil and Ergun Özbudun (eds), *Atatürk: The Founder of a Modern State*. London: Hurst, 11–36.

Karasipahi, Sena (2009), *Muslims in Modern Turkey: Islamism, Modernism and the Revolt of the Islamic Intellectuals*. New York: I. B. Tauris.

Kaymak, Özgür (2017), *İstanbul'da Az(ınlık) Olmak: Gündelik Hayatta Rumlar, Yahudiler, Ermeniler*. Istanbul: Libra Yayıncılık.

Kendi Dilinden FETÖ: Örgütlü Bir Din İstismarı (2017). Ankara: Diyanet İşleri Başkanlığı Yayınları.

Kenworthy, Scott (2011), 'Vladimir of Kiev, Prince', in George Thomas Kurian (ed.), *Encyclopaedia of Christian Civilization*. Oxford: Wiley-Blackwell, 2468–9.

Keyder, Çağlar (2008), 'A Brief History of Modern Istanbul', in Reşat Kasaba (ed.), *The Cambridge History of Turkey*, vol. 4. Cambridge: Cambridge University Press, 2008, 504–23.

Kezer, Zeynep (2015), *Building Modern Turkey: State, Space, and Ideology in the Early Republic*, Pittsburgh, PA: University of Pittsburgh Press.

Khan, Mujeeb (2018), 'The July 15th Coup: A Critical Institutional Framework for Analysis', in M. Hakan Yavuz and Bayram Balcı (eds), *Turkey's July 15 Coup: What Happened and Why*. Salt Lake City: University of Utah Press, 46–77.

Khayyat, E. (2019), *Istanbul 1940 and Global Modernity: The World According to Auerbach, Tanpınar, and Edib*. Lanham, MD: Lexington Books.

Kiprovska, Mariya (2008), 'The Mihaloğlu Family: Gazi Warriors and Patrons of Dervish Hospices', *Osmanlı Araştırmaları* 32, 194–222.

Kısakürek, Necip Fazıl (1968), 'Ayasofya', *İslam Medeniyeti*, 15 May.

Kitromilides, Paschalis (2014), 'The Ecumenical Patriarchate', in Lucian Leustean (ed.), *Orthodox Christianity and Nationalism in Nineteenth-Century Southeastern Europe*. New York: Fordham University Press, 14–33.

Klapetek, Martin (2019), 'Şehitlik Mosque and the Islamic Cemetery at Columbiadamm: Islam in Public Space', *Studia Religiologica* 52:1, 63–77.

Klaus Patel, Kiran (ed.) (2013), *The Cultural Politics of Europe: European Capitals of Culture and European Union since the 1980s*. London: Taylor & Francis.

Köprülü, Orhan F. and Mustafa İsmet Uzun (1989), 'Akşemseddin', *İslam Ansiklopedisi*. Ankara: Türkiye Diyanet Vakfı, 299–302.

Koca, Ferhat (2005), 'Molla Hüsrev', *İslam Ansiklopedisi*. Ankara: Türkiye Diyanet Vakfı, 252–4.

Kocamaner, Hikmet (2017), 'Strengthening the Family through Television: Islamic Broadcasting, Secularism, and the Politics of Responsibility in Turkey', *Anthropological Quarterly* 90:3, 675–714.

Koramaz, Turgay and Elif Kisar-Koramaz (2011), 'ECOC Istanbul: "A Commodity" for Consumers or "a Source" for All Citizens', *European Network on Housing Research*.

Kuyucu, Ali Tuna (2005), 'Ethno-religious "Unmixing" of "Turkey": 6–7 September Riots as a Case in Turkish Nationalism', *Nations and Nationalism* 11:3, 361–80.

Kuyucu, Tuna and Özlem Ünsal (2010), '"Urban Transformation" as State-led Property Transfer: An Analysis of Two Cases of Urban Renewal in Istanbul', *Urban Studies* 47:7, 1479–99.

Ladouceur, Paul (2019), *Modern Orthodox Theology: Behold, I Make All Things New*. London: T & T Clark.

Langan, Mark (2017), 'Virtuous Power Turkey in Sub-Saharan Africa: The "neo-Ottoman" Challenge to the European Union', *Third World Quarterly* 38:6, 1399–414.

Lefebvre, Henri (2016), *The Production of Space,* trans. Donald Nicholson-Smith, Malden, MA: Blackwell.

Lewis, Bernard (1958), 'Some Reflections on the Decline of the Ottoman Empire', *Studia Islamica* 9, 111–27.

Lewis, Geoffrey ([1999] 2002), *The Turkish Language Reform: A Catastrophic Success*. Oxford: Oxford University Press.

Lindstrom, Lamont (1982), 'Leftamap Kastom: The Political History of Tradition on Tanna, Vanuatu', in Roger M. Keesing and Robert Tonkinson (eds), *Reinventing Traditional Culture: The Politics of Kastom in Island Melanesia*, Special Issue *Mankind* 13, 316–29.

MacDonald, William C. (1992), 'Roman Experimental Design and the Great Church', in Robert Moore and Ahmet Ş. Çakmak (eds), *Hagia Sophia from the Age of Justinian to the Present*. Cambridge: Cambridge University Press.

Malkki, Liisa (1992), 'National Geographic: The Rooting of Peoples and the Territorialization of National Identity among Scholars and Refugees', *Cultural Anthropology* 7:1, 22–44.

Mango, Cyril (1986), *The Art of the Byzantine Empire, 312–1453: Sources and Documents*. Toronto: University of Toronto Press.

Mango, Cyril (1992), 'Byzantine Writers on the Fabric of Hagia Sophia', in Robert Moore and Ahmet Ş. Çakmak (eds), *Hagia Sophia from the Age of Justinian to the Present*. Cambridge: Cambridge University Press.

Mardin, Şerif (1994), 'The Nakşibendi Order in Turkish History', in Richard Tapper (ed.), *Islam in Modern Turkey: Religion, Politics and Literature in a Secular State*. New York: I. B. Tauris.

Markoc, Ilkim (2021), 'Poverty and Difficulties in Participation of Urban Social Life: Young Women in Istanbul', *Journal of International Women's Studies* 22:9, 49–67.

'Map: Synagogues Destroyed during Kristallnacht', *United States Holocaust Memorial Museum*, available at: https://www.ushmm.org/information/exhibitions/online-exhibitions/special-focus/kristallnacht/synagogues/how-was-kristallnacht-carried-out/map-synagogues-destroyed-during-kristallnacht, last accessed 6 July 2022.

McGuckin, John Anthony (2020), *The Eastern Orthodox Church: A New History*, New Haven, CT: Yale University Press.

McGuigan, Jim (2005), 'The Cultural Public Sphere', *European Journal of Cultural Studies* 8:4, 427–43.

Melis Uluğ, Özden and Yasemin Gülsüm Acar (2019), '"Names Will Never Hurt Us": A Qualitative Exploration of Çapulcu Identity through the Eyes of Gezi Park Protestors', *British Journal of Social Psychology* 58, 714–29.

Meyendorff, John (1979), *Byzantine Theology: Historical Trends and Doctrinal Themes*. New York: Fordham University Press.

'Milletçe Yeniden Doğuş: 15 Temmuz' (2018), Diyanet İşleri Başkanlığı, 13 July.

Mills, Amy (2010), *Streets of Memory: Landscape, Tolerance, and National Identity in Istanbul*. Athens, GA: University of Georgia Press.

Mills, Amy (2017), 'The Cultural Politics of Ethnic Nationalism: Turkish Urbanism in Occupied Istanbul (1918–1923)', *Annals of the American Association of Geographers* 107:5, 1179–93.

Mills, Amy (2018), 'Becoming Blind to the Landscape: Turkification and the Precarious National Future in Occupied Istanbul', *Journal of the Ottomand an Turkish Studies Association* 5:2, 99–117.

Moth, Laura (2013), 'What Judith Butler did not Say in Istanbul', *Today's Zaman Blog*, 17 September.

Nas, Çiğdem (2012), 'Europeanisation of Identity: The Case of the Rebuffed Candidate', in Çiğdem Nas and Yonca Özer (eds), *Turkey and the European Union: Processes of Europeanisation*. New York: Routledge, 23–44.

Navaro-Yashin, Yael (2013), 'Editorial – Breaking Memory, Spoiling Memorization: The Taksim Protests in Istanbul', Hotspots, *Fieldsights*, 31 October, available at: https://culanth.org/fieldsights/editorial-breaking-memory-spoiling-memorization-the-taksim-protests-in-istanbul, last accessed 8 July 2022.

Navaro-Yashin, Yael (2020), *Faces of the State: Secularism and Public Life in Turkey*. Princeton, NJ: Princeton University Press.

Necipoğlu, Gülrü (1992), 'The Life of an Imperial Monument: Hagia Sophia after Byzantium', in Robert Moore and Ahmet Ş. Çakmak (eds), *Hagia Sophia from the Age of Justinian to the Present*. Cambridge: Cambridge University Press.

'NGO Members March against Government Bill to Sideline Chambers in Urban Planning' (2013), *Hürriyet Daily News*, 10 July, available at: https://www.hurriyetdailynews.com/ngo-members-march-against-government-bill-to-sideline-chambers-in-urban-planning-50472, last accessed 8 July 2022.

Ocak, Serkan (2010), 'Dokuz Sekizlik Roman Açılımı', *Radikal*, 15 March.

Okumus, Bendegul and Gurel Cetin (2018), 'Marketing Istanbul as a Culinary Destination', *Journal of Destination Marketing & Management* 9, 340–6.

'Osman Yüksel Serdengeçti "Ayasofya açılsın" dediği için idamla yargılanmıştı' (2020), *Yeni Akit*, 10 June, available at: https://www.yeniakit.com.tr/haber/osman-yuksel-serdengecti-ayasofya-acilsin-dedigi-icin-idamla-yargilanmisti-1286857.html, last accessed 22 January 2022.

Ozbudun, Ergun (1982), 'The Nature of the Kemalist Political Regime', in Ergun Ozbudun and Ali Kazancigil (eds), *Ataturk: Founder of a Modern State*. London: Archon Press, 79–192.

Ozden, Pelin Pınar (2008), 'An Opportunity Missed in Tourism-led Regeneration: Sulukule', *Sustainable Tourism III* 115, 141–52.

Öncü, Ayşe (2007), 'The Politics of Istanbul's Ottoman Heritage in the Era of Globalism: Refractions through the Prism of a Theme Park', in Barbar Drieskens, Franck Mermier and Heiko Wimmen (eds), *Cities of the South: Citizenship and Exclusion in the 21st Century*. London: Saqi Books, 233–64.

Öner, Oğuz (2010), 'Istanbul 2010 European Capital of Culture: Towards a Participatory Culture?', in Deniz Göktürk, Levent Soysal and İpek Türeli (eds), *Orienting Istanbul: Cultural Capital of Europe?* New York: Routledge, 267–79.

Order of St Andrew the Apostle: Archons of the Ecumenical Patriarchate in America (2020), 'His All-Holiness Offers Uplifting Message regarding Hagia Sophia',

28 August, available at: https://www.archons.org/-/hah-thanks-order-hagia-sophia-support, last accessed 3 March 2020.

Örs, İlay Romain (2006), 'Beyond the Greek and Turkish Dichotomy: The *Rum Polites* of Istanbul and Athens', *South European Society and Politics* 11:1, 79–94.

Örs, İlay Romain (2012), '"Şehrin" Diasporası: Atina'da Yaşayan İstanbullu Rumlar', *İstanbul Rumları: Bugün ve Yarın*. Istanbul: İstos Yayınları.

Örs, İlay Romain (2018), 'Cosmopolitanist Nostalgia: Geographies, Histories, and Memories of the Rum Polites', in Nora Fisher-Onar, Susan C. Pearce, and E. Fuat Keyman (eds), *Istanbul: Living with Difference in a Global City*. New Brunswick, NJ: Rutgers University Press, 81–96.

Örs, İlay Romain (2018), *Diaspora of the City: Stories of Cosmopolitanism from Istanbul and Athens*. New York: Palgrave Macmillan.

Özal, Turgut (1991), *Turkey in Europe and Europe in Turkey*. Northern Cyprus: K. Rustem.

Özbudun, Ergun (2020), 'AKP at the Crossroads: Erdoğan's Authoritarian Drift', in Susannah Verney, Anna Bosco and Senem Aydın-Düzgit (eds), *The AKP since Gezi Park: Moving to Regime Change in Turkey*. New York: Routledge, 14–26.

Özen, Hayriye (2015), 'An Unfinished Grassroots Populism: The Gezi Park Protests in Turkey and their Aftermath', *South European Society and Politics* 20:4, 533–52.

Özil, Ayşe (2015), 'Skyscrapers of the Past and their Shadows: A Social History of Urbanity in Late Ottoman Istanbul', *International Journal of Turkish Studies* 21:1/2, 75–94.

Özkan, Behlül (2012), *From the Abode of Islam to the Turkish Vatan: The Making of a National Homeland*. New Haven, CT: Yale University Press.

Öztürk, İlker Nuri (2017), 'Şehitler kitabesi kendini yazdırdı', *Yeni Şafak*, 23 July, available at: https://www.yenisafak.com/gundem/sehitler-kitabesi-kendini-yazdirdi-2761228, last accessed 3 May 2022.

Özyürek, Esra (2006), *Nostalgia for the Modern: State Secularism and Everyday Politics in Turkey*. Durham, NC: Duke University Press.

Özyürek, Esra (ed.) (2007), *Politics of Public Memory: Production and Consumption of the Past in Turkey*. Syracuse, NY: Syracuse University Press.

Pamuk, Orhan (2006), *Istanbul: Memories and the City*, trans. Maureen Freely. New York: Vintage.

Papadopoulos, A. G. and Aslı Duru (eds) (2017), *Landscapes of Music in Istanbul: a Cultural Politics of Place and Exclusion*. Bielefeld: Transcript.

Parla, Ayşe (2013), 'Protest and the Limits of the Body', Hotspots, *Fieldsights*, 31 October, available at: https://culanth.org/fieldsights/protest-and-the-limits-of-the-body, last accessed 8 July 2022.

Parmaksız, Pınar Melis Yelsalı (2020), 'The Transformation of Citizenship Before and After the 15 July Coup Attempt', in Nikos Christofis (ed.), *Erdoğan's New Turkey: Attempted Coup d'État and the Acceleration of Political Crisis*. New York: Routledge.

Peirce, Leslie (2010), 'Polyglottism in the Ottoman Empire: A Reconsideration', in Gabriel Piterberg, Teofilo F. Ruiz and Geoffrey Symcox (eds), *Braudel Revisited: The Mediterranean World, 1600–1800*. Toronto: University of Toronto Press, 76–98.

Pekolcay, A. Necla (2004), 'Mevlid', *İslam Ansiklopedisi*. Ankara: Türkiye Diyanet Vakfı, 485–6.

Pentcheva, Bissera V. (2016), 'Liturgy and Music at Hagia Sophia', *Oxford Research Encyclopaedia of Religion*, 5 April, available at: https://doi.org/10.1093/acrefore/9780199340378.013.99, last accessed 9 February 2022.

Pentcheva, Bissera V. (2017), *Hagia Sophia: Sound, Space, and Spirit in Byzantium*. University Park: Pennsylvania State University Press.

Pew Research Center (2017), 'Orthodox Christianity in the 21st Century', available at: https://www.pewresearch.org/religion/2017/11/08/orthodox-christianity-in-the-21st-century, last accessed 27 July 2022.

Polat, Necati (2016), *Regime Change in Contemporary Turkey: Politics, Rights, Mimesis*. Edinburgh: Edinburgh University Press.

Polo, Jean-Francois (2015), 'The Istanbul Modern Art Museum: An Urban Regeneration Project?', *European Planning Studies* 23:8, 1511–28

Posocco, Lorenzo (2018), 'Museum Politics in Turkey under the Islamic Justice and Development Party (AKP): The Case of the Istanbul Museum of the History of Science and Technology in Islam', *International Journal of Politics, Culture, and Society* 32:1, 83–103.

Quataert, Donald (2000), *The Ottoman Empire, 1700–1922*. Cambridge: Cambridge University Press.

Rampton, James, Nick McAteer, Neringa Mozuraityte, Márta Levai and Selen Akçalı (2011), 'Ex-Post Evaluation of 2010 European Capitals of Culture: Final Report for the European Commission DG Education and Culture', Ecorys UK Ltd, August, pp. 1–22, 66–100, available at: https://culture.ec.europa.eu/sites/default/files/files/capitals-culture-2010-report_en.pdf, last accessed 14 July 2022.

Rizvi, Kishwar (2015), *The Transnational Mosque: Architecture and Historical Memory in the Contemporary Middle East*. Chapel Hill: University of North Carolina Press.

Ruacan, Ipek Z. (2016), 'Bringing the Empire Back In: The Gradual Discovery of the Ottoman Empire in Turkish Foreign Policy', *Welt Des Islams* 56:3/4, 466–88.

Ruacan, Ipek Z. (2020), 'Fear, Superiority, Self-Identification and Rejection: Turks' Different Attitudes to Europe Since the Late Ottoman Era', *Journal of Balkan and Near Eastern Studies* 22:5, 684–700.

Rucker-Chang, Sunnie (2014), 'The Turkish Connection: Neo-Ottoman Influence in post-Dayton Bosnia', *Journal of Muslim Minority Affairs* 34:2, 152–64.

Saatçioglu, Beken (2012), 'Turkey–EU Relations from the 1960s to 2010: A Critical Overview', in Belgin Akçay and Bahri Yılmaz (eds), *Turkey's Accession to the European Union: Political and Economic Challenges*. Lanham, MD: Lexington Books, 10–11.

Sadriu, Behar (2019), 'Shrine Diplomacy: Turkey's Quest for a post-Kemalist Identity', *History and Anthropology* 30:4, 421–33.

Şahin, Filiz and Tahir Uluç (2006), 'Contemporary Turkish Thought', in Ibrahim M. Abu-Rabi (ed.), *The Blackwell Companion to Contemporary Islamic Thought*. Oxford: Blackwell, 23–36

Said, Edward (1978), *Orientalism*. New York: Random House, 1994.

Sakıp Sabancı Müzesi (2010), 'Behind the Exhibition, *From Byzantion to Istanbul: 8000 Years of a Capital: Legendary Istanbul*, available at: https://www.sakipsabancimuzesi.org/en/exhibitions-and-events/online/16643, last accessed 15 July 2022.

Sakıp Sabancı Müzesi (2010), 'Efsane İstanbul Konuşmaları; Dr. Brigitte Pitarakis & Dr. Nazan Ölçer', available at: https://www.youtube.com/watch?v=hhgVsEpArrk, last accessed 15 July 2022.

Sakıp Sabancı Müzesi (2022), 'Legendary Istanbul; Prof. Dr. Mehmet Özdoğan & Dr. Nazan Ölçer', available at: https://www.youtube.com/watch?v=hhgVsEpArrk, last accessed 15 July.

Sariyyanis, Marinos (2013), 'Ruler and State, State and Society in Ottoman Political Thought', *Turkish Historical Review* 4:1, 83–117.

Schoon, Danielle van Dobben (2014), '"Sulukule is the Gun and We are its Bullets": Urban Renewal and Romani Identity in Istanbul', *CITY: Analysis of Urban Trends, Culture, Theory, Policy, Action* 18:6, 720–31.

Schoon, Danielle V. and Funda Oral (2018), 'The Role of Communities of Practice in Urban Rights Activism in Istanbul, Turkey', in Carl A. Maida and Sam Beck (eds), *Global Sustainability and Communities of Practice*. New York: Berghahn, 94–108.

Secor, Anna (2005), 'Islamism, Democracy, and the Political Production of the Headscarf Issue in Turkey', in Ghazi-Walid Falah and Caroline Nagel (eds), *Geographies of Muslim Women: Gender, Religion and Space*, New York: Guilford Press, 203–25.

Selection Panel for the ECoC, 'Report of the Selection Meeting for the European Capitals of Culture 2010' (2006), 1–15, available at: https://culturenext.eu/wp-content/uploads/2021/11/ECOC-2010-Selection-Report.pdf, last accessed 5 April 2023.

Shaw, Stanford ([1976] 1997), *The History of the Ottoman Empire and Modern Turkey, vol. 1: Empire of the Gazis: The Rise and Decline of the Ottoman Empire, 1280–1808*. New York: Cambridge University Press.

Shaw, Stanford (1979), 'The Population of Istanbul in the Nineteenth Century', *International Journal of Middle East Studies* 10:2, 265–77.

Shaw, Wendy M. K. (2003), *Possessors and Possessed: Museums, Archaeology, and the Visualization of History in the Late Ottoman Empire*. Berkeley: University of California Press.

Shohat, Ella (2006), *Taboo Memories, Diasporic Voices*. Durham, NC: Duke University Press.

Silverstein, Brian (2011), *Islam and Modernity in Turkey*. New York: Palgrave Macmillan.

Simsek, Ayhan (2013), 'Turkey's Kurdish Opening', *Deutsche Welle*, 19 November.

Simsir, Zeynep and Bulent Dilmac (2021), 'Experiences of post-Traumatic Growth in Witnesses to the July 15 Coup Attempt in Turkey', *Illness, Crisis, and Loss* 29:3, 220–40.

Sofos, Spyros A. (2021), 'Space and the Emotional Topography of Populism in Turkey: The Case of Hagia Sophia', *Cogent Social Sciences* 7:1, 1–15.

Solomonovich, Nadav (2021), '"Democracy and National Unity Day" in Turkey: The Invention of a New National Holiday', *New Perspectives on Turkey* 64, 55–80.

'Son Ayasofya anketi sonuçları açıklandı' (2020), *Yeniçağ*, 11 July, available at: https://www.yenicaggazetesi.com.tr/son-ayasofya-anketi-sonuclari-aciklandi-akp-chp-iyi-parti-mhp-saadet-partisi-288960h.htm, last accessed 18 February 2022.

Soysal, Levent (2010), 'Future(s) of the City: Istanbul for the New Century', in Deniz Göktürk, Levent Soysal and İpek Türeli (eds), *Orienting Istanbul: Cultural Captial of Europe?* New York: Routledge, 296–313.

Sözeri, Ceren (2016), 'Kıbrıs Meselesinin Rehineleri: Basının Gözüyle 1964 Sürgünleri', in Hakan Yücel (ed.), *Rum Olmak, Rum Kalmak*. Istanbul: İstos Yayınları.

Study Qur'an, The (2015), ed. and trans. Seyyid Hossein Nasr, Caner K. Dagli, Maria Massi Dakake, Joseph E. B. Lumbard and Muhammad Rustom. New York: HarperOne.

Sturken, Marita (1997), *Tangled Memories: The Vietnam War, the AIDS Epidemic, and the Politics of Remembering*. Berkeley: University of California Press.

Sulukule UNESCO Report (2008), Sulukule Platform, Istanbul, available at: http://inuraistanbul2009.files.wordpress.com/2009/06/sulukule-unesco-report-xx.pdf, last accessed 8 June 2022.

Syson, Damon (2010), 'Istanbul Contrast Exhibition of Work by Dice Kayek', *Wallpaper**, 10 August, available at: https://www.wallpaper.com/fashion/istanbul-contrast-exhibition-of-work-by-dice-kayek, last accessed 15 July 2022.

Szacka, Léa-Catherine (2008), 'The Architectural Public Sphere', *Multi* 2:1, 19–34.

'Taksim Through Time' (2013), *Stambouline*, 30 May, available at: https://www.stambouline.info/2013/05/taksim-through-time.html?showComment=1369998152505, last accessed 11 July 2022.

Tanyeri-Erdemir, Tuğba (2006), 'Archaeology as a Source of National Pride in the Early Years of the Turkish Republic', *Journal of Field Archaeology* 31:4, 381–93.

Taş, Hakkı and Meral Ugur (2007), 'Roads "Drawn" to Modernity: Religion and Secularism in Contemporary Turkey', *PS: Political Science and Politics* 40:2, 311–14.

Taşköprülüzade, Aḥmad ibn Muṣṭafā (1975), *al-Shaqāʾiq al-Nuʿmāniyya fī ʿUlamāʾ al-Dawla al-ʿUthmāniyya*. Beirut: Dār al-Kitāb al-ʿArabī.

Taştan, Coşkun (2013), 'The Gezi Park Protests in Turkey: A Qualitative Field Research', *Insight Turkey* 15:3, 27–38.

Taştekin, Fehim (2013), 'Turkey's Gezi Park Protestors Regroup for Ramadan', *Al-Monitor*, 4 July, available at: https://www.al-monitor.com/originals/2013/07/turkey-gezi-park-protesters-observe-ramadan-iftars.html, last accessed 8 July 2022.

Tee, Caroline (2016), *The Gülen Movement in Turkey: The Politics of Islam and Modernity*. London: I. B. Tauris.

Tee, Caroline (2018), 'The Gülen Movement and the AKP: The Rise and Fall of a Turkish Islamist Alliance', in M. Hakan Yavuz and Bayram Balcı (eds), *Turkey's July 15 Coup: What Happened and Why*. Salt Lake City: University of Utah Press, 150–72.

Tekin, Gönül (1996), 'The Motif of "Cypress-River-Beloved One-Garden" in Nevā'ī's and Aḥmed Pāşā's Poetry and its Archetype', *Oriente Moderno* 76:2, 463–83.

The Russian Primary Chronicle: The Laurentian Text (1953), ed. and trans. Samuel Hazzard Cross and Olgerd O. Sherbowitz-Wetzor. Cambridge, MA: Mediaeval Academy of America.

Tibbs, Eve (2021), *A Basic Guide to Eastern Orthodox Theology: Introducing Beliefs and Practices*. Grand Rapids, MI: Baker Academic.

'Timeline of Gezi Park Protests' (2013), *Hürriyet Daily News*, 6 June, available at: https://www.hurriyetdailynews.com/timeline-of-gezi-park-protests--48321, last accessed 8 July 2022.

'Topbaş, 15 Temmuz Şehitler Abidesi'ni İnceledi' (2017), *Haberler*, 12 July, available at: https://www.haberler.com/guncel/topbas-15-temmuz-sehitler-abidesi-ni-inceledi-9824329-haberi, last accessed 15 May 2022.

Tunç, Aslı (2015), 'In Quest for Democracy: Internet Freedom and Politics in Contemporary Turkey', in Banu Akdenizli (ed.), *Digital Transformations in Turkey: Current Perspectives in Communication Studies*. Lanham, MD: Lexington Books, 207–20.

Tunç, Aslı and Ariana Ferentinou (2012), 'Identities In-between: The Impact of Satellite Broadcasting on Greek Orthodox Minority (Rum Polites) Women's Perception of Their Identities in Turkey', *Ethnic and Racial Studies* 35:5, 906–23.

Türeli, İpek (2018), *Istanbul, Open City: Exhibiting Anxieties of Urban Modernity*. London: Routledge.

Türeli, İpek (2006), 'Modeling Citizenship in Turkey's Miniature Park', *Traditional Dwellings and Settlements Review* 17:2, 55–69.

Türeli, İpek and Meltem Al (2018), 'Walking in the Periphery: Activist Art and Urban Resistance to Neoliberalism in Istanbul', *Review of Middle East Studies* 52:2, 310–33.

Turgut, Pelin (2008), 'Constantinople's Gypsies Not Welcome in Istanbul', *Time*, 9 June, available at: http://content.time.com/time/world/article/0,8599, 1812905,00.html, last accessed 14 July 2022.

Türker, Nurdan (2020), *I Have No Country, I Have a Homeland: Istanbul Romiois: Place–Memory–Migration*, trans. Arda Akbaş and Fatima Sakarya. Berlin: Peter Lang.

Türkeş, Mustafa (2016), 'Decomposing Neo-Ottoman Hegemony', *Journal of Balkan and Near Eastern Studies* 18:3, 191–216.

'Turkey Attempted Coup: Timeline of Events' (2016), *TRT World*, 15 July, available at: https://www.trtworld.com/turkey/turkey-coup-attempt-timeline-of-events-144495, last accessed 23 May 2022.

'Turkish Court Sentences Osman Kavala to Life in Prison' (2022), *Ahval*, 22 April, available at: https://ahvalnews.com/turkey-democracy/turkish-court-sentences-osman-kavala-life-prison, last accessed 15 June 2022.

'Turkish Prosecutors Launched over 1.5 Million Terror Probes between 2016–2020: Justice Ministry' (2021), *Ahval*, 21 September, available at: https://ahvalnews.com/terror-charges/turkish-prosecutors-launched-over-15-million-terror-probes-between-2016-2020-justice, last accessed 23 May 2022.

Tüysüzoğlu, Göktürk (2014), 'Strategic Depth: A neo-Ottomanist Interpretation of Turkish Eurasianism', *Mediterranean Quarterly* 25:2, 85–104.

Utku, Hatice Ahsen (2011), 'İstanbul Concludes European Capital of Culture Stint with Achievements, Disputes', *Today's Zaman*, 2 January.

Uysal, Evrim Ülke (2012), 'An Urban Social Movement Challenging Urban Regeneration: The Case of Sulukule, Istanbul' *Cities* 29, 12–22.

Uzer, Umut (2016), *An Intellectual History of Turkish Nationalism: Between Turkish Ethnicity and Islamic Identity*. Salt Lake City: University of Utah Press.

Uzer, Umut (2020), 'Conservative Narrative: Contemporary neo-Ottomanist Approaches in Turkish Politics', *Middle East Critique* 29:3, 275–90.

Uzun, Mustafa İsmet (1994), 'Ebced', *İslam Ansiklopedisi*. Ankara: Türkiye Diyanet Vakfı, 68–70.

Vale, Lawrence J. (1992), *Architecture, Power, and National Identity*. New Haven, CT: Yale University Press.

Verney, Susannah, Anna Bosco and Senem Aydın-Düzgit (2020), 'The AKP on the Road to Presidentialism', in Susannah Verney, Anna Bosco and Senem Aydın-Düzgit (eds), *The AKP since Gezi Park: Moving to Regime Change in Turkey*. New York: Routledge, 2–26.

Voll, John O. (2013), 'Late Ottoman Istanbul: The Cosmopolitan Capital', *Turkish Review* 3:4, 362–7.

Vryonis Jr, Speros (2005), *The Mechanism of Catastrophe: The Turkish Pogrom of September 6–7, 1955, and the Destruction of the Greek Community of Istanbul*. New York: Greekworks.com.

Waldman, Simon A. and Emre Caliskan (2017), *The New Turkey and Its Discontents*. New York: Oxford University Press.

Walton, Jeremy F. (2010), 'Practices of Neo-Ottomanism: Making Space and Place Virtuous in Istanbul', in Deniz Göktürk, Levent Soysal and İpek Türeli (eds), *Orienting Istanbul: Cultural Capital of Europe?* New York: Routledge, 88–104.

Walton, Jeremy F. (2015), '"Everyday I'm *Çapulling*!": Global Flows and Local Frictions of Gezi', in Isabel David and Kumru F. Toktamış (eds), *'Everywhere Taksim':*

Sowing the Seeds for a New Turkey at Gezi. Amsterdam: Amsterdam University Press, 45–58.

Walton, Jeremy F. (2016), 'Geographies of Revival and Erasure: Neo-Ottoman Sites of Memory in Istanbul, Thessaloniki, and Budapest', *Die Welt Des Islams* 56:3/4, 511–33.

Warner, Michael (2002), *Publics and Counterpublics*, 2nd edn. Brooklyn, NY: Zone Books.

Watenpaugh, Heghnar (2013), 'Learning from Taksim Square: Architecture, State Power, and Public Space in Istanbul', *Huffington Post*, 14 August, available at: https://www.huffpost.com/entry/learning-from-taksim-squa_b_3443505, last accessed 11 July 2022.

White, Jenny (2002), *Islamist Mobilization in Turkey: A Study in Vernacular Politics*. Seattle, WA: University of Washington Press.

White, Jenny (2013), *Muslim Nationalism and the New Turks*. Princeton, NJ: Princeton University Press.

Williams, David-John (2020), 'The Use of Memory to Re-Found Hagia Sophia', *Koinonia: The Journal of the Anglican and Eastern Churches Association* 74, 15–19.

Wybrew, Hugh (2019), 'Liturgies and the Fathers', in Ken Parry (ed.), *The Wiley-Blackwell Companion to Patristics*. Chichester: Wiley-Blackwell, 385–99.

Xerri, Daniel (2014), 'The Poetry of Cities: On Discovering Poems in Istanbul, Sarajevo, and Bratislava', *Journeys* 15:1, 90–108.

Yang Erdem, Chien (2017), 'Ottomentality: Neoliberal Governance of Culture and neo-Ottoman Management of Diversity', *Turkish Studies* 18:4, 710–28.

Yanık, Lerna K. (2016), 'Bringing the Empire Back In: The Gradual Discovery of the Ottoman Empire in Turkish Foreign Policy', *Welt Des Islams* 56:3/4, 466–88.

Yanık, Lerna K. and Jelena Subotić (2001), 'Cultural Heritage as Status Seeking: The International Politics of Turkey's Restoration Wave', *Cooperation and Conflict* 56:3, 245–63.

Yaran, Rahmi (1992), 'Ömer Nasuhi Bilmen', *İslam Ansiklopedisi*. Ankara: Türkiye Diyanet Vakfı.

Yavuz, M. Hakan (1999), 'Towards an Islamic Liberalism?: The Nurcu Movement and Fethullah Gülen', *Middle East Journal* 53:4, 584–605.

Yavuz, M. Hakan (2003), *Islamic Political Identity in Turkey*. New York: Oxford University Press.

Yavuz, M. Hakan (2004), 'Opportunity Spaces, Identity, and Islamic Meaning in Turkey', in Quintan Wiktorowicz (ed.), *Islamic Activism: A Social Movement Theory Approach*. Bloomington: Indiana University Press, 270–88.

Yavuz, M. Hakan (2009), *Secularism and Muslim Democracy in Turkey*. New York: Cambridge University Press.

Yavuz, M. Hakan (2018), 'The Three Stages of the Gülen Movement: From Pietistic Weeping to Power-Obsessed Structure', in M. Hakan Yavuz and Bayram Balcı (eds), *Turkey's July 15 Coup: What Happened and Why*. Salt Lake City: University of Utah Press.

Yavuz, M. Hakan (2020), *Nostalgia for the Empire: The Politics of neo-Ottomanism*. Oxford: Oxford University Press.

Yavuz, M. Hakan (2021), *Erdoğan: The Making of An Autocrat*. Edinburgh: Edinburgh University Press, 17, 176.

Yavuz, M. Hakan and Bayram Balcı (2018), 'Introduction: The Gülen Movement and the Coup', in M. Hakan Yavuz and Bayram Balcı (eds), *Turkey's July 15 Coup: What Happened and Why*. Salt Lake City: University of Utah Press, 1–19.

Yavuz, M. Hakan and Rasım Koç (2018), 'The Gülen Movement vs. Erdoğan: The Failed Coup', in M. Hakan Yavuz and Bayram Balcı (eds), *Turkey's July 15 Coup: What Happened and Why*. Salt Lake City: University of Utah Press, 78–97.

Yayla, Atilla (2013), 'Gezi Park Revolts: For or Against Democracy?' *Insight Turkey* 15:4, 7–18.

Yazici, Berna (2013), 'Towards an Anthropology of Traffic: A Ride Through Class Hierarchies on Istanbul's Roadways', *Ethnos* 78:4, 515–42.

Yel, Ali Murat and Alparslan Nas (2013), 'After Gezi: Moving towards post-Hegemonic Imagination in Turkey', *Insight Turkey* 15:4, 177–90.

Yetiskul, Emine and Sule Demirel (2018), 'Assembling Gentrification in Istanbul: The Cihangir Neighbourhood of Beyoğlu', *Urban Studies* 55:15, 3336–52.

Yezdani, İpek (2019), 'Bakırköy'den ABD'ye başpiskopos', *Hürriyet*, 13 June, available at: https://www.hurriyet.com.tr/gundem/bakirkoyden-abdye-baspiskopos-41242370, last accessed 8 June 2022.

Yıldırım, Birge (2012), 'Transformation of Public Squares of Istanbul between 1938–1949', Proceedings of the 15th International Planning History Society Conference, 15–18 July 2012, available at: http://www.usp.br/fau/iphs/abstracts-and-papers.html, last accessed 11 July 2022.

Yildiz, Guney (2013), 'Ergenekon: The Court Case that Changed Turkey', *BBC News*, 5 August, available at: http://www.bbc.com/news/world-europe-23581891, last accessed 8 June 2022.

Yılmaz, Coşkun (2017), '15 Temmuz Şehitler Makamı', *Üsküdar Kültür, Sanat ve Medeniyet Dergisi* 4:1, 72–7.

Yılmaz, Hale (2013), *Becoming Turkish: Nationalist Reforms and Cultural Negotiations in Early Republican Turkey, 1923–1945*. Syracuse, NY: Syracuse University Press.

Young, Megan R. (2010), 'An Exploration of Govermentality and Broadcasting in the Republic of Turkey: 1923–2010', unpublished Master's thesis, University of Arizona.

Yücel, Hakan and Süheyla Yıldız (2014), 'İstanbul'da ve İmroz'da Rum Olmak, Atina'da Rum Kalmak', *Alternatif Politika* 6:2, 148–94.

Ziflioğu, Verchihan (2010), 'Istanbul Tired of Oriental Viewpoints and Debates', *Hurriyet Daily News*, 22 January.

Zilan, Akay (2021), 'Ülkede her an Terörist Olabilirsiniz', *BirGün*, 19 September, available at: https://www.birgun.net/haber/ulkede-her-an-terorist-olabilirsiniz-359165, last accessed 23 May 2022.

Zuberi, Saira (2013), 'Her Yer Taksim! Feminist and LGBTQI Engagement in the Gezi Park Protests', *Thomson Reuters Foundation News*, 26 July, available at: https://news.trust.org/item/20130726185721-m7dvq, last accessed 8 July, 2022.

Zürcher, Erik J. ([2004] 2005), *Turkey: A Modern History*, 3rd edn. New York: I. B. Tauris.

INDEX

15 July Martyrs' Bridge *see* Bosphorus
Bridge
2016 coup attempt, 2, 8–9, 17,
138–42, 218
and Islam, 159–60, 159–62
see also Monument to the Martyrs
of 15 July (15 Temmuz Şehitler
Makamı)

Abbas, Tahir
Insight Turkey, 115, 118
Abdül Hamid II, Sultan, 25–6, 27
Abdülmecid I, Sultan, 187–8
Adalet ve Kalkınma Partisi *see* AKP
Ahmad, Feroz, 29
Ahmet I, Sultan, 199
Akar, Hulusi, 139
Akın, Abdullah, 145, 149–51, 154–5
AKM (Atatürk Culture Centre), 62,
64, 99, 106
AKP (Adalet ve Kalkınma Partisi), 1–3,
5, 6, 9, 216–18

and 2016 coup attempt, 17, 138–42,
159–60
and architecture, 23
and cultural capital, 3–4, 23–4
and ECoC, 7–8, 58–9, 61–2, 70–9,
86, 87, 88–9
and EU, 56, 57
and Gezi Park, 8, 16–17, 100, 101–3,
105, 111, 112–13, 115–16
and Hagia Sophia, 171, 172, 176,
189
and *iman*, 159–60
and Monument to the Martyrs of 15
July (15 Temmuz Şehitler Makamı),
152, 153, 154, 155–6, 157
and museumification, 80–2
and non-Muslim community, 128–9
and Ottoman Empire, 20
and rise, 37–40
and Roma, 65, 66–70
and spatial politics, 118–23
and Taksim Square, 109, 110

and Turkish Islamic identity, 14–15
see also Erdoğan, Recep Tayyip
Akseki, Ahmet Hamdi, 189
Akşemseddin, 184, 197
Akşener, Meral, 196
Albanians, 43
alcohol, 101, 113, 119, 121
Alevis, 67
'All-Witnessing', 145–6, 165n32
Altınordu, Ateş, 113
Anamur, Hasan, 61
Anatolia, 26, 27, 29, 34, 40
    and conquest, 197
    and ECoC, 86
    and politics, 46
Ankara, 3, 29, 139, 142, 158
al-Ansari, Abu Ayyub, 184, 197
Anthemius of Tralles, 169, 173–4
anti-capitalists, 103, 105
anti-corruption investigations, 69
anti-Greek Orthodox discourse, 189,
    191, 192, 193, 195
Al-Aqsa Mosque (Jerusalem), 195
Arabic language, 29
architecture, 3, 7, 15–16, 19
    and ECoC, 59, 63
    and Gezi Park, 119–20
    and memorialisation, 8–9
    and mosques, 220–5
    and national identity, 21–3
    and politics, 20–1, 218–19
    see also Hagia Sophia; Monument to
    the Martyrs of 15 July (15 Temmuz
    Şehitler Makamı)
Armaoğlu, Fahir, 192
armed forces, 138–41
Armenians, 67, 108–9

arts, the, 3, 8, 59, 83, 219
Asad, Talal, 30, 31
Atatürk, Mustafa Kemal, 3, 25, 28,
    55–7
    and Gezi Park, 99
    and Greece, 127
    and Hagia Sophia, 171, 189
    and women, 29–30
    see also Kemalism
Athens, 22
authoritarianism, 39, 101–2, 217
Avni, Yeni Şehirli, 150
Ayasofya *see* Hagia Sophia
Aydın-Düzgit, Senem, 39, 102

Bahçeli, Devlet, 196
Baki, 150
Balkans, 41, 42
Balyan, Krikor, 109
Barker, Chris, 87
Bartholomew I, Patriarch, 203–5, 207
Barzani, Massoud, 67
Bayraktar, Erdoğan, 69–70
Berlin (Germany), 148, 220–3
betrayal (*ihanet*), 191, 195, 203, 207
Beylunioğlu, Anna Maria, 129
Beyoğlu, 99, 128; *see also* Pera
Bible, the, 178
Bıçakçı, Ayse Banu, 57
Bigelow, Anna, 182, 183
Bilmen, Ömer Nasuhi, 185–7, 189, 191
Boğaziçi University, 8, 102, 104–5,
    106–7
Book of Dede Korkut, The, 154
Bosco, Anna, 39, 102
Bosnians, 43
Bosphorus Bridge, 9, 17, 71, 139, 143–4

Bourdieu, Pierre, 85, 86–7
  Distinctions, 18–19
  Outline of a Theory of Practice, 3
Bozdoğan, Sibel
  Modernism and Nation Building:
    Turkish Architectural Culture in
    the Early Republic, 22–3
Braude, Benjamin, 43–4
bridge metaphor, 70–1
Brown, Wendy, 88
Bugün (newspaper), 192
built environment, 1–2, 3, 4–5, 217;
  see also architecture
Butler, Judith, 106–7
Byzantine Empire, 18, 73, 155, 202
  and Hagia Sophia, 169, 173–82

Çağaptay, Soner, 40–1, 47
calligraphy, 188, 200–1
Caucasus, 41, 71
Çelebi, Süleyman, 156
Central Asia, 27–8, 40, 71, 153, 154
Ceylan, Hasan Hüseyin
  Ayasofya İhaneti (*The Betrayal of*
    Hagia Sophia), 191, 192
Ceylan, Nuri Bilge
  Uzak, 4
Chamber of Architects and Engineers
  (TMMOB), 109–10
CHP (Cumhuriyet Halk Partisi), 129,
  171, 196
Christianity, 18, 22, 57, 76
  and Hagia Sophia, 169, 173–83, 191
  and Istanbul Greeks, 202, 203–7
  and Turkishness, 47
  see also Greek Orthodox community
Çinar, Alev, 80–1

civil society, 20, 88
civilians, 138–40
Clark, Janine, 32
Çolak, Yılmaz, 40, 41, 42–3, 44
Committee of Union and Progress, 30
Conquest of Istanbul Day, 80
conservation, 64
conservative nationalism, 46–7
Constantine I, Emperor, 169, 177
Constantinople, 18, 170, 177–8, 197
  and conquest, 183–4, 185–6, 194
  and Ecumenical Patriarchate, 180–2,
    192
Constantius II, Emperor, 169
Copenhagen Criteria, 56, 67
corruption, 69, 141
cosmopolitanism, 5–6, 8, 17, 21–2, 126
  and Gezi Park, 102, 103, 129
  and neo-Ottomanism, 42, 43
Council of Europe, 56
coup *see* 2016 coup attempt
cultural capital, 3–4, 7, 14, 24–7,
    217
  and AKP, 23–4
  and Bourdieu, 18–19
  and ECoC, 59, 63–5, 76–8
  and Europe, 84–5, 86–7
  and Islamic bourgeoisie, 32
  and Kemalism, 27–31
  and museums, 79–80
  and neo-Ottomanism, 45
  and politics, 87–90
cultural memory, 2, 14, 24–7, 19–20,
    21, 217
  and ECoC, 59, 63
  and Kemalism, 27–31
  and neo-Ottomanism, 40–4, 45

Ćurčić, Slobodan, 174
Cyprus, 127, 203

Danıştay (administrative court), 171–2
Davutoğlu, Ahmet, 196
Demir, Mustafa, 65
democracy, 38–9, 56, 105, 116, 117
Democratic People's Party see HDP
    (Halkların Demokratick Partisi)
destan (national epics), 138, 153–9
Diker, Tacettin, 75
Dilmaç, Bulent, 142
displacement, 2, 7–8, 16, 65–70
dissidents, 39
Diyanet (Turkish Directorate of
    Religious Affairs), 139, 155, 158,
    160, 197, 206
Diyanet İşleri Türk-İslam Birliği, 221
Doğan, Lütfi, 35–6
domes, 144–5, 148, 152, 188
    and Hagia Sophia, 169, 173, 175–6
dönme community, 223–4
dress, 31, 32, 55, 74, 113
Dündar, General Ümit, 140

Eastern Orthodox Christianity
    see Christianity
Eckardt, Frank
    Public Istanbul: Spaces and Spheres of
    the Urban, 4–5
ECoC see European Capital of Culture
economics, 3, 31–2, 33–4, 57, 87
    and ECoC, 64, 88–9
Ecumenical Councils, 182
education, 184–5
Eliaçık, İhsan, 113
Elpidophoros I, Archbishop, 203–7

endowment (vakıf), 171, 197–8
ENHR (European Network on
    Housing Research), 63, 64
epics see national epics
Erbakan, Necmettin, 35, 36
Erbaş, Ali, 196, 197–8, 201, 224
Erdoğan, Emine, 198
Erdoğan, Recep Tayyip, 1–2, 6, 14,
    37, 39
    and 2016 coup attempt, 139, 140,
    159–60
    and calligraphy, 200
    and ECoC, 88
    and Europe, 70, 71, 224, 225
    and Gezi Park, 8, 100–1, 111, 120
    and Hagia Sophia, 171–2, 176, 189,
    196–7, 198
    and 'Hagia Sophia Manifesto', 193–6
    and iman, 159–60, 161–2
    and Istanbul Greeks, 203, 207
    and Kısakürek, 190
    and Monument to the Martyrs of
    15 July (15 Temmuz Şehitler
    Makamı), 148, 152, 153, 157,
    159
    and neo-Ottomanism, 15, 16, 40,
    44–8, 216–17
    and patriarchy, 119
    and Roma, 67, 68, 70
    and Sunni nationalism, 17
    see also AKP
'Ergenekon' organisation, 39
Ernst & Young, 62, 76, 88–9
Ertuğrul Gazi Mosque (Ashgabat), 148
Erzen, Jale Necdet, 149
Ete, Hatem, 115–16
ethnic cleansing, 21, 41, 43

ethnic minorities, 2, 21–2, 67, 108–9
  and Gezi Park, 103, 105, 129
  and Kemalism, 30
  and museumification, 82
  and Özal, 43
  and Turkishness, 47
  see also Greek Orthodox community;
    Roma
ethnic nationalism, 46
Eucharist, 179, 182
Eurocentrism, 82–7
Europe *see* West, the
European Capital of Culture (ECoC),
  2, 7–8, 16, 57–62, 217
  and bridge metaphor, 70–2
  and Eurocentrism, 82–7
  and governmentality, 87–90
  and museumification, 78–82
  and neo-Ottomanism, 72–8, 90–1
  and preparation, 63–70
European Economic Community
  (EEC), 56
European Union (EU), 16, 38, 56–7,
  60–1
Eyüp, 25

faith (*iman*), 159–62
fashion, 32, 33
Fatih municipality, 65, 66, 69
Fatih Sultan Mehmet Bridge, 139, 143
FETÖ (Gülenist Terror Organisation),
  15, 157–8
fezes, 31, 55, 74, 77
Fırat, Hande, 139
First World War, 27, 221
Fisher-Onar, Nora, 28, 125–6
Florovsky, Georges, 178
forced migration, 202, 203

Fossatti, Gaspare and Giuseppe, 188
FP (Virtue Party), 37
Fraser, Nancy, 83, 104, 218–19
freedom (*özgürlük*), 101–2
Fuzuli, 150

Galata, 123–4
Galip, Leskofçalı, 150
Gallipoli, Battle of, 155
Gençoğlu-Onbaşı, Funda, 67–8
genocide, 21, 41
gentrification, 7–8, 58–9, 65–70
Germany, 22, 148, 220–3
Gezi Park, 2, 8, 16–17, 111–17,
  217–18
  and background, 99–103
  and movement, 107–11
  and non-Muslim community, 128–9
  and protestors, 103–7
  and resistance, 219
  and spatial politics, 118–23
  and the West, 78
al-Ghazali, Abu Hamid, 165n32
Giscard d'Estaing, Valery, 85
God, 145–6, 161, 162, 178–9
Gökalp, Ziya, 30
Göle, Nilüfer, 119
Görmez, Mehmet, 155, 161
governmentality, 87–90
Greece, 22, 125, 127, 203, 223–4
Greek Orthodox community, 2, 8, 15
  and Gezi Park, 17, 99, 129–30, 218
  and Hagia Sophia, 9, 18
  and neo-Ottomanism, 41
  and Ottoman Empire, 124–5
  and violence, 126–8
  see also anti-Greek Orthodox
    discourse; Istanbul Greeks

Greek War of Independence, 125, 127, 203
Gregory V, Patriarch, 125
Gregory of Nazianus, St, 181–2
Gül, Abdullah, 37, 101
Gül Baba, 225
Gülen, Fethullah, 17, 140–2;
    see also FETÖ (Gülenist Terror Organisation)
Günay, Ertuğrul, 70
Gunay, Zeynep, 64–5
Gündüz, Erdem, 106
gypsies see Roma

Habermas, Jürgen, 104, 218
    The Structural Transformation of the Public Sphere, 20–1
Hagia Sophia, 2, 9, 17–18
    and background, 169–72
    and Christian background, 173–82
    and Istanbul Greeks, 203–4, 205–7, 219
    and Ottoman mosque, 182–8
    and reconversion, 189–201
hainler (traitors), 155, 157
Halaçoğlu, Yusuf, 191–2
halk (common people), 155, 157
Hamas, 37
Hammond, Timur, 147
Harvey, David, 15, 218
HDP (Halkların Demokratik Partisi), 129, 196
headscarves, 32, 33, 113
healing, 146, 147, 149
Heffner, Robert, 31
Hein, Carola, 85
heritage, 219–20, 223
heterogeneity see pluralism

hierarchies, 18–19
Hintz, Lisel, 46–7
Hizbullah, 37
Hizmet movement, 141–2
homeland (vatan), 47–8, 160–1, 197
Hoyng, Rolien, 68
Hudson, Leila, 20, 23
human rights, 38–9, 56
Hungary, 225
Huntington, Samuel
    'The Clash of Civilizations', 85

Iğsiz, Aslı, 70, 82
iman (religious faith), 159–62
imperialism, 37, 42
In the Words of the Veterans of 15 July, 155
İncedayi, Deniz, 66
Iran, 37
Irmak, Hüseyin, 62
Isidore of Miletus, 169, 173–4
Islam, 41–2, 122, 186–7
    and 2016 coup attempt, 159–60
    and Gezi Park, 113–14, 116, 117
    and Hagia Sophia, 170–2
    and Istanbul Greeks, 205
    and Kemalism, 31
    and martyrs, 142
    and Monument to the Martyrs of 15 July (15 Temmuz Şehitler Makamı), 144, 145–6, 158–9
    and Ottoman Empire, 25–6
    and politics, 35–8
    see also Islamic bourgeoisie; Sunni Islam
Islamic bourgeoisie, 7, 15, 16, 31–4, 59, 104
Islamophobia, 194

Istanbul, 4–6, 28–9, 45, 216–18
  and districts, 123–4
  see also Constantinople; European
    Capital of Culture; Gezi Park;
    Hagia Sophia; Monument to the
    Martyrs of 15 July (15 Temmuz
    Şehitler Makamı)
Istanbul Greeks, 202–7, 213n97
İzzet Efendi, Kazasker Mustafa, 188

Jewish heritage, 76, 223
John Chrysostom, St, 181–2
John Paul II, Pope, 181
Justice and Development Party *see* AKP
    (Adalet ve Kalkınma Partisi)
Justinian I, Emperor, 169, 173, 174, 184

Kandili, Miraç, 113
Karaca, Banu, 61, 112
Karagöz tradition, 75
Karakoç, Sezai, 191
Karasipahi, Sena, 33
Kavala, Osman, 102
Kaya, Hüda, 196
Kayı tribe, 27
Kaymak, Özgür, 128
Kazım Paşa, 150
Kemalism, 27–31, 32, 33, 46
  and architecture, 23
  and Gezi Park, 103, 105, 116–17
  and Ottoman Empire, 81, 82
  and Turkishness, 47
Kezer, Zeynep
  *Building Modern Turkey: State,
    Space, and Ideology in the Early
    Republic*, 23
al-Khidr, 184

Kısakürek, Necip Fazıl, 190–1, 196, 197
Kisar-Koramaz, Elif, 63
Klaptek, Martin, 223
Koramaz, Turgay, 63
Kosovo, 224
Kotku, Mehmet Zahid, 35–6
Kristallnacht, 22
Kurds, 67, 103, 105
Kurt, Orhan, 75
Kurtulmuş, Numan, 196

language, 29, 55
Lewis, Bernard, 85
LGBTIQ community, 99, 101, 103, 105
lifestyle choices, 119, 121–2
literature, 40; *see also* national epics;
    poetry
liturgy, 179, 182, 206

Malkki, Liisa, 84
manipulation, 3, 6
Manzikert, Battle of, 155
marginalisation, 2, 8
martyrs, 142, 161–2; *see also*
    Monument to the Martyrs of
    15 July (15 Temmuz Şehitler
    Makamı); Şehitlik Camii (Martyrs'
    Mosque) (Berlin)
Mary the Mother of God and the infant
    Christ mosaic, 182, 199
Mass Housing Authority *see* TOKİ
mass violence, 21, 22
media, 31–2, 34, 141, 198
  and 2016 coup attempt, 139
  and Gezi Park, 104–5, 117
medreses (theological schools), 55, 170,
    184–5, 186

Mehmed I, Sultan, 26

Mehmed II, Sultan, 73, 183, 185, 186

Mehmet II, Sultan, 170, 171, 177, 183, 184, 185, 187
  and Erbaş, 197, 198
  and Erdoğan, 193, 194

memorialisation, 2, 8–9, 17, 80–1, 185–6, 218; *see also* Monument to the Martyrs of 15 July (15 Temmuz Şehitler Makamı)

memory *see* cultural memory; memorialisation; nostalgia; remembrance

Menderes, Adnan, 127

Mevlid-i Şerif, 156–7

Middle East, 71

military *see* armed forces

millet system, 42, 43–4

Mills, Amy, 5, 6, 125–6

Mısri, Niyazi, 150

MNP (National Order Party), 36

modernity, 32–3, 36, 37

Molla Hüsrev, 185

Monument to the Martyrs of 15 July (15 Temmuz Şehitler Makamı), 2, 17, 138, 143–6, 161
  and ceremony, 153–9
  and neo-Ottomanism, 146–53

moralising, 119, 120, 121–2

mosaics, 170, 182, 188, 199–200

mosques, 148, 156–7, 223–4; *see also* Hagia Sophia; Şehitlik Camii (Martyrs' Mosque) (Berlin)

mourning, 17

MSP (National Salvation Party), 36

Muhammad, Prophet, 25–6, 156, 171

multiculturalism, 7, 8, 9, 16
  and ECoC, 76, 77–8, 91

municipalities, 65–6

Murad I, Sultan, 224

museums, 79–82; *see also* Hagia Sophia

music, 74, 75, 77

Muslims *see* Islam

Myrelaion Rotunda, 174

Nas, Alparslan, 116

Nas, Çiğdem, 57

nation-states, 21–2

national epics (*destan*), 138, 153–9

national identity, 2, 5–6, 40–1
  and 2016 coup attempt, 160, 161
  and architecture, 21–3
  and Gezi Park, 17, 114, 116, 123
  and Hagia Sophia, 194, 196–7
  and Monument to the Martyrs of 15 July (15 Temmuz Şehitler Makamı), 152–3
  and Ottoman Empire, 79–80
  and Turkish Islamic, 14–15, 16
  see also national epics (*destan*)

National Outlook Movement, 35–6

nationalism, 4, 5–6, 7, 9, 217–18
  and Hagia Sophia, 190–1, 196–7
  and homeland, 160
  and Istanbul Greeks, 202
  and Kemalism, 27–8, 30–1, 42
  and non-Muslim community, 128–9
  and Ottoman Empire, 25
  and Turkish Islamic, 45–8

NATO, 56

Navaro-Yashin, Yael, 112

Necipoğlu, Gülrü, 182–3

neo-Ottomanism, 1–2, 4, 6, 7–8,
  216–18
  and ambiguities, 90–1
  and cultural memory, 40–4
  and ECoC, 58–9, 61–2, 72–8
  and Erdoğan, 15, 16, 44–8
  and Europe, 220–5
  and Gezi Park, 102, 118–19, 120
  and Hagia Sophia, 199, 200, 203
  and memorialisation, 80–1
  and Monument to the Martyrs of
    15 July (15 Temmuz Şehitler
    Makamı), 146–53
  and National Outlook Movement, 36
  and Sulukule, 65–6, 69
  and trauma, 17, 138
neoliberalism, 3, 19, 33–4, 88
New Mosque (Yeni Camii)
  (Thessaloniki), 223–4
Noah, 27
non-Muslim community, 44, 47, 99,
  128–9; see also Greek Orthodox
  community
nostalgia, 41, 118, 126

Oğuz Turks, 154
Ölçer, Dr Nazan, 73
openings, 67
Orbán, Viktor, 225
Organization for Security and
  Cooperation in Europe, 56
Oriental Orthodox Church, 178
Orientalism, 16, 62, 85–6
Osman I, Sultan, 26
Ottoman Empire, 1–2, 15, 55, 194
  and ancestry, 26–7
  and design motifs, 32

and Gezi Park, 17
and Greek Orthodox community,
  124–5
and Hagia Sophia, 170–1, 182–8
and Islam, 23–4, 25–6
and Istanbul, 16
and Kemalism, 28–9, 30, 31, 81–2
and museums, 79–80
and remembrance, 20
and romanticisation, 7–8
see also neo-Ottomanism
Özal, Turgut, 32, 33, 34, 35, 41–3
Özçay, Mehmet, 201
Özkan, Behlül, 47–8, 160
Özlen, Metin, 75
Özyürek, Esra, 81

Palmer, Robert, 60
Pamuk, Orhan
  Istanbul: Memories of a City, 4
Paradise, 144, 147, 148, 149, 150, 151,
  152, 155
Patel, Kiran Klaus
  The Cultural Politics of Europe:
    European Capitals of Culture and
    European Union since the 1980s,
    60–1
patriarchy, 119
Paylan, Garo, 196
Peirce, Leslie, 43
Pentcheva, Bissera, 179
People's Houses, 29
Pera, 123–4, 126, 127
Persian language, 29
pious generation (dindar nesil), 101
pluralism, 2, 9, 16, 126
  and ECoC, 59, 76, 77–8

and Gezi Park, 102, 116–17, 123, 129
and Hagia Sophia, 17–18
and Özal, 41–3, 44
poetry, 149–51
pogroms, 127–8, 203
police force, 69
and Gezi Park, 100, 101, 105, 106,
110–11, 117
politics, 5, 34–7, 129, 87–90, 171,
219–20
and Anatolia, 46
and architecture, 20–1
and Hagia Sophia, 196
see also AKP
polyglotism, 43
power, 15–16, 20–1, 219–20
Procopius, 174–5
Prophet see Muhammad, Prophet
Prost, Henri, 107, 108
protest see Gezi Park; resistance
public space, 1, 2–3, 4–5, 20–1, 45
and ECoC, 59, 63, 78–9
and memorialisation, 8–9
and power, 15–16
and protest, 218–19
see also architecture; Gezi Park;
Monument to the Martyrs of 15
July (15 Temmuz Şehitler Makamı)
puppetry, 75

Qur'an, 145, 149, 151–2, 186, 197, 198
and calligraphy, 201
and iman, 160
and Verse of Light (24:35), 188

Ramadan, 25, 26
regeneration, 64, 65–6

religion, 219; see also Christianity;
Islam; secularism
remembrance, 9, 138, 142, 156–7;
see also memorialisation
repression, 17
Republican People's Party see CHP
(Cumhuriyet Halk Partisi)
resistance, 1, 9, 101
and 2016 coup attempt, 138–40,
142, 157, 159–60
and Gezi Park, 111, 112–13,
123, 219
rest, 146, 147
Rizvi, Kishwar, 148
Roma, 7–8, 15, 16, 59, 65–70,
90–1
Romain Örs, İlay, 125–6, 128,
202
Roman Catholic Church, 177
RP (Welfare Party), 36–8
rule of law, 56
Rum see Greek Orthodox community
Rumi, Mevlana Jalal al-Din, 113
Russia, 22, 177, 180

Sabbati Zevi, 223
sacred law (fiqh), 185
sacred space, 146–7
sacrifice, 161
Sadriu, Behar, 224
Safa, Peyami, 195
Said, Edward, 85
saints' tombs (türbe), 147–8, 149, 152,
159, 184, 224
Sakıp Sabancı Museum, 73–4
Secor, Anna, 32, 33
sectarianism, 196

secularism, 3, 5, 15, 25, 38, 39
and AKM, 62
and Gezi Park, 16–17, 99, 101, 103,
108, 117, 128
and Hagia Sophia, 171
and Kemalism, 29, 30–1, 32
Şehitlik Camii (Martyrs' Mosque)
(Berlin), 148, 220–3
Selim III, Sultan, 107
Seljuk Turks, 155
Şemsi Efendi, Osman, 150
Şenalp, Hilmi, 145, 147–8, 150, 153, 221
Şenlikname parade, 80
Serbians, 43
Serdengeçti, Osman Yüksel, 189–90,
191, 195
Sezai, Hasan, 150
Shaw, Wendy
Possessors and Possessed: Museums,
Archaeology, and the Visualization
of History in the Late Ottoman
Empire, 79, 80
Shohat, Ella, 86
Silentiarius, Paulus, 175–6
Şimşir, Zeynep, 142
slogans, 111
social media, 104–5, 110, 139
socialists, 105
Sofos, Spyros, 183
Soğancı, Mehmet, 110
Söğüd, 26
Solomonovich, Nadav, 142
sovereignty, 194
Soviet Union, 22
SP (Felicity Party), 37
'standing man' (*duran adam*) protest,
106, 111

Station of the Martyrs *see* Monument to
the Martyrs of 15 July (15 Temmuz
Şehitler Makamı)
Stravrodromi *see* Pera
Sturken, Marita, 19
Subotić, Jelena, 225
Sufism, 31, 40, 55, 113
Süleyman the Magnificent, Sultan, 108,
225
Sulukule Gentrification Project, 7–8,
59, 65–70, 90–1
Sunni Islam, 1–2, 23–4, 45–8
and 2016 coup attempt, 159–62
and Gezi Park, 123
and Gülen, 141–2
and Hagia Sophia, 9, 182–8,
189–201
and Kemalism, 55
and Monument to the Martyrs of
15 July (15 Temmuz Şehitler
Makamı), 147–8, 149–52, 156–7
and spiritual motifs, 17
Surp Agop Armenian Cemetery, 108
symbolic violence, 85, 86–7

Taksim Artillery Barracks, 107–8, 109
Taksim Pedestrianisation Project, 109
Taksim Solidarity (Taksim
Dayanışması), 100, 109
Taksim Square, 62, 102, 127; *see also*
Gezi Park
Taşköprülüzade
Shaqa'iq al-Nu'maniyya, 184
Taşoluk neighbourhood, 8, 59, 68
Tee, Caroline, 141
terrorism, 142
Theodosius II, Emperor, 169

Timurids, 26–7
TOKİ (Mass Housing Authority), 8, 59, 65, 66–70, 90–1
Tokyo Mosque and Cultural Centre, 148
tolerance, 42
Topbaş, Kadir, 109, 152–3, 154
Topçu, Yalçın, 192
Topkapı Palace, 25–6, 185
tourism, 84
transnationalism, 195
trauma, 2, 8–9, 17, 138, 218
  and ethnic cleansing, 41
  and Monument to the Martyrs of 15 July (15 Temmuz Şehitler Makamı), 146–7
tulips, 57–8
türbe (sacred tombs), 147–8, 149, 152, 159, 184, 224
Turgut, Pelin, 65
Turkey, 4, 5–6, 40–1
  and architecture, 22–3
  and bridge metaphor, 70–1
  and ethnic minorities, 21
  and Germany, 220–1, 223
  and Greece, 223–4
  and Greek Orthodox community, 126–8
  and Kemalism, 27–31
  and the West, 55–7
  see also 2016 coup attempt; AKP (Adalet ve Kalkınma Partisi); Istanbul; Ottoman Empire
Turkish Muslims see Sunni Islam
Turkishness, 28, 30, 40, 43, 45, 46–8
  and Hagia Sophia, 190, 194, 195, 207
  and iman, 159–60
Tursun Beg, 183

umma (Islamic community), 195, 198
UNESCO, 66
urban landscape see built environment; public space
Uşaki, Abdullah Selahaddin, 150
Uşaki, Cemalettin, 150
Uzer, Umut, 42, 46, 47, 190

Vale, Lawrence, 21
vatan (homeland), 47–8, 160–1, 197
veiling, 32, 33
Verney, Susannah, 39, 102
Victory Day, 108
violence, 21, 22, 85, 86–7, 126–8
  and Istanbul Greeks, 202, 203
  see also 2016 coup attempt
Vladimir I of Kiev, Prince, 177, 180

Walton, Jeremy, 223–4
Warner, Michael, 104, 218
Watenpaugh, Heghnar, 118
West, the, 3, 8, 16–17, 29–31
  and Gezi Park, 99
  and museums, 79–80
  and neo-Ottomanism, 220–5
  and politics, 36, 37
  and Turkey, 55–7
  see also European Capital of Culture
White, Jenny, 34, 39
Whittemore, Thomas, 170
Wildner, Kathrin
  Public Istanbul: Spaces and Spheres of the Urban, 4–5
women, 29–30, 32, 33, 119, 198

Yalçın, Azat, 69
Yanık, Lerna, 225

Yapıcı, Mücella, 109
Yavaş, Mansur, 196
Yavuz, Hakan, 32, 33, 34, 39, 46
   and neo-Ottomanism, 40–1, 42, 44
Yavuz Sultan Selim Bridge, 143
Yayla, Atilla, 116
Yel, Ali Murat, 116
Yıldırım, Binali, 139

Yıldırım, Birge, 108
Yılmaz, Coşkun, 148, 153, 155
Yılmaz, Hale, 47, 48
Yılmaz, Hasan Kamil, 159
Young Turks, 25
Yüksel, Selim, 189

Zionism, 37

EU representative:
Easy Access System Europe
Mustamäe tee 50, 10621 Tallinn, Estonia
Gpsr.requests@easproject.com

www.ingramcontent.com/pod-product-compliance
Lightning Source LLC
Chambersburg PA
CBHW070842300326
41935CB00039B/1376